MW00565617

unsQuaReD

Many thanks to Erin Bennett, Steven Gillis, Elyse Guilfoyle, Ryan Howard, Katie Lorenz, Chris Oposnow, Patricia Reeb, Rich Retyi, Anne Smith, Ben Stroud, Chris Vieau, Pamela Waxman, and Amanda White. Thanks also to the contributors for generously donating their work.

Also published by 826michigan and The Neutral Zone:

Vacansopapurosophobia:
The Fear of a Blank Page

unsquared
ANN ARBOR WRITERS
UNLEASH THEIR EDGIEST
STORIES & POEMS

THE NEUTRAL ZONE

Published September 2006 by 826michigan and The Neutral Zone
© 2006 by 826michigan and The Neutral Zone
All rights reserved by 826michigan, The Neutral Zone, and the authors
Cover design by Ryan Molloy

ISBN: 0-9779289-2-6

Simply,
to our students

FOREWORD
KATHRYN HARRISON

ANYTHING CAN HAPPEN on the page—anything. Gregor Samsa wakes up as a giant cockroach; the Devil arrives in Moscow and wreaks hilarious havoc; armed with a tin drum and a window-shattering scream, three-foot tall Oskar Matzerath protests the existential nightmare of Germany in the wake of the Nazis; nurse Jenny Fields, who wants a child but not a husband, hikes up her uniform and lowers herself onto a brain dead patient's erection; with scalpel, needle, thread, and novocaine, a disfig-ured man makes himself a new face. These familiar examples, from fiction by Kafka, Bulgakov, Grass, Irving, and Pineda, are some of my *old* favorites, from enduring work dating back to the beginning of the last century, before artificial insemina-tion, face transplants, and cloning were news stories rather than fantasies. Before the prescience of a writer like George Saunders created brilliant dystopias that reveal a future in which genetic mutations have divided the populace into the Normals and the Flaweds and anyone can become a marketer of virtual reality, off-loading personal memories and selling them by the decade.

 Unsquared presents its own menu of surprises. I think Washington Irving would be amused to find his Headless Horseman subjected to the same kind of pun-ishment as Rip Van Winkle. Resigned to the workaday tribulations of the de-capitated, he makes out his "to do list" on a Post-It and negotiates the humil-iations a Singles Mixer in Sleepy Hollow's present day condo community. Not one but two relatively unknown—i.e., pre-renowned—writers contribute stories about intergenerational apprenticeships in thievery: grandfathers and fathers lead-ing sons into very peculiar lives of crime. Among work from established writ-ers is Thomas Lynch's meditation on the death of his sister's dog, so repellent and limited a representative of her species that the passing of the bitch (I am of course being literal) affords him the perfect opportunity to examine his own spe-cies and our misguided and unexpectedly redemptive tendency to succumb to the temptations of hagiography. After all, is it not in our embrace of an animal no one else can tolerate that we come to understand the love of God for hu-mankind? Peter Ho Davies discovers that among his tragically untalented work-shop students, who write of "escape goats," "death knolls," and "cops who slap on cuff-links" was the instantly infamous young man who killed his father, his class-mates, and then himself, prompting CNN to demand an interview with his teacher, and Davies' concomitant need to discover what it feels like to empty a .38 into the paper silhouette of a man at a local shooting range. And that's just a glimpse of work that spans the country, east to west, north to south, irony to elegy, comedy to tragedy and back again to comedy.

I'll confess I agreed to write the foreword to this collection of work out of a sense of moral obligation: what it earns will support two programs, 826michigan and The Neutral Zone, that hope to create and sustain . . . readers. Well, perhaps there was a little self-interest in my generosity. Whenever writers gather it's only a few minutes before we bemoan the impossibility of competing with cable and X-box and the Internet. If ever it seemed a quixotic enterprise to sit at one's desk, for many days, alone, and struggle to put a comma in the right place, surely it does today.

But, as it's turned out, while I thought I was going to do the editors of *Unsquared* a favor, the reverse has happened. Reading this collection of work from writers whose work I knew beforehand and from the generation of poets, essayists, fiction writers, and dramatists who will step forward to take our place has made me feel better about the compulsion that has eclipsed other, more gainful employment to become my life's work. It's reminded me that writers, and readers, are necessary, and that anything can and does happen on the page. Too, I've noticed something: among my fellow travelers on the subway—among the thumb-weary Blackberry addicts, glazed Game-Boy jockeys, and nodding, swaying iPod-listeners all hurtling together through the dark maze of tunnels under New York City—a lot of us still have books before our eyes. Engrossed by what we're reading, we take curves holding on with one hand, backpacks on our shoulders, briefcases between our ankles, sometimes even turning pages with our noses or our chins. Clearly, we consider finding out what happens next worth a surprising level of discomfort. *Unsquared* is what happens next.

INTRODUCTION

ANN ARBOR IS a city of readers and writers.

Sort of.

All the infrastructure is in place for a vibrant literary populace: major university with highly ranked MFA program; progressive public school system with host of terrific Language Arts and English teachers; award-winning public library; thriving youth poetry slam scene, weekly short story workshop, and visiting author series at funky and much-utilized teen center; best-selling local authors who can be spotted regularly at any number of downtown coffee shops; large-scale annual book festival; nonprofit writing center which hosts free creative writing workshops and tutoring on site, and also teaches workshops in schools; locally published literary magazines; annual Poetry Night in Ann Arbor; nationally recognized independent booksellers and a half-dozen other quirky bookshops; original Borders, Borders corporate headquarters, and a brand new Barnes & Noble; community-wide Ann Arbor Reads program; dynamic collegiate spoken word scene; countless informal bookclubs and writing groups; and the list could go on. In this smallish city, it's possible to see a different author read somewhere every night of the week.

And yet . . .

Like anywhere else, classrooms at both the university and in the public schools are dotted with reluctant readers. With Cliff Notes-instead-of-the-book devotees. With videogame, cellphone, and Ipod addicts who haven't opened a novel since Harry Potter. With freestyle rappers who fail English and claim to hate poetry. With young people who value reading no more than young people anywhere else in a country where readership is on a major decline for anyone under the age of thirty-five.

If you don't like to read, we often tell our students, *maybe you just haven't found the right book*. We think this is the right book.

Unsquared is an attempt to fight back. It's a hard left hook to the jaw of anyone who believes books are quaint relics of a bygone era. It sets *New York Times* best-selling authors like Elizabeth Kostova next to seventeen-year-old firebrand poets like Angel Nafis; august personages from the academic realm like Nick Delbanco and Charles Baxter next to innovative hustlers like Davy Rothbart. It aims to grab that nineteen-year-old kid rolling blunts in his basement (or twenty-three-year-old college drop-out scalping tickets at football games, or thirty-one-year-old coffeehouse vinyl album collector, or sixteen-year-old essay-downloader, or twenty-seven-year-old club-hopper, or thirty-three-year-old new father . . .) and yank him by the ear. *Here*, it says, *check this book out*. Now, see if you still think books are something your parents used to read "back in the day." Now, see if you still want to roll your eyes whenever you hear someone say a book changed her life.

Now, see what it's like to say, sincerely, that you truly identified with a story you read, that it spoke to you.

Unsquared is a book that wants to lead to more books, a gateway book that says, *Pay attention, there's some electric stuff out there, some stuff that's too exciting to miss.*

It is not a book for every teacher to use in a classroom. It's not for those teachers who think eighteen year olds should be reading young adult literature more approproiate for twelve year olds, for those teachers who think any cuss word disqualifies a piece of writing from the canon of great literature. It is for those teachers who want to offer students an enticing plateful of stories and poems, who want students to question, to think, to make their own attempts to write, to believe in the transformative power of the creative imagination.

Mostly, it's for those readers who aren't sure they even like reading anymore. *Try this on for size*, it says. *Find your place in it. Read. Write.*

—Jeff Kass
    director of creative writing, the Neutral Zone
    teacher, Pioneer High School
—Amy Sumerton
    assistant director, 826michigan
    executive editor, Orchid Literary Review

C⊠NTENTS

KATHRYN HARRISON..ix
  FOREWORD
JEFF KASS & AMY SUMERTON...xi
  INTRODUCTION
STEFAN KIESBYE..1
  WATER PARK
PATRICK O'KEEFFE...9
  ONLY ONE OF US
DAVY ROTHBART...11
  MAGGIE FEVER
EVELYN HOLLENSHEAD...22
  ON THE DEATH OF JORDAN COLEMAN, THE IMPRISONMENT
  OF RYAN BOWER, AND THE LOSS OF MY CITY
PETER HO DAVIES..24
  WHAT YOU KNOW
LAURA KASISCHKE..33
  IF A STRANGER APPROACHES YOU ABOUT CARRYING A
  FOREIGN OBJECT ONTO THE PLANE
SEAN NORTON...43
  BLUE TIPS
CRAIG HOLDEN..44
  COLORADO
SCOTT BEAL...54
  BULLET WITH YOUR NAME ON IT
  ASSESSMENT OF MY MASCULINITY
JEFF KASS...57
  DANNY ROTTEN
RATTAWUT LAPCHAROENSAP..64
  FARANGS
JEFF PARKER..75
  THE BRIEFCASE OF THE PREGNANT SPYLADY
STEVEN GILLIS...83
  GIRAFFES

KEITH TAYLOR..94
  THE CUSTOMER
CHARLES BAXTER..96
  A RELATIVE STRANGER
JON LIBERZON..107
  BY BIRTH
KATHE KOJA..109
  BRANDI'S BABY
CLAIRE FORSTER...114
  HANGERED
JULIE ORRINGER..117
  CARE
LAUREN WHITEHEAD..130
  STOOPDWELLERS
SAILOR J..134
  DANGEROUS MIRRORS
MOLLY RAYNOR..137
  OPEN LETTER TO THE MICHIGAN PRISON SYSTEM
  MY MOTHER'S GARDEN
LAURA PERSHIN RAYNOR..143
  ROXANNE RYDER
EILEEN POLLACK...147
  PAST, FUTURE, ELSEWHERE
ELIZABETH ELLEN...162
  WHAT I'VE BEEN TOLD WITH REGARD TO THE PIANIST
RAY McDANIEL...172
  SUPERBOY DOES NOT LOVE DUO DAMSEL
STEVE AMICK..174
  HEADLESS AND BLUE
ERICA ROSBE..178
  BUTTER KNIVES
CHRISTINE HUME..187
  A.K.A.
DEAN BAKOPOULOS..188
  HAPPY
THOMAS LYNCH...210
  THE SISTERS GODHELPUS
LAURA HULTHÉN THOMAS..218
  KISS
NICHOLAS DELBANCO..229
  X
ELIZABETH KOSTOVA..237
  DEAR MRS. BENDER-WONG
RICHARD SOLOMON..242
  ANN ARBOR ART FAIR 2005

Onna Solomon...244
   EPISTEMOLOGY OF LOVE
Paul A. Toth...245
   TELEGRAM SAM
David Lawrence Morse...250
   CONCEIVED
Deanne Lundin...259
   FOUR HOLLOWS
Heather Neff..263
   KODAI CON
Adam Falkner..271
   SOLSTICE IN A NATURAL
2006 Ann Arbor Youth Poetry Slam Team.....................................275

About 826michigan..295

About the neutral zone...297

WATER PARK
STEFAN KIESBYE

THEY'RE NICE TO me and they don't want to be near me. While we rake grass at the superintendent's house, they stay amongst themselves, two raking, another lifting the grass into the back of the E-Z-Go. It's not like they want to offend me, and maybe if you asked them about it they'd say that it's just in my head. But when I join them, they slowly stop talking and don't start up again until I have left to take care of the strip of lawn along the driveway.

The park is one hundred and fifty acres, "a good size," Dan, the super, says. Two years ago they built a small water park with slides and a wave pool, but he wishes he could build an eighteen-hole golf course. We only have a nine-hole disc-golf course, and the disc golfers come just before dark, when the gatehouse has closed for the day. They get stoned or drunk and play and we have a hell of a time getting them off the course in time to close the park at nine o'clock.

I like the park best in the mornings, when it's still a bit hazy, and no one else is around. I drive along the trails to pick up litter. Bunny rabbits scurry along or just sit in the shimmering grass and stare back at me. Bushes and trees I can't name smell sweet before it gets hot, and if you stop the cart, the trees seem to take a step toward you, as if they want to gently block your path, unscrew your head, clean it out, and keep you there.

During breaks I might sit on one of the docks by the lake and watch the fish, mostly bass, swim in the murky water. At first sight, it doesn't seem like much of a lake, but towards the middle it gets real deep. In the evenings, anglers stand along the shore. Sometimes they even grill their catch. People used to swim in the lake, before they built the docks and put up picnic tables everywhere. Now signs tell visitors it's forbidden to wade or swim.

When the other rangers are bored, they drive the E-Z-Go over to the water park to hang out with the girls, though they don't call them girls. They call them "chicks" and "bitches." They show only contempt for them, but can't stop going to our water park, where the girls show off elaborately painted toenails, killer tans and a suave attitude. They call us "immature." It's never "stupid," "dumb," or "gross," it's always "immature," as though that word gives them power over us.

My mom never mentions the park. She might say, "How was work?" or, "How was your day?" but she doesn't mention the pavilions, the pond with its new fishing docks, the vault bathrooms, the lodge or the waterslides, and when I tell her about them she finds a way to steer our conversation away from the park. She's a tall woman with wide hips, taller than I am. In the summer she wears jean shorts, and there are some green and purple blemishes on her legs she says she got when she was pregnant. I can talk to her about the rangers, the guys I went to high school with and who she knows from the time they still hung out at our place. She's curious about where Karl is going to college, if he's still playing football, or if Fred has a girlfriend now, but when I tell her that Karl was fishing plastic bags and bait boxes out of the pond with a pole he'd made from an old broom and a ski-stick, she hurries into the garage, because she "forgot to take the dry-cleaning from the car."

In Michigan, it's cold for eight months, and the rest of the time it feels like you're inside a carwash. Dad is a Ford guy, we are a Ford family. He drives a Taurus, Mom drives a Sable, and I decked out my Focus with money I earned plowing snow. It makes 240 horsepower and Dad helped me put in the supercharger. He's become quiet, and he didn't say a word when I said I wanted to work at the park for the summer. He nodded gravely, just as if I had explained relativity to him. But even though he lets me go on about work, he never answers. He just says, "Oh, that's interesting," or, "No kidding," and he seems relieved when I finally leave the room and get into my car.

We live outside Ypsilanti, in a two-story house in an older subdivision. Last fall rainwater ruined our ceilings, and every storm breaks off strips of the cheap siding. Whenever Mom cooks, my bathroom smells of whatever she's preparing. The Richardsons from next door moved away last year, and many of the families we used to invite for barbecues in the summer are gone. Every month, another "For Sale" sign is driven into one of the lawns, and each year, the cars in the driveways get a little shabbier. Dad says that the developers knew how bad their houses were, and that they were building a future ghetto. "Give it another twenty years, and you can buy crack from our neighbors," he says.

I wanted to go to the U of M, but didn't have the grades. So now I take classes at Eastern and hope I can transfer after my sophomore year. I'd like to be a mechanical engineer, I'd be happy to work for one of the Big Three, which my dad now calls the Big Two-and-a-Half, but I'd love to work for BMW. Their sedans are sweet. I'd just love to drive an M5 and have girls ride with me in the back. I'd even go to Germany and learn the language, though I'm not good at languages. I took two years of high school French and I sucked. *Voulez-vous couchez avec moi* is about the only phrase I remember and I didn't learn it in school.

Last week Dan asked me to supervise a new gate attendant. Not that she really needed my help, but Dan wants everything just so and she'd never sold vehicle passes before, so I sat with her for an hour. She was from California, a swimmer on a scholarship at Eastern, and her blond hair and skin looked as if she'd bleached them forever. But sort of pretty, in a serious kind of way. Rachel wanted to work as a lifeguard, but those positions were already filled. She asked me about the park, she'd never heard of the park before a friend of hers applied, and I told her about the trails, the pavilions that always get trashed on the weekends, and the disc golfers.

When Dan stopped by to see how we were doing, she suddenly said she'd heard about an accident here at the park a few years ago. I had no idea why she was asking, she'd said she didn't know the park. She was from California, after all. "Someone drowned?" she asked.

"Yes," Dan said real quiet.

"Even though you had lifeguards?"

"It didn't happen in the water park," Dan answered. Whenever we want an extra day off, or whenever too many workers call in sick, or people complain about the concession stand's expensive food, he lowers his head as if there's a strong wind blowing, and his voice slows down. He doesn't want to become angry and shout or brush someone off, so he answers very slowly and politely. "We didn't have it then. It happened at the pond."

"How?" Rachel asked. She wasn't trying to be mean or annoying, she just wanted to know.

"Well," Dan said, "a boy drowned." And he paused. "Let's just say it was a very tragic accident." Then he showed her how to order the different tickets so nothing gets lost. He didn't even glance at me once.

At my brother's funeral I wore a black suit my dad bought for me at the Men's Wearhouse. We went together, he needed a new one, and the whole affair lasted about ten minutes. I'd been clothes shopping with him before, and he could be very vain. He loved shoes and had gazillions of expensive ties, but at the Men's Wearhouse, he just tried on the first one the salesperson handed him, and before the guy had a chance to look at Dad's back or pants and suggest alterations, Dad said, "This one is fine." I'm sure he didn't want me to believe he was worried about the way he looked at his son's funeral.

The day was hot and sticky, and our house was full of people who, when my parents were around, fell silent or lowered their voices, but otherwise talked and ate as if it were someone's birthday. Everyone seemed itchy and uncomfortable in their suits and dresses and nobody could answer my gaze longer than a second. Only Grandma, my dad's mother, hugged me and said, "You're still here, you're still here."

Ron's classmates attended the ceremony, singing "Amazing Grace." Our pastor had tears in his eyes, and Dad had to lead Mom away halfway through the ceremony because she cried so much. You could hardly hear the pastor's speech because of her.

I had a girlfriend back then, Caysee, and the night after my brother had drowned, she came over, and we kissed and hugged, and she was all in tears and wouldn't let go of me. By the time of the funeral, each time I tried to kiss her she giggled or made helpless little sounds and moved her lips away. When Mom left the ceremony, Caysee left it too, and two days later she called and said it was over between us and I shouldn't think badly of her.

On Court TV, when criminals show remorse, the jury starts feeling bad for them, and the judge seems inclined not to punish them too harshly. As if by crying and asking for forgiveness, the world becomes again the way it was before someone got mugged or killed, as if by weeping, the world becomes better again. Maybe that way, people think the world is still working according to the laws they learned. Maybe if you don't cry, they start doubting themselves.

Our park is well hidden on Wellington Road, three miles outside of town, just at the border of the township. If you don't look hard for the brown and white signs you'll never even know it's there. But it's the only thing to do for kids in the summer, the only thing in a thirty-mile radius. Some days we even get busloads of kids from Toledo.

All the rangers and attendants and managers in the water park, those who've worked here since junior year in high school, know my brother's story and don't ask anymore, and either by will or because they've gotten used to it, they don't remember details. My brother was well liked, played in a jazz band and ran track for our school. If he hadn't died, he would have played Dr. Higgins in *My Fair Lady*. He could sing real pretty.

But this girl from Eastern kept asking about Ron. When Dan left again that first day I met her, she said, "Why didn't he tell me what happened?"

I shrugged.

"Do you know who drowned?"

"Yeah, I do. But that was three years ago. They don't let people swim in the pond anymore. It doesn't look like much, but it's real deep in the middle."

Rachel was quiet for some time, staring at her toenails, which were done in red, with white, blue, and yellow flowers painted on them. She didn't look very girly, so I asked who'd painted her toes.

"My roommate," she said, suddenly smiling. "Do you think they look cheesy?"

"No, they're fine," I said.

"So how did the boy drown?" she asked.

"Why do you want to know?"

She shrugged. "It's creepy. Kind of cool." She laughed, shaking her head at what she'd said. "Do you mind telling?"

She really has no idea, I thought, no idea at all. And I said, "He was a good athlete, but he couldn't swim."

"Then why did he go swimming in the pond?"

"He wanted to save his brother," I said. "His name was Ron."

The car I had back then, an old Escort, was keyed the first day of school after my brother's death, the headlights were kicked in. They never found out who did it. I left the car just as it was, only replacing the lights, and the next day the windows were smashed in. I transferred to Belleville that same fall, my father made the arrangements. On the advice of my old school's counselor, he also paid for sessions with a shrink, Al Larsen. He was a decent guy, maybe in his thirties, maybe a bit older, with pale skin, quivering lips, and beard. Whenever he took off his glasses, which shrank his eyes, he looked like a bearded frog. After I told him the story of Ron's death, he said, "That must be hard for you," and I felt relieved because finally someone was talking about me and not only of my brother. I said yes, I had been afraid when my car was smashed and I didn't play roller hockey with the other guys anymore, on Sundays, in our school's lot. But the guy looked at me in this blank way, eyes not blinking and without expression. "That's not what I meant," he said, and then asked, "How are things between you and your parents?" His computer in the back of the office was running, and every once in a while, an e-mail would come in with a "bing." Right after he asked, another mail arrived, and he went over to mute the sound.

"So his brother was drowning and he tried to save him?" Rachel said.

I would have liked to ask her out right there in that gatehouse with its sticky floor and the bees always coming through the window. I wanted to drive around with her, maybe to Ford Lake or Ann Arbor, maybe go see a movie. It was nice she wasn't from here, and nice that she was asking me all these questions without knowing that I could answer them all. "No, Ron's brother wasn't drowning," I said. "He jumped out of their inflatable boat and started screaming, 'I can't move, I can't move.' And then he let himself sink under water."

"And?"

"Ron jumped after his brother. He must have. Nobody knows how it could have happened so fast. But when his brother came up again, it was all silent. No screaming, no thrashing, nothing. The boat was empty, and Ron was gone."

Rachel noticed the rhyme and repeated, "Ron was gone," and laughed, I think, despite of herself. She shook her head as if she could shake off the laughter, but kept laughing. "Ron was gone."

And I laughed too, it was so good to see someone laughing about it. I was happier in that moment than I had been in a long time, and she looked pretty laughing. People stopped at the gatehouse window and paid for the ticket and I showed Rachel how to handle errors by printing a receipt and how to fold our leaflets. She had big and strong hands, nice hands, even though she was biting her nails.

The shrink, after I told him that I thought my mom blamed me for Ron's death, asked what my opinion was. Did I blame myself?

"I guess," I said.

"You guess?" His eyes were strangely focused, almost like those of the disc golfers when they leave the course at nine or after nine and are all stoned. Their eyes jump at you, look really mean, and yet somehow they are not seeing anything, there's nothing behind those eyes.

"Yeah," I said. "If I hadn't played with him, he'd never have drowned."

"It could have happened anyway," Al said. "Do you and your folks believe in God? Some people believe in fate, or that God takes people when he decides to."

"But that would make me his tool. That'd be pretty fucked up," I said. "I was pretending I was drowning, that's all. Nobody made me. I just did."

"Do you ever wonder why?"

"It was fun. He was always so worried and scared, and I knew he would get all upset."

"Did it ever occur to you that he might love you?"

"I don't know. I guess," I said.

We had good times together; Ron wasn't a pain in the ass or anything. He was pretty cool, knew a ton about computers and cars, and designed a website for me. Apart from running track, he was more of a geek, but a popular one, not one of those pimply nerds with grimy glasses and a gut. He was pretty, even though he was real thin and didn't play football and didn't know how to swim. He was two years younger than me and bugged me that summer about showing him how to drive. But my Escort had a stick, and I didn't want him to ruin the transmission. It was an '89 GT and pretty fast, and I said he should buy his own car and I would teach him alright. I mean, we played pranks on each other as kids, and he was always there, but when I thought of my family, or told friends about Mom and

Dad, Ronnie was never part of that. We got along, though, didn't fight much either. When I told him to shut up or get off the phone, he usually would, and most of the time he'd be in his room anyway.

Dad cleaned out Ronnie's room even though Mom cried and hit him with her fists when he did. He got rid of the posters, the CDs, the Cleveland Indians blanket he'd won at a church raffle, and even Ron's photo albums. He didn't want to erase him, but he didn't want Mom to spend her evenings locked in Ron's room, and he didn't even look at the things he threw out. Nobody has used the room since—we don't have many visitors. My uncles and aunts and grandparents all live close by, in Manchester and Saline. Dad bought a bed, a wardrobe, and a desk, but there's nothing in the wardrobe, and no one ever sits at the desk. Mom refuses to clean the room, and Dad doesn't take the time. Ronnie's room is dusty and empty.

The next time I saw Rachel, she came out of the water park's staff room. I was running change to the gatehouse, and she spotted me and came over to say hello. She looked very cool in her bathing suit and white shirt—they'd let her lifeguard because one of the guards had busted his shoulder playing hockey. Her eyes were a bit red, maybe she'd been in the water all day, and she jumped from one foot onto the other, as if she had to pee, but I guess she was just nervous, and I thought she was pretty that way. Her hair was almost white and held back in a pony tail, and she blinked her eyes because of the sun behind me.

That night we went to see *Charlie's Angels*. Even while the movie was still playing, we were already bitching about how silly it was, but somehow it was really fun, and we moaned and groaned and rolled our eyes in the darkness, and everyone was shushing us, and we just kept laughing harder. Afterward we went to Big Boy's and she said she would like to lifeguard on a real beach out in California or in Myrtle Beach or Miami, and Ypsilanti suddenly felt very small, and for a moment I saw our park and I saw pictures of the ocean, and my souped-up Focus looked real silly, and I thought that if not for that scholarship, Rachel would have never come to Eastern, or Michigan, for that matter. She was only here for a short time, and I wondered if I would ever make it to Germany, or if I would buy a house somewhere here and still drive over to the water park and watch families spread out their blankets near the concession stand and stuff their faces with nachos.

"I'd really like to get a tattoo," she said suddenly. "I just don't know where." She dipped one of her last fries in a big heap of ketchup, and sucked the ketchup off the fry before chewing it. There weren't many people left at Big Boy's, it was almost closing time.

"Oh," I said.

"Do you think that's stupid?"

"No," I said. "I just don't think that I could wear any one symbol or picture for the rest of my life. Or a name. I mean, if you don't like the person anymore, it's still there, and you're constantly reminded of them."

"I'd like a shape, a simple one," she said. "Maybe a triangle, a circle, or a square."

"A square. Simple," I repeated stupidly.

"Yeah, a black square. Doesn't have to mean anything. Just a square."

"'Hey, what's that mean?'—'Why, I love squares,'" I said, and we both laughed. "Yeah, a square," she said.

We both ordered strawberry milkshakes, although the waitress seemed really annoyed, and while we were waiting for them, I said, "I'd like to see somebody tattooing his body onto his body."

"What do you mean?" she said.

"The shape of his body tattooed onto his skin, just a bit smaller, so it fits. His fingers are drawn onto his fingers, his arms onto his arms. Well, the face would be difficult."

She looked at me, as if I were completely nuts, but smiled real sweet, and said, "The eyes, yeah. The nose—you could do that."

"And one thing would be missing. You know, he'd have the whole body tattooed on his body, but one hand would be missing, or a calf. And everybody would look at the missing limb, because it's just missing."

"That's creepy," Rachel said. "Like tattooing your skeleton, I mean, all your bones, onto your skin."

"Maybe," I said. "But there would be two people, only one is incomplete."

Rachel put her hands on my ears and shook me and laughed, and there was some of her fry lodged between two teeth.

When I dropped her off that night, she said, "That was fun. Let's do it again." I said, "Any time," and meant it.

But there was no other time. The next day at the park she was all weird. When I came to work in the afternoon and looked for her in the staff room, she didn't look my way, just turned around when I knew she'd seen me. She just turned to another girl and kept talking. Maybe someone had seen us together, or maybe she had told a friend about me. And of course they would have told her about Ron. Whenever I ran into Rachel that afternoon, she passed by me, as though I was only a customer, someone you don't want or need to know and don't see anyway.

The night of the funeral, I'd gone driving around, speeding on back roads, trying to feel anything special when I thought of Ron. Fireflies exploded on my windshield, swarms of them, their squished bodies glowing for a second or two, before turning into smudges. When I came home around one or two in the morning, Mom was still sitting in the kitchen, a glass of pickles and a jar of mayonnaise in front of her. She'd put bread and lunchmeat on the table too, and I could see that she hadn't touched anything. Dad's plate was full of crumbs and he'd left it on the table, and hers was clean, and she sat there as if she were waiting for something to happen, as if she were waiting for the mayonnaise to make sense.

I sat down across from her, because she was sad, and I was responsible for it, and I had not wanted to make her unhappy. But she got up real quick, as if the table had suddenly gotten hot and burned her arms. And she looked at me with her mouth open, and for a long time, no words came. Finally she spoke, but it was a hissing noise, like a hot kettle. Maybe she didn't want to wake Dad or maybe she was afraid of what would happen if she raised her voice. At first I couldn't understand, but she was repeating what she said, over and over again, staring at me as though she were frightened.

"Why don't *you* cry?" Mom said. "Why don't *you* cry?" Although there were no tears coming, I was sure she was crying. And I stared at her, didn't respond, didn't go upstairs to my room, but waited for her to stop, waited until she was all cried out. Then I poured her a glass of iced water and sat it down in front of her.

"Thanks," she said, and got up, leaving the kitchen to sit by herself on the back porch, without the water. She never asked again afterward, but she didn't need to. When I sit on the fishing dock by the pond and the other rangers come by, I can hear them ask the same question. And I wish I could have cried with Mom after the funeral, wish I could have told her that I never wanted to hurt Ronnie and how much I missed him. Maybe she would have slapped me, maybe even beaten me, but then she would have hugged me and cried for Ronnie and for me. I knew I would have been forgiven.

She wanted to see me cry to find her peace or to be consoled or to be reassured that the world was still what she thought it was, that I was still who she thought I was. I never cried for Ron though, and that night I just emptied her glass into the sink and went to my room. I didn't cry for him. People can smell I never did.

Stefan Kiesbye is the author of the novel *Next Door Lived A Girl* (Low Fidelity Press 2005). He studied drama, performed on stages in Hamburg and Berlin, hosted a morning show for a Gay and Lesbian radio station, and worked as a coffeehouse reader, drag queen, and nude model. His stories have appeared in *Hobart, Pindeldyboz, Best of Carve Magazine,* and the anthology *Stumbling and Raging: More Politically Inspired Fiction,* edited by Stephen Elliott. Kiesbye currently lives in Ann Arbor with his wife Sanaz, and teaches at Eastern Michigan University. For more info, go to www.skiesbye.com.

ONLY ONE OF US

PATRICK O'KEEFFE

When my brother kisses me,
his hands are on my hips.
We both know that we may never
see each other again.

Rows of poplars are behind us,
that unchanged sway of our childhood.

He is the only one of us
who claims he saw the sputnik
dive over the poplars
some years before we got television;
he was the dreamer,
saying he'd leave,
but I did.

He had a concertina once
that I gave to some kid on the school bus
for a pack of cigarettes.

Now he holds me;
His belly is swollen against mine.
He has four children and a wife
who live on the dole.

The kiss is brief.
He's looking right at me.
I see his tears rise,
but I made a choice:
I do not cry over leaving anymore.
What I feel is his swollen belly
falling away from mine
and I remember he showed
me his first erection:
dropped his shorts
one summer's day
before the poplars

and waved it over and back
like a cigarette
between his fingers,
as if he was the only boy
who had one,
as if he was the only one of us
getting older.

Lexington, 1996

Patrick O'Keeffe grew up in Co. Limerick, Ireland, but moved to the United States in his twenties. He lives in Ann Arbor and teaches at the University of Michigan. His first book, *The Hill Road*, a collection of four linked novellas published by Bloomsbury in June 2005, is the winner of the 2006 Story Prize.

MAGGIE FEVER

DAVY ROTHBART

I LIVED WITH my older brother and his wife in Gulfport, Mississippi, from when I was seven to fourteen years old, but then my brother got stationed on an aircraft carrier off the coast of Bahrain, and I got sent out to Albuquerque to live with my grandpa. My grandpa was weird and scary; he hardly ever said a word, just spat and grunted. He looked like a tiny viking—barely five feet tall, with beady eyes and an enormous, ragged silver beard with yellow stains. Three or four days a week he worked at the McDonald's at Central and Coal while I went to school; all the other days we went to the airport and returned carts. These carts, the way it worked was folks would put a buck in the machine and unhitch one to push their luggage around in. When you returned them, you got twenty-five cents back, but most people just left them in the parking lot and drove away, so me and my grandpa would spend all day collecting them and pushing them back to the terminal, filling our pockets with the quarters that the cart machine spat out. Together we could make more than fifty bucks in a day.

There was no camaraderie between us out there in the blazing parking lot, no buddy-buddy, no whistling while we worked. I kept as far from my grandpa as I could. If he took notice of me, it was only to grumble about my laziness and long hair. My grandpa was sixty-eight years old but for some reason told everyone he was ninety, and he looked it, so they believed him. He wasn't even really my grandpa, but he'd raised my mom and my older brother, so that's what we called him. All he ever did besides work was read and listen to basketball on the radio and play with his cat. He loved his cat more than anything in the world. The cat was named Gilbert, and it was an old, scrawny, tiger-striped stray he'd found in the McDonald's lot. Gilbert strutted around the house, constantly wheezing and mewling, and my grandpa followed him from room to room, carrying on the other side of the conversation. They talked about sports, the weather, the crystal-meth freaks who worked at McDonald's with my grandpa, and sometimes they talked about me.

Gilbert was sick all the time and required special foul-smelling potions to keep him going. My grandpa mixed these on the back porch, and twice a day he had me hold Gilbert down while he squirted murky purple juice down the cat's throat with an eyedropper. Gilbert blamed me—not my grandpa—for medicine time; whenever he saw me, he'd run from the room, or else stand there arching his back wickedly and hissing.

One morning, on our way to the airport in my grandpa's ancient, clattering pickup truck, my grandpa cocked his head at me and growled, "We're not doing carts today."

"Then why are we going to the airport?" I said. "Or are we not going to the airport?"

My grandpa said, "We're going to the airport, but we're not doing carts."

"Okay." I waited for him to explain. It was the middle of October. The night before, I'd figured out that I'd been in Albuquerque for exactly two months, which meant I had thirty-four months left on my sentence before my brother came home and I could move back to Mississippi. "Wait," I said, bolting up in my seat, doing the arithmetic. "Am I going somewhere? Am I going back to Gulfport?" Maybe my brother had quit the navy, I thought, and come home to Mississippi. Or maybe my mom had gotten an early release. Or maybe my dad had even drifted back from wherever he was. My grandpa didn't say anything, and I took his silence as a no and sat back, disappointed. Then it occurred to me that I wasn't going home, but was being shipped off somewhere else, most likely Yuma, Arizona, where my grandpa's friend owned an emu farm. For two months I'd been telling anyone who'd listen how much Albuquerque sucked, but now the thought of leaving—being jettisoned again—lodged a lump in my throat and made my nostrils sting. I couldn't believe I hadn't been allowed to at least get my stuff together. Was my grandpa just going to box it all up and send it on? I was furious and near tears.

Finally my grandpa gave me his viking snarl, "Okay, listen. Gilbert needs surgery. That's right. They're telling me it's going to be fifteen hundred dollars. At the least. That's what they say." We were getting near the airport. In front of us, a plane shot straight skyward, catching a blinding glare from the morning sun. "Here's what we're going to do," my grandpa went on. "We're going to pull up at the baggage claim at American. You go in and pull the first two bags you see off the belt, bring them out here, and throw them in the back of the truck. Then we'll do the same thing at Delta. And then we'll go home. And when I say the first two bags, I mean the first two nice bags, bags that belong to folks with money. And grab ones that look like all the others, so if someone stops you, you can just say you made a mistake. Right?"

"Why can't we just do carts?" I said, though I was thrilled to be part of the heist like this, and giddy with relief that I wasn't headed for Yuma to tend emus. Still, I told my grandpa we could return enough carts to get the money together, no problem; we could do carts every day; I could miss a few weeks of school.

"Gilbert doesn't have a few weeks," my grandpa snapped at me. "We need this now!" He merged into the lanes for arriving flights and fixed me with a look of grizzled menace. "Nice bags," he said. He spat out the window, then looked back. "Heavy bags. And nice."

An hour later we pulled up in the alley behind our house and dragged the airport haul inside to my grandpa's hot attic bedroom—four big suitcases plus a little green backpack. My grandpa was especially pleased about the backpack. "Why would someone check a backpack?" he said. "That's the lucky charm. That's our ace in the hole. We're saving that one for last."

We hoisted the first suitcase up onto his bed, and my grandpa fought with the shiny clasps for a moment, then disappeared from the room and came back with his ten-inch hunting blade. He stabbed the suitcase once, drew the knife out, stabbed it again, and sawed from the second puncture back to the first. Together we tore the case open and dumped its contents out on the bed: sweatshirts, sweatpants, socks, women's underwear, a red umbrella, a tennis racket, a couple of skirts and dresses, a couple of pairs of shorts, a few pairs of jeans, and a little plastic case that held makeup and toiletries. "Fuck," said my grandpa. With his forearm he rubbed the sweat around on his face. "Come on," he said. "Bring another one over."

The next suitcase was filled with men's suits and business papers. We tried the pockets of every suit jacket and every pair of slacks but found only business cards, pens, and paper clips. The third suitcase was lighter than the first two, which gave me hope that it might have something besides clothes, but all it held was about thirty cardboard tubes; inside each tube were architectural blueprints for what appeared to be an enormous mall. Gilbert stalked into the room, crowing loudly. "I know," said my grandpa. "You're telling me."

He brought the last suitcase over to the bed and squatted on top of it, the same way I'd hold Gilbert down when we gave him his medicine. As my grandpa plunged his knife through the bag's black nylon skin and ripped into its contents, I wondered if he had ever killed a man before, and I decided that yes, he almost certainly had, but that it had probably been during World War II, when he was in the army, fighting the Germans in Africa. This revelation filled me with both greater fear of him and greater respect.

"That's what I'm talking about!" my grandpa cried suddenly. He raised a black Nikon camera high in the air like the head of an enemy soldier. Then he added, a bit more composed, "There's a whole bunch of lenses, too." I jumped up on the bed and helped him dig. There were two smaller cameras and some camera equipment: flashbulbs, film, two tripods of different sizes. In the little zipper pocket of a pouch filled with batteries, I discovered a wad of cash—ones, fives, tens, and twenties. My grandpa snatched the money out of my hand and counted it up. "Three hundred and thirty-three bucks," he said. "And I'll probably get a thousand for the cameras, and I can get a couple hundred bucks for some of these suits." He stuffed the cash in the breast pocket of his shirt and gave me a black-toothed smile. "You did good." His eyes shifted. "Hey," he said, "what's in that backpack?"

I scooped it off the floor and tugged it open. Inside were a couple of lined notebooks filled with writing, a sketch pad, a beat-up copy of *Guitar World* magazine, and a walkman with a few loose cassette tapes. "This might be worth a few dollars," I said.

"Tell you what," said my grandpa, "you keep that stuff. You did okay today." He grunted and pivoted and clomped out of the room and down the stairs, Gilbert at his heels, wailing. I closed up the backpack and slipped it over my shoulders like it was mine. For a long time I stood there, looking over the carnage of the four suitcases strewn across the bed and the floor. I heard the radio in the kitchen crackle to life—a noontime sports call-in show—and the tiny, clanking noises of my grandpa preparing Gilbert a meal. Then the heat seemed to suck all sound out of the room. A powerful stillness descended. I became gently aware of my breath, and of the beat of my heart. The light through the drapes was red and soft and made the walls shimmer. The quarters piled on my grandpa's nightstand and card table and dresser and on the floor all hummed with a dull shine. I touched my face and found that I was crying. With my forefinger, I brought a tear to my tongue and tasted it—sweet, salty, like a hot raindrop. That was the first time I'd ever done that; now I always taste my tears.

Much later, after the sun had gone down and left the city smoldering, I walked out of the house and headed down Central Avenue a ways toward the McDonald's where my grandpa worked; my grandpa was home asleep, but sometimes his boss gave me hamburgers at the end of the night. I was wearing my new walkman and listening to the tape that had been inside—a series of low, melancholy trance beats. The world around me crashed and surged in time with the music. I glided past all the pawnshops and gun shops and residential motels, action in each tiny parking lot. A hundred and five degrees, hookers out hooking in twos and threes, a stream of red brake lights in the near lane as dudes slowed to check them out—passenger-side windows open, one hand on the wheel, faces hidden. Lowriders rumbled with bass; kids shouted giddy threats from car to car in Spanish; lights slipped red to green; engines buzzed like saws. Every half block white men like dead stalks—every last drop of moisture squeezed from them—poked skinny arms from the sleeves of their jackets to grab at my new green backpack and ask me for change. I wondered if one of these men was my dad, if he'd choose this night to appear. Long hair, matted beards, camo fatigues, logoless mesh baseball caps, purpled eyes, scars, black scabs and wicked burns, brown teeth, missing teeth—each face rocked me like one of the barroom-brawl punches or collisions with motorcycle handlebars that had caused all that damage to them in the first place. This had to be the saddest stretch of road in all of America. It was as if the country was deeply tilted, and Albuquerque was at the bottom corner; in time, the most lonely and desperate of drifters would always drift here.

At the McDonald's I sat on the weedy cement in the back of the parking lot and listened to the walkman and watched cars whirl through the drive-thru. The contents of the backpack called to me; I dumped the stuff out, shuffled through the cassette tapes for a minute, then started flipping through the composition notebooks. They were covered with punk-rock stickers and turned out to be a pair of journals that belonged, according to the return-address labels stuck inside the covers, to a girl named Maggie Smith. With blue and black ballpoint pens, she'd filled page after page in wild cursive scrawl. The very first sentence I read pulled me right in: "Well, that stupid fucker died today." It went on from there. "I was in the room with him and he died right there in front of me. He was alive and then he was dead. Not like he was moving much anyway, but when he died he was just gone, and I was there in the room with a fucking dead body. My dad's dead body. I sat there for about twenty minutes. Then I called for the nurse."

I did what I always did when I picked up a book: skipped to the last page. The entry was from early that morning. She was talking about getting packed up, heading back to Albuquerque from wherever she'd been. "If there's one thing that's bound to improve my mood and my outlook on life," she'd written, "it's being stuck on fucking airplanes for ten fucking hours. Well, at least I'll be home and can get fucked up. And I can finally sleep in my own bed again. Or Noah's, if he still remembers I exist."

Before I flipped back to begin at page one, I fished another tape from the little pile and popped it in. This one was labeled with a marker "shitty opera." But it wasn't shitty at all; it was beautiful. A man sang. I cranked up the volume and drowned out the sounds of rattling exhausts and the drive-thru speaker.

Maggie's journals only covered a span of a few weeks. She'd written incessantly—ten, fifteen, sometimes twenty pages a day, two full notebooks. Reading them was like being dunked right inside her head. She'd gone to Maine for a month because her dad had cancer and she wanted to be with him during his final days, even though she hardly knew him in the first place. But what had seemed like a shot at becoming friends, getting to know each other a little bit, had become a disaster. The whole time she was there up until he died, her dad had been unrelentingly nasty—not grumpy and sour, like my grandpa, but outright vicious and cruel. "You know, you're even uglier than your mother was"—that's the type of shit he'd actually say to her, which Maggie a few minutes later would record into her journal. It sounded like about the most excruciating, punishing stretch of time I could ever imagine; I could understand how keeping her journal always close at hand had brought some relief.

For the most part, though, Maggie didn't write about her dad. She wrote about Noah, her on-again, off-again boyfriend. She fantasized about sex with him—the details were so raw, I started getting turned on right there in the parking lot. She wrote about Noah's hands, his arms, his chest. She dreamed of vacations they could take together. Then, in nearly the same breath, she'd write about what an asshole he was and how much she hated him, and plot ways to destroy him. She didn't seem confused, just equally intense in her love and her anger.

I'd never been so riveted. Every page I read, I felt Maggie press closer and closer to me. Maybe it was the music—her tapes—mixed with all the lowriders' blue fumes, or maybe it was the simmering haze of Albuquerque at night, just being there in this desert city so far from everything I knew, but I felt dizzy and hollow. Maggie's every thought, every one of her tiny hopes and fears and sadnesses, ripped at me and consumed me. I felt gripped with a wild, desperate longing to be next to her, to hold her in my arms, to listen to shitty opera together in her warm and calm bed. I wanted to reveal myself to her as clearly and honestly and crushingly as she was revealing herself to me, page after page after page.

It occurred to me that she'd been delivered to me, that the universe had guided us together. At the airport there'd been a hundred little bags I could have snatched off the conveyor—what force had compelled me to choose hers? I'd never been superstitious, but I felt a wave of gratitude toward whatever spirits were behind this. Was she sixteen years old? Was she twenty-four? It was hard to know. Nothing in her journals pinned it down. My only clues to her daily life were that she worked at a veterinary clinic answering phones and mopping up urine, and that she had a car. I guessed she was seventeen. I didn't even know what she looked like, but I didn't care; I was achingly in love.

I finished reading the journals and turned right back to the beginning and read them all the way through again, then switched tapes in the walkman and read the journals a third time through. I paged carefully through her sketchbook—filled mostly with intricate drawings of spiders—and even read her *Guitar World* magazine cover to cover. Just as I was about to open the journals again, someone yanked the headphones off me; it was like being jarred out of a dream. My grandpa's boss—a young black guy named Calvin—squinted down at me; behind him, the McDonald's was dark. "Hey, Anthony," he said. "Didn't know you was out here, kid. We done threw all the burgers away." He shook his head. "I got some McNuggets. You want some McNuggets?" A black Cadillac bumped into the empty lot. "Come on," Calvin said, reaching out his hand. "Get up. My brother and me, we'll give you a ride home."

Over the next few days, I slipped into a kind of Maggie fever. Cool, vivid visions of the future came to me: Driving with her through the desert at sundown, then sleeping next to her in the back of a truck, a billion stars overhead; the truck itself seemed to click and sigh. Looking at rabbits in cages at a county fair; they pressed wet noses to our fingers through the wire. Floating for a long afternoon down a lush Texas river on blow-up rafts. Sipping flat orange juice at a sad midnight diner outside of Baton Rouge. And early one morning, we watched from the runway as a small navy plane touched down and came to a stop and a door popped open and stairs folded down and my brother's unit filed down the steps, one at a time. "Is that him?" she said after each of them appeared. "Is that him? Is that him? How 'bout this guy—is this one him?" These crisp scenes were what was real to me; the rest of the world faded into an underwater dream. Dimly I was aware of pushing carts around the baking-hot airport lots, sitting in algebra class, holding Gilbert down while my grandpa gave him his poison, but I wasn't there at all; I was with Maggie.

I'd discovered that the tape labeled "shitty shit" contained her own tentative fumblings on the guitar. She'd play a couple lines from a Beatles or a Paul Simon tune and then get tripped up and say, barely audibly, "Oh shit," and start over again. I felt closest to her when I listened to this tape; soon I stopped listening to the others. I got to know all the moments where she talked to herself. At one point she said, "I suck at this"; at another point she said, "This is hopeless"; and near the end of the tape she said, in a moment of sudden triumph, "That only half sucked!" I lay in bed for hours with her walkman on, listening to shitty shit and touching the pages of her journals, feeling the ridges her pens had dug. Every time I looked at her name on the return-address labels, a bolt of nervousness flapped from my belly up through my lungs—I knew I was going to have to make contact with her, and the thought of that was terrifying.

My grandpa hadn't been able to sell the cameras from the stolen suitcases for as much as he'd figured. When he wasn't at McDonald's or with me doing carts, he wandered around the house batting at flies with his hunting blade and talking about robbing a pimp. He could see that something had changed in me. He thought I was on meth. One morning he pinned me down and started chopping off all my hair. I kicked and screamed and flailed my arms, knocking stacks of quarters everywhere. My grandpa pulled his blade back. He couldn't understand why I cared so much.

"Maggie likes my hair long," I said.

"Who's Maggie?" he asked, softening.

"My girlfriend." I knew it was a little crazy, but saying it out loud almost made it feel true.

"Oh." My grandpa bit his lip and thought about that for a minute, still kneeling on top of me. "Okay, then," he said, "let me just even it out." He went back to hacking at my hair and I tuned out, so that I was with Maggie again. Now we were at a drive-in movie, tossing popcorn up, trying to land it in each other's mouths. Light from the screen played color across her hair and her face. Movie voices boomed from a little speaker mounted outside her window. Maggie laughed, then drew back in her seat for a moment, and her eyes, wide and whirling, gathered me in.

Late that night—after doing carts with the walkman on, giving Gilbert his purple juice, and lying in bed reading Maggie's journals for hours—I tiptoed up to my grandpa's bedroom while he was asleep and snagged the keys to his truck off the floor. I rolled the truck in stealth halfway down the block before cranking the engine and rattling down Central. I stopped at McDonald's. Calvin was at the drive-thru window; he had on a silver football helmet and jersey. It was Halloween. He squinted at me. "Is that your costume? You look like you done got chewed up and spit out. Who gave you that haircut, Stevie Wonder? Hey, your grandpa know you got his truck? Look, we been closed for an hour. I ain't got no burgers for you. Want some McNuggets?"

"Sure."

"Going to a party or something?"

"I'm going to my girlfriend's house." As I said it, I realized that this was it—I was really going to Maggie's house—and a jolt went through me, but then I felt extremely calm. Calvin passed me a little ten-piece box of chicken McNuggets, and I pulled away.

It was two in the morning. Everywhere half-costumed revelers crept home. Ghosts and a samurai warrior waited at a bus stop; three witches crowded around an ATM; Batman and Bill Clinton tussled in the middle of the road. The drive to Maggie's street took less than fifteen minutes. I'd expected a house, but her address matched a wide, crumbling, three-story apartment building. I parked and got nervous again. What would I say to her? Where could I start? I felt sick. I grabbed the green backpack and climbed out of the truck and stood in the street for ten long seconds, then climbed back in and sprawled across the seat, near tears. Finally I gathered myself. I remembered something I had to do: I unzipped the backpack and took shitty shit out of the Walkman and put Maggie's trance mix back in, just like it had been when I got it. She wouldn't have to know I'd listened to her tapes or read her journals, though one day I was sure I would tell her.

The apartment building had the look of a halfway house where I'd once visited my mom—a thick main gate of wire mesh with a mess of barbed wire rolled at the top, all for nothing, since someone had propped the gate open an inch with a pizza box. The entranceway led to a little gravel-filled courtyard with eight apartment doors, each numbered with its own reflective sticker. But Maggie's address label hadn't listed an apartment number. Cinders shifted in my chest; every sound made me jump. Back inside the entranceway I found the mailboxes for the whole building. A few of them listed names, a few of them didn't, and there was no Smith. There was no way to know—she probably lived with her mom or another relative who didn't even share her last name. I felt hopeless and clutched at my butchered hair.

Someone crashed through the gate behind me, and I cried out in surprise—it was an old, drunk Navajo woman. I asked her if she knew where Maggie Smith lived. I said the name a few times, and soon she was repeating after me, "Maggie Smith, Maggie Smith, Maggie Smith," but she had no idea what she was saying. She kept banging into walls and falling down. I helped her up. She barged across the courtyard and started hammering on doors, crying out now, "Maggie Smith, Maggie Smith!" She understood I was looking for someone. Doors opened and slammed shut. The old woman careened back and forth across the dirt.

Then I heard, from somewhere above, a little voice: "Hi, I'm Maggie." The world fell into a hush. I looked up but couldn't see anything except dark windows and the purple night sky. "Here. I'm here," she said. The voice was unmistakably hers.

"I can't see you," I called. The old woman, deed done, lurched back across the courtyard and out the front gate. "Hey," I said into the deep silence, "I've got something that belongs to you. Your stuff."

"Is that my backpack?"

"My grandpa made me take it. To save Gilbert."

"Who's Gilbert?"

"His cat." I hadn't intended to confess everything all at once, but I felt I knew Maggie, and I had nothing to hide from her.

"Oh," she said. "Well, why don't you come inside for a minute? Wait, I'll come down."

I turned slow circles in the night, raked with chills, unsure which door would open. I thought of bolting off. Then I began to savor the moment, this tiny half-beat interlude before Maggie and I came face to face. It was like being perched at a swing's highest point back, waiting to rush the air.

A door squeaked open behind me. Halfway in and halfway out stood a middle-aged woman.

"Is that—is this—does Maggie live here?" I said.

She leaned a little further out into the light and peered at me and nodded. Her face was open and moonlike.

"Oh, well, I have her backpack. Could I give it to her? She was just talking to me out the window."

"I'm Maggie," the woman said.

I looked up again. She stepped out of her door and craned her neck back to follow my gaze toward the high window. The sky rippled, and the stars clustered in. I felt light. I felt far away from everything. "Well, come on in," she said.

I followed her inside. The apartment air tasted of damp earth and cigarette smoke. We went down a long, dark hallway into a little room with two couches and two TVs stacked totem pole–style with the sound off. On one a weatherman waved his hand; on the other, a black-and-white Frankenstein staggered down a hillside while lightning flashed and wild rain whipped around him. The woman kicked one of the couches, and the cushions seemed to sit up and arrange themselves into the shape of a man. He had a mask of orange face paint, and his hair was dyed green. "Noah," the woman said, "you got to wake up for this." She disappeared and came back with a glass of water. "Here," she said, "have a seat and drink this and tell me how you ended up with my backpack. I was so mad that they'd made me check it. I thought it was gone forever."

My heart jangled; I felt immersed in flame. I started into the story—telling her about Gilbert and how he was sick and all—and then the fever sacked me and the world seemed to turn inside out. In my mind it was three months later and I was collecting carts with my grandpa in the curling heat, my pants heavy with quarters. I was listening to Maggie's shitty shit tape with her playing the guitar. But I was also still there, talking to that woman in the den. Everything had become layered, like two different movies playing on the same TV. It was all real and it was all happening at the same time. More layers spooled out: I was climbing into my grandpa's truck an hour later, and the old Navajo woman was asleep across the front seat. Then I was back in the den, asking the woman for another glass of water. She brought her guitar out and was playing it for me and Noah, tapping a beat on its body, and singing tunelessly, "Hey, you've got to hide your love away. Oops. I fucked that up." It really was Maggie; I could tell from her voice. I asked how old she was; she said she was thirty-six. I asked the woman—Maggie—if I could keep one of her tapes. I lied and said I wanted the opera tape, then reached into the backpack and drew the shitty shit tape out and wedged it in my back pocket.

"What else can I do to thank you?" said Maggie. I was done with my story; the fever had cooled; we were in the den with the two TVs, but at some point she'd shut them off. "What would you most want? Anything. Just tell me, out of curiosity."

"But I stole your bag," I protested. "I'm just giving it back."

"He did steal your bag," Noah agreed sleepily, his lids hanging low.

"And you gave me a tape," I added. "That's a lot."

"Yup, baby," said Noah, "you did give him the tape."

The woman stared at me with owl eyes.

"Well," I said, "I'd like to talk to my brother. But that's impossible." I explained that he was on an aircraft carrier—the Independence—halfway around the world. Suddenly, unexpectedly, I was on the edge of tears.

Noah came alive. "That's not impossible," he said. "Calling him. A guy I work with, Frank Tavarez, his son's on a battleship somewhere, like Japan or the Persian Gulf. They talk every few weeks. It's always in the middle of the night." He jumped to his feet. "Hold on. Frank's maybe up right now." He headed down the hallway into a back room, and I heard the beeps of a phone being dialed and Noah's muffled voice: "Hey, Frank? You sleeping? Sorry, man. Right. Yeah. Hey, Frank, I got a question for you."

Maggie and I sat across from each other for the next twenty minutes, listening to Noah's conversations as he made one call after another; I could barely make out

his words, but I was hanging on every pause and intonation. At one point Noah
came back in and asked me for my brother's full name and the name of his unit,
then disappeared again down the hall. Here and there Maggie strummed her guitar
for a bit and hummed, as though to gently accentuate the action in the other room.
I was twitchy with nervous excitement. Every time I heard Noah dialing another
number, I imagined my brother at a command post in some dark, hot room deep
within his ship—the kind of red-lit chamber where people shouted things in submarine movies. I pictured a phone clanging to life in the middle of a vast circuitry
board, and my brother picking it up and saying, "This is Mabry," the same way
he'd answered the phones when he'd worked at Robert's Refrigeration & Cooling
Service in Gulfport.

Finally Noah sidled back down the hall, cradling the cordless phone between
his ear and his shoulder, a strange smile on his orange-painted face. "We found
him!" he said. "But your brother's actually not on the Independence. He got transferred to a base in Greece. We're on right now with the front desk at his barracks.
They're going up to his room to get him. It's past noon there. Guess they had a late
night last night. Life of a sailor, right? Here you go." He handed me the phone.

My heart flailed this way and that; the room rocked side to side. I pressed the
phone tight to my ear and absorbed the quiet buzzing silence. Maggie took Noah's
hand, and the two of them watched me, hopeful, open-faced. For a moment I
thought of the Maggie Smith I'd expected to meet that night, the Maggie my age,
and I wondered if I would ever find her, and if so, how and where and when it
would happen. The silence on the other end of the phone dragged on. My eyes
began to water again, and I turned my head away so Maggie and Noah wouldn't
see me cry. "Is he there?" asked Maggie. "Did he pick up?"

How can I describe what that silence was made of? It was thrilling, awful,
crushing. It brought every blow, every scrape, every nick, every pummeling that my
heart had ever taken straight to the surface. I found myself gasping. All I wanted was
to hear my brother's voice.

The rest of it is easier to tell: An hour later, at dawn, 5:15 in the morning, I
pulled the truck up in front of my grandpa's place, Maggie and Noah beside me.
Maggie wanted to look at Gilbert and see if she could figure out what was wrong
with him. But there was my grandpa on the front steps, cradling the cat in his arms.
The cat was dead. We got shovels and piled silently, all four of us, into the cab of
the truck—Noah at the wheel, Maggie next to him, then me, then my grandpa
at the passenger-side window, Gilbert on his lap. We took Central to I-40 to the
Turquoise Highway and headed up the back side of the mountain. We parked and
hiked a long, long ways up, taking turns carrying the cat. Finally we agreed on
a spot and dug a hole. My grandpa, breathing heavy, spread out on his belly and
lowered Gilbert in.

But that was all still to come. In Maggie's den, the silence on the phone hissed
and rumbled and crashed in my ear—it's the silence I still hear, always in the middle
of the night, when I'm walking down an empty highway, or rowing across the center of a lake, or holed up in the last, darkened Amtrak car, looking out the window

at distant twinkling lights. Some call it longing; I call it silence. That night, though, on the phone, there was a clattering sound, a pause, another little clatter, and then I heard my brother's voice, clear as a trumpet: "Hello? Hello? Anthony? Hello?"

Davy Rothbart is the author of the national bestseller *Found*, and creator of the magazine of the same name. A contributor to public radio's *This American Life*, he is also the author of the story collection *The Lone Surfer of Montana, Kansas*. He lives in Ann Arbor, Michigan.

ON THE DEATH OF JORDAN COLEMAN, THE IMPRISONMENT OF RYAN BOWER, AND THE LOSS OF MY CITY

EVELYN HOLLENSHEAD

I. To the Murdered, 10:40AM

The whispers ran like water through Michigan leaving me empty in Indiana.
I didn't hear the gun fire.
I didn't see the bullets wrap around your brain, tear apart your chest, destroy your
    organs.
I'll admit to you now that I don't even know where you were shot.
And yet I remember how the metal entered your body, opened your bones,
pressed against your ribcage.
Your cooling veins forced the muscles in your face to harden and
the abandonment of your heartbeat might have curled your lips into a smile
were it not for your best friend hovering above you,
your father's rifle clutched in his hands.

II. To the Murderer, 10:40AM

His screams made ripples in the pool of blood threatening to stain your sneakers.
The pads of your running feet failed to absorb the shock
of the sidewalk, of the situation.
The ringing in your ears swallowed the severity of bullet shells
hidden in your backpack.
The imprint of the gun in your hand heavy and malicious
caused the fear of imprisonment to curl around your neck like a python.
Your panic is no surprise but it is enough to age you two years in the eyes of the
    law.
It is strange, I know.
I have seen your buried high school a thousand times and never thought of
    retribution.

III. To the Boys, 10:40AM

I do not know how much grief I can justify for two people who, for me,
exist only in newsprint.
You are both strangers for whom I have already shed too many unexplained tears.
But I am in love with the way summertime graces this city and
I imagine that we all walked on the same sidewalk, once.
You, the boy torn open on the ground,
ate a Superman ice cream cone from the dairy I loved as a child.
You, the boy behind bars,
basked in the amber autumn offered by my neighborhood like a trophy.

But something went wrong and though
the ice that covered the tiny branches of trees dazzled for me,
to you it was nothing more than the cold devastation of winter.
This city which raised me failed you,
and it is for this I feel the need to express my sorrow to the street corners.
This city will never be a warm memory for you, and it is for this I am sorry.
But it is for myself that I weep,
because I cannot look joyfully upon the graffiti splashed buildings
when I am wondering how much blood is mixed in the paint.

Evelyn Hollenshead is a student at Earlham College in Indiana. She is a founding member of the performance poetry troupe Ann Arbor Wordworks, a two-time member of the Ann Arbor Youth Poetry Slam Team, and a former coach of the Ann Arbor Youth Poetry Slam Team.

WHAT YOU KNOW

PETER HO DAVIES

PEOPLE SUDDENLY WANT to know all about my students, what they're like. What do I know, I want to say. I'm just a writer, a writer-in-the-schools. All I see is their writing.

So what are they like as writers?

They're shocking. Appalling, in fact. Indescribably awful—and when a writer, even one of my low self-esteem, says that, you know it's serious. The good ones are bad, and the bad ones are tragic.

When at the start of each class I ask them their favorite books their fifteen-year-old faces are as blank as paper. The better students struggle to offer a "right" answer: *Catcher*, *Gatsby*, the Bible (!). The honest ones—the stupid, arrogant honest ones—tell me, *For the Love of the Game* by Michael Jordan, or the latest Dean Koontz.

The most voracious readers among them are the science-fiction fans, the genre nerds, the heavy-duty book worms (all those sequels and prequels; trilogies and tetrologies), but none of them are deterred for a nano-second when I tell them that good science-fiction is one of the hardest things to write. After all, they're thinking—I can see it in their eyes—it's just a matter of taste, isn't it?

As a matter of fact, no. I believe in the well-made story. Have your character want something, I tell them. Have a conflict. Have the character change. Learn these simple rules, and you can spend the rest of your life breaking them.

But most of the time I find myself telling them what not to write. All the narrative clichés. No stories about suicide. No narrators from beyond the grave. No, "And then I woke up," endings. No, "I woke up and then...," beginnings. No psychedelic dream sequences. The list of boringly bad stories ("But it's supposed to be boring, life is boring") goes on and on.

"No suicides?" they say in their flat, whiny voices, as if there is nothing else, nothing better. "How can suicide be boring?"

Maybe not in life, I explain quickly, but in fiction? Sure. It's a cruel world of readers out there—callous, heartless, *commuting* readers, who've been there, seen that, read it all before. "I'm not saying you can't try to write about suicide," I console them. "I'm just saying it's hard to do well, that you owe it to the material to do it justice, to find a way of making it real and raw for readers again."

They nod in complete incomprehension. Yes, they're saying. Yes, we see now that there is absolutely no chance we'll understand a word you say. We're just here for the extra credit. It's the nod you give a crazy man, a lunatic with a gun.

What redeems it? My love of teaching? I do love teaching, but for all the wrong reasons. I love the sound of my own voice. I love to pontificate about writing, get excited about it, argue about it (and usually win) with people who have to listen to me, more or less (unlike my parents, my friends, my wife). But always, behind their acquiescence, behind the fact that however bad my taste I'm still the coolest teacher they have (the competition is not stiff), lie the awful, numbing questions: "What have you published? Why haven't we heard of you?"

What really redeems it, then, are the laughs. The laughable badness of their prose. The moose frozen like a *d-e-a-r* in the headlights. The cop slapping on the *cuff-links*. The *viscous* criminal. The *escape* goat.

It's as if they're hard of hearing, snatching up half-heard, half-comprehended phrases, trusting blindly in their spell-checkers to save them. (Think! Think who designs spell-checkers for a moment. Were these people ever good spellers?)

I once had a heated argument with a student about the death KNOLL.

"Knell," I said.

"Knoll," he insisted with vehemence, until finally we determined that he was thinking of the *grassy* knoll. My way might be right, he conceded grudgingly, but his way made more sense. We took a vote in class (they love democracy) and the majority agreed. And perhaps this is the way that language, meaning, evolves before our very eyes and ears. "It's the death mole of literacy," I told them, but they didn't get it. Sometimes, I despair of language. If only there was some way for what I know to just appear, instanteously, in their heads.

So *that*, if you really want to know, is what my students are like. Does any of it explain why one of them last week shot his father in the head across the breakfast nook, rode the bus to school with a pistol in his waistband, emptied it in his homeroom, killing two and wounding five, before putting the gun in his mouth and splashing his brains all over the whiteboard?

In the moments after the crisis no one thinks to call me—as the other staff, the *full-time* staff are called—to warn me not to talk to the media. No one, in fact, thinks to call me *apart* from the media. "It's CNN," my wife says passing me the phone, then stepping back as if I hold a snake in my hands. But we're *watching* CNN, I want to say. I look at her and she mimes helplessness. It never occurs to me that all my fellow teachers have been asked to say nothing to the media, that this is why some bright spark in Atlanta after trying five or six names and getting the same response has slid his finger down the faxed list before him to "Other" and found me, not quite a teacher, but better than a janitor.

What he wants to know is if I had taught the killer, the dead boy, Clark, and when I admit, and it feels like an admission, nothing to be proud of, that yes I have him—*had him* (watch those tense changes)—in a writing workshop, I can hear the reporter lean forward in his chair, cup his hand around the mouthpiece. I wonder for a second about him, this young journalist, probably around my age, looking for his big break. This could be it, I realize, and I feel an odd vertiginous jealousy, almost wanting to hold back. But later, listening to my voice over and over on national TV—a grainy photo from the latest yearbook and a caption identifying me as a writer, floating over a live shot of the blank school buildings—I'm glad I talked to him, glad I didn't say anything stupid, that I come across as dignified and responsible. I answer all his questions in the first person plural. "We're shocked and appalled. We'll all be doing our best to help our students through this awful period. Our hearts go out to the families in the tragedy." Later my mother will call from Arizona, then my colleagues, even the principal with a warning not to say anything else, but an off-the-record pat on the back for "our unofficial spokesman." "A way with words," my mother will say. "You always had a way with words." Even though she's never read one of my stories. I tell her it was easy and it was. It comes naturally. For months now I've been talking in the first person plural. We're pregnant, my wife and I. We're expecting. We're about to be parents ourselves.

"CNN," my wife says, touching her stomach. "Something to tell the kid." It's not often she's proud of me, and I'm pleased, even though I despise the network, its incompetent staff. I heard one anchor a couple of years back talking about a first in the "anals" of country music. Another time I caught a piece in which the President was described as being "salt and peppered" with questions at a news conference. Someone wrote that, was paid to. "I suppose I should be grateful," I tell my wife. "My caption could have read 'waiter,' not 'writer.'" And she smiles uncertainly, not sure who this particular joke is on.

What I tell no one, though, not even my wife, is the reporter's last question, off air, quietly into my ear after he has thanked me and double-checked the spelling of my name. Only the tone alerted me, otherwise this could have been the same as any of the previous questions—"Was he a good student? What was he like?" This final shot: "Do you have anything he wrote for you? A poem or a story?"

I said, "No," but something in my voice must have made him wonder because he added softly, "It could be worth a great deal." So I said, "No," again, more forcefully and then, "I'm sorry," and hung up.

Why was I sorry? Easier to explain why I said, "No," with that catch of hesitation. Because I couldn't remember, that's why. I had work upstairs, ungraded stories, the response to an exercise. Something by Clark might be there, if he'd done the assignment. They often didn't. And, indeed, when I look there's nothing, just a note—brief—he'd been sick, and below his own signature, another—larger, flowing. It takes me a second to realize; it's his father's.

So why was I sorry? Because I'm a writer-in-the-schools. I earn $16,000 a year ($3000 less than my wife's bookstore job pays) and we are pregnant. I was sorry I hadn't had the nerve to say: "How much?" He might have even been bullshitting me, the reporter. CNN would never do business like that right? But something in his voice, the shift of register, made me think he might have just slipped into freelance mode. The phone was hot where I was pressing it against my head, but for a second I could have sworn it was his warm breath in my ear. Now I wondered—$1000, $5000, $10,000? Who knew? I was only sure it would be more than anything I'd ever gotten for my own work. And out of this irony, of course, came this idea. *I* could write a piece by Clark. I could write it and sell it. I could. His letter was typed, printed. He was a loner, without friends. His father was dead. He was dead. Who would know?

As a plan it seemed so simple at first, at least if you separate it from the issue of morality. And separating from that issue is something I teach my students. Don't stop yourselves writing something because it might hurt someone; your family, your friends. Don't stop yourself writing it because you think it's too personal, sexual, violent. Don't censor yourselves, I tell them, at least not alone when it's just you and the paper. No one else has to see it.

"But what's the point?" I remember one of them asking, "what's the point writing it if you're not going to show it to someone?" And I have sympathy with this. I believe in writing for an audience. Writing fiction is an act of communication—not just facts or opinions like a newspaper, but emotions. I tell them this. And in truth once something is written, actually expressed, showing it to someone—the desire to do that—is hard to escape. It's the momentum of the act. So I tell myself that writing a piece as Clark isn't the same as passing it off to others as Clark's, but once you've got it—especially if it's good—what else is there to do with it? So perhaps the moral problem does lie behind this practical one: it should be easy to write this piece—it doesn't have to be *good* after all; it needs, in fact, to be bad to be good—yet, after all the mockery I've heaped on their work, I can't do it. I can't imitate my students.

God help me, I'm blocked.

Here's the trouble. If I'm to write this and overcome the lie of it I need it to mean something. I want to offer, coded, buried, subtly perhaps, an answer, a psychological, sociological subtext, that will explain these deaths, and in explaining offer some hope or comfort to us all. It may not be *the* meaning, but surely any meaning, even a sniff of meaning is what we want. It is the writer's instinct to offer these things and, beyond mere morality, I can't quite shrug off this duty to, of all things, art.

Which is why I find myself in my '88 Subaru wagon, driving out to a gun range on the interstate called the Duke's Den. I have never fired a gun before and I decide that this—everything else not withstanding—is the problem. If I want to understand Clark, take on his voice, I should at least try to understand how he expressed himself.

And this, too, is what I teach them. Show don't tell. Write what you know. Did Clark's baseball cap bob at that one? Did he take notes? Some of them do and it still amazes me, makes me think they're making fun, when in truth they only set down what they don't understand. Show, they write carefully, and Tell.

Write what you know is even worse.

"So is that why we can't write about suicide? Because if you know it, you're, like, dead?"

"Yeah, and there're no narrator's from beyond the grave, right?"

They look at me, so pleased, so earnest, like they've figured it out and I feel my heart clench.

At least, I don't get any suicide stories. (Although as one smart guy recently pointed out: "It's ironic, don't you think? Considering how many writers kill themselves.") Instead, I get first kiss stories, first joint stories, the death of pets, the death of grandparents, sad fat girls, thin sad girls. The tone is always the same—life is tragic; tragically small or epicly tragic (the chasm, come to think of it, that suicide bridges).

What else do I teach them? I teach them what Forster says: that there are stories and there are plots. That stories are simple sequences of events (this happened and then this and then that), but that plots are about causes, motivation (this happened because of this, on account of that). And the truth is that life is all stories and fiction is all plots, and what we're looking for in Clark's story is the plot that makes sense of it. Which is why it has to be someone's fault—his, his father's, the NRA, Nintendo, Hollywood—all the escape goats. This happened because of that or that or that. Or all of them.

So that's what I teach them; how to plot.

And if that's beyond them, what I try to leave them with is this; when in doubt, when stuck, blocked or fucked, to always ask themselves, "What if?" (Even if their instinct is to ask, "So what?")

What if I pick up a gun and fire it?

The range is quiet. It's the weekend after the shooting, we're still in shock. I show my driver's license and join for twenty-five bucks, which entitles me to rent guns from behind the counter for five dollars an hour. It seems so cheap—what can you get for five bucks?—but as I buy ammunition for my choice, a thirty-eight caliber revolver (I just pointed to the first gun I recognized from TV), I realize that this is what costs.

The man behind the counter is unfailingly polite and helpful. He reminds me of a hardware salesman, the kind of guy in a brown apron who'll show you how to use a tool, dig out exactly the right size of wrench or washer for your job. The kind of guy who loves what he does and who'll tell you all about it if you're not careful. His name is Vern, and above his head, hanging up like so many hammers and saws on a workshop wall, are all manner of guns—not just pistols but rifles, even a replica Tommy gun, the kind of thing Al Capone might have used. There's an air of fancy dress about the display; an air of the toy store, the magic trick. On a ledge at the very top of the wall is a line of model railway rolling stock. Vern is a train enthusiast, a hobbyist.

After the gun and the shells, he hands over a pair of ear defenders and then asks, "Target?" I must look puzzled, because he repeats himself. "What kind of target?"

"What kinds do you have?"

He grins, glad I asked, and starts to show me. There's a simple roundel, each ring marked with a score, the "classic" silhouette, a sheet covered in playing cards for "shooting poker," a double silhouette of a gunman and a woman, his hostage, and finally a set of caricature targets of everyone from Saddam Hussein to Barney. I take the classic silhouette and Vern rolls it for me and secures it with a rubber band. He hands me the lot—gun, shells, target, ear defenders in a plastic tray—and points me back toward the range which is separated from the shop by double-glazing. Through the glass I can see one man, broad shouldered, graying, balding, firing. "You put your headset on in the booth," Vern tells me, indicating the double set of doors between the shop and the range. "Take lane three."

Inside, with the ear defenders pinching my skull, the shots from the other man in the range sound like a distant throbbing pulse. I set up in the lane beside him.

Place the gun on the counter and the shells beside it, work the toggle switch that brings the target toward me on a wire. All this is familiar from the movies. When the target board arrives I'm momentarily at a loss as to how to fix the silhouette to it. I look around and there's Vern on the other side of the glass pointing and when I look again I see a tape dispenser mounted to the shelf.

I run the target back about halfway to the rear concrete wall. It's ridged, corrugated, and it takes me a slow moment to realize that this is to prevent ricochets. The concrete makes the range cooler than the shop, like a bunker and it smells, but only faintly, of Fourth of July, fireworks. And this creeping nostalgia, the insulation of the ear defenders, the odd underground cool, give the experience an air of unreality.

The target jumps about on the wire for a few seconds like a puppet and I wait until it's still before turning to the gun. Vern has taught me how to load it, flipping out the cylinder and dropping in the shells. It's a six shooter, but he warned me to put five shots in and leave the chamber under the hammer empty, "to save your toes." The bullets go in very easily and quickly—the whole thing feels well made in a way that very few things do these days—and I slide the cylinder back into the gun. I hold it away from me and down and then slowly raise it. Vern has shown me how to cock the hammer and fire, or how to pull the trigger all the way back. He has advised me to keep my trigger finger outside the guard until I'm ready to shoot. I'm frightened of it going off before I'm ready, of seeming dangerous. But once I have it in position, cocking it is simple and when I fire my first shot I'm surprised how easy it comes. (Vern is a good teacher.) There's a crack and a small flash from the gun, but the recoil is almost playful in the way it bats my hand up. I've hit serves that jarred worse. I look last at the target and see a small neat puncture in the shoulder of my silhouette. Almost too neat, but for the slight tearing of the paper. I fire again. And again and again and again. Because after all, what else is there to do? By my fifth shot I'm not cocking, but experimenting with pulling the trigger back. Two of my shots score tens in the target's chest. With my next set I take aim at the head and put all five on target. I feel like Dirty Harry, or Steve McGarrett. Just not Clark.

Beside me as I'm loading again, the other shooter reels in his target, unrolls another and tapes it up. He's old, grandfatherly, dressed in polyester, metallic blue sansabelt pants and a teal polo shirt. He nods and I nod back. He looks like a bowler and I realize that's exactly what this experience is reminding me of, bowling. I'd laugh at him rather than nod back, that slightly too portentous nod, except that he has a loaded weapon on the counter before him, a tool with which he could kill me. It occurs to me that if he took that into his head the only thing stopping him would be the fact that I might shoot back.

I try to ask myself what this might have meant to Clark, but I can't guess. The experience isn't inspiring, just deadening, mechanical. I feel my writer's-block panic rising again, and with it the greed. We need the money. I think of my own son, my unborn son (I wanted to know the sex; not for me the surprise ending), for whom I'm doing this, and I wonder what might possibly ever drive him to kill me. I know I thought about killing him. We talked about it, about a termination, an abortion. We hadn't planned on this. I kept thinking something would come up; a new job, a major publication. I had a story with one of the slick magazines and they had held it for weeks, months, so long my hopes were rising day by day. A score like that—thousands of dollars—could change our lives. I found myself putting my imaginative energy not into new work, but into visualizing that moment, the letter in the mail, not in my own self-addressed envelope, but the magazine's embossed one, telling me blah, blah, blah, *delighted*. I didn't say so, but I think I'd decided we'd keep the baby if I sold the story. When the rejection letter ("too familiar") finally came with that sudden rushing inevitability they all have, I couldn't stop shaking. My wife, used to rages or resignation, was speechless. But later, lying in bed I realized, *how insane*. In the morning, we talked it through again and I told my wife I thought we should go ahead and she cried and held me and I felt saved.

So the thought that one day in some world this child might kill me, might shoot me in the face, who wants to imagine that? And yet, and yet, when I think of my own father, there have been . . . moments. If I had a gun, knew how to use one. Oh yes. But petty reasons, anger over a grounding, over using the car, disappointing him. Not worth killing for. Not worth going out and buying a gun and laying in ambush for. But if the gun were at hand? Not worth running upstairs for, perhaps, not worth crossing the hall for, but if it were in the drawer, on the counter, in my hand? I did punch my father once. I'd come in late and he waited up, barred the door to my room. We yelled at each other and I raised a fist. There was a moment when I could have lowered it, merely threatened, but having made it I couldn't stop. I hit him and he took a step back, out of surprise, I think. "Do that again," he told me when he'd recovered himself, and I did—bowing to that curious complicit male desire to make a bad thing worse, to transform an accident, a mistake, into a tragedy, to render ourselves not hapless, not foolish and vain, but heroic, grand, awesome. And he took the next shot too, and then he beat me unconscious (in fact, he only raised his own fist and I took a step back, fell down the stairs and knocked myself cold—so close is tragedy to farce—but the first version makes a better story). Except if it hadn't been a fist, if it had been a gun I'd raised, he wouldn't have had the chance, would he? And all over nothing.

He's dead now, my father, and as I empty the gun I'm thinking of naming my son after him.

Shooting is actually duller than bowling, I'm finding, duller and easier. I can daydream while doing it. There's something effortless and magical in the seemingly instantaneous bang and the appearance yards away of a small hole. I fire another twenty rounds. I move the target back, forward. I shoot to kill, I shoot to wound, I shoot from the hip. I suddenly understand why someone might rent a machine gun. What I want most in the world I realize is a moving target, a more interesting target. The idea on the range is marksmanship, but there's no real challenge here. I look down the barrel of my gun, but watch the shots of the man next to me. He doesn't seem much better, and I've only been shooting for twenty minutes. I watch him cluster his shots in the high scoring body of the target, one, two, three, four. Nothing. And something about the rhythm, my focus on his target, makes me swing my gun over and put a fifth shot into the face of his target. Perhaps because of the angle I'm firing from, the bullet makes a ragged hole, tearing loose a strip of paper that curls slighty, flaps like a tongue. I hold my breath, horrified. I keep the gun raised, keep sighting down it. I can't hear anything from my neighbor behind his screen. Perhaps he's reloading, hasn't noticed. The pause goes on and eventually, I empty my revolver, slowly and methodically into my target. When I'm done and my gun is down and I'm pushing out the shells, I feel a heavy tap on my shoulder. It's him. He's waited for me to empty.

He mouths something, and I shake my head, lift an ear cup.

"What the hell was that back there?" he asks again, gesturing toward the target, without taking his eyes off me. His hand is huge and mottled red and white where he's been gripping his gun. His other hand is out of sight.

"Sorry," I tell him, and it sounds as if I'm speaking in slow motion. "A. Mis. Fire?"

He looks at me for a long moment, waits for my eyes to meet his, the dark muzzles of his pupils behind their yellow protective goggles. It occurs to me that they are the exact same shade as my computer screen, and I imagine my precious last words drifting across them, the letters springing into existence under the beating cursor: "like a d-e-a-r in the headlights." Finally, he nods and says, "All right, then," vanishes back behind his booth.

I reload, pressing the shells home, letting their snug fit steady me, and wait for him to start firing again. And wait and wait and wait until my hand begins to tremble, and finally I can't not fire. The gap between thought and action is so fine. It's like standing on a cliff, the way the fear of falling makes you want to end the tension, take control, jump before you fall. I felt the death mole, if you like. I felt it burrowing forward, undermining me.

Only when I'm empty, do I see my neighbor's target beside me jerk finally. He puts five rounds into the head of his target in a tight fist, then draws it toward him, packs up and leaves. I still have ammo left. Unfinished business, like a chore. I pick the gun back up and fire round after round after round like hammering nails.

Sometime in there—after the fear wears off and then the elation, and the boredom sets in—I realize there's nothing to learn here. This won't tell me anything about Clark. And the thought of the continuing failure fills me with sudden despair. I put the gun down for a moment, afraid of it. I have about one suicidal thought a year, but this isn't a good time to be having it. And then the moment passes, because I know with an adrenaline fueled clarity that killing myself won't make any kind of difference. I know my wife will go on, my son will be born. My work won't suddenly be discovered. There's no point. And it's a crushing feeling. Knowing that the ultimate gesture, the very worst thing you can do is nothing special, a failure of imagination.

I fire five more times, reel in my target, roll it up in a tight tube.

When I return my gun and pay, Vern gives the name on my credit card a long look.

"I thought I knew you. You're the teacher from that school. You were on TV." He shakes his head sadly, and for a second I think it's a moment of contrition, and then he says, "What are you teaching those kids, anyway?"

I pass behind school on my way home and I have to stop, I'm shaking so much. It's in my bones now, the distant ringing shudder of the gun. My hands smell of powder, my hair, my shirt, and I clamber out of the car before I gag. There's an old pack of Marlboro Lights in the glove compartment from before my wife got pregnant, and I fumble for a cigarette, suck on it until all I can taste is tobacco smoke.

The storm fence here has been festooned with tokens; flowers, cards, soft toys hang from the wire. Damp from the dew, a little faded already, they ripple in the breeze, fluttering and twisting against the chain-link as if caught in a net. I lean on my hood, watching the twilight seep up out of the earth toward the still bright sky.

What do I teach them? I teach them that telling stories is the easiest and hardest thing in the world, and among the looks of disbelief and confusion there's always one who nods, who gets it, like the teenage fatalist who asked me once, "Because there are only so many stories, right? Like seven or something." Seven, or ten, or a dozen, although no one can agree what they are and there's countless ways of telling them wrong. But the theory feels right. A finite number of stories, which writers try to tell over and over again. So suicide is boring? Then how do you make it not boring? How do you make it exciting? How do you make it new? So original, so vital, that it speaks to an audience?

Before the light fades completely, I step up to the fence to read the messages. The first moves me close to tears, and I sag against the wire. It's such a relief. I read another and another, hungrily, but by the time I've read a dozen, my eyes are dry as stone. I snatch at them, plucking them down, the ribbon and colored wool they dangle from gouging through the soft card. Taken together they're clichéd, mawkish, misspelled. There are hundreds of them stretching forty, fifty yards in each direction, as far as I can see in the gloom, like so much litter swept here by the wind. And I want to tear them all down, I want to rip them to shreds. Every awful word.

Peter Ho Davies is the author of the story collections, *The Ugliest House in the World* and *Equal Love*, and the novel, *The Welsh Girl*. He teaches Creative Writing at the University of Michigan, where he's grateful his students aren't anything like the students in his story (and fervently hopes he's nothing like the teacher).

IF A STRANGER APPROACHES YOU ABOUT CARRYING A FOREIGN OBJECT ONTO THE PLANE . . .

LAURA KASISCHKE

ONCE THERE WAS a woman who was asked by a stranger to carry a foreign object with her onto a plane:

When the stranger approached her, the woman was sitting at the edge of her chair a few feet from the gate out of which her plane was scheduled to leave. Her legs were crossed. She was wearing a black turtleneck and slim black pants. Black boots. Pearl studs in her ears. She was swinging the loose leg, the one that was tossed over the knee of the other—swinging it slowly and rhythmically, like a pendulum, as she tried to drink her latte in burning sips.

By the time the stranger approached her and asked her to carry the foreign object with her onto the plane, the woman had already owned that latte for at least twenty minutes, but it hadn't cooled a single degree. It was as if there were a thermonuclear process at work inside her cup—the steamed milk and espresso somehow generating together their own heat—and the tip of her tongue had been stung numb from trying to drink it, and the plastic nipple of the cup's white lid was smeared with her lipstick.

Her name was Kathy Bliss. She was anxious. At home, her two year old was sick, but she'd had to go to Maine, anyway, because she'd been asked to speak on behalf of the nonprofit for which she worked, and possibly thousands upon thousands of dollars would be gifted to it by her hosts if she were able to conjure the right combination of passion and desperation with which she was sometimes able to speak on behalf of her nonprofit. She didn't much believe in what they were doing, which was, to her mind, mostly justifying the spending of their donations on computers and letterhead and lunches with donors, but she had her eye on another nonprofit, one devoted to curing a disease (or at least *publicizing* a disease) which no one knew about until it was contracted, at which time the body attacked itself, turning the skin into a suit of armor, petrifying the internal organs one by one. The vice president of this nonprofit had his eye on the regional directorship of the American Cancer Society, she knew, and with some luck his position would be open, and she would be ready to move into it.

Still, she'd always understood that you have to put your energy into the place you are if you want to move on to another place; and, on occasion, she could be convincing—something about the podium, a bottle of water, a few notes, and all eyes on her—and there was clearly no one else at her nonprofit who could even remotely have been considered for this engagement. (Jen, with her multiple piercings? Rob, with his speech impediment?) She had to go.

The baby was sick, but the baby would be fine. Kathy Bliss had a husband, after all, who would take care of their baby. He was the baby's father, for God's sake. This wasn't 1952. The man had a Ph.D. in compassion; who was she to think the baby would be any better off with her there just because she was *of a certain gender*? And if she hadn't had to go to Maine, Garrett would have gone to work himself, which would have left only one parent at home, anyway, doing the same thing either way—cuddling, cleaning up puke, taking the temp, filling the sippy cup with cold water.

Still, Kathy Bliss felt a pain, which she knew, intellectually, was imaginary, but nonetheless was excruciating, hovering around a few inches above her breasts, as if only moments ago something adhesive—a bandage, duct tape, a baby—had been ripped away from her bare flesh and taken a top layer of cellular material with it.

The latte had scalded her tongue (just the tip) to the point that she could feel, when she moved it across the ridge behind teeth, the rough little bumps of it gone completely dead—just a prickling dullness. Without the taste buds to interfere, Kathy Bliss could really feel the ridge behind the back of her teeth, the place where the bone smoothed into flesh, the difference between what was there for now and what, when she was dead, would be left. She took another sip. Better. Maybe it had cooled down a bit, or maybe her tongue couldn't register the heat of it anymore. That was probably dangerous, she thought. The way people got scalded. Their nerve endings dulled, and they stepped into the tub without knowing it would cook them.

"Sorry," the stranger said after his pant leg brushed her knee, but she didn't really look at him, not yet. His tan belt was at eye level, nothing remarkable about it, and then he was gone.

As was always the case in airports, there was a small crowd of confused people (the elderly, the poor, some foreigners) standing patiently in a line they didn't need to stand in, and a woman behind a counter who was waving them away one by one as they approached her with their fully sufficient pieces of paper.

"We'll be boarding in forty minutes," the woman said over and over, refusing to smile, make eye contact, or answer questions. The woman had a spectacular hairpiece on top of her head. A kind of beehive with fronds. When she waved, the fronds shivered, caught the light, looking fountain-like, or like incandescent antennae. Although the woman had dark skin (tanning booth?), her real hair was a pale pink-blond beneath the hairpiece, which was the synthetic blond of a Barbie doll. What had the woman been thinking, Kathy Bliss wondered, that morning at the mirror, placing it atop her head. What had she believed she would look like with that thing on her head? Had she *wanted* to look the way she did—shocking, alien, a creature out of an illustrated Hans Christian Andersen?

Many years before, when Kathy Bliss was a college student, in an incident that had, she believed, changed and defined her forever, she'd come across a dead body in the Arboretum. A woman. Stabbed. Mostly bones and some scraps of clothing—and she (Kathy Bliss, not the dead woman) had run screaming.

It had been a very quick glimpse, so of course she hadn't known at the time that the body was that of a woman, or that the woman had been stabbed, knew nothing of the details until she was given them later by the police. Still, she knew that she must have stood there open-mouthed for at least a second or two (she had been running on a trail but gone off of it to pee) because she clearly saw, or *remembered* seeing, that there were bees in that dead woman's hair.

When a few people left the line, a few more entered it. All over the airport, there were such sad, small crowds. They hesitated together at every counter, not ready to believe that all was well, not able to so easily accept the assurance that they already had what they needed, that they had found their proper places so quickly and had only now to wait. Kathy Bliss herself had forced one such crowd to part for her when she entered the terminal, pulling her luggage on wheels behind her as she made her way to security. She could feel their eyes on her back as she passed, knew they were probably loathing and admiring in equal measure her swift professional purposefulness. *She* knew where she was going. *She'd* done this a million times.

But, to her ears, anyway, the wheels of her luggage made the sound of a spit turning quickly (but with some effort) over a burning pit, as she dragged it behind her. She had no idea why. They weren't rusty. It was a fairly new bag. It had never been left out in the rain or pulled through the mud. But there it was, the sound of a spit, turning. A pig on that spit. An apple in its mouth. That final humiliation: *We shall eat you, Pig.*

She couldn't believe it when, at the *SAVe a LIFe!* picnic that summer, that they'd actually *done* that, actually roasted a pig on a spit with an apple crammed into its mouth.

At first, she hadn't noticed it because she'd been busy meeting and greeting. ("Yes, yes, of course I remember. Nice to see you again. Thank you for coming.")

But after she'd filled her glass with punch and had just tipped the glass to her lips, she'd seen it out of the corner of her eye, taken one step toward it, seen it fully then, and reeled—literally reeled—and splashed pink punch onto her chest, where it trickled down in a sweet zigzagging rivulet between her breasts.

Luckily, she'd been wearing a low-cut dress, also pink.

"Whoa," the college president she'd been standing next to said when she reeled. "Friend of yours or something? Are you a vegetarian?"

"Jesus," she'd said, "I am now," turning her back to the spit, trying to smile. But there was a cool film of sweat all over her body, as if each pore had opened in a moment, coating her with dew. "What a spectacle."

"Isn't that the point?" the college president had said.

"*Because of heightened security measures,*" the ceiling droned, "*we ask that you report any unattended luggage. If a stranger should approach you and ask you to carry a foreign object with you onto a plane, please contact a member of security personnel immediately.*"

"Excuse me?" the stranger said, taking a seat beside her.

Kathy Bliss turned, swinging her leg off her knee, placing both black boots beside one another on the floor.

"Yes?"

The stranger was young and handsome. He had dark hair and tan skin and large brown eyes. Slender fingers. What appeared to be an actual gold Rolex on his wrist. He was wearing a white shirt with a red tie and a black leather jacket. An Arab, she thought right away, and then felt bad for thinking it. He had no accent; she could tell that already from the two words he'd spoken. He was an American, not an

"Arab." He was probably more American than she was, her mother's parents having stumbled into this country from Liverpool, broke, in the twenties, her paternal grandparents having dashed across the Canadian border in the thirties in search of higher-paying employment with the US Postal Service.

Still, it must be awful, she thought, to *look* like an Arab in an airport these days. It must have felt, she supposed, like wearing a scarlet *A*. Everyone staring, either wondering suspiciously about you and feeling guilty about wondering, or feeling suspicious and self-righteous about staring and wondering. "I'm sorry to bother you," the stranger said. "Are you, by any chance, going to Portland?"

"Yes," Kathy Bliss said.

"Well—" he smiled, and then his breast pocket began to play the theme from *The Lone Ranger* loudly and digitally, and he reached into it and fumbled around for a moment until it stopped and he said, "Sorry," shaking his head. For a crazy second Kathy Bliss thought of asking him to check the caller ID, to make sure her husband wasn't trying to reach her with some news about the baby (she'd turned her own cell off to conserve the battery, and would check it just before she got on the plane)—but, of course, this stranger had nothing to do with her baby.

"Can I help you?" she asked.

The man had a tiny gold cross in his left earlobe. It was really very beautiful—and strange, too, how masculine that little earring made him look with the dark shadow of beard on his chiseled jawline, and how masculine he made that earring by wearing it in his ear, with its foiled brilliance. A small, bold statement. It might have been a religious statement or a fashion statement, what difference did it make?

"Yes, but please," he said, "if this sounds strange to you, just send me away."

"Okay?" she said. A question.

"Okay," he said. "I'm supposed to be going to Portland for my mother's seventieth birthday, but I just got a call from my girlfriend telling me"—he smiled ruefully, rolled his eyes to the ceiling—"I'm sorry, I should make something up here, but I'll just tell you the truth: she's pregnant. And she's flipping out. And I feel like"—he tossed some emptiness into the air with his palms, making a gesture she'd seen men make many times in response to women's emotional states—"honestly—I think I ought to go buy her an engagement ring *today*, and get my butt back to our apartment. I mean, this isn't a disaster. Or it doesn't *have* to be. We were getting married, anyway, and we knew we might get pregnant. We weren't even using any—" He shook his head. "I'm sorry, *really* sorry, to be filling you in on all these details. I'd made it through security, I was planning to just go and come back maybe even tonight, and then I realized—I just realized I shouldn't go at all. That I should go straight back to my girlfriend right now." He inhaled, looked at Kathy Bliss as if trying to gauge her reaction. "I'm sorry," he said, "to fill you, a complete stranger, in on these sordid details."

Kathy Bliss tried to laugh sympathetically. She shook her head a little. Shrugged. "It's okay," she said. "Been there, done that!"

The stranger laughed pretty hard at this. His teeth were very straight and white, although one of the front ones had what looked to be a hairline crack in it. A very thin gray crack. Her two year old, Connor, had just recently gotten so many new teeth that it surprised her every time he opened his mouth. The teeth were like little dabs of meringue. Clean and white and peaked. She liked to smell his breath. It was as if there were a pure little spring in there. His mouth smelled like mineral water.

"Well, there you have it," the stranger said. "I guess, if nothing else, we're all here because *somebody'd* been there and done that."

"That, too," Kathy Bliss said. "But, I mean, I have a child. It's a great thing."

"Yeah," he said. "I'm starting to forget, in all this hysteria, the great fact that I'm going to be a dad—"

"Well, congratulations from me," Kathy Bliss said. She felt the warm implication of tears starting somewhere around her sinuses, and swallowed. She changed her latte cup from her right hand to her left, reached over the metal armrest, and offered her hand to him. He shook it, smiling. Then he shook his own hand as if it had been burned. "Jeez," he said, "that's one burning handshake."

"My latte," she said. "It's like molten lava."

"I guess so," he said.

The stranger was wearing khaki pants with very precisely ironed creases. For a quick second Kathy Bliss wondered if his girlfriend was also an Arab, and then she remembered that she had no way of knowing that *he* was an Arab, and far more evidence, anyway, that he *wasn't*—and reminded herself that it didn't matter, anyway. So, maybe his parents had been born in Egypt, or Iran. The color of his skin was beautiful! A warm milky brown. She felt a pang of jealousy about the girlfriend, lying on their bed at home, not knowing that this beautiful stranger was making desperate plans to buy her a diamond that day. What a thing, this life. Love. God, when it worked, it really worked! She had, herself, fallen in love with her husband upon first sight. She'd been given his name as the best shrink in town for the kind of problem she was having—which was spending every minute of her day trying not to think about the dead body in the Arboretum for two solid years after she'd seen it—and she had no sooner settled herself in the chair across from his, and he'd crossed his legs, looking more anxious and frightened than she, herself, the *patient*, felt, that she knew she wanted to marry him. And he'd cured her, too. Without drugs. A few behavior modifications. A rubber band around her wrist, a mantra, a series of self-punishments and rewards.

"Well, to make a long story short," the stranger said, "my girlfriend's freaking out back at our apartment, and my mother's turning seventy in Portland, and I'm her only son, who's such a scoundrel and an ingrate, not to mention morally reprehensible for impregnating someone he's not married to, *yet*, that he's not even showing up for her party, so"—and here he shook his head and looked directly into Kathy Bliss's eyes—"I wonder if I, a stranger, could ask you, a passenger, to carry a foreign object with you onto the plane?"

"Oh my God," Kathy Bliss said. "All these years I was wondering if anyone was ever going to ask me that."

"I think," the stranger said, "now is the point at which you ought to contact security personnel—like, right away."

"Yes," she said, "I think I may have heard an announcement pertaining to that. And I've always wondered to myself what kind of idiot would actually do such a thing, like carry a foreign object onto a plane."

"Well," the stranger said, "here's the object you've been waiting your whole life to carry with you onto the plane."

Out of a pocket in the inner lining of his coat, the stranger produced a narrow rectangular box wrapped in gold paper. He sighed. "It's a gold necklace, and if you'd be so foolhardy as to carry it with you onto the plane, I'd call my brother and have him meet you at baggage claim and get it to the party this evening. *But*"—he waved his slender fingers around over the box—"I totally understand if you think that's nuts."

"I have no problem with it," she said. "Don't worry, I won't contact security personnel."

"Let me open it for you, at least," he said, "so you know you're not carrying a bomb—"

"If you managed to get a bomb in that little package," she said, "you deserve to have it carried by a passenger onto the plane."

She regretted the joke even as she said it, saw the Towers dissolving into dust on her television again. It had been on the floor because the entertainment center had not yet arrived (it was being custom-built somewhere in Illinois) and there was no table or counter big enough to put the television on. The baby was crying (eight weeks old), so she'd had to stand and pace with his hot little face leaking tears onto her shoulders as those Towers collapsed at her feet. The front door had been open, and it had smelled to her as if the stone-blue perfect sky out there were dissolving in talcumish particles of dried flowers—such a beautiful day it horrified her. An illusion dipped in blue. She could have walked with her baby straight out the front door or right into the big-screen TV of it, and they might have turned themselves into nothing but subatomic particles, blue light, perfume.

There was nothing funny about terrorism. Nothing even remotely funny about terrorism. Still, she was from the Midwest, and it seemed like a long time ago already. No more National Guard in the airport—those boys with their big weapons trying not to look bored and out of place around every corner. She had, herself, only been to New York a few times, and never to those Towers, having only glimpsed them from her plane as it banked into LaGuardia. From the plane, they'd looked like Legos, and no matter how real she knew it all was, on the television, on the floor, it had not looked real. And the least likely plane a terrorist would want to blow up or hijack was one traveling from Grand Rapids, Michigan, to Portland, Maine. Right? "Don't unwrap that," she said. "It's exquisite. I trust you."

"I insist," he said. "This is too weird and too much of a . . . cliché! I have my dignity!" He laughed. "And in any case, I will doubt your sanity if you don't let me open it. I can't have a crazy woman delivering my mother's birthday present—"

"No," Kathy Bliss said, snatching the little present off his lap. "You'll never get it wrapped like this again. It's like a little dream. I'd be insane if I thought you could get anything *but* a necklace in that box."

He made his mouth into a zero, and sighed, loosened his tie a little by inserting his index finger between the knot and his collar. From somewhere on the other side of the wall of screens that listed arrivals and departures, a baby began to cry, and the feeling came back to her—the ripping, intensely, as if yet another layer of skin, or whatever was underneath her skin, were being pulled off her torso in one quick yank. The stranger took the cell phone out of his pocket and said, "I'll call my brother. Can I tell him your name? I'll have him at baggage claim—I mean—" He interrupted himself here. "I'm assuming that's where you'll be going—" He looked at the black bag at her feet. "Did you check luggage?"

"Yes," she said. "I mean no, but I can go to baggage claim, no problem. Tell him—"

"I'll have him carry a sign, with your name on it, okay?"

"Yes. Kathy Bliss."

"Bliss?" He smiled. "Like, 'bliss'?"

"Yes," she said. "Like the Joseph Campbell thing. 'Follow your bliss.' "

He smiled, but she could tell he hadn't heard of Joseph Campbell, or the advice of Joseph Campbell. She had, herself, been in graduate school when the PBS series with Bill Moyers had aired, and gotten together every Tuesday night with a group of women from her Mind, Brain, and Violence Seminar to watch it. A lot of joking about Bliss, and following it, had been made. When she'd get up to go to the bathroom or to get a beer out of the refrigerator, someone always pretended to follow her.

"*We would like to begin boarding passengers on Flight 5236 to Portland, Maine. Passengers traveling with small children or needing special assistance . . . *"

"That's me," she said.

"Yes," he said. "Of course. I'll make the call after you board. But let me tell you, my brother—he's twenty-two, but he looks a lot like me. I haven't seen him in a year, and sometimes he has long hair and sometimes he shaves his head, so"—he shrugged—"who knows. But he's about five-nine, one hundred sixty pounds—"

Kathy Bliss slipped the gold-wrapped box into her black bag carefully, so he could see that he could trust her with it. "Well," she said, "he'll have my name on a piece of paper, right? It'll be simple."

"Am I right, the plane's supposed to land at 12:51?" the stranger asked, peeking into the inner lining of his suit coat again, as if to look at his own unnecessary itinerary.

"Yep," she said. "12:51, assuming we're on time."

"Here," he said, hurrying with a piece of paper and a pen he'd taken from the pocket of his suit coat, "my brother's name is Mack Kaloustian. He'll be there. Or I'll kill him, and he knows it."

Kaloustian. Armenian. Kathy Bliss blinked and saw a spray of bullets raking through a family in a stand of trees on a mountaintop, a mother shielding her child, collapsing onto him: That child might have been this stranger's grandmother. And then they were boarding her row—twelve. Kathy Bliss stood up and extended her hand to the stranger. "Good luck to you," she said with all the warmth she could generate with only four words. The second word, *luck*, caught in her throat—a little emotional fishhook made out of consonants—because it was all so lovely, and simple, and lucky. Nothing but goodness in it for anyone. And her part in this sweet small drama moved her deeply, too—this gesture she was making of pure human camaraderie, this nonprofit venture, this small recognition of the cliché *We're all in this together.* That it mattered. Love. Family. The stranger. The favor. The bond of trust between them. He knew she wouldn't disappear into Portland with his gold necklace. She knew he wouldn't—what? Send her onto a plane with an explosive? He shook her hand so warmly it was like a hug. He said, "I can't tell you how much I appreciate this," and she said, "Of course. I'm happy to be able to help," and then she walked backward so she could extend the moment of their smiling and parting, and then turned, inhaling, and began the dull and claustrophobic process of boarding her plane.

Kathy Bliss had been born and raised in a little stone house at the edge of a deep forest. "Honest to God," she always had to say after giving someone this piece of information about herself for the first time. "But it was nothing like you're imagining."

Her father had worked for a minimum-security prison, and the prison had been the thing her bedroom window faced, its high cyclone fencing topped by hundreds of yards of coiled barbed wire. In the summer, the sun rising in the east over the prison turned that barbed wire into a blinding fretwork, all spun-sugar and baroque and glitter, as if the air had been embroidered with silver thread by a gifted witch. She'd squint at it pretending that what her bedroom faced was an enchanted castle, as if the little stone house at the edge of the dark forest really were something from a fairy tale. But it was a sedentary childhood. Her parents wouldn't let her play in the yard or wait outside for the bus because, if there were an escape, she would make too good a hostage, being the prison director's daughter. For this reason, Kathy Bliss rarely had the chance to see the prisoners milling around behind that barbed wire, wearing their orange jumpsuits, and was able, therefore, to imagine them handsome and gallant as knights.

She and her mother had moved, when Kathy was nine, after her father died from an illness that announced itself first as bleeding gums, and then paralysis, and then he was just gone. She was thinking about this blip in her first years—the stone house, the barbed-wire castle—and watching the other passengers struggle onto the plane, shoving their heavy luggage into overhead compartments, the fat ones sweating, the thin ones trembling, the mothers with babies and little children looking blissfully burdened, when a voice came over the plane's intercom and said, "If there is a Katherine Bliss onboard, could she please press the flight attendant call button now?"

"Oh my God," Kathy Bliss said so loudly that an old woman standing in the aisle next to her whirled around and hit the call button for her. "Is that you?" the old woman said, as if she knew what they were calling Kathy Bliss about, as if everyone knew. "Yes," she said. "I forgot to check my messages." "Oh dear," the old woman said. The skin hung off her face in gray rags, and yet she'd made herself up carefully that morning, with tastefully understated foundation and blush, the kind of replica of life that would cause all gathered around her casket to say, "She just looks as if she's sleeping."

There began a cold trickling at the tip of Kathy Bliss's spine, and then it turned into a fine mist, coating every inch of her. She could not close her mouth. She tried to stand, but there were so many people in the aisle she couldn't get out of her seat, although the old woman had turned to face the strangers surging forward and put a bony arm in front of her as if to try to block their passage. "Ma'am," a flight attendant said from ten feet behind that line, looking at the old woman. "Are you Mrs. Bliss?"

"No," the old woman said, and pointed to Kathy. "This is Mrs. Bliss."

"We have a message for you, Mrs. Bliss," the flight attendant called over the shoulders of the passengers in the aisle. She was a huge blond beauty, a Norse goddess. Someone who might stand on a mountain peak with a bolt of lightning in her fist. The crowd in the aisle dissolved to make way for her, and she pressed a folded piece of paper into Kathy Bliss's shaking hand: *Baby in hospital. Call home now. Husband.*

It was a week later—after the long pale nights at his crib-side in the hospital, taking turns pretending to sleep as the other paced, the tests, and the antibiotics, and the failure of the first ones to fight off the infection, and the terrifying night when the baby didn't wake during his injection, and they could clearly see the residency doctor's hand shaking as he punched the emergency button. It was after they'd begun a whole new life on the children's floor. *Sesame Street* in the lounge all day, as if the world were being run by benevolent toys, and then CNN scrolling its silent, redundant messages to them all night below images of the cynical and maimed. After they'd gotten to know the nurses. It was after Kathy Bliss had fallen in love, madly, with one doctor after another—not a sexual love, but a deep wild worship of the archetype, a reverent adulation of the Healer—and then grown to despise them one by one, and then to see them merely as human beings. It was after she'd spent some self-conscious moments on her knees in the hospital chapel, which turned into deep semiconscious communions with the Almighty as the hospital intercom called out its mundane codes and locations in the hallway behind her—and the baby was taking fluids, and then solids, and then given a signature of release, and the nurses hugged Kathy Bliss and her husband, and let their hands wave magically, baptismally, over the head of the baby, who laughed, sputtered, still a little weak, scarlet-cheeked, but very much of this world, and cured for the next leg of the journey into the future, when they packed up the stuffed animals and picture books and headed for home—it was after all these events had come to an end that Kathy Bliss remembered the foreign object, given to her by the stranger, which had stayed where she'd tucked it into her carry-on luggage, where she'd left it in the hallway of her house, tossed under a table, in a panic, on her brief stop there between the airport and the hospital.

Garrett had gone to work, and the baby was napping in a patch of sunlight that poured green and gold through the front door onto the living room floor. It was a warm late-summer day. The phone had been unplugged the night before, and stayed that way. She hadn't turned the television on once since they'd come home. The silence swelled and receded in a manner that would have been imperceivable to her only two weeks before, but which now seemed sacred, full of implication, a kind of immaculate tableau rolled out over the neighborhood in the middle of the day when no one was anywhere, and only the cats crossed the streets, padding in considerate quiet on their starry little paws. She glanced at the black bag.

She got down on her knees and pulled the bag to her, and removed the umbrella, and the pink makeup bag, and the folded black sweater, the brother's name, *Mack Kaloustian* (but hadn't the stranger said he was his mother's only son?), and saw it there, the box, in its gold paper, and recognized it only vaguely, as neither a gift nor a recrimination, a threat, or a blessing.

She didn't open it, but imagined herself opening it. Imagined herself as a passenger on that plane, unable to resist it. Holding it to her ear. Shaking it, maybe. Lifting the edge of the gold paper, tearing it away from the box. And then, the certain, brilliant cataclysm that would follow. The lurching of unsteady weight in the sky, and then the inertia, followed by tumbling. The numbing sensation of great speed and realization in your face. She'd been a fool to take it with her onto the plane. It could have killed them all.

Or, the simple gold braid of it.

Tasteful. Elegant. A thoughtful gift chosen by a devoted son for his beloved mother. And she imagined taking the necklace out of the box, holding it up to her own neck at the mirror, admiring the glint of it around her neck—this bit of love and brevity snatched from the throat of a stranger—wearing it with an evening gown, passing it down as an heirloom to her children:

Who was to say, she thought to herself as she began to peel the gold paper away, that something stolen, without malice or intent, is any less yours than something you've been given?

Laura Kasischke has published three novels and six collections of poetry. She teaches in the MFA Program and the Residential College at the University of Michigan, and lives in Chelsea with her husband and ten-year-old son.

BLUE TIPS

SEAN NORTON

In nature there always seems to be some time to waste.
I played with Ohio Blue Tips waiting for the tea to boil.
Fire was a surprise. Fire is a surprise. Being so distinct, it can only be itself,
not earth   not water   not air. Being so itself it is quietly indestructible.

Like Bergman's *The Virgin Spring,* with a blue film cast over it, the pines,
the grass   the picnic table   black and white and blue. Oh the indestructible
        Max von Sydow
after the dull-witted thugs unable to comprehend his daughter's beauty
after the slaying builds a church to the God beyond suffering.

Max von Sydow continually building and rebuilding.
There is a blue fire in a man who must remake his ability to live,
cursed by both the action beyond his control and his own action. Silence,
that absence, is an action, a space qualified with implosion, fire.

Where does the heart go when it caves in, where does the mind go?
Raw material for the woodland cathedral that's superior to the city,
made with the exact earth where loss ruled and bit down the innocent wildly.
I'd be surprised now to sense it where we walk though the forest is capacious.

We miss renewal below the needle blanket and fern floor.
Quickly, quickly, we need the consolation in fire-treated stone.
Urgency is flattened as time goes rolling on, the weight of it.
But time too goes up in blue flame by the hour.

Sean Norton received his MFA in Poetry from the University of Michigan and his BA from the University of Oregon after a couple of false starts at other schools. In the past he has taught poetry, fiction, and essay writing at the University of Michigan. He is currently the Assistant Director of the University of Michigan's MFA Program in Creative Writing. His debut collection is called *Bad with Faces.*

COLORADO
CRAIG HOLDEN

FIVE MILES DOWN there is an exit and a light. "Food," the sign says. "Diesel. Showers." Five miles has never seemed so long. In the days when I was running, five miles was a warm up, a blip. Now this civilization looming in front of us out of the black nothingness of the Nebraska night has seemed forever in coming. I look over at Father, though, and his expression is set, no reaction. Perhaps it is a mirage. I could understand that. I'm about to say something to him, to ask, when he flips on the blinker. There is no other traffic in this wasteland but I appreciate his being so careful, having seen what we have just seen. On the exit ramp our old station wagon drifts on some invisible black ice then catches concrete with a jolt. I go stiff, and I see his jaw line and his hands tighten, knuckles white at the skid. There is death in this night, in these gasoline engines, on this three thousand mile long strip of concrete. But the tension in my father's face is nothing more than veneer. His wide and watching eyes betray a deeper something, a pathological peacefulness, a childish joy at the disruption of routine. I wonder if any memory of the carnage we have just seen lingers in him, in his eyes, or if he has already, in his peculiar power, put away those grisly visions.

There are a few trucks in the parking lot, one semi and some four wheelers. We bust without a word out into the frigidness and head for the lighted doorway.

I was dreaming when Father stopped at the accident. In my dream I was at home. Mother, my brother, and my sister were all there with me, but not Father. We were standing in the section of living room Father had made over into a library—the red leather chair, the shelves of books, the ashtray on its stork stand. We were smiling. Mother held a large volume open in her hand, reminding us of something. This was not a dream in need of interpretation, I can tell you, no deep subconscious thing. I was sleeping lightly and the movie played just inside the surface of my eyelids, more a thought, a remembrance, than a dream.

"Wake up, boy," Father said when he stopped. "Jack, wake up."

I opened my eyes. I was lying in the back of the station wagon, off to one side, against the tire well where we had built a bed of dark green mover's quilts and some blankets. I sat up. Through the hoary frost on the rear window I could make out the lights of a tractor-trailer rig a hundred feet behind us. Other than those, this was the blackest place I had ever seen.

"Up," said Father. "Wreck. Dandy one." Then he opened his door and stepped out in his LL Bean mackinaw and wool trousers. He rapped on the rear window as he walked past.

I went from my waking dreams and groggy staring into sudden motion. I leapt from under the covers, over the back seat, and out the door. I was not in sound mind. Consider the dreaming, the darkness, the motion of traveling. I didn't think until my tube-stockinged feet hit the pavement. I was already in a run so I kept moving, but the shock of it almost knocked me down. The radio out of Grand Island had said twelve degrees with a wind chill thirty below that. I breathed in hard, then coughed harder. With quickly numbing fingers I buttoned my flannel over-shirt and ran after Father.

"We're the first," he said. He held between his teeth the meerschaum lined pipe my mother had given him for Christmas last year, so he had to speak without moving his jaw. He didn't seem to notice that I was only half-dressed in this arctic mess, that I would freeze to death quickly like this.

Three men sit at the counter and one behind is washing dishes.

"There's a wreck," I say. I point, west.

The men turn around and look at me. "Mile marker 435," Father says, upstaging me, but I can't help being impressed that in all this he remembered to check the mile marker. "No one's been radioed yet. There's a truck but his radio's out," he says.

"Truck wreck?" one of them says.

"He was parked," says Father. "Some little gal in a car. She either dozed off or saw his tail lights and thought he was in a lane."

"She rear-ended him?" the counter man says.

"There you go," says Father.

"Fast?"

"Ho," Father says, "fast is a word for it." The three men at the counter all jump up and grab their coats and run out. They have been waiting for this. It is their life on nights like this, in Nebraska. The counter man turns and works his CB radio, which is next to the grill. It is silver with black knobs, and grease and coagulated dust coat its top.

I go into the men's room and turn on the hot water. It is too hot. I add cold. I keep adding cold. Finally I have the hot off almost completely and I run my hands under until I can feel them. The bowl is stained with icicles of rust which point down from the base of the faucet. The whole sink is pulled away from the wall. I can look down and see the pipes there. Next to it is a condom machine with a picture of a tanned and blond woman and a man embracing on a beach with the sun setting red behind them. Protect yourself, the machine warns. Increased strength, increased sensitivity. I wash off my face and dry on the smudged roller towel. I don't mind; it is honest dirt, Father would say. The mirror, polished stainless steel, is creased down the middle, creased from behind as if someone laid an ax through the other side of the wall. I can only get an approximate image of myself. My face is broadened in the distortion, my nose flat, my eyes wide-set and Asian looking. But still I can see it is me. I can't help watching. I am seventeen years old. It is 1978. There is trouble. But my face is whole. It is a thing to fall down on your knees and thank God for. Father would be proud to know I have realized this.

"She moved me," the trucker said, jogging toward us, his legs bowed and crab-like, not used to moving quickly. "She moved me goddamn fifteen feet. I was sleeping."

My father walked past him, toward the car which had bounced backward an awful distance. The front end looked gone at first but the chassis and wheels were still there. There was the firewall at the front of the passenger compartment. There was the hood twisted up over the windshield and the windshield itself exploded but hanging in one milky piece. Fingers of smoke rose from what was left but the wind and the cold sucked them away. I felt the horror in my cheekbones and my lips.

It was hard to see here, behind the truck. Father in his green mackinaw and natty trousers looked incongruous. I couldn't help thinking of the leather-bound copies of James Fenimore Cooper and Charles Dickens he loved to sit and read, or of how sometimes he would just hold them, feeling the leather and the sharp gilded edges of the pages in the evenings after he got home from work at the stamping plant. He held a job that could have been done by a man with one-tenth his intelligence.

There were engine parts everywhere. I could make out the crankcase and block on the concrete. I saw other parts scattered in the ditch. The road felt blistering. I had cramps in my chest and stomach from the hard cold. My father approached the window on the driver's side. I stood shoulder to shoulder with the trucker, a few yards back. I shivered so hard the world was moving. The wind came down on us. But standing thus, freezing quickly to death, frightened at the sights and at the world, when you would think I would be most aware, most there, I found my mind drifting to other places, thinking other times.

Back in the diner my father is at the counter sipping coffee. I sit, too, but he ignores me.

"Do you think she was dead?" I say.

"Don't you talk about that," the counter man says. "Wait 'til they get her in someplace. No point guessing when you got no way to know." He refills Father's cup. "You just wait," he says.

"There's some advice for you, boy," Father says. He has been staring off but now he looks at me. "Care for anything?" he says.

"Coffee," I say. The counter man serves it up black. I shiver a little still, but it is bright and warm in the diner. We sit for a few moments and just sip. When our cups are down an inch the counter man serves us up again, then turns back to his grill.

Father takes out a hot-pink bandanna and wipes at his nose. Then he folds it carefully and tucks it into his shirt pocket. I hear a ticking up on the roof; the wind outside sounds like it is coming through a huge set of teeth.

"Somebody here ran away from home," Father tells the counter man.

The counter man stops what he is doing. He has been scraping away at the griddle, pulling the grease with long parallel strokes into the trough that runs around the edges. He stops but he does not turn around. I feel the muscles at the base of my head, where it joins my neck, tighten in the way that fingers would grip there. I feel a dizziness come up over me.

"What's that?" says the counter man. He tries to look uninterested.

"Someone." Father enunciates carefully. "Ran away from home."

The counter man turns and looks me up and down. His pig eyes linger on my face and then on my hands which fidget in front of me, middle fingers clawing at thumb cuticles. His breathing is thick. "Mm hm," he says as if he has decided something. But he has no idea.

"Loaded up the car one day while the rest of the family were away."

"Note?" says the counter man.

"Not right away," Father says, solemnly. "Came in the mail."

"Mm hm," says the counter man.

I sip at my coffee and I can feel the heat from my face reflecting back up from its surface. I can feel this heat in my eyes. They are drying. The fingers at the base of my head tighten painfully. I can feel my heart beat.

"I was angry," Father says. Mad, I think, is more like it.

Standing shoulder to shoulder with the trucker, watching Father, freezing, the wind screaming and tearing at my face, my mind running wherever it wanted out there because there was nothing to stop it, I remembered another time with Father by an expressway. In the dream of it he is always stealing across the side yard (I am watching from my room) and he is shrouded in a dark cloak of some kind, his face obscured. In the reality of six years ago, though, he was walking, only walking. But it was a strange and unnatural walk, in a direction he never went, toward the warehouse district that bordered the neighborhood where we lived in a house a little too small for the five of us. I knew, somehow, that I had to follow. Through gloomy rain-wetted streets we walked, me shadowing him, him not suspecting. We came to the great embankment of the expressway that had gone through a few years before. I heard the rumbling of the traffic blocks away. The steel-walled warehouses were shut up tight. At the embankment he did not pause. I broke into a run; I knew what he was after. As he climbed over the guardrail at the top he sensed my presence. I do not know if he was relieved or angry but he didn't stop what he was doing. He looked into me and then turned. I tackled him at the berm. I tackled him in the very shadow of a semi screaming past at eighty miles per hour, tackled him as he prepared to step out in its path and to be knocked two hundred feet through the air, knocked clear out of this world and up to heaven. Except you don't go to heaven like that because God knows. I told him that, berm stones imbedded hotly in my knees and the butts of my hands. He was crying, hugging me and weeping and choking. A police cruiser stopped but the cop knew things were okay now. When a man cries in that way it is because he has gotten past something monumental.

I became his savior at that moment and this has been my job since. Martha, my sister, knows. She is my manager.

"Jack!" my father shouted from the broken car in the Nebraska night. The trucker shined his light in my father's face. "Jack," Father yelled again, "I want you to look at this." He motioned for me to move closer, to look first-hand at the horror of naked and primary violence.

The trucker and I stepped up closer. The trucker shined his light into the car. Everything was jumping. My eyes watered from the cold. My head ached. My stomach hurt and my neck hurt and my knees hurt. We stepped closer yet. It was dark, a black interior, black vinyl. I saw teeth in the white of the trucker's flashlight. I saw blood and hair, but I couldn't see a face.

"Moved me fifteen feet," the trucker said. "Look at the marks."

I looked at him, then turned to where he was pointing the light, behind us, at the marks on the berm concrete where the impact of the passenger car had shoved the huge truck along when it hit. I gagged with the hardness of the cold and the thought of the impact.

"Hey," said Father. "Pay attention here."

"I can see where a guy'd be mad," says the counter man. "And hurt. You got to consider hurt."

He is looking me over, peeling me, as he speaks.

"Nah," says Father, "anger was the thing." He clutches a napkin in his left hand, wadding it up and letting it go. His fingers leave lines on the napkin marked in motor oil ink.

The counter man turns to the sink and washes his hands and dries them carefully on a clean towel. He tops off our mugs, pours himself one, lights a cigarette and leans on his elbows on the counter. "Don't mind my askin'," he says, "I'm interested. You go get him?"

"We're driving back home now," Father says.

"And a blizzard coming at us," says the counter man. His face, up to within an inch of his eye sockets, is blackened by a day's growth of heavy beard; his cigarette hangs from his meaty lip; his eyes are puffy and sore looking. I push myself away from the counter and stand up.

"Been out there a good month," my father says. "Lived near a bunch of, what you call 'ems, beatniks, you know." Do not think Father isn't aware of the embarrassing outdatedness of the term.

"Them," the counterman says. He licks his lips.

I turn and look toward the bathroom.

"Talk," says the counter man. He reaches over and pokes me in the shoulder.

I walk carefully back toward the bathroom, feeling each step as I go, noticing details—empty tables, plastic napkin holders, the snow starting outside, white bullets whipping past the glass door.

"He don't want to hear it," the counter man says. He can't wait until the boys get back.

I have always been estranged from people by my language. My brother and sister and I were raised on the page, the image, the lathed phrase. We sucked on the great myths, teethed on the Bible.

I remember sitting in my father's lap when he'd come home from work, turning pages and smelling the queer mingling of musty book and machine grease.

The bathroom feels much colder now than the dining area. I can see borders of frost on my breath. From in here the wind sounds very near, held at bay by plaster and wood but only a thin and brittle shell of it. If the wind were to suddenly splinter the wall and come ripping in, I would not be surprised; I would be so un-surprised, in fact, that I would not even go out and tell anyone until I was ready to go out anyway. The walls move like breathing under the wind. I go into a stall and lock the door. I sit on the stool with my hands on my knees and my head lowered into my lap.

What I saw, when the trucker and I moved closer, I would have thought would make me puke, like people on TV. But I didn't. I only looked. Father was waving me closer. My feet were numb now. My face was numb and my hands were numb and the top of my head was numb. I only looked at the face of a girl, a blond-headed girl, maybe young, maybe old, the teeth pointing out in strange directions, the jaw torn savagely down from the face and hanging loose like a necklace, the tongue stuck to it, profoundly out of place. One eye was cocked off to the right, the eyelid gone so you could see the sphere of it. Her hair hung down witchy. Her nose was smashed out broad.

"Look at this, boy!" Father shouted at me. "This is the world we're talking about." Hanging from the rearview mirror, mounted on a loose spring, was a little monkey made of pink feathers and plastic. It still moved slightly, up and down on its spring swing, its head rolling back and forth on its shoulders. I saw snatches of blond hair stuck in the fractures of the windshield.

"Is she dead?" I hollered. The wind stole my words away and flung them across the prairies.

"Let's find out!" he shouted back.

I didn't want him to. I pulled his hand off the handle and hugged him tight. "Is she, you think?" I said. "Probably, huh?"

"You got to find out," he said. I imagined my father hit by a semi at eighty miles per hour, flying through the air or going under, crushed out of shape, looking no longer like anything he ever looked like. I thought I saw the girl move.

"Is she dead?" I said.

"Study this, son. Let it scare you good."

"I'm scared," I said.

"That's the boy," he said. "Now we can go."

"Is she dead?" I said.

"Come on," he said, walking me toward the trucker, who had hung back just enough. My father had his arms around me.

"Hey, kid," the trucker said, falling in step with us, apparently glad to be leaving that car behind him. "Hey, boy, ain't you cold?"

"He is," said Father.

"You ever seen a thing like this before?" the trucker asked. "I been drivin' for prit near twenty years. One time I saw a man in a tree, jus hangin' there, his car down under him." The trucker leaned into me, his breath hot and coffee smelling.

"Get in the car, son," Father said. "I'll have a word with this man." He turned to the trucker. "Farmer," I heard him say. "My name is Frank Farmer."

I sprinted as fast as I could. But in the big winds and the hard cold I moved slowly. In the wide prairies I moved slowly. I used to be a runner when I was fourteen, fifteen, back when I thought I could do everything; I was fast, powerful, a quarter miler. But here there was so much space. In Ohio, where we lived, there wasn't this much space. In the mountains of Colorado where I met Father there wasn't this much space. It's too much, I thought. It needed something to break it up. Our car was still running and it was warm. I crawled in and huddled on the front seat, waiting for the heat to thaw me.

Someone comes into the john and sits in the stall next to mine. I know who it is. Beneath the dividing wall I can see a familiar old pair of Red Wing work boots, scuffed up and worn into softness, and dropped around them the black wool trousers and the boxer shorts with hearts. I can hear him grunting and clearing his throat.

"What am I going to do with you?" I ask.

The throat clears again, a grunt, and then, "What's that?"

"You," I say. "What is to be done?"

Again a cleared throat and then a grunt.

"Do you understand me?"

"What do you want from me?" he says.

"I just want t o know what to do. Nothing is any better, is it?"

Grunt. "I don't know what you mean."

"Why did you lie to him like that?"

"I didn't lie. I never said it was you who went. I said somebody did."

"But you knew what he'd think. What he'd assume."

He clears his throat again.

"Should I just let you go?" I say. This is a thing I have never asked him before, and hearing it out loud I am just as surprised by it as he must be.

He is quiet for a few moments, then says, "I don't know."

"I'm sick of this shit," I almost yell. "This isn't something I should have to be doing."

My sister, Martha, came home from college when I called her and told her. She booked a flight for me on Northwestern and got me on a shuttle up to Detroit. From there I flew into Denver Stapleton, a place I did not know. This time Father had taken the old wagon and run a long way.

"Listen, you," he says. "How do you think the world is?" His legs bounce, keeping time to some song I can't hear. He dropped clues all along, buttons in the woods: a map with notes, a postcard. I took a bus from Denver out to Golden where I found him holed up in a Best Western, eating fried chicken and watching game shows on the television and waiting for something to happen.

"I just thought about it in here," I say. "I decided the world doesn't have to be this hard."

"Haw," he says. His legs stop for a moment, then pick up again. "It's no question of has to," he says. "These are just the things you have to do."

"Forever?" I say.

"If you need," he says. "This is all there is. You'll see."

"Going after," I say.

"That's it," he says.

"Just going," I say.

"Yes," he says. "Yessirree," the legs moving.

From the place called Golden he took me out to see what he called the purple mountain majesties. And even in their fearful whiteness, with snowy caps running all the way down to where the trees started, the mountains did have a purplish cast to them if you went right at dusk, which we did. It just matters to know that there is a place like this, he told me. A place you can go to and see it. I asked him why he came all the way out here, so far to go. The air, he said. I always heard about the air. It was cold on the ledge where we stood, a widened spot in a curve in the road with a sign there saying "Scenic Lookout." The mountains reached up before us, and down below the trees folded lower and lower into the haze of a valley, darkening, wisps of clouds below us rushing by. And down there with the clouds a huge dark bird sailed easily on the updrafts, never moving its wings but to twitch the end feathers.

"She wasn't dead, was she?" I say.

His legs stop. I hear nothing. I think about why we didn't do something for her right there, why we looked and left. I think of asking him this but I know. He could talk about how there was nothing we could do, about the need for help, but all he would say is: it's enough to save yourself.

This is the old him. I am used to it. What I can't understand, cannot reconcile, is how he is treating me. "Why the abuse?" I ask.

"You want me to stop?" he says. "I'll just stop," he says, but he says it in a way that tells me he knows that I know he's just moving air. Like a guilty kid denying.

"Shit," I say. I stand up and uncramp my legs and leave the stall. My head hums with anger. "I'm leaving you here."

"Jack," he says after me. I walk out into the diner and past the counter man, who pauses in his wiping to watch me. He looks ready to say something but I give him a glare that shuts him up. I lift my coat from the stool and walk out.

The front edge of the blizzard which has been nipping at our heels since we left Denver is here. Snow is everywhere, the path of each flake nearly horizontal. It is banked against the driver's side windows of the station wagon. I keep waiting for myself to stop, to go back in, to wake up. But I brush the snow away and get in and start the car.

The highway is a different place than it was an hour ago. Instead of the flat dry black empty frigidness it is now a wonderland of flashing and piling white. The expanse of it has been broken. The blizzard is coming out of the northwest, whipping across the prairies and building its head of steam all the while and then slamming into my car. No one should be driving in this but I keep on. I am able to think little because I have to concentrate so hard on driving, on keeping it straight. My father left the pipe in the ashtray for some reason, probably his hurrying to get into the warmth of the diner. I find his tobacco pouch on the seat, pack the pipe full, and light it. My lips pop as I suck. The smoke makes my mouth feel like it is lined with a thick membrane but I like the taste.

I have really left him this time. I think this: it is good. It will be good for us to be rid of him. He has been nothing but trouble. I think I will miss him but I won't miss the going after. Martha and I will have to explain it to Mother. She has no idea. We have protected her, somehow, improbable as it seems. Football games. Antique book shows. Tool and die conventions. We have lied. Once a precedent is set it is not hard to sustain.

Some trucks are still moving and a car here and there. Then, after a long gentle curve in the highway, the visibility now limited to a dozen yards or so, the snow several inches deep even on the road where the traffic has passed, my speed reduced to the thirties, my windshield fogged and iced all around the edges, the wind bleeding in through chinks in the door, the smoke from the pipe coating my throat so thick it is making me gag, my hands tight on the wheel, I see a Greyhound bus that has slid in the snow and ice over in the westbound lane, and tipped over on its side in the median. I pull off to the right and watch although it is hard to see. People are crawling up through the windows which they have punched out. I know how these Greyhound windows work; I once spent six hours reading the signs on my way down to Cincinnati, chasing Father. That was one of his longer trips, before this jaunt to Colorado. Once a few years ago he went as far as Nashville, Tennessee. "Real music," he said when I found him in some worn-out bar listening to a fake blond with lines in her face sing slurred and dragging heartbreak songs.

His running is not a routine thing, however. It is not something we have got used to. He has left us six times since the day I saved him on the highway, and each time, although Martha and I have come to be able to sense his discontent, to predict his flight, it is a shock and a crisis to us. Most of these times have been to fairly nearby places, places within a few hundred mile radius of where we live, places like Chicago, say, or Cleveland. He always goes to cities. It used to be Martha would drive me, before I was sixteen. She is three years my elder. I was the one who had to go though. She couldn't bring him in. She tried it once, when he was holed up in Detroit, only forty miles away, and he wouldn't budge from his motel room. She came home and got me and took me back and I spoke with him for five minutes. I asked him what he was watching on the television and after he told me I said couldn't he watch it at home. He said he supposed so and packed up and went out to the car where she waited. It is not that he doesn't love her as much. It is something else. I don't know what.

Then I think I am wrong. He hasn't been all trouble. He has been our father. He has provided.

In all his leaving he has never lost his job. He manages it so I can get him back by the time he has to work again—he leaves on long weekends or vacations or he uses sick time. He is not careless.

These bus people are so bundled and wrapped up they do not look human. They remind me of insects crawling out of an underground hive. I strain to see through the wind and snow. The turning red lights of the highway patrol bloody the whiteness. I should help. But other cars and trucks are stopping, good samaritans running all over the place, pulling bugs out. I feel guilty, as if they will see me if I leave, as if they will chase me and accuse me of not caring, of abandoning the needy. But in the confusion and the blizzard I figure they can't really see who I am.

In some tiny town, thirty miles from the truck stop where I ditched my father, I pull in for gas and coffee. It is slow going in the storm. I sit at the counter and sip and think.

I think of something else, then. I think that my brother Davey is thirteen now, older than I was when I first followed Father to the berm of the expressway and saved him and brought him home.

When I am tired of smoking my father's pipe and watching the little waitress hustle about, I stand up and stretch and pay up and walk out. The blizzard is coming hard. Only crazy people will be on the road now.

Father will not come home on his own; it is a hard fact to explain but it is true. All I have ever had to do was go where he was and he would come along. Always I have known that if I didn't go he would disappear. I say I have known this but it hasn't been a physical knowledge, a knowledge in the body. It has been something I thought but never could have acted on. Now I can feel this knowledge in my hands and in the foot I will use to press the accelerator.

The snow whips into my face, stinging, waking me up, steeling me. I brush off the car and am ready. If I go out the driveway and head straight I will be going east, homeward, alone. If I turn left I can catch the westbound on-ramp and go back and get him. I stand still.

The decision is mine. I am seventeen years old. How is it that a seventeen year old can hold in his mind power over the fate of a man and his family? To release into exile or to reunite? And where has this power come from? I ask myself. It is a thing to turn over.

There is something else, too. I could do neither. I could turn the car south, say, and never look back to any of it. I could fade into the world. Who would know? I look up into the sky, where flakes of snow become visible only when they cross into the room of light put up by this little oasis. "Who would know?" I say. It is this sudden swelling moment of disconnection that keeps drawing him out. Perhaps he only feels it for one instant on each trip. I can see how that would be enough. The air, he said.

It is all one thing.

I am cold again. I see no reason not to go back.

I know where he will be when I get there—sitting at the counter, telling the whiskered man about the purple mountain beauty of Colorado. Imagine standing above the clouds, my father will say.

The car starts fine and the wind is hard and the snow is thick all around.

Craig Holden has published five novels, the latest of which, *The Narcissist's Daughter*, came out last year. Though he is in the odd position of having a publisher (Simon & Schuster) but no editor, his next novel should appear in 2007. He is a recipient of the Great Lakes Book Award in Fiction, and in 2004 was a guest at the Festival International du Roman Noir in Frontignan, France. He teaches occasionally at the University of Michigan, and lives with his wife and four kids and two dogs and one cat in York Township.

BULLET WITH YOUR NAME ON IT
SCOTT BEAL

When you are a preprinted address label,
you have no sense
of wonder or time.
When the lid of a box
closes over your face,
and opens again,
that dark may fill four minutes
or forty years. Death
could be like that. When you are
a preprinted address label, nine-tenths of your personality
is fixed in early infancy—
your squat shape, dull finish, the birthmark
on your left side in the form of a precious orchid or
the UNICEF logo. You are born in makeup, tint and font
that inscribe for you one expression. In a window envelope
you arrive unbidden, an orphan dropped
on the doorstep among a colony of orphans,
tucked in with dire pleadings and a perforated
payment stub. You are less
than a dime a dozen. Peeled from a sheet, you reveal
a desperate, clingy side—once you're stuck,
you're stuck. Odds are you'll be bagged
with spoiled leftovers. Shredded. Incinerated.
You'll never make it out of the envelope. But suppose
you do: a practical thumb smoothes you in place to lend
the proper bureaucratic distance to
a holiday family newsletter. The deadest
of dead end jobs. Or suppose you are pressed upon
a skewed prayer bound
for a certain Francine in Topeka. She takes in
your poker face, sets the package on her palm
as if to weigh a memory.
Scrawls RETURN TO SENDER. Lets it clunk in the box.
And as the carrier delivers you back into the hand that sent you,
the instant you actualize your potential,
the man accepts his own package like a ticket
to a lonely grave. Better to lie

buried in a drawer with paper clips and ugly stationery,
and the dim hope of being retrieved one day
by a child too young to discriminate among stickers.
A kid like that may smack you
to the handlebars of a tricycle. You soak up
a season of sprinkler mist, shouts of neighbors,
the fragrance of lawnmowers. Left
in the yard in a storm, cloudlight bleaches you blank
as droplets crash all around. And after the garage sale,
scraped away by new owners, you leave
a sticky patch on the bar no sponge
or sandpaper can scrub clean. Death could be
like that. Or instead she fastens you
in rings of red ink and glitter.
You brighten the fridge until you're taken down
to make space for a grocery list. The lid of a box
closes over your face, and opens again.
And there the man finds you,
red loops tangling over alphanumerics
as ivy would climb a headstone—
and in an instant his mind nails together
the house your digits plot,
fills it with lamplight and cinnamon.
He folds you into a package. He sends it to that house,
to a certain Francine in Topeka as if she's always been
there waiting for her childhood to
arrive and reopen in her hands,
as if death could ever be like that.

ASSESSMENT OF MY MASCULINITY

I have been drinking my coffee black
since the eleventh grade, my whiskey straight
since graduation. I have never killed anyone.
I did not, during the gulf war, display
a flag decal in the window of my pickup.

I've never driven a pickup. I don't
own a car, or an uncommonly large penis,
and the one I have has not been
stuck into a vast array of girls.

I don't holler about those it has.

I have broken bones playing football,
long ago, not in high school, not on a team.
I never wore pads. I have
medical insurance. I have been drinking
my coffee black, my whiskey straight,

for years. I have never killed
anyone. I don't have any business
sense. I just write my goddamn poems,
but they are not just poems, they are
my goddamn poems. I stop

and ask directions. I have never
liked fishing. I have been drinking my coffee
black since the eleventh grade. This doesn't matter
until I tell you, man, and then
I am one of you, even though I have

never killed anyone. In primary school
I got battered. I didn't fight back.
One time, this guy knocked me down.
I got up, he knocked me down, a lot of times.
I only snickered at him, sore but

thinking I felt like a man.

Scott Beal is a poet and educator who lives and works in Ann Arbor. A number of his poems have appeared in journals, anthologies, and his chapbook, *Two Shakespearean Madwomen Vs. The Detroit Red Wings* (White Eagle Coffee Store Press 1999). He holds an MFA in Creative Writing from the University of Michigan.

DANNY ROTTEN
JEFF KASS

UNDER THIS SHIRT is skin, and under this skin is heart. And under this heart, is
nachos. My own full plate with hot jalapeños and the six of us—my two brothers,
my sister, my parents and me—heading out to dinner in Mamaroneck on Saturday
nights. It was a twenty-minute drive, the inside of the station wagon warm, dark
and fluid—a womb. We'd park for free on the street atop a hill a couple hundred
yards from the restaurant, and walk down through a metered parking lot. Often, I
held my mother's hand, or that of my little sister; but what burned under my shirt,
skin, heart, and silent tongue, was the anticipation of nachos. My own plate. And
not a heaping mound of cheese-sauce and fake salsa slop, but a dozen individual
chips, each with its own slather of fresh melted cheese, refried beans, and a single
bold jalapeño in the center—juicy and staring, like an eyeball.

The back of the restaurant's menu taught me Mexican history I never learned
in school, tales of Emiliano Zapata and Pancho Villa zooming across the countryside on horseback, shooting rifles and liberating farmers from beneath the heel of
fat and greedy landowners. My parents would split a pitcher of Sangria, a quarter-
chunk of lemon floating on the surface like a rowboat. A Mariachi trio circulated
through the dining room and when the three broad-faced men hovered near our
table, my father slipped them a few dollars to play Guantanamera.

No dining experience will ever compare to the ecstasy of that one—for years
the only full meal I'd eat each week during wrestling season. My mouth would start
to water sometime late Wednesday afternoon as I thought of the warm womb-like
car ride, the trek through the parking lot, and, at last, the restaurant's stiff high-
backed chairs, faux stone arches, and smooth tiled floor. Then, minutes after we
were seated, the hot metal platter would swoop down over my left shoulder and
land in front of me like a holy gift.

It was always worth it, those nachos. That first tentative nibble of the cheese's
soft goo and the crisp of the chip's mildly resistant crunch, the combined flavor filling my mouth with a pleasant surge, as if I'd woken mid-morning from a long and
particularly satisfying sleep. It was worth the grunt and sweat of a week eating little
but lettuce, ice cubes, and peanut butter-and-jelly on whole wheat. It was worth
the desperation that came with learning how to break down an opponent's base
with a sharp arm-chop, knocking the kid off-balance and digging his shoulder and
face, nose-forward, into the mat.

Under that desperation, was Danny Rowton.

We called him Danny Rotten. He called himself that too, and bit the alligators
off chests of preppy golf shirts worn by kids whose asses he could kick. Which was
pretty much every kid who wore that kind of shirt. Which was pretty much why

I never wore that kind of shirt. In front of a lunch-line of sixth graders, he once broke the arm of Timmy Anders—a semi-retarded kid—snapped it like a wishbone, apparently for no other reason than he wanted to hear what sound it would make when it splintered. Word had it that, at thirteen, he stole a car when he was drunk and crashed it through a police roadblock, then killed a cop and shattered his own collarbone in the ensuing scuffle. Whether or not the story is true, it's why I joined wrestling. So I could learn how to apply pressure to Danny's already once broken collarbone, and crack that fucking thing all over again if he ever tried to mess with me.

Under that fear was the paralyzing notion there were two sides of town, and I lived in the wrong one—the soft cheese one. The other side, where Danny lived, was Battle Hill, so named for the bravery of George Washington, who allegedly held the high ground there and beat the Redcoats back to their tea and crumpets. Perhaps in that tradition, perhaps because of the proximity to the train station, kids who lived on Battle Hill grew up tough and restless; squeezed in cramped homes with well-worn rugs and the only television in the living room, the only telephone hanging on a wall in the kitchen. Kids from Ridgeway—my side of town—attended Hebrew school, played tennis at country clubs, and, in the winter, ping-pong in their spacious and finished basements. But not me.

Under our living room, the uncarpeted dampness held a lightbulb without a fixture and a beat-up bench-press. I calloused my hands there, banging my head to AC-DC and Zeppelin, ten sets of ten every other day until no wimp-ass alligator shirt could contain my bulging pectorals. Shoulder-blades pushing into the bench's sweat-stinking vinyl, I shaped my vision around the bar cutting into my palms, a cold iron line that blocked my view of the ceiling and its chipped paint. The only sight I could conjure anyway, as I breathed in and out through my reps, was Danny, hand over hand, scaling the rope in our middle school gymnasium, pulling himself all the way to the top where—incredibly—he held on with one hand, and with the other inked his name onto the support beam with a Sharpie.

He scrawled his name everywhere at that middle school—just the first name, Danny, in six aggressive capital letters, the Y at the end winding backward beneath the two Ns and terminating in a downward pointing arrow so it looked like a cartoonish devil's tail. Danny on the basketball backboards in the parking lot. Danny on the heating and cooling vents. Danny on the drinking fountains and bathroom stalls. Danny on the fire-alarm boxes and Danny on as many desks in as many classrooms as he could possibly inhabit. It was art and it was vandalism and it scared the shit out of the rest of us who believed Danny could be anywhere, at any time, ready to ink his name into your face with his fists, and to add to his legend by kicking your ass.

He was fond of wearing a black t-shirt, emblazoned with the slogan "Death to Disco," a sentiment I could not understand back then—a year before AC-DC, Zeppelin and the bench-press. I was just discovering disco, celebrating the fun of its party-hard back-beats with an uncontainable ear-to-ear grin. I boogied *down* at Bar Mitzvah receptions, my penny-loafered feet spinning like propellor blades. My clip-on tie whipped back and forth with the crazed energy of a boy who knew Danny would never be invited to the Jewish kids' dance, and who also was beginning to understand that those bra straps bumping out of the back of the strapless dresses the girls wore, portended something powerful, something wonderous, some glorious hint of the future. What quarrel could Danny Rotten have with *that*?

He disappeared for a year after seventh grade, a vanishing which birthed the rumors of the stolen car, broken collarbone and dead cop. I spent the mysterious interval of his absence convinced he'd return any minute, feeling him like a dark ball of jagged teeth lurking in my head—ready to pounce and chomp on my chest. I discarded Donna Summer for Eric Clapton and pumped up in the basement, wanting to take advantage of every moment Danny wasn't ubiquitous with his Sharpie, wasn't pouncing and chomping; so I got busy growing amusement park dizzy on first kisses, and trembling a little too much to let my fingers do anything but graze the outside of the beckoning bra-straps. Even now, I shiver thinking of it, the thrill.

At the onset of high school, Danny was back. Like me, he was beefier than before, none of it fat, and a scar that stretched across the front of his right hand looked like it could have been a knife-wound. We were assigned lockers in the same cul-de-sac, though I'm not sure why Danny needed one. He rarely carried books or wore a coat. Still, he checked in at his empty locker every day, opening and closing it with violence, turning to hiss at me: "Kass, you're a pussy."

I never said anything in return, pretended I didn't hear and hoped Danny wouldn't decide to shove me, to cross over into the physical where I'd have to test my bench-pressed strength and the techniques I'd learned in wrestling practice. I could see my reponse developing already, visualize it like pro golfers did before they hit their shots. He would lunge at me and I would attempt to grab his right wrist with both my hands, tie him up in a Russian two-on-one so I could leverage his head toward the ground. He would resist, trying to push back up, and I would use that momentum, rise up with him so I could drive his wrist behind his back and fold it like a chicken wing. He'd react by trying to jolt forward and break my hold on his wrist. When he lurched, I'd let go with my left hand and circle it around the top of his head, yanking his neck backward and—pop—there would go his collarbone, neatly split at its most vulnerable point.

It never came to that and I never wanted it to, until Danny stopped opening and closing his locker and used it instead as a surface he could slide his girlfriend against as he leaned in and sucked on her tongue. He was surprisingly tender toward her, holding her face with both hands as he kissed her, moving slow, talking quietly. I'd pretend to organize my textbooks, or dig for homework, and watch them. I'd imagine she was good for him, would calm him enough to curb his desire to beat the piss out of me. When the warning bell sounded for first hour, he'd place an arm around her shoulder as if she'd break if his touch weren't light enough, and massage circles onto her back. Then he'd turn his head and mouth, "You're still a pussy, Kass, still a pussy."

Whatever—I was used to ignoring his taunts. But I couldn't ignore his girlfriend, who was tender toward him as well, ruffling her fingers though his hair as they kissed, or slipping her hand into the backpocket of his blue jeans as they walked. Danny Rotten's girlfriend was Caroline Haas, and I'd been in love with her since elementary school. Half-Filipino/half-Dutch, she was gorgeous. Athletic, she slid through the hallways like a dancer and starred for the cross-country team. Smart, she took all A.P. classes, labored through reams of homework, and earned a four-point. She had huge brown eyes, long dark hair that cascaded across her forehead, soft round lips and a way of breathing that lifted her chest and made me want to bang my face against the sharp corner of my locker-door until I drew blood. It was her bra-strap I'd always focused on back at the Bar Mitzvahs. I had no idea why she was dating Danny Rotten.

For the most part, upon reaching high school, he'd stopped writing his name everywhere. One morning though, I arrived at my locker to find it covered with his scrawl—a huge heart and several smaller ones surrounding it like satellites. Each was filled with his aggressive handwriting. Danny loves Caroline. Danny loves Caroline. Danny loves Caroline. All over my locker. I felt like I was staring at my own tombstone. What had died was whatever sense of manhood I'd been trying to cling to. My pussification was complete.

That afternoon after class, as I stuffed my back-pack with homework assignments it was doubtful I'd ever get to, and made ready to hustle down to wrestling practice, he showed up at the lockers, leering.

"Hey, pussy," he said. "What're you doing? You wanna come hang out with me and Caroline? I got beer."

"What do you mean?"

"I mean, dumb-ass, she's got a cousin from the city who wants to hang out. We need another dude to make shit even."

I didn't drink beer. The whole thing could have been a trap. Danny wanted to take me somewhere off school grounds so he could beat my ass without getting suspended. Plus, I had practice, and we had a match in a couple of days against New Rochelle. But New Rochelle sucked. It didn't matter who they'd try to run out there, it would be quick—forty-five seconds maybe, a minute at most. Nothing fancy. Circle, circle, shuffle-step, shoot for a double-leg takedown. Arm-chop to knock him from his base. Then a simple half-nelson to turn him over. A simple half would do.

I looked at Danny. He was a devious fuck, but his face looked open, pleading a little. He had a serious problem. If he couldn't find another dude, his afternoon with his girlfriend might get totally screwed up. Maybe he'd stop hassling me if I helped him out. Plus, maybe Caroline's cousin would look like her. I threw my backpack into my tombstone locker and followed him.

We walked through the hallways and headed toward the gym area where the wrestling room was. I stayed behind Danny and kept my head down, hoping none of the coaches or any of my teammates would see me. We slipped out through a side-door and Danny started jogging toward a tree-line about a half-mile away. "Hurry up, dude," he urged. "We gotta grab some food before they get there."

It was grey out and about forty degrees, but I'd broken a sweat by the time we reached the woods. It made me feel loose and happy. Yeah, I was skipping practice, but I was getting a bit of conditioning in anyway. We kept jogging in the woods on a small foot-path I hadn't known existed, and I was surprised at the kind of shape Danny was in. I knew he was strong, but I hadn't known he had endurance. He seemed hardly tired and I picked up the pace to see if he could keep up. "Good," he said, "yeah. Let's move."

We ran faster. My lungs and legs were fine, but my stomach began to cry out in hunger. I hadn't eaten anything all day but a piece of dry toast for breakfast. The pangs worsened when the sound of automobile traffic linked itself to fumes bearing the tell-tale grease of a fast-food restaurant as we neared the edge of the woods. The path dumped us into a Burger King parking lot. We slanted past the drive-through line, slowed, and walked in. "I'm gonna get Caroline and Alisa—that's the other chick's name, Alisa—some burgers and fries," Danny said, holding the door open for me. "What about you? Want anything?"

It was strange, this kindness coming from a kid who'd perpetually branded me a pussy. Maybe it wasn't kindness though. Maybe he knew there was no way I could eat anything like that and maintain my weight. I shook my head and tried not to breathe, not to smell anything as he stood on line and then ordered, but I couldn't take it, felt the words pushing up toward my teeth to say hey, on second thought, I'll have a milkshake, vanilla, so I slinked back outside to wait. He emerged after a few moments with a couple of bags and handed me one to carry before starting to jog back toward the woods. "Wait," I said, angling a thumb toward the market across the road. "I thought you said you had beer, or were getting it, or something like that."

"I do, dumb-ass, don't worry."

Again I followed Danny Rotten into the forest—each of us holding a paper bag of steaming burgers and fries—and this time, after we'd jogged a few minutes back on the path toward school, he veered left onto another trail I hadn't known existed. Who was he? Freakin' Ranger Rick? A couple of minutes later, he turned and spoke to me. Finally, his breath seemed uneven, as if he were tiring. "Caroline would be kicking our ass right now," he said. "Girl can run forever. She's a fuckin' mutant."

I nodded because, yeah, she was a mutant. Not because of her running. But because she was beautiful and smart, and yet somehow attracted to this idiot. At least I knew how he got into the shape he was in, and how he knew how to navigate the forest. Clearly, he'd been running with her, and these trails must be where her team trained. That depressed me for some reason—the two of them running together— as if their relationship might be deeper than just making out by my locker.

A few more minutes and we were out of the woods, this time opposite a chain-link fence which I recognized immediately. It was the out-of-bounds barrier behind the fifteenth green at my parents' country club. I'd played the hole dozens of times but didn't say anything when Danny led me to an opening in the fence, shushing me as he peeked to see if any nutcase members were out in the fairway, braving the cold. It felt moronic to sneak onto property I could've walked onto through the front door, but there was no way I was going to mention that to someone known for biting alligators off golf shirts.

Nobody was around—"no Jewbags," Danny said—so we strolled across the green and a couple hundred yards down the middle of the fairway, before cutting into the rough and heading toward a grove of trees that I knew hid a pond where I'd deposited many a slice from the tee-box. Danny led me on yet another thin trail, around to the back of the pond where I was stunned to see what looked like the ruins of an old stone house. Part of it had sunk into the brack on the edge of the pond, leaving a roof that looked like a mound of dirt about six feet off the ground. We clambered up easily, put our Burger King bags to the side, and sat looking over the water. "It's from the revolutionary war," Danny said. "Soldiers hid supplies."

"No shit?"

"Yeah, man, you gotta know about stuff like this. Chicks love these fuckin' places."

Suddenly, the smell of the french fries overwhelmed me. Probably they were emitting a last steam of warmth, like a pheremone, before beginning to cool. I felt like grabbing both bags, ripping them open with my teeth, and scarfing. Nachos, I chanted to myself, nachos. Just a few more days 'til the weekend. Hold out for the nachos. Then I wondered, after skipping practice, if I deserved them.

"I'm gonna get the beer," Danny said, and rolled off the side of the roof, jumping to the ground. I watched him push up the sleeves of his sweatshirt and scramble to where a log poked a branch out of the pond. With one foot on the bank, he stretched his other across to stand on the log, reached down to hold onto the branch and steady himself and, then, balanced precariously, dipped his other hand into the water and pulled out a six-pack of Budweiser, the cans attached to each other with plastic rings. It was an astounding feat of athleticism, and I began to doubt the probable success of my busting-his-collarbone battleplan.

He ducked inside the house on his way back up and ascended to the roof with the six in one hand and what looked like a ratty horse blanket in the other. "I steal these from a snack-bar over there," he said of the beer, pointing in the direction of the halfway house between the tenth and eleventh holes, "and this is for fucking."

He unfolded the blanket and spread it out next to him. "I fuck Caroline a lot here," he said. "I mean, so many times. She's good too. Alisa, yeah, you'll get something off her. She probably won't do you. Not on the first date. But you'll get something. You can watch us though. You like that, don't you? Watching me and Caroline?"

There were stones on the roof. I grabbed one by my feet and threw it deep into the pond. No matter what, I could always throw. "Nah, man," I said. "That's sick."

"Are you a faggot, dude? Seriously, 'cuz you're, like, ripped as hell. I mean, you look like you could bench-press a Buick, but I never see you with any females."

It was a legitimate question, one I can't say I hadn't asked myself. I'd loved dancing to disco, after all, but hadn't been laid yet. It was as if I'd loved the dancing just *for* the dancing. I hadn't treated it as a prelude to anything else. I mean, look—too afraid to venture inside a bra—I hadn't even made a serious attempt to get laid. And there was the wrestling thing too. All the rolling around with other male bodies. The tight singlets. Group showers.

"You want to touch it?" Danny said. "I'll pull it out right now. I don't give a fuck. Friction is friction."

I wondered if the girls were going to show up. If they *ever* were going to show up. If Alisa even existed. I threw another rock into the pond and stood.

"We can do this right here," I said. "You think you can kick my ass? Let's go."

Danny stood up too, a little annoyed it seemed, as if he had to handle an unpleasant task he'd rather have someone else deal with. He cricked his neck one time from side to side, then flexed. His forearms were taut and he was light on his feet, toes balled against the dirt roof. It felt then like the house had not been built for soldiers, but for us; for the tall leafless trees to ring us under the grey sky, right here, right where he'd fucked Caroline Haas so many times.

I was calm though, like, okay, maybe I was about to get my ass kicked, but maybe I wasn't. Either way, I could no longer be called a pussy. I circled and watched his hands, waiting to see which wrist I could grab and twist.

"Dude, chill," Danny said. "This ain't no WWF. I was just fucking with you. Have a beer."

I took one. I didn't like beer, still don't. And I knew the empty calories would mean twenty more minutes of conditioning. But that didn't matter, there was no way I wasn't going to hit the basement bench for hours that night anyway. And there was no way I was going to turn down that beer. I knew what it meant.

We drank and I asked him why he didn't write his name everywhere any more, only on my locker. "In middle school, you want everyone to know you," he said. "In high school, it's like, fuck it, leave my ass alone. I got shit to do."

The sound of the girls' voices, their clatter through the woods, was like The Lord sending Abraham a ram through the thicket. A miracle. Or maybe a disappointment. "That's so sweet," Caroline said to both of us, when she saw the fast food.

Alisa wasn't as pretty as her cousin, but Danny was right, she would give me something. Or, more like—huddled in a sand-trap, far from Danny and Caroline—she would offer, and I would take. More than I ever had before.

Caroline would go on to med school and marry an orthodox Jew. I have no clue what happened to Danny Rotten. Maybe he got married too. Maybe he's fat and happy and sells carpets. Maybe he has kids who steal cars and break into snackbars. Maybe he's dead, or in prison. Maybe he leads wilderness trips for at-risk teenagers, and hasn't eaten a french fry in years.

The only thing I know for sure is his name's still on top of the gymnasium, black ink staring into history, devil-tail "Y" pointing to the floor. And under that, is me, the middle school wrestling coach, looking up and wondering if I can still react quickly to a whistle, chop an arm, and break another kid down.

Jeff Kass is a teacher of English and Creative Writing at Pioneer High School in Ann Arbor and currently works as the Poet-in-Residence for Ann Arbor Public Schools. He is a two-time Ann Arbor Poetry Slam Grand Slam Champion, the winner of the 2005 *Current* Fiction Contest, a runner-up in the 2006 *Georgetown Review* Fiction Contest, and an editor's honorable mention for the 2006 E.M. Koeppel Short Fiction Award.

FARANGS

RATTAWUT LAPCHAROENSAP

THIS IS HOW we count the days. June: the Germans come to the Island—football cleats, big t-shirts, thick tongues—speaking like spitting. July: the Italians, the French, the British, the Americans. The Italians like pad thai, its affinity with spaghetti. They like light fabrics, sunglasses, leather sandals. The French like plump girls, rambutans, disco music, baring their breasts. The British are here to work on their pasty complexions, their penchant for hashish. Americans are the fattest, the stingiest of the bunch. They may pretend to like pad thai or grilled prawns or the occasional curry, but twice a week they need their culinary comforts, their hamburgers and their pizzas. They're also the worst drunks. Never get too close to a drunk American. August brings the Japanese. Stay close to them. Never underestimate the power of the yen. Everything's cheap with imperial monies in hand and they're too polite to bargain. By the end of August, when the monsoon starts to blow, they're all consorting, slapping each other's backs, slipping each other drugs, sleeping with each other, sipping their liquor under the pink lights of the Island's bars. By September they've all deserted, leaving the Island to the Aussies and the Chinese, who are so omnipresent one need not mention them at all.

Ma says, "Pussy and elephants. That's all these people want." She always says this in August, at the season's peak, when she's tired of farangs running all over the Island, tired of finding used condoms in the motel's rooms, tired of guests complaining to her in five languages. She turns to me and says, "You give them history, temples, pagodas, traditional dance, floating markets, seafood curry, tapioca desserts, silk-weaving cooperatives, but all they really want is to ride some hulking gray beast like a bunch of wildmen and to pant over girls and to lie there half-dead getting skin cancer on the beach during the time in between."

We're having a late lunch, watching television in the motel office. The Island Network is showing *Rambo: First Blood Part II* again. Sylvester Stallone, dubbed in Thai, mows down an entire VC regiment with a bow and arrow. I tell Ma I've just met a girl. "It might be love," I say. "It might be real love, Ma. Like Romeo and Juliet love."

Ma turns off the television just as John Rambo flies a chopper to safety.

She tells me it's just my hormones. She sighs and says, "Oh no, not again. Don't be so naive," she says. "I didn't raise you to be stupid. Are you bonking one of the guests? You better not be bonking one of the guests. Because if you are, if you're bonking one of the guests, we're going to have to bleed the pig. Remember, luk, we have an agreement."

I tell her she's being xenophobic. I tell her things are different this time. But Ma just licks her lips and says once more that if I'm bonking one of the guests, I

64

can look forward to eating Clint Eastwood curry in the near future. Ma's always talking about killing my pig. And though I know she's just teasing, she says it with such zeal and a peculiar glint in her eyes that I run out to the pen to check on the swine.

I knew it was love when Clint Eastwood sniffed her crotch earlier that morning and the girl didn't scream or jump out of the sand or swat the pig like some of the other girls do. She merely lay there, snout in crotch, smiling that angelic smile, like it was the most natural thing in the world, running a hand over the fuzz of Clint Eastwood's head like he was some pink and docile dog, and said, giggling, "Why hello, oh my, what a nice surprise, you're quite a beast, aren't you?"

I'd been combing the motel beachfront for trash when I looked up from my morning chore and noticed Clint Eastwood sniffing his new friend. An American: her Budweiser bikini told me so. I apologized from a distance, called the pig over, but the girl said it was okay, it was fine, the pig could stay as long as he liked. She called me over and said I could do the same.

I told her the pig's name.

"That's adorable," she said, laughing.

"He's the best," I said. "*Dirty Harry. Fistful of Dollars. The Outlaw Josey Wales. The Good, the Bad and the Ugly.*"

"He's a very good actor."

"Yes. Mister Eastwood is a first-class thespian."

Clint Eastwood trotted into the ocean for his morning bath then, leaving us alone, side-by-side in the sand. I looked to make sure Ma wasn't watching me from the office window. I explained how Clint Eastwood loves the ocean at low tide, the wet sand like a three-kilometer trough of mud. The girl sat up on her elbows, watched the pig, a waterlogged copy of *The Portrait of a Lady* at her side. She'd just gone for a swim and the beads of water on her navel seemed so close that for a moment I thought I might faint if I did not look away.

"I'm Elizabeth. Lizzie."

"Nice to meet you, Miss Elizabeth," I said. "I like your bikini."

She threw back her head and laughed. I admired the shine of her tiny, perfectly even rows of teeth, the gleam of that soft, rose-colored tongue quivering between them like the meat of some magnificent mussel.

"Oh my," she said, closing that mouth, gesturing with her chin. "I think your pig is drowning."

Clint Eastwood was rolling around where the ocean meets the sand, chasing receding waves, running away from oncoming ones. It's a game he plays every morning, scampering back and forth across the water's edge, and he snorted happily every time the waves knocked him into the foam.

"He's not drowning," I said. "He's swimming."

"I didn't know pigs could swim."

"Clint Eastwood can."

She smiled, a close-mouthed grin, admiring my pig at play, and I would've given anything in the world to see her tongue again, to reach out and sink my fingers into the hollows of her collarbone, to stare at that damp, beautiful navel all day long.

"I have an idea, Miss Elizabeth," I said, getting up, brushing the sand from the seat of my shorts. "This may seem rather presumptuous, but would you like to go for an elephant ride with me today?"

Ma doesn't want me bonking a farang because once, long ago, she had bonked a farang herself, against the wishes of her own parents, and all she got for her trouble was a broken heart and me in return. The farang was a man known to me only as Sergeant Marshall Henderson. I remember the Sergeant well, if only because he insisted I call him by his military rank.

"Not Daddy," I remember him saying in English, my first and only language at the time. "Sergeant. Sergeant Henderson. Sergeant Marshall. Remember you're a soldier now, boy. A spy for Uncle Sam's army."

And during those early years—before he went back to America, promising to send for us—the Sergeant and I would go on imaginary missions together, navigating our way through the thicket of farangs lazing on the beach.

"Private," he'd yell after me. "I don't have a good feeling about this, Private. This place gives me the creeps. We should radio for reinforcements. It could be an ambush."

"Let 'em come, Sergeant! We can take 'em!" I would squeal, crawling through the sand with a large stick in hand, eyes trained on the enemy. "Those gooks'll be sorry they ever showed their ugly faces."

One day, the three of us went to the fresh market by the Island's southern pier. I saw a litter of pigs there, six of them squeezed into a small cardboard box amidst the loud thudding of butchers' knives. I remember thinking of the little piglets I'd seen skewered and roasting over an open fire outside many of the Island's fancier restaurants.

I began to cry.

"What's wrong, Private?"

"I don't know."

"A soldier," the Sergeant grunted, "never cries."

"They just piggies," Ma laughed, bending to pat me on the back. Because of our plans to move to California, Ma was learning English at the time. She hasn't spoken a word of English to me since. "What piggies say, luk? What they say? Piggies say oink-oink. No cry, luk. No cry. Oink-oink is yummy-yummy."

A few days later, the Sergeant walked into my bedroom with something wriggling beneath his t-shirt. He sat down on the bed beside me. I remember the mattress sinking with his weight, the chirping of some desperate bird struggling in his belly.

"Congratulations, Private," the Sergeant whispered through the dark, holding out a young and frightened Clint Eastwood in one of his large, chapped hands. "You're a CO now. A commanding officer. From now on, you'll be responsible for the welfare of this recruit."

I stared at him dumbfounded, took the pig into my arms.

"Happy birthday, kiddo."

And shortly before the Sergeant left us, before Ma took over the motel from her parents, before she ever forbade me from speaking the Sergeant's language except to assist the motel's guests, before I knew what "bastard" or "mongrel" or "slut" or "whore" meant in any language, there was an evening when I walked into the ocean with Clint Eastwood—I was teaching him how to swim—and when I looked back to shore I saw my mother sitting between the Sergeant's legs in the sand, the sun a bright red orb on the crest of the mountains behind them. They spoke without looking at each other, my mother reaching back to hook an arm around his neck, while my piglet thrashed in the sea foam.

"Ma," I asked a few years later, "you think the Sergeant will ever send for us?"

"It's best, luk," Ma said in Thai, "if you never mention his name again. It gives me a headache."

After I finished combing the beach for trash, put Clint Eastwood back in his pen, Lizzie and I went up the mountain on my motorcycle to Surachai's house, where his uncle Mongkhon ran an elephant-trekking business. MR. MONGKHON'S JUNGLE SAFARI, a painted sign declared in their driveway. COME EXPERIENCE THE NATURAL BEAUTY WITH THE AMAZING OF OCEAN OF FOREST VIEW AND SPLENDID FROM ELEPHANT'S HORIZON BACK! I'd informed Uncle Mongkhon once that his sign was grammatically incorrect and that I'd lend him my expertise for a small fee, but he just laughed and said farangs preferred it just the way it was, thank you very much, they thought it was charming, and did I really think I was the only huakhuai who knew English on this godforsaken Island? During the war in Vietnam, before he started the business, Uncle Mongkhon had worked at an airbase on the mainland dishing lunch to American soldiers.

From where Lizzie and I stood, we could see the gray backs of two bulls peeking over the roof of their one-story house. Uncle Mongkhon used to have a corral full of elephants before the people at Monopolated Elephant Tours came to the Island and started underpricing the competition, monopolizing mountain-pass tariffs, and staking their claim upon farangs at hotels three stars and up—doing, in short, what they had done on so many other islands like ours. MET was putting Uncle Mongkhon out of business, and in the end he was forced to sell several elephants to logging companies on the mainland. Where there had once been eight elephants roaming the wide corral, now there were only two—Yai and Not—aging bulls with ulcered bellies and flaccid trunks that hung limply between their crusty forelegs.

"Oh, wow," Lizzie said. "Are those actual elephants?"

I nodded.

"They're so huge."

She clapped a few times, laughing.

"Huge!" she said again, jumping up and down. She turned to me and smiled.

Surachai was lifting weights in the yard, a barbell in each hand. Uncle Mongkhon sat on the porch bare-chested, smoking a cigarette. When Surachai saw Lizzie standing there in her bikini, his arms went limp. For a second I was afraid he might drop the weights on his feet.

"Where'd you find this one?" he said in Thai, smirking, walking toward us.

"Boy," Uncle Mongkhon yelled from the porch, also in Thai. "You irritate me.

Tell that girl to put on some clothes. You know damn well I don't let bikinis ride. This is a respectable establishment. We have rules."

"What are they saying?" Lizzie asked. Farangs get nervous when you carry on a conversation they can't understand.

"They just want to know if we need one elephant or two."

"Let's just get one." Lizzie smiled, reaching out to take my hand. "Let's ride one together." I held my breath. Her hand shot bright, surprising comets of heat up my arm. I wanted to yank my hand away even as I longed to stand there forever with our sweaty palms folded together. I heard the voice of Surachai's mother coming from inside the house, the light sizzle of a frying pan.

"It's nothing, Maew," Uncle Mongkhon yelled back to his sister inside. "Though I wouldn't come out here unless you like nudie shows. The mongrel's here with another member of his international harem."

"These are my friends," I said to Lizzie. "This is Surachai."

"How do you do," Surachai said in English, shaking her hand, looking at me all the while.

"I'm fine, thank you." Lizzie chuckled. "Nice to meet you."

"Yes yes yes," Surachai said, grinning like a fool. "Honor to meet you, madam. It will make me very gratified to let you ride my elephants. Very gratified. Because he"—Surachai patted me on the back now—"he my handsome soulmate. My best man."

Surachai beamed proudly at me. I'd taught him that word: "soulmate."

"You're married?" Lizzie asked. Surachai laughed hysterically, uncomprehendingly, widening his eyes at me for help.

"He's not," I said. "He meant to say 'best friend.'"

"Yes yes," Surachai said, nodding. "Best friend."

"You listening to me, boy?" Uncle Mongkhon got up from the porch and walked toward us. "Bikinis don't ride. It scares the animals."

"Sawatdee, Uncle," I said, greeting him with a wai, bending my head extra low for effect; but he slapped me on the head with a forehand when I came up.

"Tell the girl to put on some clothes," Uncle Mongkhon growled. "It's unholy."

"Aw, Uncle," I pleaded. "We didn't bring any with us."

"Need I remind you, boy, that the elephant is our national symbol? Sometimes I think your stubborn farang half keeps you from understanding this. You should be ashamed of yourself. I would tell your ma if it wouldn't break her heart.

"What if I went to her country and rode a bald eagle in my underwear, huh?" he continued, pointing at Lizzie. "How would she like it? Ask her, will you?"

"What's he saying?" Lizzie whispered in my ear.

"Ha ha ha," Surachai interjected, gesticulating wildly. "Everything okay, madam. Don't worry, be happy. My uncle, he just say elephants very terrified of your breasts."

"You should've told me to put on some clothes." Lizzie turned to me, frowning, letting go of my hand.

"It's really not a problem," I said, laughing.

"No," Uncle Mongkhon said to Lizzie in English. "Not a big problem, madam. Just a small one."

In the end, I took off my t-shirt and gave it to Lizzie. As we made our way toward the corral, I caught her grinning at the sight of my bare torso. Though I had been spending time at the new public gym by the pier, I felt some of that old adolescent embarrassment returning again. I casually flexed my muscles in the postures I'd practiced before my bedroom mirror so Lizzie could see my body not as the soft, skinny thing that it was, but as a pillar of strength and stamina.

When we came upon the gates of the elephant corral, Lizzie took my hand again. I turned to smile at her and she seemed, at that moment, some ethereal angel come from heaven to save me, an angel whose breasts left round, dark damp spots on my t-shirt. And when we mounted the elephant Yai, the beast rising quickly to his feet, Lizzie squealed and wrapped her arms so tightly around my bare waist that I would've gladly forfeited breathing for the rest of my life.

Under that jungle canopy, climbing up the mountainside on Yai's back, I told her about Sergeant Henderson, the motel, Ma, Clint Eastwood. She told me about her Ohio childhood, the New York City skyline, NASCAR, TJ Maxx, the drinking habits of American teenagers. I told her about Pamela, my last American girlfriend, and how she promised me her heart but never answered any of my letters. Lizzie nodded sympathetically and told me about her bastard boyfriend Hunter, whom she'd left last night at their hotel on the other side of the Island after finding him in the arms of a young prostitute. "That fucker," she said. "That whore." I told Lizzie she should forget about him, she deserved better, and besides Hunter was a stupid name anyway, and we both shook our heads and laughed at how poorly our lovers had behaved.

We came upon a scenic overlook. The sea rippled before us like a giant blue bedspread. I decided to give Yai a rest. He sat down gratefully on his haunches. For a minute Lizzie and I just sat there on the elephant's back looking out at the ocean, the wind blowing through the trees behind us. Yai was winded from the climb; we rose and fell with his heavy breaths. I told Lizzie about how the Sergeant and my mother used to stand on the beach, point east, and tell me that if I looked hard enough I might be able to catch a glimpse of the California coast rising out of the Pacific horizon. I pointed to Ma's motel below, the twelve bungalows like tiny insects on a golden shoreline. It's amazing, I told Lizzie, how small my life looks from such a height.

Lizzie hummed contentedly. Then she stood up on Yai's back.

"Here's your shirt," she said, tossing it at me.

With a quick sweeping motion, Lizzie took off her bikini top. Then she peeled off her bikini bottom. And then there she was—my American angel—naked on the back of Uncle Mongkhon's decrepit elephant.

"Your country is so hot," she said, smiling, crawling toward me on all fours. Yai made a low moan and shifted beneath us.

"Yes, it is," I said, pretending to study the horizon, rubbing Yai's parched, gray back.

....

After *Rambo*, lunch with my mother, and a brief afternoon nap, I walk out the door to meet Lizzie at the restaurant when Ma asks me what I'm all dressed up for.

"What do you mean?" I ask innocently, and Ma says, "What do I mean? Am I your mother? Are you my son? Are those black pants? Is that a button-down shirt? Is that the silk tie I bought for your birthday?"

She sniffs my head.

"And is that my nice mousse in your hair? And why," she asks, "do you smell like an elephant?"

I just stand there blinking at her questions.

"Don't think I don't know," she says finally. "I saw you, luk. I saw you on your motorcycle with that farang slut in her bikini."

I laugh and tell her I have hair mousse of my own. But Ma's still yelling at me when I go to the pen to fetch Clint Eastwood.

"Remember whose son you are," she says through the day's last light, standing in the office doorway with her arms akimbo. "Remember who raised you all these years."

"What are you talking about, Ma?"

"Why do you insist, luk, on chasing after these farangs?"

"You're being silly, Ma. It's just love. It's not a crime."

"I don't think," Ma says, "that I'm the silly one here, luk. I'm not the one taking my pet pig out to dinner just because some farang thinks it's cute."

I make my way down the beach with Clint Eastwood toward the lights of the restaurant. It's an outdoor establishment with low candlelit tables set in the sand and a large pit that the bare-chested chefs use to grill the day's catch. The restaurant's quite popular with the farangs. Wind at their backs, sand at their feet, night sky above, eating by the light of the moon and the stars. It's romantic, I suppose. Although I'm hesitant to spend so much money on what Ma calls second-rate seafood in a third-rate atmosphere, Lizzie suggested we meet there for dinner tonight, so who am I to argue with love's demands?

When we get to the restaurant, Lizzie's seated at one of the tables, candlelight flickering on her face. Clint Eastwood races ahead and nuzzles his snout in her lap, but Lizzie's face doesn't light up the way it did this morning. The other customers turn around in their seats to look at Clint Eastwood, and Lizzie seems embarrassed to be the object of his affections.

"Hi," she says when I get to the table, lighting a cigarette.

I kiss one of her hands, sit down beside her. I tell Clint Eastwood to stay. He lies down on his belly in the sand, head resting between his stubby feet. The sun is setting behind us, rays flickering across the plane of the sea, and I think I'm starting to understand why farangs come such a long way to get to the Island, why they travel so far to come to my home.

"Beautiful evening," I say, fingering the knot of my tie.

Lizzie nods absentmindedly.

"Is there something wrong?" I finally ask, after the waiter takes our order in English. "Have I done anything to offend you?"

Lizzie sighs, stubs out her cigarette in the bamboo ashtray.

"Nothing's wrong," she says. "Nothing at all."

But when our food arrives, Lizzie barely touches it. She keeps passing Clint Eastwood pieces of her sautéed prawns. Clint Eastwood gobbles them up gratefully. At least he's enjoying the meal, I think. On weekend nights, I often bring Clint Eastwood to this restaurant, after the tables have been stowed away, and he usually has to fight with the strays that descend on the beach for leftovers farangs leave in their wake: crab shells, fish bones, prawn husks.

"Something's wrong," I say. "You're not happy."

She lights another cigarette, blows a cloud of smoke.

"Hunter's here," she says finally, looking out at the darkening ocean.

"Your ex-boyfriend?"

"No," she says. "My boyfriend. He's here."

"Here?"

"Don't turn around. He's sitting right behind us with his friends."

At that moment, a large farang swoops into the empty seat across the table from us. He's dressed in a white undershirt and a pair of surfer's shorts. His nose is caked with sunscreen. His chest is pink from too much sun. There's a Buddha dangling from his neck. He looks like a deranged clown.

He reaches over and grabs a piece of stuffed squid from my plate.

"Who's the joker?" he asks Lizzie, gnawing on my squid. "Friend of yours?"

"Hunter," Lizzie says. "Please."

"Hey," he says, looking at me, taking another piece of squid from my entree. "What's with the tie? And what's with the pig, man?"

I smile, put on a hand on Clint Eastwood's head.

"Hey you," he says. "I'm talking to you. Speak English? Talk American?"

He tears off a piece of squid with his front teeth. I can't stop staring at his powdered nose, the bulge of his hairy, sunburned chest. I'm hoping he chokes.

"You've really outdone yourself this time, baby," he says to Lizzie now. "But that's what I love about you. Your unpredictability. Your wicked sense of humor. Didn't know you went for mute tards with pet pigs."

"Jesus."

"Oh, Lizzie," he says, feigning tenderness, reaching out to take one of her hands. "I've missed you so much. I hate it when you just leave like that. I've been worried sick about you. I'm sorry about last night, okay baby? Okay? I'm really sorry. But it was just a misunderstanding, you know? Jerry and Billyboy over there can testify to my innocence. You know how Thai girls get when we're around."

"We can talk about this later, Hunter."

"Yes," I interject. "I think you should talk to her later."

He just stares at me with that stupid white nose jutting out between his eyes. For a second, I think Hunter might throw the squid at me. But then he just pops the rest into his mouth, turns to Lizzie, and says with his mouth full:

"You fucked this joker, didn't you?"

I look over at Lizzie. She's staring at the table, tapping her fingers lightly against the wood. It seems she's about to cry. I stand up, throw a few hundred bahts on the table. Clint Eastwood follows my lead, rises clumsily to his feet.

"It was a pleasure meeting you, Miss Elizabeth," I say, smiling. I want to take her hand and run back to the motel so we can curl up together on the beach, watch the constellations. But Lizzie just keeps on staring at the top of that table.

I walk with Clint Eastwood back to the motel. We're the only ones on the beach. Night is upon us now. In the distance, I can see squidding boats perched on the horizon, searchlights luring their catch to the surface. Clint Eastwood races ahead, foraging for food in the sand, and I'm thinking with what I suppose is grief about all the American girls I've ever loved. Girls with names like Pamela, Angela, Stephanie, Joy. And now Lizzie.

One of the girls sent me a postcard of Miami once. A row of palm trees and a pink condo. "Hi Sweetie," it said. "I just wanted to say hi and to thank you for showing me a good time when I was over there. I'm in South Beach now, it's Spring Break, and let me tell you it's not half as beautiful as it is where you are. If you ever make it out to the U S of A, look me up okay?" which was nice of her, but she never told me where to look her up and there was no return address on the postcard. I'd taken that girl to see phosphorescence in one of the Island's bays and when she told me it was the most miraculous thing she'd ever seen, I told her I loved her—but the girl just giggled and ran into the sea, that phosphorescent blue streaking like a comet's tail behind her. Every time they do that, I swear I'll never love another, and I'm thinking about Lizzie and Hunter sitting at the restaurant now, and how this is really the last time I'll let myself love one of her kind.

Halfway down the beach, I find Surachai sitting in a mango tree. He's hidden behind a thicket of leaves, straddling one of the branches, leaning back against the trunk.

When we were kids, Surachai and I used to run around the beach advertising ourselves as the Island's Miraculous Monkey Boys. We made loincloths out of Uncle Mongkhon's straw heap and an old t-shirt Ma used as a rag. For a small fee, we'd climb up trees and fetch coconuts for farangs, who would ooh and ahh at how nimble we were. A product of our Island environment, they'd say, as if it was due to something in the water and not the fact that we'd spent hours practicing in Surachai's backyard. For added effect, we'd make monkey noises when we climbed, which always made them laugh. They would often be impressed, too, by my facility with the English language. In one version of the speech I gave before every performance, I played the part of an American boy shipwrecked on the Island as an infant. With both parents dead, I was raised in the jungle by a family of gibbons. Though we've long outgrown what Ma calls "that idiot stunt," Surachai still comes down from the mountain occasionally to climb a tree on the beach. He'll just sit there staring at the ocean for hours. It's meditative, he told me once. And the view is one-of-a-kind.

"You look terrible," he says now. "Something happen with that farang girl?"

I call Clint Eastwood over. I tell the pig to stay. I take off my leather shoes, my knitted socks, and—because I don't want to ruin them—the button-down shirt and the silk tie, leaving them all at the bottom of the trunk before joining Surachai on an adjacent branch. As I climb, the night air warm against my skin, I'm reminded of how pleasurable this used to be—hoisting myself up by my bare feet and finger-tips—and I'm surprised by how easy it still is.

When I settle myself into the tree, I start to tell Surachai everything, including the episode on the elephant. As I talk, Surachai snakes his way out onto one of the branches and drops a mango for Clint Eastwood down below.

"At least you're having sex," Surachai says. "At least you're doing it. Some of us just get to sit in a mango tree and think about it."

I laugh.

"I don't suppose," Surachai says, "you loved this girl?"

I shrug.

"You're a mystery to me, phuan," Surachai says, climbing higher now into the branches. "I've known you all these years, and that's the one thing I'll never be able to understand—why you keep falling for these farang girls. It's like you're crazy for heartache. Plenty of nice Thai girls around. Girls without plane tickets."

"I know. I don't think they like me, though. Something about the way I look. I don't think my nose is flat enough."

"That may be true. But they don't like me either, okay? And I've got the flattest nose on the Island."

We sit silently for a while, perched in that mango tree like a couple of sloths, listening to the leaves rustling around us. I climb up to where Surachai is sitting. Through the thicket, I see Clint Eastwood jogging out to meet a group of farangs making their way down the beach. I call out to him, tell him to stay, but my pig's not listening to me.

It's Hunter and his friends, laughing, slapping each other's backs, tackling each other to the sand. Lizzie's walking with them silently, head down, trying to ignore their antics. When she sees Clint Eastwood racing up to meet her, she looks to see if I'm around. But she can't see us from where she's standing. She can't see us at all.

"It's that fucking pig again!" Hunter yells.

They all laugh, make rude little pig noises, jab him with their feet. Clint East-wood panics. He squeals. He starts to run. The American boys give chase, try to tackle him to the ground. Lizzie tells them to leave the pig alone, but the boys aren't listening. Clint Eastwood is fast. He's making a fool of them, running in circles one way, then the other, zigzagging back and forth through the sand. The more they give chase, the more Clint Eastwood eludes them, the more frustrated the boys become, and what began as jovial tomfoolery has now turned into some kind of bizarre mission for Hunter and his friends. Their chase becomes more orchestrated. The movements of their shadows turn strategic. They try to corner the pig, run him into a trap, but Clint Eastwood keeps on moving between them, slipping through their fingers like he's greased.

I can tell that Clint Eastwood's beginning to tire, though. He can't keep it up much longer. He's an old pig. I start to climb down from the mango tree, but Sura-chai grabs me by the wrist.

"Wait," he says.

Surachai climbs out to one of the branches. He reaches for a mango and with a quick sweeping motion throws the fruit out to the beach. It hits one of the boys squarely on the shoulder.

"What the fuck!" I hear the boy yell, looking in the direction of the tree, though he continues to pursue Clint Eastwood.

They have him surrounded now, encircled. There's no way out for my pig.

I follow Surachai's lead, grab as many mangoes as I can. Our mangoes sail through the night air. Some of them miss, but some meet their targets squarely in the face, on the head, in the abdomen. Some of the mangoes hit Lizzie by accident, but I don't really care anymore, I'm not really aiming. I'm climbing through that tree like a gibbon, swinging gracefully between the branches, grabbing any piece of fruit—ripe or unripe—that I can get my hands on. Surachai starts to whoop like a monkey and I join him in the chorus. They all turn in our direction then, the four farangs, trying to dodge the mangoes as they come.

It's then that I see Clint Eastwood scurry away unnoticed. I see my pig running into the ocean, his pink snout inching across the sea's dark surface, phosphorescence glittering around his head like a crown of blue stars, and as I'm throwing each mango with all the strength I have, I'm thinking: Swim, Clint, Swim.

Rattawut Lapcharoensap was born in Chicago and raised in Bangkok. He was educated at Triamudomsuksa Pattanakarn High School in Bangkok, Cornell University, and the University of Michigan, where he received an MFA in creative writing. His stories have appeared in *Granta*, *Zoetrope*, and *Glimmer Train*, as well as Harcourt's *Best New American Voices* series. He lives in Ann Arbor, Michigan. *Sightseeing*, his first collection of short stories, was published in January 2005 by Grove Press.

THE BRIEFCASE OF THE PREGNANT SPYLADY

JEFF PARKER

LET'S PLAY A game, his father says.

The game, Hryushka wants to say, a specific member of a group. But two things his father will never figure out: articles and customer service. So Hryushka says nothing. He goes and gets his scoop.

Six burlap sacks are prearranged in the old chest freezer they've converted into storage. The cooling fans no longer work and Hryushka himself severed the power cord which his father used to power a bucket that he turned into a leaf blower. Each sack contains a different granule: sugar, flour, salt, dog food, buckwheat, semolina. His father has sewn zippers into the sacks and locked them with little padlocks.

His father zips Hryushka along with his keychain flashlight and scoop into a seventh sack, then lifts him, with some difficulty, into the freezer and closes the lid. Hryushka's job, once zippered into a seventh sack and closed in the freezer, is to unzip himself from the seventh sack, to jimmy the little padlock on the other sacks one-by-one, taking one scoop of granule from each, depositing it into a Ziplock bag, rezipping and relocking each sack—if he breaks a little padlock while jimmying it he has to superglue it back together—then to rezipper himself, the keychain flashlight and scoop, and the six Ziplocks of granule into the seventh sack.

He has done it so many times he doesn't get claustrophobic or break a sweat even when his father kicks the freezer, even when he tips it all the way over and then rights it. Hryushka stays focused. He spills one scoop of dog food. He knows one scoop holds roughly thirty-two kibbles. He feels around on the floor, counting as he retrieves them, until he hits thirty-two, then he feels around more, shining the keychain flashlight to where he can't reach. When he's done, his father will check the floor carefully. For now Hryushka doesn't even think about what might be happening on the outside. That is how his father taught him.

Even when he breaks a little padlock and glues two of his fingers together while trying to glue the lock back together he doesn't spaz. He has plenty of time actually, and he sits long after he's done, zippered in the seventh sack with his single scoop of sugar, flour, salt, dog food, buckwheat, and semolina, sucking on his glued-together fingers before rocking himself back and forth against the side of the freezer, signaling to his father that the game is over.

Itchy, this guy in a pick-up says to Hryushka.

I don't know what you mean, Hryushka says from the sidewalk, unsure what language the guy is speaking.

Hey, chief, he says. Where's the library?

Oh, Hryushka says. You're right in front of it. It's here.

Then he walks into the library and sits down with the ESL pamphlets. He is trying to rid himself of reflexive particles. He knows he should not feel himself bad. He should feel bad. He should not feel himself like his bones are exploding in the night. He should feel like his bones are exploding in the night. His father never spoke Russian to him, only self-taught English with his thick accent, the same accent that home-schooled him, and now he's the only kid around who doesn't really speak English or Russian, no native language, just a thick accent all his own. Or maybe he should reflexive particle when he's writing but not in speech?

Hryushka heard somewhere that his name means piglet. He feels it but can't directly translate. He feels the pigletness in the sound of his name. He hears things all the time around him, in The Briefcase of the Pregnant Spylady, from the luggage compartment of the Greyhound, he hears them.

Once some grandma, one of the émigrés who used to shop in The Briefcase of the Pregnant Spylady, gave him a Russian language textbook. She felt sorry for him because he couldn't speak what he could understand. His father caught him reading and burned it in the wood stove.

We not emigrate so you beet Russian, he said. Want that we go anywhere.

When Hryushka hears a word in either language, it's not like he hears the word. It kind of bypasses his ears and an image pops into his head. When he hears his own name a piglet pops into his head.

The library is across the street from The Briefcase of the Pregnant Spylady and their attached apartment. Now that he's twelve his father lets him go on his own in the mornings to study. There is no need for him in the shop. It used to be the only Russian store in the city. There were always frozen pelmeni to sweep up (the bags break and they skid across the restaurant floor like hockey pucks) or farmer's cheese to rotate (the old stuff he opens out back for the pigeons). Now there's two other stores. Even though his father's prices are cheaper, no one comes anymore.

At noon Hryushka walks across the street for lunch. His father has prepared kielbasa and cheese sandwiches and the stereo is blasting "There is No God," his father's favorite song, the only song he ever listens to. It's a seventies rock ballad repeating the words—and only the words, There is no God. It's in Russian, so Hryushka is not sure how he knows what's being said, he just knows. His father's got a whole tape with that one song taking up both sides. Everyday he plays it, over and over, the only pauses the time it takes after the cassette stops to walk to the stereo and flip it. His father sings along as he slices deli meats. It's why none of the other émigrés shop here. They're all Orthodox and that kind of thing gets to them. Like articles, his father doesn't understand.

They eat and Hryushka cleans the store. He feather dusts shelves and boxes of instant pancake mix, vinegars the glass on the freezer doors. His father wipes off the cash register keys.

Sometimes, an utterance comes out of Hryushka's mouth and he has no idea why he said it. Before they play the game again, his father says, No fur, no feathers, and Hryushka replies, To the devil. He has no idea why he says it.

Hryushka knocks himself against the side of the storage cabinet when he's done. His father lifts him out of the seventh sack and brushes him off with the back of his hand.

How legs? his father asks.

Cramped, he says. It's hard to turn around.

Not much time, he says. Your body wants grow. His father dumps out the seventh sack and checks the bottom of the storage cabinet. We do a real thing now. Once more.

The real thing, Papa, one more time.

The trick to the prices is logistics. Every two weeks Hryushka and his father take a trip to New York on the Greyhound. When they get there, Hryushka's father one-way rentals a van and drives product back, direct from the wholesalers; they pick it up themselves at the warehouses in Brooklyn. It's still expensive but cheaper than dealing with distributors. The other stores have the goods shipped in and poppy seed buns go for two bucks each. The Briefcase of the Pregnant Spylady sells them for one dollar.

The weather broke tonight, a freak cold snap on the heels of a front, rain then ice. On the way to the Greyhound station, Hryushka keeps bending down to pick up bracelets off the sidewalk but they're frozen worms glittering under the street lights. He pockets them and they break like pencil leads in his pocket. Before they reach the station they step into an alley and his father opens up the suitcase, which is insulated with rabbit fur. Hryushka climbs in and his father snaps it shut.

As his father rolls the suitcase across the asphalt, Hryushka loses himself. He forgets where he is, does not turn on the keychain flashlight, closes his eyes as tight as possible so as not to witness all the dark. He thinks how the cold snap came on like his growth spurt, from nowhere, pang to the bone. He shot up three inches this month. He cries in the night, massaging his legs and starving. His father brings him carrots and tells him to think small. He tries to think small. He tries to imagine his legs the size they used to be, but he finds that he has a great deal of trouble picturing his legs without looking at them.

It is easy to tell when his father hands him off. The driver is never as careful with the suitcase. He is dropped, then flipped upside down, then thrown. He hears his father ask the driver to be more careful. The driver gives the suitcase an extra hard shove to the back of the compartment.

This is the part that always seems to take forever, idling at the station. His father watches where his son is positioned in the luggage compartment and tries to sit above him. The bus is full of other émigrés going from Cleveland to Squirrel Hill. His father talks so loud that Hryushka can actually hear him over the engine noise.

The real thing is quite a bit different than the game. For one, there is no scoop. The scoop was his father's idea, to get Hryushka to concentrate on process and technique. There are no prearranged bags of granule; instead piles of suitcases, most of them locked at best with a little padlock, which Hryushka can easily pick. The little padlocks his father buys for the game are much higher quality than these.

Other things are similar. He is only to take one thing from each bag, just one thing, his father always said. If you took just one thing, he said, no one notice. He wanted them no notice as much as possible. If it was just one thing, they could never be sure they hadn't left it, no one could make a case. It should be something valuable, usually jewelry. Sometimes he found cash, a laser pointer, massagers, a prosthetic hand. Another of his father's rules: if there is nothing of value, he still has to take something from each bag for consistency and fairness. Here Hryushka's own rule comes into play: he never takes anything he himself wants. He leaves the candy. Once he happened on a porno collection—he looked, but left it. Instead, from these bags, he takes toenail clippers, Rogaine, and XXL t-shirts, which were too big for him even to sleep in.

The first leg of the trip—mostly Russians—he is to stay put. His father always told him to forget about what's going on outside, to relax, because he can feel by the speed of the bus how fast it's going. If it slows, it's getting off the highway and a stop will come soon. If it slows, he's to climb immediately back into the suitcase. As long as the speed is constant, they're still on the highway and everything's fine. Highway = fine. He should forget about what's going on outside, relax. The first time they pull off the highway—you cannot miss that from the luggage compartment—they will be in Pittsburgh, some bags will be pulled off, others put on, better bags. But there will be plenty of time from that first slowing to Pittsburgh, so he can relax.

Hryushka does not stay put this time. His legs are cramping. There is a special pocket on the top of the suitcase, which looks like a zipper pocket. The zipper is on the inside. He squeezes his skinny body out of the pocket like a stick of chewing gum from its pack. The compartment vibrates and he bangs his head on the steel sheet of flimsy metal separating the luggage from the people.

He turns on the keychain light and looks around. He knows how to spot the good bags, the kind kids his age or a little older pack. They're like sports bags athletes carry. They say *Nike* or *Reebok* or *Fine Young Thing* on the outside. They are never locked. He shines his keychain flashlight on a green one. He pulls up the side of the bag and reads: *Phuket Thailand*. The bus is barreling, maybe seventy-five, eighty.

Ordinarily he would avoid the temptation of a *Phuket Thailand* bag, but his legs are stretched and better feeling, though he's hungry again. Hryushka can barely remember a time before he had taken this trip in the luggage compartment. It was always there, something he understood but couldn't explain. He tried to remember the first time he'd played the game, but he couldn't remember that either. He might never get the chance to root around in another kid's bag. And this bag—he can't figure out how to pronounce this word. It wouldn't hurt to peek, he figures.

He opens the zipper and crawls in. There is no sound more exciting to him than that of a zipper. Inside, the bag smells of pecan. To him, the flannels and jeans are softer than his father's fur. His head knocks against something hard and flat. He reaches under a stack of undershirts and removes a CD player with headphones, something he's always wanted. He can't understand why the kid wouldn't take the headphones with him to listen on the bus. If Hryushka had headphones and he was riding on the bus with a ticket, he would surely take them with him. Hryushka hits the open/close button.

As the CD player opens, Hryushka hears the squeal-hiss of the bus brakes, then the slow pull as it merges into the exit lane. He removes a length of frozen worm from his pocket and shines the flashlight on it. It's beginning to thaw and come back to life, writhing almost imperceptibly. He places it under the stack of undershirts then climbs out of the *Phuket Thailand* bag, rezips it, scales the stacks of luggage back to his own suitcase. Still clutching the CD player, he dives back in.

He is sweating and nervous as the brakes—Hryushka imagines the collective whine of a million beagles—bite then release. He hears the driver pop the luggage compartment door, toss out bags around him, chuck others in. Then, to his shock, his own suitcase and he himself are removed, plopped to the ground briefly then picked up and carried, a circuitous route by very sure steps, indistinguishably his father's calculated steps. The suitcase is dropped to the ground again, then the latches snapped and the top lifted open.

Hryushka blinks. He is in a stall next to a toilet, his father standing over him, saying, Come out, Hryushka. You have a whole life to ride bus. Might well as start now. His father leaves the stall and washes his hands. Hryushka steps out of the suitcase, sticking the CD player and headphones down his pants. Then they leave the bathroom together.

Hryushka's father buys an additional ticket from the attendant, and Hryushka watches the driver's face as he and his father emerge from the terminal, a place awash in such white a light—Hryushka can hardly imagine having seen a place so bright before. His father hands the driver his stub and Hryushka's ticket. Then he hands over the empty suitcase.

I deposited some things for my wife and picked my son, his father says, motioning toward Hryushka.

Fine, the driver says. He frisbees the suitcase into the compartment. It lands right on top of the *Phuket Thailand* bag.

Hryushka doesn't understand what's going on, but since he has never ridden in a bus like a normal ticketed person he doesn't worry. He takes the window seat beside his father and absorbs all the silence, amazed at how quiet the bus is from up here. He always thought he heard so much talking. He glances at his father, whose eyes are closed, his head held perfectly straight, not bent to the side sloppily like other people.

He closes his eyes and briefly imagines himself back inside the *Phuket Thailand* bag. He looks over the seatbacks for a little boy to go with it. He goes to the bathroom and on his way stares intently at the crooked sleeping heads of the other passengers. No boy. He balances the CD player on the little bus-bathroom faucet. Something occurs to him then as he's peeing: perhaps whoever's bag that was, was someone like him, another boy whose father hides him in the luggage to steal what there is to steal. Suppose that little boy snuck out of the bag before Hryushka, and he was investigating another suitcase—maybe even his own—as he stole the kid's CD player. More likely, the kid rode the bus the first leg, then had his accomplice—someone like his own father—install him in the luggage at the same time as Hryushka's father inexplicably let him out. The idea was just outrageous enough. Hryushka had never considered a possibility like this before.

On the way back down the aisle he looks not for people like himself, but for people who look like his father. They pretty much all could be him in one way or another.

Hryushka's father has ordered special pies from the distributors. He is taking the store in this direction, in the direction of desserts. He's specifically ordered Napoleon, Stump, and Kiss of an African Man. He asks the wholesaler in English for his pies, and the guy replies something about credit and then Hryushka's father shoos Hryushka out and he and the wholesaler argue in Russian.

Hryushka and his father leave with no Napoleons, Stumps, or Kisses of African Man. They have a couple boxes of candy Squirrels and frozen chocolate bars filled with farmer's cheese. They rent a Kia rather than the minivan because they have only a trunkful of product to transport and Hryushka sleeps most of the way across New York when something else strange happens: In a town called Corning above the Finger Lakes, Hryushka's father pulls off the highway and into the parking lot of the Corning Museum of Glass.

The building itself, surprisingly, is brick. But inside everything is glass. Hryushka can see, across the room, a glass Egyptian pharaoh at least four times bigger than himself. His father, for the second time in so many days, hands him a ticket. On this one is written, *Corning Museum of Glass: After spending time here you will understand glass in a very different way.*

Hryushka looks down at the ground as he's stocking the candies and chocolate covered farmer's cheese in the reach-in cooler. He gets slightly dizzy then walks over to the mark on the wall his father uses to track his height.

Hryushka presses his back against the wall trim. His father is flipping the tape and restarting "There is No God."

Can you measure me, Papa? he says.

His father runs a pencil across the top of Hryushka's head. He steps away from the wall and they both look at it. The new mark is separated from the old one by approximately the height of one poppy seed bun.

His father falls back into a corner, then slides down to a sitting position below a speaker. Both of them stare at the bun-sized space. His father's legs are stretched out in front of him. The only sound, except for the There is No God refrain, is the reach-in cooler fans.

Hryusha wants to ask why he was pulled off the bus in Pittsburgh, but he doesn't. He is thinking about *some* and *any*. He is not sure when to say *Is there any problem?* or *Is there some problem?* He's not sure what the difference is.

His thoughts are interrupted by his father's voice in Russian, explaining something, though at first Hryushka is not sure what. Then he realizes that he is telling him the story of the store's name. Hryushka listens, and it is difficult, but images begin to appear in his head: His father's father used to put him in the luggage compartment on trains. In those days he wouldn't get much but everything was worth something. He'd be happy if he found half a loaf of bread wadded in a head scarf. But there came a time—as with Hryushka—when he started to grow. Hryushka's father was sad not because he particularly liked stealing from people, but because he liked being among their things and imagining them based on that. On what Hryushka's father's father said would be his last trip in the luggage compartment, he made a fabulous discovery, one that stands to this day as his most exciting moment. While burrowing through the wool socks and musty suitcases tied together with rope, he discovered a small shiny black briefcase. The locks on it were difficult to pick, but he had a good knife, and though his father would have killed him if he had found out, he broke the locks to get in. In that briefcase was the most strange combination of items. He first noticed a pistol and a kind of radio, both made by Japanese. There were also stacks of folders containing documents labeled *secret*. Underneath them, smushed at the bottom of the briefcase were women's underwear and a pacifier with a piece of ribbon around it, a gift tag that read, *For Mashinka—my favorite pregnant spylady—and offspring.*

Hryushka's father goes on with the story, but Hryushka stops listening. He now has an image in his head of his father as a little kid, sitting cross-legged over an open briefcase, fumbling through the belongings of a pregnant KGB. He takes that image with him to bed, where he gets under the sheet and toys with the CD player he'd stolen from the *Phuket Thailand* bag. Inside is a CD with a piece of tape and the word *Rach* written on it. He puts the headphones on and hits play. He'd expected Van Halen or Aerosmith, but it's classical, piano. He lies there listening.

Later he pads down the hall and across the corridor into The Briefcase of the Pregnant Spylady, where his father is still hunkered in the corner, his back to the wall, his hands on his knees, mouthing the words to his favorite song.

Let's try one more time, Papa, Hryushka says.

Hryushka's father tells him to take a pillow but he says it like *pilaf*. He can curl around it since he is really too big for the suitcase and with the CD player again shoved down the front of his pants it cushions things. During the hand-off he hears the driver ask his father what the hell he's got in there.

Weights, his father says. Sorry.

Hryushka waits through the idling, until they've pulled out and he knows they're on the freeway by the vibrations of the flimsy sheet metal lining the luggage compartment and the whoosh of air beneath him. Then he slides himself out of the suitcase and shines the flashlight around.

Mostly the usual stuff. He eyes an expensive looking silver metal set, and beside it is the very same *Phuket Thailand* bag he stole the CD player from. This had never happened before, that he'd seen the same bag twice.

He climbs over the expensive silver luggage set and punches the *Phuket Thailand* bag, not knowing exactly what to expect. It does not react. He unzips it and shines the flashlight in. It's packed much like it was before, like it's missing something about the size of a body. He climbs in and pushes his shoulders back into the flannels, extends his legs as far as they'll go. He zips himself in. The bag is longer and stretchier than his father's suitcase.

He takes out the stolen CD player, fits the headphones over his ears, and starts the piano music again, dulling the bus noise to a background buzz. He breathes in the smell of this kid's bag—not nuts, more like the underneath of library desks. He closes his eyes. He grips denim, feels his hands into a small cardboard box. He shakes it and it flutters. Band-Aids, he guesses. He sees only dark and hears only this strange piano music. He puts the box of Band-Aids into his pocket.

It's more comfortable in this bag, Hryushka thinks. I feel, all there.

When the Greyhound comes to a full stop—how did he miss the pulling off the highway?—he doesn't hit pause on the CD player. The door on the luggage compartment roars open, annoying him. I'm the bag, Hrushka says. Me's it. He doesn't know how loud he says it because he can't hear himself with the headphones. But he guesses the driver doesn't catch it. He's lifted with the *Phuket Thailand* bag and thrown on the sidewalk.

Hryushka hears people move all around him, picking up other cases that are not him. It seems like he waits forever, for all of the buses to pull away, for someone to give the now seventy-pound heavier *Phuket Thailand* bag a puzzled tug, and then comes the unzippering.

When the bright bus station lights shine in, Hryushka prepares a big smile for a boy who turns out to look exactly like he expected him to look. They stare into each other's faces, each of them thinking the other is something he is not. Hryushka breaks the silence. A pancake in general, he says.

Jeff Parker's stories have appeared in *Ploughshares, Tin House, Hobart,* and *The Best American Nonrequired Reading 2006.* His novel *Ovenman* will be published by Tin House Books in spring 2006. He teaches creative writing and hypermedia at Eastern Michigan University.

GIRAFFES
STEVEN GILLIS

M.E. HUNG THE children in the yard. The girl was anxious and twice told not to kick. M.E. strung her beneath the arms, watched until the blue in her face disappeared and she seemed again almost normal.

The boy was weighed and measured next, a few stones placed in his front pockets, the rope looped over the highest branch rubbing the bark down to smooth white fibers. M.E. stood near the exposed taproot of the Juniper bush and explained resonant pendula to his students. "Every pendulum has an intrinsic frequency," he said. "When two pendulums are placed side by side, with one set in motion, the energy from the first is transferred to the second until it also starts to swing. The exchange continues until the first body surrenders all its energy and stops moving completely. At that point the situation is reversed and the energy acquired by the second body is stolen back again. It is," M.E. said, "a natural occurrence."

The first time M.E. tried kissing Mimi Bell, she laughed and slipped off her shoes. Mimi's skin was thick and smooth and tan, her breasts large, her cheeks round and lush as apples. In M.E.'s apartment, near the couch, a half step from the window, Mimi asked "Where? Here?" and pulled her sweater over her head.

M.E. phoned the next day and invited Mimi for a swim at the Fenview High pool.

"I can't," she said. "I have a date."

He waited until noon Sunday then called again.

"You can take me to dinner," she told him, then put him off until Friday night. They went to Dominique's on the waterfront. Mimi wore a green skirt and thin blue sweater. When she undressed this time, he had her lay her clothes down neatly on the back of his bedroom chair.

Saturday M.E. graded papers, ate a burger at the House of Meat, then phoned Mimi at seven. "I thought I'd stop by."

"Sorry."

"Are you?"

"On my way out."

"I see." M.E. checked the children in the yard, the new ones hanging and the others waiting. Afterward, he went to Huber's Market and bought groceries for the week. He remembered Mimi liked Oreos and tuna, and left a bag outside her front door with a note. Mimi phoned just before one in the morning. "What are you doing?"

"Sleeping."

"That's not what I meant. What are you doing bringing me groceries?"

M.E. sat up. "I thought you liked."

"That isn't the point."

He switched on the lamp beside his bed, heard Mimi turn from the phone and tell someone else to, "Just go!" A second later she was back on the line. "You can't bring me groceries."

"Why?"

"It's too transparent."

"But I."

"Happened to be at the store."

"And just."

"What?"

"Wanted to bring you."

"Because?"

"Because."

"Because, because, because, because, because," Mimi sang, "because of the wonderful things she does!"

"That's not it."

"Really? You don't want?"

M.E. considered his choices, said "No," then quickly, "That is, of course, I want."

"And so you brought me groceries," Mimi in her kitchen heard M.E. breathing through the line, all swift and eager as a puppy dog's pant. "Listen," she ran down a list of his deficiencies, how he was too thin for her, his shoulders and chest, his hair too neat and hands too soft. "Two dates," she said, and so what if she liked him better than the others? "You're just sniffing around the hen house," she held the phone out in front of her. "You don't even know me."

M.E. went to his window, saw the children where he left them, the girl now swinging higher but the boy catching up. The moon made them silver and black, silver and black, silver and black. "I know enough. I know I like being with you."

"You like playing pin the tail to the bedsprings."

"That's not it. It's more than that," M.E. recalled the first time he saw her, at a seminar on Electron Configuration and the Discoveries of Sir William Ramsay, which Mimi's company—Just Desserts—catered. Watching her across the room, in a pink cotton skirt and white chef's top, looking much as her own perfectly purveyed confection, M.E. experienced a series of involuntarily chemical reactions: the monoamine in his brain dancing like carbonated fizz, the dopamine, norepinephrine and serotonin shooting off electric charges, while his PEA count soared and accelerated his pulse. An hour after the conference, M.E. found the nerve to ask Mimi out. "We seemed to hit it off."

"A couple of dinners."

"I thought maybe if we spent more time together."

"You're assuming."

"You like me."

"Who said?"

M.E. whispered her name into the phone. "Mimi, Mimi, Mimi."

"Don't do that," she reached into the grocery bag, brought out a can of tuna, held it for a moment then dropped it back inside. "You got the wrong stuff."

"I don't think."

"I'm going to hang up," she had her finger on the button, hesitated then cradled the phone close again. "You can't just bring me things and expect," she spoke loud enough to keep her voice from dropping down into her belly. "What's your problem?" she insisted he tell her. "What do you want?" but M.E. didn't answer, was already searching for his shoes.

In the morning, M.E. fixed breakfast and filled Mimi's car with gas. He taught Newton's theory of gravity to eleventh grade students, explaining by way of cannonballs dropped and then fired from the roof of Fenview High how any two objects in the universe can exert gravitational attraction on one another. ("Fg = Gm1m2/r2. Look at the pull, look at the drag.") The boy and girl still testing resonant pendula were fed through rubber tubes in order not to disrupt their motion. Their progress charted, their endurance earned them extra credit.

"Alright then, loverboy," Mimi behind the door last night, let M.E. rattle the knob before undoing the lock and pulling him inside. "If we're going to do this," she handed him a mop and bucket, had him clean her kitchen and take out the trash. Surprised, M.E. did as told, anticipating Mimi waiting for him in the bedroom, naked and with candles lit, he pictured the pout of her mouth, the sweet swell of her nipples and deep green pool of her eyes. Afterward, M.E. undressed in the bathroom, went and found Mimi beneath the sheet, rubbed a hand along her shoulder and toward her hip, only to realize she was sleeping. Each additional overture proved futile. When M.E. kissed her cheek, Mimi squirmed and farted against his leg.

Ha! Who couldn't help but laugh? What a pip she was! What a pistol! M.E. consoled himself by wrapping his body around Mimi's curves, waited until the next day when he drove over from Fenview High, cleaned the rest of Mimi's apartment, picked up two more bags of groceries at Huber's and made steaks on the grill. In bed that night, Mimi wore grey sweats and a flannel pajama top instead of the see-through nightie and sheer silk thong M.E. hoped for. "Let's talk," she said.

M.E. leaned over and nibbled on her shoulder, ran a hand up her thigh.

"What are you doing?" she slapped at his wrist. "Can't you?"

"Yes, of course," he moved his hand to her knee. "I just thought."

"I know what you thought."

"We had a nice evening."

"So you figured."

"It would be fun."

"To smack hips? Hide the salami? Bang the monkey?"

"Make love."

"It's all about getting laid still, isn't it?"

"That's not."

"Because you promised."

"I know."

"You said."

"I remember."

"Then what?"

"I just."

"And now you won't even talk to me unless."

M.E. apologized, said "You're right," and hoping to salvage what he could from the situation, told her, "If you want to talk. If you need to. How are things then?"

That Saturday, after cleaning the windows and re-grouting the tub, M.E. invited Mimi to the zoo. She wore baggy blue shorts and a yellow top one size too small, her white canvas sneakers large and wide, flapping like clown shoes when she walked. "You like?" She raised her arms above her head and did a pirouette.

"I'm speechless. Maybe a sweatshirt," M.E. suggested. "In case it rains."

Mimi stopped her spin, set her hands on her hips, her blue shorts flapping, the bottom of her shirt ending three inches above her waist, the small folds of her belly exposed. "What are you saying?"

"Nothing. Just. The forecast," M.E. muttered.

"There isn't a cloud."

"There's a chance."

"You don't like the way I look?"

"That's not it."

"I spent a lot of time."

"I'm sure you did."

"You don't like it."

"No, I do."

"Really?"

"Yes."

"Then tell me."

Between the cages and outdoor exhibits at the zoo, M.E. held Mimi's hand as they walked past the llamas, the ocelots, polar bears, and zebras. Standing later by the leopards, eating a Zoo Dog wrapped in silver foil and thick with mustard, M.E. apologized for not responding with more immediate favor to the way Mimi dressed. His reaction, he said, was uncalled for, petty and unkind. Why should it matter what she wore, especially when she was trying so hard to look nice for him? (How she got the shirt on to begin with, he couldn't imagine.) What a treat she was! What a corker! M.E. wiped mustard from her chin, said "Mimi, I," only she stopped him, shook her head and covered his mouth. "Please M.E., not while I'm eating."

At the giraffe exhibit, they watched one of the male giraffes follow the female around the yard, saw him stretch his neck and reach to rub his head against the female's rump, lick her tail and sniff her urine in the standard mating ritual. M.E. told Mimi, "The giraffe's heart is over twenty-four pounds on average, bigger than it's head. The giraffe heart pumps more than sixteen gallons of blood a minute, up through a series of back-flow preventor valves in the neck and on to the brain. Physiologically, the giraffe is an anomaly. No other animal is put together quite this way. Any disturbance to the rhythms of the heart, the flow of blood or drop in pressure, and the giraffe will instantly pass out."

Mimi stared, imagining the fall, while M.E. rubbed his chest and agreed, "It can be a problem."

Mimi wore black chaps and a green cotton sports bra to bed that night. A tiny cowboy hat, red and white, was clipped to her hair, a blue string dangling under her chin. Her bottom was bare beneath the sheet, the leather of her chaps covering just her shins and thighs. She gave M.E. the curve of her back, her body turned for him to fit around again like the frame of a painting. M.E. slid into position and wrapped himself tight. Despite her outfit, Mimi insisted M.E. leave his shorts on. She pressed against him, making him hard. M.E. maneuvered around her shoulder and murmured softly, "May I?"

"You like?"

"Very much. Is it okay if I?"

"No."

"But Mimi."

She pushed harder against him. "What is it? Is there something you want to tell me?" She squirmed again, did a little backward wiggle and said, "Funny how eager you are to tell me now."

M.E. lined himself up, an explorer with his purple helmet poking at the mouth of a cave. "I tried telling you at the zoo."

"So? I suppose you think all this sweet chatter will get you inside the magic kingdom."

M.E. in retreat, wondered "Why are you?"

"What? So hard?" Mimi laughed.

"I just want."

"I know what you want, but you can't talk your way in."

"You let me in, remember?"

"You pestered me until."

"If we're going to do this, you said."

"You brought me groceries."

"You opened the door."

"It doesn't matter."

"Why?"

"Because, I know how these things wind up."

"They wind up as we let them."

"Wrong, they go as they will."

M.E. moved his chin further down Mimi's arm and asked her then, "What are you so afraid of?" The question caught her by surprise. M.E. could feel her beneath him, breathing out, collapsed and still. He waited a moment, wondering if he'd gone too far, and losing his nerve, said "Mimi, I."

"Ha!" she rolled right and tossed back the sheet, stood over M.E. with legs wide, her sex covered by wild hair, all tangled and glistening. "I knew it. Who's afraid?" She hopped twice on the bed, bouncing M.E. who, rising and falling, thought of kinetic energy, the force created by the translational flow and the speed of Mimi's leaping mass. All objects in motion acquired kinetic energy—KE=1/2*m*v2—yet here M.E. considered the transference, how dormant he was laid out on the bed before Mimi started jumping, the way he had no motility at all until she moved him.

"If you'd only let me," he ached, his underwear tented, his hands curved like bird wings rising slightly while Mimi squatted lower, reached down and tugged off his shorts.

"Let you what, M.E.?" she grabbed hold of his member with her right hand, her left arm raised for balance, a bull rider at the rodeo seizing the rope. She dropped lower, settled directly on top of M.E., sinking with an, "Ooff," and an, "Ahh," and a "Wow-wee!" When she finished, well after M.E. who came in a series of quick, full body shudders, Mimi released a final, "Yee-ha!" and fell onto his chest. M.E. wrapped his arms around her, tender and triumphant, until Mimi bit him hard on the ear and rolled away. "Don't confuse any of this," she warned him, and tossing off her cowboy hat, slid over to the far side of the bed and fell asleep.

In the yard, the children fixed an additional three ropes to the surrounding trees. M.E. stood beneath their feet, each student hoping he would teach them now how to turn resonant pendula into perpetual motion. "We want to continue moving," they called from the branches. "We understand the give and take," they said, "but how do we keep things going?"

"That's the problem," M.E. looked up. "There's no such thing as perpetual motion. Resonant pendula allows for a sharing of energy between two bodies only for a time. The energy created produces friction, and while it seems counter intuitive, the truth is all motion causes resistance which leads to drag and ultimately forces a moving object to stop."

"But there must be a way," the children were convinced, believing as they did that everything in nature was eternal, the force and flow of objects, the sun and air, all energy immutable and constant. M.E. smiled at this, watching the children test the effect of resonant pendula on two classmates not of equal mass. ("What if the bodies are different?" they were curious.) For a moment M.E. was tempted to encourage them, imagined human emotion having a self perpetuating orbit built into its center, neutrons and electrons circling the nucleus of an atom. Nothing in physics actually denied the existence of perpetual motion, M.E. nearly confessed. Einstein's E=MC^2 exposed the possibility of converting light into mass, and so, too, in theory the possibility existed for creating a perfect mirror through which mass could be converted into light. The light could then be gathered and reflected skyward where, at its apex, the light would change back into mass and drop to earth attached to a pulley, creating energy and force. By repeating the process through an indefinite production of light, perpetual motion could be created.

It was however, only a theory.

M.E. grabbed the foot of a tall girl in a short red corduroy dress and black and white saddle shoes strung some four feet overhead, and giving her a yank, said "Modern physicists insist energy can never be created or destroyed, but simply altered in form." He told them how Pascal tried building a perpetual motion machine in the seventeenth century, only to wind up inventing the roulette wheel, and picturing Mimi on the bed, thought of the energy expended and the way objects dropped from a great height produced friction and risked disintegration before landing. The girl swung against the drag of her partner. M.E. stared at the children, shrugged and said, "Let me think. Let's see if there isn't something."

The following Thursday, Fenview High held an end of the year faculty dinner. Mimi wore a strapless purple dress, a pink belt and red pumps. Her hair was pulled back over her shoulders and clipped in the center by an oversized bow. "You like?" she twirled around.

"It's you," M.E. couldn't deny.

The cafeteria was decorated with blue and orange crepe paper. Student volunteers in Fenview High band uniforms served boiled chicken, mackerel salad and bright yellow corn out of large electric crock pots. M.E. introduced Mimi to his colleagues who complimented her on her dress. Music was piped through the intercom from the stereo in the main office. Mimi heard Springsteen's "Born in the USA" and wanted to dance. M.E. did his best to keep up, tossing his arms high and low as Mimi covered the floor with pulsating pyrotechnics; Newton's theory of gravitational attraction in full effect, the drag constant across the top of her gown. Halfway through the second song, Lloyd Nedhure tapped M.E. on the shoulder and asked to cut in. Soon a line formed along the north wall where a dozen of M.E.'s colleagues waited eagerly to give Mimi a whirl.

M.E. watched Mimi dance with Bill Teruss and Al Farre, Buck Wile, and even Charity Wentworth who helped Mimi with her dress when most of her right boob popped out. "Some outfit," Dickie Davis loosened his tie, slapped M.E. on the shoulder and took his place in line. Driving home afterward, Mimi hummed tunes from Santana's "Abraxas." "That was fun," she said.

"I'm glad."

"What about you?" Mimi's feet were sore and she'd a bit of mackerel salad stuck between her front teeth. She undid her bow and tossed it in back. "Did you enjoy yourself?"

"Sure, yes."

"You liked watching me with everyone then?"

"You seemed happy."

"That isn't what I asked. Were you jealous?"

"Of my friends?"

"Of my dancing with them. Did it bother you?"

M.E. turned the wheel, glanced at Mimi, wondered how he was supposed to respond. He pictured her again whirling around the cafeteria, dipping and grinding with Buck Wile, arching as Larry Wein set his hands on her hips, laughing as Dickie Davis had her slide through his legs in the middle of MC5's "Kick Out the Jams, Motherfuckers." "I would have preferred," he told her.

"But you let them," Mimi adjusted the front of her dress, pulled it down then up and asked again, "Were you jealous?" She took hold of M.E.'s middle finger, picked at the fish in her teeth, then clamped down hard. "Because you should."

"Yoww-icch!"

"What am I supposed to think if you're not jealous?"

"But Mimi," M.E. retrieved his finger and massaged it with his thumb. "You know that I."

"Stop. You can't tell me now."

He reached for her with his sore hand, braving another bite, yet hoping to provide perspective, said of the evening, "It was all just dance."

At this Mimi laughed, shook her head and told M.E., "Of course it was. Everything is dance."

M.E. slept that night on his side, touching only Mimi's hip. He dreamed of the children in the trees and new ways to produce perpetual motion, imagined a couple making love, the kinetic energy from their sex transferred through their hump-hump-hump up into the branches. The couple's constant rhythm created an endless force, a long assembly of volunteers ready to take their place the second they tired.

Three days later, Mimi told M.E., "I have to work this weekend in Bristol. There's a convention."

M.E. had on a pink cotton apron and large rubber gloves. He was kneeling to clean Mimi's oven, a can of Campbell's tomato soup cooking on the rear left burner. "Alright," he said. "I'll drive up with you, if you like."

"That's okay," Mimi stirred the pot. "I'm going with a friend. Roy Fiske. We'll be back Sunday night."

"Roy?"

"Fiske."

"And Roy is?"

"I just told you."

"A friend?"

"And co-worker."

"Is he?"

"What?"

"I mean, did you ever?"

"Date him?"

"Date him."

"You could say that."

M.E. scraped the muck, finished with the oven, washed his hands, and made tuna sandwiches to go with their soup. Later, in bed, he thought again what a pip Mimi was, how clever the way she set him up. ("Everything is dance," she told him.) He recalled the conference where they first met, how the lecturer spoke on valence shells and atoms merging, at one point joking that the process was like falling in love. "Chemicals bond in order to satisfy specific needs. Atoms with fewer than eight valence electrons look to fill their void by establishing a practical partnership. Chlorine for example, with seven valence electrons, seems a perfect fit for Sodium which has but one, and yet if Sodium took on Chlorine's seven electrons, the resulting electrical charge would be -7, too unstable given Sodium's number of protons." For the bond to work certain adjustments were required. Sodium first had to empty its third electron shell, surrender its one valence electron and become a +1 ion before bonding with Chlorine. So much calculation and modification, yet ultimately M.E. knew the pairing worked.

Eager to offer more than minor mewling as proof of his jealous reflex, certain what Mimi needed, M.E. focused on the task at hand, set out his strategy and did not complain—despite other immediate desires—when Mimi came to bed that night dressed in armor.

Roy Fiske had short blond hair, cut close and standing on end like the hooked spikes of rodent fur. Early the next morning, Mimi packed while M.E. fixed breakfast. Roy pulled up in a red La Sabre, honked the horn and popped the trunk by pressing a button on the dash. M.E. came down the steps while Mimi tossed her overnight bag inside the trunk. Approaching the passenger door, M.E. put his arm on the roof and his hip against the paneling.

"What are you doing?" Mimi tried getting by.

M.E. grinned, found her protest almost believable. (What a pistol! What a card!) "I don't want you to go," he nearly winked. "I think, that is, I feel."

"You don't want what?"

"I'd rather take you myself."

"Why?"

"Because."

"Don't you trust me?"

"It's not that."

"Are you trying to suffocate me?"

"No, of course not."

"Then what?"

"It's just. Didn't you say?"

"I said? Jesus, M.E., where is all this coming from?"

Surprised, M.E. extended his free hand to touch Mimi's cheek, only she ducked underneath and came up feinting and weaving like a boxer. "Stop it, M.E.. I have to go."

"But Mimi."

"What?"

No longer certain she was bluffing, M.E. set his hand down firmer, still startled when Mimi squeezed his wrist and tugged at his arm. "You have to move. What are you doing?"

Roy finished his cigarette, flicked the butt into the street. He had a gravely voice, not so much deep but rough in the center, like a tenor delivering notes through sandpaper. "Are you coming or not girl?" he called to Mimi who continued tugging on M.E.'s arm. Put off, baffled and unsure, M.E. thought, "What a muddle. What a can of worms." He shook his head, the sound of Roy's voice on top of everything else triggering in him a chemical reaction. Exothermic. The way Sodium bonded with water, sending blue and white flames skyward. Activation energy. Aluminum and Bromine steaming together. M.E. slapped the roof hard and shouted for Roy to, "Just wait!"

Shocked, Mimi almost peed her pants. The dog tattoo on Roy's muscled arm did a four-legged samba and leaped several inches. "What the fuck!" Roy shot from the car as Mimi tried pushing M.E. back. Roy raced around the trunk. "Are you out of your fucking mind?"

M.E. replied by banging the roof twice more.

Mimi shouted for M.E. to, "Stop!"

M.E. took his hand from the roof, raised both arms and began shuffling in a stationary moonwalk, much as the giraffe at the zoo, the Giraffa Camelopardalis which, when confronted by a rival, marched in place with its neck stretched high. "Now what?" he wondered, still hoping Mimi would intervene and send Roy away. Instead she rolled her hips and sniffed the air. Roy went up on his toes, forcing M.E. to climb onto the hood of the car and then the roof in order to appear tallest.

"God damn it!" Roy lunged for M.E.'s ankle.

Mimi moved in a circle.

M.E.'s chest pounded as if filled with all twenty-four pounds of the giraffe's heart. The preventor valves failing, the blood flowing back, his head went light, the chemicals in his brain—the endorphins and opioids—doing their best to block the pain. M.E. stared at Mimi, tried quickly to assess his situation, the sudden awkwardness of it all. He thought in terms of resonant pendula and questioned if, at any point, two bodies paired together were ever in equal motion, where the one transferring and the one stealing energy became perfectly aligned.

Mimi turned and showed M.E. her tail.

Roy howled and grabbed again for M.E.'s leg. "You're fucking crazy! Get the hell off my car!"

M.E. danced in order to avoid Roy's grasp. In the cadence of schoolgirls reciting rhymes as they skipped rope, he presented a list of the inert elements. "Neon and Radon, Argon and Krypton, Helium and Xenon," he sang out, each atom incapable of bonding, their shells neutral and complete. M.E. asked Mimi, "Do you understand?"

He thought more about chemical reactions, how all false wishes aside, the end result was invariable. When Magnesium mixed with Hydrochloric Acid there was always fire, and when Urea and Ammonium Chloride bonded there was always ice. What kept people mixing and matching as mad scientists was the off chance of something remarkable occurring, the way lethal Chlorine gas reacted with Sodium to form Sodium Chloride, harmless table salt, and who would have guessed?

Roy sprinted around to the driver's side and yelled at Mimi to, "Get in the car!" When he hit the gas the old La Sabre flew forward, sending M.E. off the rear, suspending him briefly in midair like a diver at the top of a perfect pike. A half second later, M.E. crashed in a tumble, flipped and landed hard on his back. The force drove the air from his lungs and left him gasping. He lay by the curb, stunned and listening to the car roar off.

The sun passed in and out from behind a cirrus cloud shaped as a silver-white trout. M.E. groaned. His ribs ached and his tailbone burned. He checked his arms and legs, tested his faculties, relieved to have not hit his head. "Barium Hydroxide and Ammonium Chloride," he felt the chill, groaned again and thought next of Vasopressin, the chemical in the blood which promoted two animals mating exclusively for life. Less than 3 percent of all animals had Vasopressin, the prairie vole yes, but neither giraffes nor humans; the majority of creatures still fundamentally feral when it came to ways of the heart.

Mimi stood where the car had been, staring down at M.E., smiling as she heard him go, "Ooff," and "Aarrgh," while attempting to sit up. "Look at you," she said. "Alright, alright. I'm ready. So tell me."

M.E. gazed up the street, squinting and unsteady. His body ached, the pavement beneath him somehow harder than he expected. "Too hard," he decided, and recalled the afternoon Mimi and he spent at the zoo, how they watched the male giraffe rub his head against the female's rump, licking her tail, nudging and gently bumping, resting his neck on her back, how each time he did this, he thought he was in love.

Steven Gillis likes to kill flies with a machete. He is the author of the novels *The Weight of Nothing* and *Walter Falls*, both finalists for IPPY and ForeWord Magazine National Book of the Year. Currently at work on a new novel, *Temporary People*, Steve's stories, articles, and book reviews have appeared in over two dozen journals. A collection of stories, *Giraffes*, will be published this fall by Atomic Quill Press. He teaches writing at Eastern Michigan University and is the founder of 826michigan. He lives in a glass house and likes to throw stones.

THE CUSTOMER

KEITH TAYLOR

SHE'D BEEN A customer at the shop for a few years, not a major one, but a regular who bought a book or two a month. Mostly the $2.98 or $3.98 remainders we kept on the tables outside. Inside, she bought novels, mainline middle–of–the–road fiction, the kind that gets to the bottom of the paperback bestseller list and stays there for a couple of weeks. She always paid in cash, so I never learned her name from checks or credit cards. I was polite when I waited on her. I'm always polite.

She had spectacular hair, black and thick and shiny. It was the kind that couldn't be cut into a fashionable style, unless she cut it very short. She kept it clean and brushed and often let it fall wherever it fell. Sometimes she'd pull it back in a loose ponytail, with strands coming free and blowing around the edges of her face. I figure she might have been Greek or Italian, something Mediterranean.

Early last fall, I started walking home instead of taking the bus. I walk most of the year. But in summer I sweat too much. I like walking in the fall, watching leaves change, then drop. I still enjoy kicking the leaves that collect in gutters or on the edges of sidewalks. In the fall I'll often walk several blocks out of my way, just for exercise.

That first time, after I'd punched out, I saw her a block ahead, walking north. I started in the same direction. She walked four or five blocks, then turned left down one of the small side streets lined with old Victorian houses subdivided into over-priced apartments. By the time I turned after her, she was gone.

The next day I walked the same way but didn't see her. The third day, just as I was going down the small street, I saw her coming out of the fourth house on the left. She locked the door. When she passed me on the sidewalk, we exchanged a hesitant nod.

I didn't walk that way again for over a week.

As the weather grew colder and the first snows began, I started walking down her street regularly. Not every day, but at least two or three times a week. Usually I didn't see her. Once, though, I was right behind her, a hundred yards or so. I figured that if she noticed me, she would assume I was on my regular route. But it was cold. She wore a heavy coat, the fur lined collar pulled up around her ears. Her hair looked wild and wind blown, some of it under her coat, some flying out above her collar. She turned quickly into her house. Just as I was passing in front, I saw the upstairs light come on. She was in the room, and I could see her clearly. She took her coat off and threw it on a chair. She shook her hair out and brushed her hand back through it. I stopped and looked up. Just for a second.

As the days grew shorter, it was dark, almost night, when I walked home. I continued passing her house a couple of times a week. Her light was usually on, and the shades were drawn. Sometimes I found myself on the sidewalk looking up at her window. But I tried not to, tried to keep walking. Casual.

The heavy snows started a few days before Christmas. Most of the students who lived in that neighborhood had already left for vacation. She had been walking home again, a block or two in front of me. Snow twisted around the street lamps and drifted on the sidewalk. When I passed in front of her house, I looked up. The window was still dark. I stopped. The light came on, suddenly illuminating a new swirl of snow. I caught a glimpse of her. She glanced toward the window, and she looked frightened. Then she quickly reached over and turned out the light. I sensed that she moved closer to the window and thought I heard her say something. Maybe she yelled.

I stood for a moment, then walked away quickly. It was still snowing. I never walked that way again.

Keith Taylor published two books this year. He is the coordinator of undergraduate creative writing in the English Department at the U of M and the director of the Bear River Writers Conference.

A RELATIVE STRANGER

CHARLES BAXTER

I WAS SEPARATED from my biological mother when I was four months old. Everything from that period goes through the wash of my memory and comes out clean, blank. The existing snapshots of my mother show this very young woman holding me, a baby, at arm's length, like a caught fish, outside in the blaring mid-day summer sunlight. She's got clothes up on the clothesline in the background, little cotton infant things. In one picture a spotted dog, a mongrel combination of labrador and dalmation, is asleep beside the bassinet. I'd like to know what the dog's name was, but time has swallowed that information. In another picture, a half-empty bottle of Grain Belt beer stands on the lawn near a wading pool. My mother must have figured that if she could have me, at the age of seventeen, she could also have the beer.

My mother's face in these pictures is having a tough time with daylight. It's a struggle for her to bask in so much glare. She squints and smiles, but the smile is all on one side, the right. The left side stays level, except at the edge, where it slips down. Because of the sunlight and the black-and-white film, my mother's face in other respects is bleached, without details, like a sketch for a face. She's a kid in these pictures and she has a kid's face, with hair pulled back with bobby pins and a slight puffiness in the cheeks, which I think must be bubble gum.

She doesn't look like she's ever been used to the outdoors, the poor kid. Sunlight doesn't become her. It's true she smiled, but then she did give me up. I was too much serious work, too much of a squalling load. Her girlish smile was unsteady and finally didn't include me. She gave me away—this is historical record—to my adoptive parents, Harold and Ethel Harris, who were older and more capable of parental love. She also gave them these photographs, the old kind, with soft saw-tooth borders, so I'd be sure to know how she had looked when the unfamiliar sunlight hit her in a certain way. I think her teenaged boyfriend, my father, took these pictures. Harold and Ethel Harris were my parents in every respect, in love and in their care for me, except for the fact of these pictures. The other children in the family, also adopted, looked at the snapshots of this backyard lady with curiosity but not much else.

My biological father was never a particle of interest to me compared to my adoptive father, Harold Harris, a man who lived a life of miraculous calm. A piano tuner and occasional jazz saxophonist, Harold liked to sit at home, humming and tapping his fingers in the midst of uproar and riot, kids shouting and plaster fall-ing. He could not be riled; he never made a fist. He was the parental hit of any childhood group, and could drive a car competently with children sitting on his shoulders and banging their hands on the side of his head. Genetic inheritance or not, he gave us all a feeling for pitch. Ask me for an F-sharp, I'll give you one. I get the talent from Harold.

I went to high school, messed around here and there, did some time in the Navy, and when I was discharged I married my sweetheart of three years, the object of my shipboard love letters, Lynda Claire Norton. We had an apartment. I was clerking at Meijer's Thrifty Acres. I thought we were doing okay. Each night I was sleeping naked next to a sexual angel. At sunrise she would wake me with tender physical comfort, with hair and fingertips. I was working to get a degree from night school. Fourteen months after we were married, right on the day it was due, the baby came. A boy, this was. Jonathan Harold Harris. Then everything went to hell.

I was crazy. Don't ask me to account for it. I have no background or inclination to explain the human mind. Besides, I'm not proud of the way I acted. Lynda moved right out, baby and all, the way any sensible woman would have, and she left me two empty rooms in the apartment in which I could puzzle myself out.

I had turned into the damnedest thing. I was a human monster movie. I'd never seen my daddy shouting the way I had; he had never carried on or made a spectacle of himself. Where had I picked up this terrible craziness that made me yell at a woman who had taken me again and again into her arms? I wrote long letters to the world while I worked at home on my model ships, a dull expression on my face. You will say that liquor was the troublemaker here and you would be correct, but only so far. I had another bad ingredient I was trying to track down. I broke dishes. My mind, day and night, was muzzy with bad intentions. I threw a light bulb against a wall and did not sweep up the glass for days. Food burned on the stove and then I ate it. I was committing outrageous offenses against the spirit. Never, though, did I smash one of the model ships. Give me credit for that.

I love oceans and the ships that move across them. I believe in man-made objects that take their chances on the earth's expanses of water. And so it happened that one weekday afternoon I was watching a rerun of *The Caine Mutiny*, with my workboard set up in front of me with the tiny pieces of my model *Cutty Sark* in separated piles, when the phone rang. For a moment I believed that my wife had had second thoughts about my behavior and was going to give me another chance. To tell the truth, whenever the phone rang, I thought it would be Lynda, announcing her terms for my parole.

"Hello? Is this Oliver Harris?" a man's voice asked.

"This is him," I said. "Who's this?"

"This is your brother." Just like that. Very matter-of-fact. This is your brother. Harold and Ethel Harris had had two other adopted sons, in addition to me, but I knew them. This voice was not them. I gripped the telephone.

Now—and I'm convinced of this—every adopted child fears and fantasizes getting a call like this announcing from out of the blue that someone in the world is a relative and has tracked you down. I know I am not alone in thinking that anyone in the world might be related to me. My biological mother and father were very busy, urgent lovers. Who knows how much procreation they were capable of, together and separately? And maybe they had brothers and sisters, too, as urgent in their own way as my mother and father had been in theirs, filling up the adoption agencies with their offspring. I could never go into a strange city without feeling that I had cousins in it.

Therefore I gripped the telephone, hoping for reason, for the everyday. "This is not my brother," I said.

"Oh yes, it is. Your mother was Alice Barton, right?"

"My mother was Ethel Harris," I said.

"Before that," the voice said, "your mother was Alice Barton. She was my mother, too. This is your brother, Kurt. I'm a couple of years younger than you." He waited. "I know this is a shock," he said.

"You can't find out about me," I said. The room wasn't spinning, but I had an idea that it might. My mouth was open halfway and I was taking short sweaty breaths through it. One shiver took its snaky way down and settled in the lumbar region. "The records are sealed. It's all private, completely secret."

"Not anymore, it isn't," he said. "Haven't you been keeping up? In this country you can find out anything. There are no secrets worth keeping anymore; nobody *wants* privacy, so there isn't any."

He was shoving this pile of ideas at me. My thoughts had left me in great flight, the whole sad flock of them. "Who are you?" I asked.

"Your brother Kurt," he said, repeating himself. "Listen, I won't bore you to explain what I had to do to find you. The fact is that it's possible. Easy, if you have money. You pay someone and someone pays someone and eventually you find out what you want to know. Big surprise, right?" He waited, and when I didn't agree with him, he started up again, this time with small talk. "So I hear that you're married and you have a kid yourself." He laughed. "And I'm an uncle."

"What? No. Now you're only partly right," I said, wanting very hard to correct this man who said he was my brother. "My wife left me. I'm living here alone now."

"Oh. I'm sorry about that." He offered his sympathies in a shallow, masculine way: the compassion offered by princes and salesmen. "But listen," he said, "you're not alone. It's happened before. Couples separate all the time. You'll get back. It's not the end of the world. Oliver?"

"What?"

"Would you be willing to get together and talk?"

"Talk? Talk about what?"

"Well, about being brothers. Or something else. You can talk about anything you please." He waited for me to respond, and I didn't. This was my only weapon—the terrible static of telephone silence. "Look," he said, "this is tough for me. *I'm not a bad person.* I've been sitting by this hone for an hour. I don't know if I'm doing the right thing. My wife . . . you'll meet her . . . she hasn't been exactly supportive. She thinks this is a mistake. She says I've gone too far this time. I dialed your number four times before I dialed it to the end. I make hundreds of business calls but this one I could not do. It may be hard for you, also: I mean, I take a little getting used to. I can get obsessive about little things. That's how I found you."

"By being obsessive."

"Yeah. Lucille . . . that's my wife . . . she says it's one of my faults. Well, I always wanted a brother, you know, blood-related and everything, but I couldn't have one until I found you. But then I thought you might not like me. It's possible. Are you following me?"

"Yes, I am." I was thinking: here I am in my apartment, recently vacated by my wife, talking to a man who says he's my brother. Isn't there a law against this? Someone help me.

"You don't have to like me," he said, his brusque voice starting to stumble over the consonants. That made me feel better. "But that isn't the point, is it?" Another question I didn't have to answer, so I made him wait. "I can imagine what's in your head. But let's meet. Just once. Let's try it. Not at a house. I only live about twenty miles away. I can meet you in Ann Arbor. We can meet in a bar. I *know* where you live. I drove by your building. I believe I've even seen your car."

"Have you seen me?" This brother had been cruising past my house, taking an interest. Do brothers do that? What do they do?

"Well, no, but who cares about looks where brothers are concerned? We'll see each other. Listen, there's this place a couple of miles from you, the Wooden Keg. Could we meet there? Tomorrow at three? Are you off tomorrow?"

"That's a real problem for me," I said. "Booze is my special poison."

"Hell, that's all right," he said. "I'll watch out for you. I'm your brother. Oh. There's one other thing. I lied. I look like you. That's how you'll recognize me. I have seen you."

I held on to the telephone a long time after I hung up. I turned my eyes to the television set. Jose Ferrer was getting drunk and belligerent at a cocktail party. I switched off the set.

I was in that bar one hour before I said I would be, and my feelings were very grim. I wasn't humming. I didn't want him to be stationed there when I came in. I didn't want to be the one who sauntered in through the door and walked the long distance to the bar stool. I didn't want some strange sibling checking out the way I close the distance or blink behind my glasses while my eyes adjust to the light. I don't like people watching me when they think they're going to get a skeleton key to my character. I'm not a door and I won't be opened that easily.

Going into a bar in the midsummer afternoon takes you out of the steel heat and air-hammer sun; it softens you up until you're all smoothed out. This was one of those wood-sidewall bars with air that hasn't recirculated for fifty years, with framed pictures of thoroughbreds and cars on the walls next to the chrome decorator hubcaps. A man's bar, smelling of cigarettes and hamburger grease and beer. The brown padded light comes down on you from some recessed source, and the leather cushions on those bar stools are as soft as a woman's hand, and before long the bar is one big bed, a bed on a barge eddying down a sluggish river where you've got nothing but good friends lined up on the banks. This is why I am an alcoholic. It wasn't easy drinking Coca-Cola in that place, that dim halfway house between the job and home, and I was about to slide off my wagon and order my first stiff one when the door cracked open behind me, letting in a trumpet blast of light, and I

saw, in the doorframe outline, my brother coming toward me. He was taking his
own time. He had on a hat. When the door closed and my eyes adjusted, I got a
better look at him, and I saw what he said I would see: I saw instantly that this was
my brother. The elves had stolen my shadow and given it to him. A version of my
face was fixed on a stranger. From the outdoors came this example of me, wearing
a coat and tie.

He took a bar stool next to mine and held out his hand. I held out mine and we
shook like old friends, which we were a long way from becoming. "Hey," we both
said. He had the eyes, the cheek, and the jaw in a combination I had seen only in
the mirror. "Oliver," he said, refusing to let my hand go. "Good to meet you."

"Kurt," I said. "Likewise." Brother or no brother, I wasn't giving away anything
too fast. This is America, after all.

"What're you drinking?" he asked.

"Coke."

"Oh. Right." He nodded. When he nodded, the hat nodded. After he saw me
looking at it, he said, "Keeps the sun out of my eyes." He took it off and tried
to put it on the bar, but there wasn't enough room for it next to the uncleared
beer glasses and the ashtrays, so he stood up and dropped it on a hook over by the
popcorn machine. There it was, the only hat. He said, "My eyes are sensitive to
light. What about yours?" I nodded. Then he laughed, hit the bar with the broad
flat of his hand, and said, "Isn't this great?" I wanted to say, yes, it's great, but the
true heart of the secret was that no, it was not. It was horrifyingly strange without
being eventful. You can't just get a brother off the street. But before I could stop
him from doing it, he leaned over and put his right arm, not a large arm but an arm
all the same, over my shoulders, and he dropped his head so that it came sliding in
toward my chest just under the chin. Here was a man dead set on intimacy. When
he straightened up, he said, "We're going to have ourselves a day today, that's for
sure." His stutter took some of the certainty out of the words. "You don't have to
work this afternoon, right?"

"No," I said, "I'm not scheduled."

"Great," he said. "Let me fill you in on myself."

Instead of giving me his past, he gave me a resume. He tried to explain his
origins. My biological mother, for all the vagueness in her face, had been a demon
for good times. She had been passionate and prophylactically carefree. Maybe she
had had twenty kids, like old Mother Hubbard. She gave us away like presents to
a world that wanted us. This one, this Kurt, she had kept for ten months before
he was adopted by some people called Sykes. My brother said that he understood
that we—he and I—had two other siblings in Laramie, Wyoming. There might be
more he didn't know about. I had a sudden image of Alice Barton as a human stork,
flying at tree level and dropping babies into the arms of waiting parents.

Did I relax as my brother's voice took me through his life? Were we related
under the skin, and all the way around the block? He talked; I talked. The Sykes
family had been bookish types, lawyers, both of them, and Kurt had gone to Michigan State University in East Lansing. He had had certain advantages. No falling

plaster or piano tuning. By learning the mysterious dynamics of an orderly life, he had been turned out as a salesman, and now he ran a plastics factory in Southfield, north of Detroit. "A small business," he said in a friendly, smug way. "Just fifteen employees." I heard about his comfortably huge home. I heard about his children, my nephews. From the wallet thick with money and credit cards came the lineup of photos of these beautiful children.

So what was he doing, this successful man, sitting on a barstool out here, next to his brother, me, the lowly checkout clerk?

"Does anybody have enough friends?" he asked me. "Does anyone have enough *brothers?*" He asked this calmly, but the questions, as questions, were desperate. "Here's what it was," he said. "Two or three times a week I felt like checking in with someone who wasn't a wife and wasn't just a friend. Brothers are a different category, right there in the middle. It's all about *relatedness*, you know what I mean?" I must have scowled. "We can't rush this," he said. "Let's go have dinner some-where. My treat. And then let's do something."

"Do what?" I asked.

"I've given that a lot of thought," he said. "What do you do the first time out with your brother? You can't just eat and drink. You can't shop; women do that." Then he looked me square in the eye, smiled, and said, "It's summer. Maybe we could go bowling or play some baseball." There was a wild look in his eye. He let out a quick laugh.

We went in his Pontiac Firebird to a German restaurant and loaded up on sau-erbraten. I had a vague sense he was lowering himself to my level but did not say so. He ordered a chest-sized decorated stein of beer but I stayed on the cola wagon. I tried to talk about my wife, but it wouldn't come out: all I could say was that I had a problem with myself as a family man. That wasn't me. The crying of babies tore me up. Feeding time gave me inexplicable jitters. I had acted like Godzilla. When I told him this, he nodded hard, like a yes man. It was all reasonable to him.

"Of course," he said. "Of course you were upset and confused." He was un-derstanding me the way I wanted to be understood. I talked some more. Blah blah blah. Outside, it was getting dark. The bill came, and he paid it: out came the thick wallet again, and from a major-league collection of credit cards came the white bank plastic he wanted. I talked more. He agreed with everything I said. He said, "You're exactly right." Then I said something else, and he responded, "Yes, you're exactly right."

That was when I knew I was being conned. In real life people don't say that to you unless they're trying to earn your love in a hurry. But here he was, Kurt Sykes, visibly my brother, telling me I was exactly right. It was hard to resist, but I was holding on, and trying.

"Here's how," he said. He lifted his big stein of beer into the air, and I lifted my glass of Coke. Click. A big blond waitress watched us, her face disciplined into a steel-helmet smile.

After that, it was his idea to go outside and play catch. This activity had all sorts of symbolic meanings for him, but what was I going to do? Go home and watch television? I myself have participated in a few softball leagues and the jock way of life is not alien to me, but I think he believed he could open up if we stayed at my level, throwing something back and forth, grunting and sweating. We drove across town to Buhr Park, where he unloaded his newly purchased baseball, his two brand-new gloves, and a shiny new bat. Baseball was on the agenda. We were going to play ball or die. "We don't have to do any hitting," he said. While I fitted the glove to my left hand—a perfect fit, as if he had measured me—he locked the car. I have never had a car worth locking; it was not a goal.

The sun having set, I jogged out across a field of darkening grass. The sky had that blue tablecloth color it gets at dusk just before the stars come out. I had my jeans, sweatshirt, and sneakers on, my usual day-off drag. I had not dressed up for this event. In fact, I was almost feeling comfortable, except for some growing emotional hot spot I couldn't locate that was making me feel like pushing the baseball into my brother's face. Kurt started to toss the ball toward me and then either noticed his inappropriate dress-for-success formality or felt uncomfortable. He went back to the car and changed into his sweat clothes in the half-dark. He could have been seen, but wasn't, except by me. (My brother could change his clothes out in the open, not even bothering to look around to see who would see. What did this mean?)

Now, dressed down, we started to hustle, keeping the rhythms up. He threw grounders, ineptly, his arm stiff and curious. I bent down, made the imaginary play, and pivoted. He picked up the bat and hit a few high flies toward me. Playing baseball with me was his way of claiming friendship. Fine. Stars came out. We moved across the field, closer to a floodlit tennis court, so we had a bit of light. I could see fireflies at the edge of where we were playing. On the court to my right, a high school couple was working their way through their second set. The girl let out little cries of frustration now and then. They were pleasurable to hear. Meanwhile, Kurt and I played catch in the near-dark, following the script that, I could see, he had written through one long sleepless night after another.

As we threw the ball back and forth, he talked. He continued on in his resume. He was married but had two girlfriends. His wife knew about them both. She did not panic because she expected imperfection in men. Also, he said, he usually voted Republican. He went to parent-teacher-organization meetings.

"I suppose you weren't expecting this," he said.

No, I thought, I was not expecting you. I glanced at the tennis court. Clouds of moths and bright bugs swarmed in insect parabolas around the high-voltage lights. The boy had a white Huron high school t-shirt on, and white shorts and tennis shoes, and a blue sweatband around his thick damp hair. The girl was dressed in an odd assortment of pink and pastel blue clothes. She was flying the colors and was the better player. He had the force, but she had the accuracy. Between his heat and her coolness, she piled up the points. I let myself watch her; I allowed myself that. I was having a harder and harder time keeping my eyes on my brother.

"You gonna play or look at them?" Kurt asked.

I glanced at him. I thought I'd ignore his question. "You got any hobbies?" I asked.

He seemed surprised. "Hobbies? No. Unless you count women and making money."

"How's your pitch?"

"You mean baseball?"

"No. Music. How's your sense of pitch?"

"Don't have one."

"I do," I said. "F-sharp." And I blew it at him.

He leaned back and grimaced. "How do you know that's F-sharp?"

"My daddy taught me," I said. "He taught me all the notes on the scale. You can live with them. You can become familiar with a note."

"I don't care for music," he said, ending that conversation. We were still both panting a bit from our exertions. The baseball idea was not quite working in the way he had planned. He seemed to be considering the possibility that he might not like me. "What the hell," he said. "Let's go back to that bar."

Why did I hit my brother in that bar? Gentlemen of the bottle, it is you I address now. You will understand when I tell you that when my brother and I entered the bar, cool and smoky and filled with midsummer ballplayers, uniformed men and women, and he thoughtlessly ordered me a Scotch, you will understand that I drank it. Drank it after I saw his wad of money, his credit cards, his wallet-rubbed pictures of the children, my little nephews. He said he would save me from my alcoholism but he did not. Gentlemen, in a state of raw blank irritation I drank down what God and nature have labeled "poison" and fixed with a secret skull and crossbones. He bought me this drink, knowing it was bad for me. My mind withdrew in a snap from my brain. The universe is vast, you cannot predict it. From the great resources of anger I pulled my fund, my honest share. But I do not remember exactly why I said something terrible, and hit my brother in the jaw with my fist. And then again, higher, a punch I had learned in the Navy.

He staggered back, and he looked at me.

His nose was bleeding and my knuckles hurt. I was sitting in the passenger side of his car. My soul ached. My soul was lying facedown. He was taking me back to my apartment, and I knew that my brother would not care to see me from now on. He would reassert his right to be a stranger. I had lost my wife, and now I had lost him, too.

We stumbled into my living room. I wobbled out to the kitchen and, booze-sick, filled a dish towel with ice cubes and brought it to him. My right hand felt swollen. We were going to have ugly bruises, but his were facial and would be worse. Holding the ice to his damaged face, he looked around. Above the ice his eyes flickered on with curiosity. "Ships," he said. Then he pointed at the work table against the wall. "What's all that?"

"It's my hobby," I said. The words came slow and wormlike out of my puzzled mouth.

He squinted above the ice. "Bottles? And glue?"

"I build ships in bottles." I sounded like a balloon emptying itself of air. I pointed at the decorator shelf on the west wall, where my three-masted clipper ship, the *Thermopylae*, was on display.

"How long have you done this?" he asked.

"So long I can't remember."

"How do you do it?"

He gave me a chance. Even a bad drunk is sometimes forced to seize his life and to speak. So I went over to the worktable. "You need these." I held up the surgical forceps. I could hardly move my fingers for the pain. Alcoholic darkness sat in a corner with its black bag waiting to cover me entirely. I went on talking. "And these. Surgical scissors." Dried specks of glue were stuck to the tips. "Some people cheat and saw off the bottom of the bottle, then glue it back on once the ship is inside. I don't do it that way. It has to grow inside the bottle. You need a challenge. I build the hull inside. I have used prefab hulls. Then you've got to lay the deck down. I like to do it with deck furnishings already in place: you know, the cabin doors and hatch covers and cleats and riding bits already in place on the deck. You put the glue on and then you put the deck in, all in one piece, folded up, through the neck; then you fold it out. With all that glue on, you only have one shot. Then you do the rigging inside the bottle. See these masts? The masts are laid down inside the bottle with the bottom of the mast in a hole."

I pointed to the *Cutty Sark*, which I was working on. I did not care if my hands were broken; I would continue this, the only lecture in my head, even if I sounded like a chattering magpie.

"You see, you pull the mast up inside the bottle with a string attached to the mast, and there's a stop in the hole that'll keep the mast from going too far forward. Then you tie the lines that are already on the mast off on the belaying pins and the bits and the cleats." I stopped. "These are the best things I do. I make ships in bottles better than anything else I do in my life."

"Yes." He had been standing over my worktable, but now he was lying on the sofa again.

"I like ships," I said. "When I was growing up, I had pictures on the wall of yachts. I was the only person in the Harris family who was interested in ships."

"Hmm."

"I like sailboats the most." I was talking to myself. "They're in their own class."

"That's interesting," he said. "That's all very interesting, but I wonder if I could lie down here for a while."

"I think you're already doing it."

"I don't need a pillow or a blanket," Kurt said, covered with sweat. "I can lie here just as is."

"I was going to turn on the air conditioner."

"Good. Put it on low."

I went over to the rattletrap machine and turned it on. The compressor started with a mechanical complaint, a sound like *orrr orrr orrr,* and then faster, *orrorrorr.* By the time I got back into the living room, my brother's eyes were closed.

"You're asleep," I said.

"No," he said, "no, I'm not. My eyes are just closed. I'm bruised and taking a rest here. That's all. Why don't you talk to me for a minute while I lie here with this ice. Say anything."

So I talked against the demons chittering in the corners of the room. I told my brother about being on a carrier in the Navy. I talked about how I watched the blue lifting swells of the Pacific even when I wasn't supposed to and would get my ass kicked for it. I was hypnotized by seawater, the crazy majesty of horizontal lines. I sleepwalked on that ship, I was so happy. I told him about the rolling progress of oceanic storms, and how the cumulonimbus clouds rose up for what looked like three or four miles into the atmosphere. Straight-edged curtains of rain followed us; near the Straits of Gibraltar it once rained for thirty minutes on the forward part of the ship, while the sun burned down on the aft.

I talked about the ship's work, the painting and repairing I did, and I told him about the constant metallic rumble vibrating below decks. I told him about the smell, which was thick with sterile grease stink that stayed in your nostrils, and the smell of working men. Men away from women, men who aren't getting any, go bad, and they start to smell like metal and fur and meat.

Then I told him about the ships I built, the models, and the originals for them, about the masts and sails, and how, in the water, they had been beautiful things.

"What if they fell?" my brother said.

I didn't understand the question, but thought I would try to answer it anyway. It was vague, but it showed he was still awake, still listening. I wanted to ask, fell from where? But I didn't. I said if a man stood on the mainmast lookout, on a whaler, for example, he could lose his balance. If he tumbled from that height, he might slap the water like he was hitting cement. He might be internally damaged, but if he did come up, they'd throw him a lifebuoy, the white ones made out of cork and braided with a square of rope.

I brought one of the ships toward him. "I've got one here," I said, "tiny, the size of your fingernail."

He looked at it, cleated to the ship above the deck. He studied it and then he gazed at me. "Yes," he said. It was the most painful smile I'd ever seen in an adult human being, and it reminded me of me. I thought of the ocean, which I hadn't viewed for years and might not, ever again. " Yes," my brother said from under the icepack. "Now I get it."

Like strangers sitting randomly together in a midnight peeling-gray downtown bus depot smelling of old leather shoes, we talked until four in the morning, and he left, his face bruised dark, carrying one of my ships, the *Lightning*, under his arm. He came back a week later. We sat in the park this time, not saying much. Then I went to see him, and I met his wife. She's a pleasant woman, a tall blond who comes fully outfitted with jewels I usually see under glass in display cases. My brother and I know each other better now; we've discovered that we have, in fact, no subjects in common. But it's love, so we have to go on talking, throwing this nonsense into the air, using up the clock. He has apologized for trying to play baseball with me; he admits now that it was a mistake.

When I was small, living with Harold and Ethel Harris and the other Harris children, I knew about my other parents, the aching lovers who had brought me into my life, but I did not miss them. They'd done me my favor and gone on to the rest of their lives. No, the only thing I missed was the world: the oceans, their huge distances, their creatures, the tides, the burning water-light I heard you could see at the equator. I kept a globe nearby my boy's bed. Even though I live here, now, no matter where I ever was, I was always homesick for the rest of the world. My brother does not understand that. He thinks home is where he is now. I show him maps; I tell him about Turkey and the Azores; I have told him about the great variety and beauty of human pigmentation. He listens but won't take me seriously.

When my brother talks now, he fingers his nose, probably to remind me where I hit him. It's a delicate gesture, with a touch of self-pity. With this gesture he establishes a bit of history between us. He wants to look up to me. He's twenty-eight years old, hasn't ever seen Asia, and he says this to me seriously. Have you ever heard the sound of a man's voice from a minaret? I ask him, but he just smiles. He's already called my wife; he has a whole series of happy endings planned, scene by scene. He wants to sit in a chair and see me come into the room, perfected, thanking the past for all it has done for me.

Charles Baxter is the author of *Saul and Patsy*, published in September 2003 by Pantheon. His previous novel, *The Feast of Love* (Pantheon/Vintage), was a finalist for the National Book Award in 2000 and will be made into a film by Robert Benton, starring Morgan Freeman. He has published two other novels and four books of stories, most recently *Believers*, published by Pantheon in hardback and Vintage in paperback. He has also published essays on fiction collected in *Burning Down the House* (Graywolf) and the forthcoming *Beyond Plot*. He now lives in Minneapolis and is currently the Edelstein-Keller Professor of Creative Writing at the University of Minnesota.

BY BIRTH

JON LIBERZON

Most nights, before you left
we slept at the old house near campus
where we joked about ghosts.

Sometimes, when I woke up first
in the small, dusty bed,
the blankets would make a great effort
to cover you, then they'd fail and retreat.
Other times, I'd wake up
and find you all made of cloth.

It was the same the ten weeks you didn't see blood
and had to keep checking the window
to make sure the moon hadn't fallen off
like a loose button—

Sometimes you shined like a sword
unsheathed, a cloudless peak
unsummitable and exposed.
Sometimes your heart was all cloth
and I folded you over and over in my hands.
You had always been leaving,
like late summer, or a very old dog.

You loved the intermittent pace of morning
and you were brave then—
ran around naked and laughed.
We spent a long time eating breakfast.
I looked around too much and saw no children, you folded
your hands over your belly and smiled.
I put my ear there and tried to hear the blood flowing.
Soon enough, it came apart and the fear
and you changed your mind.

Meanwhile the winter felt its first contractions.
My mother was as private as an orgasm
and my father, who divorced her, stared at his sons

as if thinking: "Maybe I can do that again," and was gone
on long vacations. None of this is any of my business.

Later on you bled and we settled back into place
like untethered skiffs that were lifted by the tide
and came down again not far from where they'd lain
Panicked, I had swallowed many large stones, and you
begged for them, your hands upturned.

Today you are across the sea, waiting
and I am once again a house wondering
if it is possible to be haunted

Jon Liberzon graduated from the University of Michigan Residential College in 2006. When he isn't writing, Jon spends his time working in the out
of doors or conducting research in the environmental sciences. His poem "by
birth" was included in a manuscript that was awarded the 2006 Undergraduate
Hopwood Award for Poetry at the University of Michigan and the 2006 Paul
and Sonya Handleman Award. Jon resides in Ann Arbor.

BRANDI'S BABY
KATHE KOJA

YOU NEED TO *take these*, the doctor said, his warm hand closing over her cold one, gently trapping the pills inside. Rainbow Clinic doctor, rainbow decals on the walls; the pills were shiny blue. *One right now and then one at night, okay?*

Okay.

And then come back in the morning and get two more. Okay?

Okay, she said, obedient and soft, like a sleepwalker, sleep-talker, hypnotist's subject, blinking her long-lidded eyes. She wore two grimy sweaters, a grey and a gold; jeans from the kids' department, a Winnie-the-Pooh appliqué. Dirt under her nails. In the corner sat an infant stroller, cheap umbrella stroller in a faded birds-and-bears print, and in it like a parody of a child a rubber baby doll, lurid pink in a pink dress.

Can I have another one? she said.

You only need two, he said. *One in the morning and one at—*

No, shaking her head, long hair, a matted cornsilk blonde. *For my baby.*

The doctor thought a minute, then reached behind to the counter, to a parti-colored jar and *Here,* he said, handing Brandi two paper-wrapped candies, one purple, one red. *Give her these.*

Outside the air tasted of bus fumes. A murmuring wind came down between the stores and the buildings—empty, boarded, or named NAILS'N'MORE, PACKAGE LIQUOR LOTTO—and fluttered the doll's dress. She bent and tucked the hem solicitously close to its feet, one of them scarred with ink, deep marking-pen lines as black as a prison tattoo.

There there, she said. *Let's go.*

Some days the baby's name was Caitlin, sometimes it was Marie; sometimes it was Eugenia, her own grandma's name. Sometimes the baby was bad, wailing and fussing, trying to play with nasty stuff she found on the street—broken glass, garbage, old torn-up paper bags. But mostly she was good, happy in her stroller, pleased to be pushed from one end of the block to the other: in sunshine, in the misty rain, in the dry or muggy winds and breezes that rose and sank, the city's invisible tides. Only hard rain, or cold, could start her crying, a frail rubber cry like a squeaking toy's: and then Brandi would hold the baby, hold her tight beneath her sweaters and *There there,* she would say, more sound than words; deeply content in the comfort, in the gift of a mother's warmth. *Don't cry. There there.*

From one end of the block to the other, that was how it was. Just like when she was little: *Don't leave the block, Brandi!* from her grandma watching through the screen door, watching out for her. Cheese sandwiches, chocolate milk. Cartoons on TV. Grandma making sure she got on the bus every morning, the "short bus" kids called it, sometimes the kids made fun of her but *You leave my Brandi alone*, Grandma would say, shooing them off and *There there*, she would say to Brandi, held warm against her broad soft breast. *Don't you listen to those bad boys.*

She and Grandma lived together in the house, for a long time, a timeless time. But then Grandma got sick, Grandma coughed and coughed and went at last to the doctor and then there was only Brandi, alone in the house, trying to figure out how to work the stove, trying to remember which days were school days—until someone from The County came, a lady in a dark red dress and *Your grandmother's gone*, the lady told Brandi, hands on her shoulders; thin hands, a hard gold ring. *Do you understand me, hon?*

She went to the doctor. Is she better yet?

Come with me, hon, the red-dress lady said.

It took awhile, but finally Brandi understood that when the red-dress lady, when the lady from school said "gone" they meant "dead," like when Tweety had died, Grandma's old cockatoo, dead in his cage and buried in a spaghetti sauce jar since they couldn't find a shoebox, oh they had cried . . . but if Grandma was dead like Tweety, dead and buried in a jar then what would happen to Brandi? Hiding under the blanket they gave her, too frightened to talk to the red-dress lady, too frightened even to cry, she hid until they found her and took her someplace else: to a house with another lady and two big girls, *Oh great now we gotta share the room with a retard* but she didn't stay there very long; she never stayed anywhere long, one foster home to another to another—kids she didn't know, beds she never slept in—until she was big enough to just climb out the window and go: across the weedy back yard, out into the dark. She had never been afraid of the dark.

How long, from there to here?—from climbing out the window to the Rainbow Clinic?—a long time, but not so long when you counted day by day, night by night, soup kitchen coffee and a St. Vincent's coat, from one end of the block to the other, trying to keep warm, to stay clear of the drug boys, the bad boys who called her names (*fuckin' space case, Out-to-Lunch*) then tried to touch her, back and forth in loneliness so great she cried sometimes without knowing it, felt tears thin and cold on her own cheeks as if waking into a dream. A long time; no time at all.

Finding the baby—her baby—had made all the difference to her, all the difference in the world. Flung to the curb as if dead—for a moment Brandi thought she *was* dead, this silent naked ink-marked infant, people did things like that all the time . . . but when she picked up the baby it cried, cried out, squeaking and forlorn and *Baby*, she said, with a certain wonder, feeling it pink and chill inside her arms. *What are you doing there? What's your name?*

At once the baby stopped crying; in a moment it was asleep. She watched it for a moment, not thinking so much as held by thought; then with a brief triumphant sigh tucked its body beneath her coat and walked on, careful to keep her steps even, and not jog the baby—her baby—awake.

A baby needs clothes, of course, and toys; these things she gathered as best she could, some from St. Vincent's or Open Arms or the Mothers' Shoppe at the downtown Baptist church; some she found, like the stroller, slewed flat at the curb by LIQUOR LOTTO, one of its wheels was mildly warped but the wobble was almost jaunty and anyway the baby loved the stroller, loved to ride as much as Brandi loved to walk her: up and down, up and down, no wanderer now but a mother, busy caring for her baby in the teeth of the careless world.

With the baby she was happy, a calm happiness she had not felt since her time in Grandma's house; but with happiness came a new fear, the fear of loss, of Caitlin-Marie-Eugenia somehow snatched from her saving arms. The fear made her wary, the wariness kept her safe, kept them both safe on nights when there was no safety anywhere, not in the streetlight shadows of the buildings, or the close and noisy confines of the women's shelter, where Brandi woke in the heart of one miserable night, woke from a dream of crying to find a woman close beside her cot—on all fours, teeth gleaming—*Hey baby doll* the woman said and Brandi erupted, one arm hooked hard around the little body, the other raised and striking, slapping, driving off the other woman in a fury of fear so great that though the woman was easily twice her size there was no question of resistance, so great that when it was over she felt emptied, as if a huge wind, a tornado had rushed through her, and blown everything away . . . everything but that body still jammed tight beneath her arm and *Don't cry,* she said, though the baby was not crying at all. *There there. Don't cry.*

Nothing bad had happened since then, in fact nothing had happened but what happened every day: rise and stand in line for coffee, change the baby's dress (pink or yellow, she had two), then start walking the block until it was time to find something to eat, or a place to get out of the rain, or somewhere to sleep until it was time to get up again. Everything was as it always was, each day a wheel to the next, like interlocking gears, thin sunshine or heavy rain, the pink dress or the yellow; until Brandi started to cough.

The rubber van, that was what the hookers called it, a pale green van that drove around handing out condoms and bottled juice and sandwiches. WOMAN-TO-WOMAN stenciled big on the side, beneath a drawing of two ladies standing arm-in-arm; like Brandi and Grandma, Brandi and her baby grown up. Brandi never took the condoms, but she did like the cheese sandwiches, and the sweet fruit drinks; she liked talking with the WOMAN-TO-WOMAN ladies, especially the youngest one, who had lush black braids and barrettes shaped like butterflies, as if a bright flock had landed in her hair. She gave one to Brandi, a pink one to match the baby's dress, and then *You gotta wicked cough,* she said. *You better do something about that.*

A wicked cough: like Grandma had? and *No,* Brandi said, eyes wide: thinking of her baby, what would Caitlin-Marie-Eugenia do without her? Go with the red-dress lady, go where no one would watch her, feed her, listen for her tiny cry? and *No,* she said again, voice trembling. *I'm not sick, I'm fine.*

The young woman squinted in a shaft of sun, an autumn light, bright but without true heat; she raised her hand to adjust the butterfly barrette but Brandi flinched away and *Listen,* the young woman said; her voice sounded sad, like the sunlight was somehow sad, trying its best but unable to give full warmth. *A cough like that, it can turn into pneumonia. Especially now it's gettin' cold. You know about the Rainbow Clinic?*

She did not know, she did not want to know: go to the doctor and never come back. . . . In her arms the baby seemed restless, emitting once or twice a nervous squeak as Brandi turned away from the van, and hurried, coughing, down the street, the block, up and down in a rhythm as restless as the baby's until the night she woke herself coughing, a wet chugging sound like an engine just about to break down, a sound that frightened her even more than a visit to the doctor. People died on the street; she knew that; she had seen them. Maybe Caitlin-Marie-Eugenia's first mother had died that way too.

But in the end it was all right: the doctor, the blue pills, the baby had liked the candies and Brandi even came back the next morning, still coughing hard but *Better,* she told the doctor when he asked. *I feel better now.*

Good, he said. He listened to her breathing with the stethoscope; he sighed a little. *We're going to need an x-ray, okay, a picture of your lungs. . . . Come on in here,* leading her from the small bright exam room, pausing in the doorway as she maneuvered the stroller but *Leave your d—your baby here, okay? We'll be back in just a second.*

No.

It has to be just you in the x-ray, the doctor said but Brandi refused and kept refusing, hand on the stroller, shaking her head again and again, her cough growing loud as a second voice until *Wait a minute,* the doctor said, and *Janice!* sharp, until a kind of nurse appeared, fuzzy red hair, impatient put-upon frown and *Janice will watch the baby,* the doctor said, *Okay? Now come on, it'll just take one minute to—*

But my baby, I can't—

I'll watch it, said red-haired Janice, was she a nurse? or some other kind of worker, she didn't look like a nurse. Still frowning, she tugged the stroller aside, half-way between one door and the next and truthfully Caitlin-Marie-Eugenia was not at all unhappy to go, she never cried, she never stirred so *Okay,* said Brandi in an agony of indecision, watching the stroller recede, *just for one minute* but it didn't take just one minute, first there was some other nurse to set things up, to ask the doctor questions and then Brandi had to take off her sweaters and *stand still, stand still again, turn around please* and all the time like humming black bees the worry for her baby swarmed behind her eyes, making her palms wet, making her cough but *Hold still,* the x-ray nurse said. *We have to do that one again.*

Finally—sweaters yanked on, the butterfly clip tangled in her hair—she hurried back into the hall, looking for the stroller, found not Janice the redhead but a different woman, a tall black lady writing something on a clipboard and *My baby,* Brandi cried. *Where's my baby?*

I don't know. Is that yours? gesturing with the pen, the stroller pushed haphazard by the door and—did she know already? from the black bees' buzz?—the stroller was empty, its sagging lap belt lolling like a soiled tongue.

Her baby was gone, her baby was *gone*

like Grandma in reverse, like Tweety and the house and everything ever clung to or loved, everything cherished all *gone* and in its place, her place, the heart's place nothing as she stood in the hall of that huge nothing tiny as a mote, a speck, a dwindle shrinking down to less than nothing and she could have screamed but no sound came out, just the wet ghost of a cough, death's rattle rehearsal to match the look on her face

my fault I left like Grandma oh oh oh Caitlin-Marie-Eugenia I'm sorry I'm sorry

as around the corner came Janice the not-nurse, a blue towel bundled in her hands and *Listen,* she said to Brandi, then stopped when she saw her, stopped the way a car brakes for a wreck on the road and *Hey,* she said, and opened the towel, blue and moist pink at its heart like some tropical flower and *I washed it,* Janice said. *It was pretty dirty. No offense.*

And inside the towel, like the miracle that never happens, was her baby: naked and bright as a boiled shrimp, the pen marks on her feet almost gone, scrubbed clean away and *Here,* said Janice, handing her the yellow dress that now looked very soiled. *Maybe you want to wash this too.*

You okay? said the doctor; he had come into the hall, they were all watching Brandi, he and Janice and the lady with the clipboard, even the x-ray nurse had stuck her head into the hall and *I'm fine,* Brandi said, tried to say but no sound came out, *I'm very fine.* In rapture she pressed her baby to her, right against her heart, emptied heart now full to surfiet: and Caitlin-Marie-Eugenia gave a squeak, a funny musical wheeze but no one laughed and *Tomorrow morning,* the doctor said. *Come back for more pills, okay?*

Okay, said Brandi, still radiant with relief. *Okay, sure.*

When she had left the hall, the clinic, the woman with the clipboard turned to the doctor and *How old is she?* the woman asked.

I don't know, the doctor said. *Sixteenish, maybe. . . . You know,* on a sigh, *it could be a real baby she was toting around.*

It is a real baby, said Janice the not-nurse.

In the street the wind had changed again, the dark fretful ripple that means rain so *We better hurry,* Brandi said. If they hurried they could get to the library, and maybe look at picture books until the sun came out again. . . . One last glance at the sky, one more for Caitlin-Marie-Eugenia and they were off down the block again, Brandi tugging the empty stroller behind, unwilling for even a moment to lose the weight of love in her arms.

Kathe Koja's books for young people include *Straydog, Buddha Boy, The Blue Mirror, Talk,* and the newest, *Going Under.* She counts Harriet the Spy, Zooey Glass, and Flannery O'Connor among her influences. She lives in the Detroit area with her husband, artist Rick Lieder, and their three companion cats. Her son attends the College for Creative Studies (Class of '07).

HANGERED

CLAIRE FORSTER

the full moon knocks at my door
every twenty-eight days to mock me
she hangs her lunar womb
in dark skies
ripe
she lights my uterus on fire
cackles at how I am swept by her flames
month after month.

your ghost marks the scars
like prisoners' tallies
counting the days
you have crawled through me

I would have swallowed my arms to cradle you

Fifty-six of my seventy-two years I've starved
there are only shards of moon in my stomach
there are no sympathy cards
for girls with blank ring-fingers
and runaway lovers

we didn't say the word abortion in 1949
so I let you go on a Tuesday morning
opened wide for his metal tools
to rust inside me
the coat hanger turned me to sand
his hands were unblemished
and jabbed me like he was stoking a fire
he told me not to scream
like he was a museum guard shushing noisy children
he put it so far in me I felt it in my ears
like butcher knives on a chalkboard
he sewed a devil into me
while the ribbons in my hair loosened

I saw your empty body

unzipped
dangling from the wire
As my eyes rolled in my head like marbles
I felt you pound on my vocal chords
but he was hanging us

I
a silent, threadbare coat
strewn on a motel bed

he painted my dress the most incredible crimson
if only blood didn't dry brown
and crack like a wasteland

I wanted to mummify myself with your umbilical chord
and hang by the final thread
in your no-name

you bring me wire-bound nightmares
of your soft fingernails slashing my womb
your blank face presses behind my taut skin
you tessellate
a million soldiers
with coat hanger hooks for hands

I've reached years
past the clouds for you
but all I've got is moon dust the scent of rotten baby powder
pressed in my creases

my thighs have ten crescent indentations
where my fingernails cut you from my daydreams
you have stamped your footprints into my caves
drawn your outline on my walls like primitive paintings

men who have loved me
wonder why I am silent
when they are in me
I tell them
there is nothing sacred
in love with a barren woman

you are the bloodied sweater in the back of my closet
its rusted hanger slits my womb

these scars have a pulse
like your heart is still in me
in the moon
lighting my deserts on fire
etching another tally.

Claire Forster (a.k.a. inky billows) is a thinker before anything else and writes poems because otherwise she'd lack most proper human social and behavioral functions. She was a member of the 2004 Ann Arbor Youth Poetry Slam Team and was the 2005 Ann Arbor Youth Poetry Slam Champion. In her second year in the Residential College at the University of Michigan, she hopes to craft her own concentration entitled "Creative Language" combining the forces of foreign language and creative writing to philosophize upon expression and understanding. Being a member of Ann Arbor Wordworks performance poetry group keeps her in the deuce for the time being but she will heed the call of NYC for graduate school.

CARE
JULIE ORRINGER

HOW TO CROSS the street with a six year old: take her hand, look both ways, wait until it's safe. Then stay within the crosswalk as you cross. Tessa does all these things as she guides Olivia across the street toward the cable car stop. There's a right way to take care of a child, she knows, and a wrong way. Many wrong ways. What you do not do: take the drugs that are in your pocket, the Devvies and Sallies in their silver pillbox. She can make it through the day without them. Even bringing them was wrong—another wrong thing. But it makes her feel better to have them close by.

The heel of Tessa's left shoe is coming loose, so she's been walking on the ball of her foot ever since she left her apartment. She has a blister already. At the stop she sits on a bench and examines the broken shoe. The tips of tiny nails glint in the space between heel and sole. Olivia sits next to her, zipping and unzipping her lavender jacket.

"What's wrong with your shoe?" Olivia asks.

"Nothing," Tessa says, straightening the heel. She stuffs her hands into the pockets of her leather jacket—Kenji's jacket, actually, heavy and familiar and smelling of his cigarettes—and feels for the pillbox. There it is in the right-hand pocket, round and familiar, a relief.

"Can I get a souvenir?" Olivia says, eyeing a shop across the street.

"Maybe later. We have to wait for the cable car."

"Can we just look for a second?"

Tessa glances down the street in the direction of the car turnaround. A cable car is just beginning to make the climb up the hill. "We have to stay here."

"I want a t-shirt and a light-up snow dome," Olivia says.

"You'll get what I give you," Tessa says, and Olivia goes silent. She slides down the bench, as far away from Tessa as possible.

Tessa tries to concentrate on the distant clang of the bell. She wills the cable car to hurry up. All her joints feel dry and sore, her mind whitely empty. She bites the inside of her cheek just for the distraction.

The cable car glides uphill through the intersection of Post and Powell and comes to rest at their stop. It's packed with tall boys in green-and-white sweatshirts that read *Bonn Jungenchor*. The boys are belting out a peasant tune in three-part harmony. Tessa and Olivia squeeze onto the side-rail and grab the brass pole as the cable car begins to move. All around them the boys sing the lilting chorus with its repeating nonsense line, *o-di-lon tee-lee, o-di-ion tee-lee*. Tessa's head begins to pound. She wonders if Olivia is too young to be standing on the side-rail of a cable car, hanging onto a pole as they ascend Nob Hill. Maybe they should be inside the car, not standing here, where Olivia could fall onto the tracks or be jostled to the pavement. The bell of the cable car is like a pickax inside Tessa's head. "Clay Street, Clay," the driver calls, yanking the wooden brake. For a long moment, a metallic screech drowns out the German boys' song.

They roll through Chinatown, with its dead-eyed fish on ice and its mysterious herb stores, its smells of frying meat and fruity garbage and wet boxes. Farther along, the German boys stop singing. Olivia knocks and knocks her toe against the brass pole. Tessa wants to make her stop, but she can't move. There's a hot fast clawing inside her chest. She takes one hand off the pole and feels for the silver pillbox. With her thumb she flicks the lid open. She can feel the difference between a Devvie and a Sallie, the Devvie like a chalky little submarine, the Sallie hexagonal and coated. She works a Devvie out with her index finger. It calms her just to hold it. Clenching it in her hand, she wraps her arm around the pole and braces herself for the next hill.

Her shoes keep slipping on the smooth side-rail, and the narrow skirt makes it hard to get her balance. God, if only her mind had been working that morning, she would have worn something different, more casual. Her plan had been to dress as if she'd otherwise be spending the day at a job. When she got to the hotel, though, Gayle was busy zipping Olivia into her jacket and folding her socks down and putting her hair up into a ponytail. She'd hardly glanced at Tessa's clothes. It was a good thing, too, because Tessa hadn't gotten it right. She couldn't find any stockings or a convincing jacket. And if she *had* a job, and this were really her day off, wouldn't she just be wearing jeans and a t-shirt? But Gayle had her mind on the lecture she was going to deliver that afternoon, something about *Mrs. Dalloway*, and Tessa left before she could notice much of anything.

The German youths move on to another song, this one in English. Tessa doesn't recognize it, but it has the predictable swelling cadences of a show tune. One of the teenagers beside her belts out the baritone. Olivia stares at the rows of pink and yellow houses, at the blue expanse of bay opening before them. They can see an antique sailing vessel docked near Ghiradelli Square, and the white masts of fishing boats bobbing alongside a pier. The cable car is going downhill now, mashing Olivia against the brass pole and Tessa against Olivia.

"You're hurting me," Olivia says.

Tessa pushes herself away, feeling the Devvie like a smooth pebble in her fist. "We're almost there," she says. "We can get some ice cream, okay?"

Olivia rubs a hand under her nose. "I'm not allowed," she says. "It'll spoil my appetite."

"Not today it won't. Not while you're with me."

Olivia gives her a skeptical look.

"I'm your adult today," Tessa says. "I make the rules."

At last the cable car reaches its turnaround. Tessa and Olivia get off and walk toward Ghiradelli Square, leaving the German choir-boys behind. Each step sends a burning jolt through Tessa's foot. She'll never make it through the day in these shoes. There's a line at the ice cream shop entrance, of course, and they have to wait outside in the wind and the blinding sun. The other people in line are parents and children, shivering in their bright t-shirts and shorts. They're all strangely quiet. They edge against the brick wall of the ice cream shop, away from a man with dun-colored dreadlocks and milky eyes. Around his neck is a sign that reads, simply, "AIDS." He moves in Tessa's direction, shaking a coffee can. Tessa takes a crumpled dollar from her pocket. When the man reaches her, she drops it in his can. He grins and says, "Thank you, beautiful." Though she's never seen him before, something seems to pass between them, a kind of uneasy recognition. Tessa pulls Kenji's jacket tighter around herself as the man moves off down the line.

"He smelled like pee," Olivia says.

"You would too, if you were him," Tessa says. It gives her a strange satisfaction to see how much this disturbs her niece. Olivia takes another look at the man, then moves behind Tessa, out of sight.

It's another fifteen minutes before the host shows them to a booth. As soon as he leaves, Tessa slides her shoes off and tucks her throbbing feet under her thighs. Olivia seems nervous, glancing at the families in other booths, humming a tight little song to herself. Will no one quit singing? Tessa lowers her forehead onto her fist.

When the waiter comes and asks what she'll have, Olivia shakes her head and looks down at the table. Tessa orders a hot-fudge-and-Oreo sundae for her, and coffee for herself. As they wait, Tessa takes sugars from the little ceramic sugar-holder and rips them open one by one, lining them up on her napkin. She's not thinking about it, just getting into the rhythm of it, the feeling of paper in her hands, the sound of tearing. Olivia stares at her. Tessa looks down at the row of sugars, the little nest of torn-off strips of paper. This is not normal behavior. She puts a hand in her pocket and rolls the Devvie between her fingers, thinking how easy it would be to take this one white pill. Olivia would never even notice. It couldn't hurt anyone. In fact, she'd be worse off without it. And Olivia would be worse off. Olivia needs her to take this Devvie. Who knows what will happen otherwise?

The waitress brings the ice cream and the coffee, and Olivia seems relieved. She picks up the long spoon and lifts a delicate peak of whipped cream from the sundae. When she tastes it, she smiles and then scoops up a bite of ice cream and hot fudge. Quickly, with a feeling of inevitability, Tessa puts the Devvie on her tongue and washes it down with coffee. She takes a long breath and leans back in her chair. In a few minutes she'll begin to feel it. She glances at her wrist where she once wore a watch. She remembers the watch, an oversized Swiss Army chronometer, and wonders how it got away from her.

Across the table Olivia eats her ice cream with deliberation, spooning hot fudge and whipped cream with each bite. Tessa watches her, waiting for the first quickening of the drug, that flutter at the center of her chest. Soon she will be able to handle anything, including taking care of her niece, her sister's child. She squints at Olivia, trying to imagine her as a six-year-old Gayle. But Gayle was a thin, sly-eyed girl, her mouth full and pink, her hands agile. This girl is sturdy and round-faced. Pure Henry.

Oh, her brother-in-law is valiantly good, doesn't smoke or drink; he is devoted to the study of imaginary numbers and to the building of handy gadgets. In his house, each family member's preferred bathwater temperature is programmed into a special faucet, and the toaster-oven responds to voice commands. "Black," Tessa said, last time she visited, and the toaster complied. Henry's responsible and compassionate, a good father. Right now he's back home taking care of Ethan, the younger child, who has chicken pox. He's the kind of husband who can be trusted to take care of a sick child. Tessa can almost stand him, though for a long time she wanted to kill kim. Gayle had met him in college. For years Tessa felt like he was the one who'd taken Gayle away, made Gayle forget that she and Tessa were supposed to go to Barcelona when they finished school, get a tiny apartment there, teach English, go out with dark-eyed men, give the world of careers and babies and husbands a grand and permanent *adios*.

Of course, if it hadn't been Henry, it would have been someone else. Or something else. Tessa understands that now. Gayle started talking about graduate school when Tessa was still a freshman. She applied and got in right out of college. Stupidly, Tessa kept talking about Barcelona as if they might still go, as if Gayle might ditch her boyfriend and her PhD in favor of a wild life in Catalonia. When Tessa was a senior herself, she asked Gayle what she was supposed to do next. She'd majored in computer programming, but she couldn't imagine getting a normal job, working in an office. Gayle suggested Tessa go to Barcelona and teach English, just like they'd talked about. But that wasn't what they'd talked about, and Gayle knew it. Instead, Tessa dropped out of school and moved to San Francisco. And just look at her now.

Tessa can feel the Devvie coming on, the flush in her face that means her veins are dilating, the flutter in her diaphragm as the drug gets down to business. She can't avert her eyes from Olivia, sated and pale, the empty ice cream bowl in front of her. They'll go look at the sea lions, they'll shop for souvenirs. She can do those things.

She pays the bill and wipes Olivia's face with a napkin, and then they're back out into the wind and sun. The light has become brighter and hotter and she's drinking it in like milk. Now she's the one who's singing, a hand-clapping song from when she and Gayle were little girls, *Miss Lucy had a steamboat, the steamboat had a bell*. It's a song where you say all the bad words but not really, *Miss Lucy went to heaven, the steamboat went to hell-o operator, please give me number nine* . . . She and Gayle used to sing it at the top of their lungs when their father wasn't home. She should teach it to Olivia. *Behind the frigerator there lay a piece of glass, Miss Lucy sat upon it and broke her little ass me no more questions, tell me no more lies* . . . but she can't remember what comes after that. And these shoes are killing her. Why is she still wearing them? She pauses to take them off, and the sidewalk is mercifully cold against her burning feet.

"You're barefoot," Olivia says. "You can't go barefoot."

"Why not?"

"You might step on glass. Or a bee. Or doody."

"I'm not going to step on doody," Tessa says. "Believe me."

"You could get an infection," Olivia says, pausing at the door of a crowded t-shirt shop. On a tall rotating stand beside the door, pink and turquoise and yellow novelty flip-flops hang on individual hooks. Tessa turns the stand, looking. Maybe Olivia is right. Maybe what she needs is a new pair of shoes.

"What do you think of these?" Tessa pulls off a pair of pink flip-flops with palm trees stenciled in black on the footbed. *California Dreamin'*, they say in looping script.

"You should get them," Olivia says. "And I could get a souvenir."

"I just got you ice cream," Tessa says.

"I'm going to look in here," Olivia says vaguely, and wanders inside toward a shelf of plush toys. Tessa glances at the price tag on the flip-flops. Twelve dollars, but maybe they're worth it. She goes to the register and waits in line, shifting from foot to foot, biting her nails. When she gets to the front of the line, she pays for the shoes with the twenty Kenji gave her that morning. There are still a couple of crumpled bills in her pocket. How much does she have left? Ten bucks? Fifteen? She doesn't even want to check. She still has to buy a present for Olivia and lunch for both of them and the cable car ride back, and her bank account is history, and her credit card won't accept new charges ever again. The rush in her chest becomes a pounding, the beginning of panic. Tessa takes her flip-flops and goes to get Olivia, who's struggling with another child at the rack of plush toys. The child is a blond boy, perhaps three inches taller. He pulls a toy otter away from Olivia and holds it against his chest.

"I want that bear," Olivia says.

"That's not a bear," Tessa says.

"I want him," Olivia says, her voice low and dangerous. The boy takes a step back, holding the otter. His hair is cut like a hockey player's, short and scruffy on top, long in back. A thin blond woman rushes toward him and grabs him by the wrist.

"Wayne Christopher," the woman says. "You put that thing back where you got it."

Baring his teeth at Olivia, the boy shoves the otter back onto its shelf, deep behind the other animals. His mother takes his wrist and pulls him out of the store, scolding. Olivia goes to the shelf and digs through the animals until she's found the otter, a glossy brown thing with deep, live-looking eyes. "I want him," she says, holding the toy against her chest.

There's no way Tessa can afford the otter. She's sure it must cost fifteen dollars, at least. But she doesn't feel like arguing about it. What she wants is to get outside and put on her new flip-flops. She glances around the store and takes Olivia's hand. Nothing is going to make her drop the otter. Tessa leads her toward the door, through a group of women in sun visors, past the racks of magnets and postcards, then out onto the sidewalk.

Olivia glances back over her shoulder toward the store. "Hey," she says. "Stop."

Tessa pulls her along. Without a word, they walk toward Pier 39, Tessa still barefoot, the new flip-flops in a plastic bag in her hand, the broken pumps forgotten somewhere inside the store. When they've gone two blocks, Tessa sits down on a bench and puts on the flip-flops. They feel so much better she wants to cry. Olivia looks down at the otter she's still holding in her arms.

"You made me steal him," she says.

"No, I didn't," Tessa says. "You stole him all by yourself."

Olivia draws her eyebrows together. "You made me leave while I was holding him."

"You could have dropped him," Tessa says.

Olivia says nothing, looking down at the otter. Tessa feels a kind of triumph. "It's time to go now," she says. "We have to go see the sea lions."

"I have to put him back," Olivia says.

"No, you don't. You said you wanted him. Now you have him. Give him a name or something." Tessa stands and puts a hand on the back of Olivia's neck. "Let's go," she says.

"You're pinching me," Olivia says, squirming out of her grasp. She hides the otter under her jacket and holds it there as they make their way down the wharf.

The flip-flops do the trick. It's crazy how much better Tessa feels. She could walk for miles, for hours. Olivia trots beside her, trying to keep up, the otter concealed beneath her jacket. She keeps glancing back in the direction of the store as if someone might still come after them. Tessa knows she should be worried about what Olivia will tell her mother, and what Gayle will believe. But she almost *wants* Olivia to tell her mother. It feels good to know she's made Olivia do something her parents would punish her for. This is not right, she knows—not the way to take care of a six year old. There's no time to think about it, though—the Devvie has filled her with shimmering urgency. They need to see the sea lions and think about lunch and maybe she should take a Sallie. There's nothing quite like a Sallie after a Devvie, that lucent pink infusion that makes her almost come, every time. They've spent hours doing this, she and Kenji. At first it was just on Sundays in the Arboretum, but after they quit their jobs at Oracle they started doing it every day. One Devvie, then a Sallie, then another Sallie, and another Devvie. Then the feeling of each other's bodies. It's better than Ecstasy, cheaper than meth. She wasn't going to do it today, not both, not even a Devvie, but now that she's started maybe she should go ahead and take the Sallie, because that's what she's used to now.

Pier 39 is teeming with parents and children and teenagers and cops and vendors. There's the smell of hot dogs, waffle cones, saltwater taffy. Above the accordion music and children's shouts, Tessa can hear the frantic braying of sea lions. Olivia should be loving this. Instead she's looking anxious and pinched, her hand cold in Tessa's. They make their way down to the end of the pier, where families have gathered at the railing to watch the sea lions down in the bay. They lie on wooden floats in a protected cove, hundreds of them, molasses-brown, their glossy bodies heaped upon the floats and upon each other. They smell like elephants in the zoo. Fat with fish, they drowse in the sun or crow at the tourists, their faces small and canine. Spoiled, Tessa thinks. Tame. Hardly even animals anymore. Olivia sidles up to the railing, staring. Behind her there's a free spot on a bench. Tessa sinks into it, stretching her legs out in the sun. It's too hot for Kenji's jacket now. She takes it off and holds it on her lap. She cannot close her eyes to feel the crescendo of her buzz, as much as she wants to. She has to watch Olivia. The Devvie surges in her, flushing her cheeks, and she concentrates on the dark brush of her niece's ponytail. Olivia's egg-blue ponytail holder matches the blue edging of her socks. She is a child cared for in great detail. Tessa likes the sound of that in her mind: *cared for in great detail.* She wonders what Olivia would look like if she were *her* kid, if Tessa were the one responsible for raising her. Worse, maybe. No matching ponytail holder, no cute windbreaker. But she'd be happier, Tessa's sure of that. She wouldn't be worrying about everything she ate and everything she might step on and this rule and that rule. She'd be a girl, a little girl, not a tiny adult.

Olivia seems completely absorbed in the sea lions now, ready to stand there at the railing for a long time. Long enough, maybe, for Tessa to do what she wants to do. She works a hand into the pocket of Kenji's coat. There, like a promise, is the pillbox, the Sallies waiting inside. She flips the top and slides one out. The smoothness of it. The regularity of its six corners. She lays it on her tongue to taste the sweet coating before she swallows. Olivia crouches at the railing now, poking a finger through the wooden slats. Beside her, other children scream and laugh and point.

Tessa closes her eyes, letting the sun come down upon her. She can feel the waves of the Devvie still breaking over her, the flutter in her chest that means it's working, and it's lovely, and it's making her lovely and gone. The Sallie will take a little while to work, but when it does work, what joy. She will sit here and wait. She will let her niece watch those braying dogs of the sea. But she can't sit still or get comfortable, and she can't help thinking about what they'll have to do next, and after that, and after that, and she can't help thinking about Gayle back at the hotel, her sister, who seems so far from her now.

She opens her eyes. Olivia's pulling on her hand. "Stand up," she says.

"What is it?"

"I have to go bathroom."

"Right now?"

In answer, Olivia presses a hand between her legs.

"Okay, okay," Tessa says. When she stands, her vision crowds with blue sparks. She steadies herself against the bench. "We'll find one," she says. "Come on."

They weave through the tourists, looking. Olivia's mouth is pursed with the effort of holding it in. Tessa keeps forgetting what they're looking for—not ice cream, they've had that, not the sea lions, not souvenirs. She sees a line of girls and women extending from a door and suddenly she remembers, but this is not the bathroom, it's a fudge shop. She looks for signs and finds none. She asks a small woman with a broom and dustpan, but the woman shrugs and says, "No speak." Olivia is dancing now, making urgent noises in her throat. Finally, coming around a corner, they find it: the women's bathroom, a blue door and then a long silver cavern of stalls. Olivia breaks away from Tessa and locks herself inside one of them.

Tessa takes a stall nearby and closes the door behind her. She leans against the door, trying to slow her breathing. She doesn't have to pee. What she wants is to feel that Sallie. If she can get it, just the beginning of it, right here alone in the stall, it will be perfect. She will receive the shock of it in her groin, the tightening heat of it in her belly. She puts Kenji's jacket on again, trying to think about being in bed with him when this day is over. Instead she imagines Henry with his hands on Gayle. His broad white face, his small damp mouth. The chalkdust smell of him. She imagines him panting and sweating, whispering equations to stave off his orgasm.

Tessa sits down on the toilet and puts her head in her hands. From all up and down the row of stalls comes the roar of flushing, the banging of metal against metal, the raised voices of mothers and children. What would her own mother think if she saw Tessa now? Sometimes it almost seems better that she died when she did, when Tessa was four. Tessa remembers her mother playing with her in a kiddie pool, holding her on her knees as Tessa splashed. She's sure she remembers this, though Gayle always said she only *thought* she remembered it because they had a picture of it. It was one of the photographs they'd had in their secret closet altar, back in their room at home. They also had a pair of their mother's dancing shoes, silver; an old pink plastic hairbrush with strands of her hair; an empty wallet with a broken snap; a pair of malachite earrings. For years they kept finding small things of hers around the house, and at night they'd sneak into the closet and add them to the altar. There, crouched in the dark, they'd talk about her in whispers and see who could remember more. Gayle always won, of course.

There were times when Tessa would go into the closet by herself and look at the photos, try on the shoes and earrings, feeling like that might help her remember something. It was hopeless, though. Tessa could never catch up. And after a while it all began to seem beside the point. As Gayle grew older she seemed to think about their mother less and less. Instead of creeping into the closet with Tessa, she would stay up late with their father in his study. She'd brew weak tea, which Tessa wasn't allowed to drink yet, and she'd sit on the leather ottoman and talk about what had happened at school or what she'd read in the newspaper that day. Their father would talk to Gayle almost as if she were another adult, asking her opinions and listening to her responses. A few times he even let Gayle come to the political science classes he taught at the university. When Tessa had finally asked him, a few years ago, why he'd never brought *her* to his classes, he'd looked at her with surprise and said he never knew she was interested.

Tessa can feel the Sallie beginning to come on, but it's coming on wrong because she's sitting here in a bathroom stall and thinking about the wrong things. The Sallie ices her veins and makes her toes cramp up. She needs some water. She needs money. Her skin prickles cold. Something is happening and she cannot make it stop.

From outside the stall Olivia calls something, words Tessa cannot make out. *Hold on,* she tries to say, but her voice is not working properly. A wave of shudders breaks over her, and then another, and then they keep on coming. She has to get her niece and get out of there. They need to go someplace quiet and alone. She is ready for that. She will open the door on three.

One.

Two.

Three.

But where is Olivia?

Not in the corridor between the line of stalls, and not in the open stalls, and not by the sinks washing her hands or by the dryers drying them. Not hiding under the Changin' Station or in the utility closet. She must be outside, waiting by the entrance. That is where she has to be. Tessa steps into a blinding crush of sun, a cataract of men and women and children. She looks beside the restroom door, behind the trash can a few feet away, behind the planter with its tiny sick palm. She sits down on the bench beside the palm. Under the surge of the Sallie she can feel the rhythmic thwick of panic in her chest, the wingbeats of an insect. Maybe this is a game. *Ass me no more questions, tell me no more lies.* Tessa goes back into the restroom and makes her way up and down the row of stalls. Women are staring at her, she realizes, giving her looks of concern or fear, pulling their children away. They think she's crazy, and why not? Her hair is a wind-nest, her jacket a bulky male thing, her shirt half-untucked from her tweed skirt, her feet dirty in pink flip-flops.

"Olivia," she screams. "This is not a joke!"

The noise and bustle of the restroom continue around her. She waits, but her niece does not appear.

She has to look outside again. She shoulders through the door and out into the wind. The fronds of the sick palm tree rustle like paper. What color jacket is Olivia wearing? Is it blue? Purple? Is that her, standing by the rail? No, a different child, an older child. The sea lions. She must have gone back to see them, to wait for Tessa there. How to get back to that place? She remembers a confusion, a frantic search for restrooms. Where did they end up? She can hear the sea lions' sound, their fretful barking, and she follows it through a twist of shops and wooden staircases and restaurant patios, looking for that jacket all the while, the jacket that might have been light blue or lavender or pale green, something green, maybe the dress underneath. She should never have let Olivia go into a stall alone. How could she keep it straight, what you were and weren't supposed to do? There are things she should be doing now, smart ways of trying to find Olivia. She has to think of what they are. If she could just lie down somewhere, in a cool dark room. But she cannot lie down.

Olivia is not standing by the rail watching the sea lions. Tessa leans forward over the rail, staring into the lapping water. A child, leaning out too far, could fall in. Would anyone notice? Would anyone notice if she, Tessa, dropped herself into that black-blue, if she let herself sink to the bottom?

What about the otter, that toy she made Olivia steal from the t-shirt shop? That must be where she is, in the shop, putting that thing back on the shelf. That can be the only place. She knows where it is. Back in the direction of the cable car. Olivia would have remembered. And Tessa can find it. It's the only t-shirt shop in San Francisco that has her broken shoes. She slaps along the pier in the direction of the shop, her flip-flops threatening to fly off her feet, the rubber thongs cutting into her skin. Get out of her way. She is a woman in a hurry, a person trying to beat fate. She scans the crowds for a glimpse of purple or of sea-green, for a head of tight dark curls, a ponytail, an egg-blue ponytail holder. Her sister, sitting in a conference room in a hotel downtown, has no idea what is happening. Perhaps Olivia is headed there right now, running to tell her mother what Tessa's done. Here's what Tessa knows: no child of hers would run off into a crowd, lose herself in a strange city.

All along Beach Street there are t-shirt shops and t-shirt shops and t-shirt shops. Three of them have flip-flops displayed out front. Two of these have stuffed animals inside. One of these has otters. None of them has Olivia. Tessa stands on the sidewalk, looking out toward the bay. There, passing between the shore and Alcatraz, is a rust-red oil tanker with the word TANAKA on the side in high white letters. A million gallons of oil. She can almost taste it, bitter and black.

Tessa shuffles along Beach Street. She should tell the cops. She needs help. But look at her, in her crazy outfit, with Devvies and Sallies in her pocket. They'll think she's a kidnapper, a criminal. They'll handcuff her and throw her in a cell. Then they'll search the apartment. Kenji will be arrested too. She has to call him. Maybe he can make it all stop. Up ahead there is a payphone, a little man shouting into it. She bounces on her toes, waiting, looking, willing Olivia to walk by. She'd like to take her by the shoulder, shake her, wake her up: *this* is the world, not what your parents have told you. This is what exists just outside the borders of your pretty life. It's what she's had to learn herself, the hard way, through Gayle's slow and steady pulling-away, through all that time since college when she didn't know what to do with herself, the hated jobs in offices, her father's quiet disappointment, those deadened months at Oracle, and the months since she quit, months of her and Kenji in the apartment during the day, fucking and fighting and tweaking and reading the paper and watching movies and lying to everyone. She knows she's getting closer to a new kind of truth, a real discovery, a kind of knowledge Gayle will never have.

The little man gets off the phone and runs down the street, cursing. Tessa picks up the phone. She can smell food, sweet and greasy, on the receiver. She can't speak into the hum of the dial tone or decide which buttons to press. Her head feels like it's hurtling in fast-forward, her breath coming so fast her vision is going black at the edges. She can't explain why she's standing on the street holding this phone instead of searching for Olivia. A recording comes on and tells her what to do if she'd like to make a call.

"Get Kenji," she says to the voice. "Dial Kenji."

Please hang up and try again.

Try what? She can't hang up. Someone else is already waiting for the phone. *If you'd like to make a call.*

She jams the receiver onto the hook, then picks it up again and presses numbers. *Please deposit thirty-five cents.* She digs in her pocket for change and finds a quarter and a dime. She fumbles them into the slot and dials again. Seven numbers. She can manage them. She does. The phone is ringing, and then, like a reprieve from everything awful, Kenji's voice. She can hardly believe he still exists in this world. She tries to say something but all she can do is cough out sobs.

"Tessa? Is that you?"

"It's not my fault," she cries into the receiver.

"Hey," he says. "Come home. Where did you go?"

"You have to come get me," she says.

He gives a faint, panicked laugh. "Come get you? I can't come get you! I'm extremely fucking fucked up at the moment."

"You have to come," she says. "Olivia's gone."

"Who?"

She hangs up and sits down on the curb. Behind her, someone else picks up the phone and begins punching numbers. There are cars passing in the street just beyond Tessa's flip flops, almost running over her feet as they pass. Crushed bones, blood, a wreck. She almost wants it.

She stands and crosses the street, making the cars swerve around her. There's a small park sloping down toward the water, with pigeons coming down like shattering slate. Weathered green benches stand between beds of blue and yellow pansies. She sits down on a bench, looking out toward the flat metallic expanse of the bay. She feels something going wide and empty in her chest, the Devvie slipping out from beneath the Sallie, the cartoon moment just before you fall, when the cliff's already gone but gravity has not yet got you. A horror goes through her: a child somewhere, screaming, lost. Not just a child, her own niece. She takes the pillbox from her pocket, looks inside. Two Devvies, one more Sallie. She looks at the flowerbed beside the bench, then kneels on the grass. With her finger she digs a hole in the loose soil of the flowerbed, turning up dirt and curled-up bugs and roots. Then she packs the pillbox into the hole, and tamps the soil down on top of it. She fixes this spot in her mind: the park with its beds of pansies, the flowerbed near the center of the park. She picks the dirt from beneath her fingernails, then walks down to the beach and washes her hands in the cold water of the bay.

The waiting room is plastered with posters of missing children, of wanted men and women wearing numbers. She sits in an orange plastic chair, looking down at her wrists. Uncuffed. Beside her on the floor is a cup of black police-station coffee. This is where the police brought Olivia when they found her wandering the wharf alone, crying for her mother, and it is where they brought Tessa when she told them what had happened. She, Tessa, has not been treated like a criminal; she's been allowed to sit here while someone goes to get Olivia. She cannot shake the feeling that someone might come in at any minute and take her roughly by the back of the neck and shove her into a cell. Her policeman acted as if things like this happened all the time: children wandering away from their harried guardians at Pier 39, everyone reunited soon afterward. Now the policeman carries Olivia into the waiting room, her small face grim and scrubbed, her pale purple jacket torn at the sleeve, the stolen otter tucked under her arm. When the officer sets her down she looks at Tessa with shamed, fearful eyes. Tessa pulls her close and holds her there. The girl's arms come around her. It amazes her to think Olivia would trust her after what has happened.

"See that?" the officer says to Olivia. "I told you she wouldn't be mad."

She feels Olivia's breath, quick and hot, against her neck. "I'm sorry," she says.

"It's okay," Tessa says. "It's okay."

They step back out into the sun, into the blinding afternoon, and walk down Bay Street back toward the water. Olivia is stunned and silent, holding Tessa's hand. She seems uninterested in the shops and houses. There are no tourists on this part of Bay Street, only women and men going about the business of their lives. Now would be the time to take Olivia back to the hotel, to get her cleaned up in Gayle's hotel room, to wait for her sister to be finished with her conference. They could both pretend everything was fine, and maybe Gayle would believe them. Or maybe she wouldn't, and everything would begin to change—the nightmare that has become Tessa's life might crack open and begin to fall away. Part of her wants to surrender to that, to let Gayle know at last what has happened to her life, to make her have to recognize it and do something about it, finally. Maybe that's what she's been hoping for all day, maybe that's why she let herself lose Olivia: to make things so terrible they'd have to change. But Olivia is back now, and Tessa feels almost as if she's been tricked. She feels as if she doesn't have the power to decide anything anymore, as if she's being pulled along slick tracks by a strong and twisted steel rope underground, like the cable car. All she can think about are the pills in their silver box, dark and safe beneath the soil. She has to have them, and she has to keep having them. She feels like she'll die if she doesn't. The Devvie is long gone now, and her nerves crackle with the afterburn of the Sallie. A cold white pain gathers behind her eyes. She hurries Olivia along the sidewalk, toward the park.

"I went to put my animal back," Olivia says. "I went back to that store."

"But you didn't put him back," Tessa says. "You decided to keep him."

Olivia looks down at the otter, saying nothing. At an intersection she and Tessa stop to watch the cars pass. Olivia fingers the ripped sleeve of her jacket, trying to hold the edges of the fabric together. "I tore this," she says. "My mom's going to be mad."

"Maybe she won't be," Tessa says, not really listening.

"Yes, she will."

Tessa is at the end of kindness. Her temples pulse with pain. As she looks down at Olivia, a fine sharp cruelty gathers in her chest. "At least you have a mother," she says. "When I was your age, my mother was dead."

Olivia's mouth opens and closes. Tessa will not watch her start to cry. When the light changes, she takes Olivia's wrist and pulls her across the street. As they enter the park, Tessa walks faster. Her flip-flops make their muffled slap against the pavement. In the distance she can see the bay, bright-scaled with afternoon light. She heads toward the row of benches along the park path, each with its crowd of pigeons, each separated by a bed of pansies. The benches are empty now. Tourist families hurry along the path, looking as if they mean to get somewhere before the sun gets any lower.

At a flowerbed near the center of the park, Tessa gets to her knees to examine the soil. She can't tell if this is the right place or not. The bench beside the flowerbed looks familiar, but they all have the same weathered green paint, the same brass plaques. She scrabbles through the loose soil. Nothing. She moves to the next flowerbed, kneeling down to dig again while Olivia watches, holding the otter.

"What are you doing?" Olivia asks, her voice a dry whisper.

"Looking for something," Tessa says. She turns up clods of dirt, but her pills are not there. She leads Olivia along the path, then stoops beside the next flowerbed. She thinks she remembers these flowers at the edge, these yellow pansies with their dark velvet hearts. Olivia sits down on the grass and holds the otter, her eyes glassy with fatigue. The wind is sharp against Tessa's neck as she kneels beside the flower-bed. Her fingers are going numb, her nails are packed with soil, but she lowers her head and digs.

Julie Orringer is the Helen Hertzog Zell Visiting Professor at the University of Michigan. Her short story collection, *How to Breathe Underwater,* was a New York Times Notable Book and the winner of the Northern California Book Award. Orringer is a graduate of Cornell University and the Iowa Writers' Workshop, and was a Truman Capote Fellow in the Stegner Program at Stanford. Her stories have appeared in *The Paris Review, McSweeney's, Ploughshares, Zoetrope: All-Story, The Pushcart Prize Anthology, The Best New American Voices,* and *The Best American Non-Required Reading.* She was the recipient of a 2004–5 NEA grant for her current project, a novel set in Budapest and Paris in the late 1930s.

STOOPDWELLERS

LAUREN WHITEHEAD

Amy wanted to teach second grade since she was in it
I didn't know her then
She came to me four summers after
Her daddy's alcohol yellowed body was lowered into its grave

I knew her days of Tweety shirts and velcro Nikes
Of Extra bubble gum and incarcerated teeth
I knew her before school cigarettes on the air conditioner units
I knew her bus rides busting spades and her high score on calculator Tetris
I knew her vanilla chapstick'd lips
And two mists of Joven White Musk on her wrists

Seven winters I'd spent
Wandering through school buildings
Never thinking I'd find anybody so much like myself
        Nice shirt, it began
While we both tried to snatch a handful of sky
From our swings

I knew her before her fingers wore gold rings
And still shaped silver like mine
Back when I tried to convince her not to spend twenty minutes
Killing her cowlicks natural wave with sprits and spray
That the half circle that bounced off her face
Didn't have to be perfect
She'd always insist that it did
I'd get perturbed
But I'd never get mad at her

Back then we'd spend hours trying to unlock her tongue
From accent thick of Minnesota
I'd attempt to teach her to talk shit back
And not get punk'd for asking for soda
        It's all, I'd begin, in the way you say it
Like I knew at thirteen the key to life or something

But even then

Before we worried about boobs boys or bras
Before we traded games of four square for squares
Before hide-n-go-seek became hide-n-go-get-it
Before she became the girl that always got got
And I became the girl that got lost
She wanted to teach
Give back
   Second or tenth grade, she began
   That way I can either influence
   Or I can save

I didn't know how she could know
So I just used to roll my browns at her blues
As if to say
   Okay psychic lady
   Tell your crystal clear balls
   To look into my future too
      I'ma get off the block for real though, she began
      I'ma either teach second graders to tread water
      Or show sophomores how to stay afloat

In her I saw possible
So when she told me that Big T was ill destined
'Cause he couldn't swim
I was disquieted
Not convinced
Cause see she didn't predict
That Diamond would be a feather feast for a black cat
But she let my tears fill her lap when it happened
She didn't foretell
Katie's teeth getting expelled by a Slugger's bat
But together we laughed
She didn't prophesize that Johnny would never come back
That Richard and Chad would leave
That Marci would be twenty, two kids and tubes tied
Or that Uncle Mike would die at the hand of a drunk who drives
But now
That Big T is 120 miles in an ironbound ocean
Of servitude
I wonder if her third eye caught a glimpse of our friendships' demise
Arriving before graduation too

High school divided us
She got high
I went to school

People would have assumed our fates different
That somehow the white girl would have found success
And the black girl only found herself stuck to the steps
But daily
I scribbled plans in my assignment notebook
Marked my busy weeks with paperclips

While she and her clique
Cut class to cut coke with student IDs

I unlaced spikes to dump sand
Opened my hand to batons

She dodged round wands but also ran
Ducked and tucked between East Court's buildings
To dodge police

While I was barely making it through science
Being tutored and schooled by salutatorians so I pulled no C's in Chem.

She was learning from the local smackmaster to boil crack
On stolen Bunsen burners

Everyday I grappled with fraction subtraction
While her drug transactions became more complicated than algorithms

How did it happen so quick
How did I end up   here
Trying to wrap my hands around happiness
          Here
Alone scribbling rhymes on napkins
While she's stuck on East Court
Still thinking about her daddy

Wonder if the next time she's twenty-three pills and three Bloody Marys
Closer to yellowing her own body
She'll think to call me
          See I, I'd begin
          Have never been
          But I am angry with you now, Amy
          'Cause there you are on the curb
          With the rest of the stoopdwellers
          And I know you know better
          I know you slang rocks and not at a hopscotch
          And I know you've terminated more bright futures

Than just your own
I know you haven't changed
But also
That you're not the same
And that I don't know you
Anymore
You were going to save, Aims
But you never even made it to tenth grade

I wish I would have known to teach her
That actions
Speak louder than words
Cause when I see her now
On East Court's defiled curbside
Third step
Legs open
Feet in dingy white sneaks
Future faded in her once bright eyes
From Newport smoke floating over gold rings
I hope she understands
That the only reason
I come around the corner to just sit and not say shit
To just dwell
From time to time
Is to tell her that I miss her
Hope she knows that I throw pounds when I dip
Only so I can try to give her
Half my handful
Of sky

Lauren Whitehead is a student at the University of Michigan currently pursuing dual degrees in Words and People Moving (with a minor in superstardom). On her journey to be somebody, Lauren has had the distinct pleasure of sharing the stage with some of the most talented and rising stars, including but not limited to: Gabriel Peoples, Tiffany Edwards, Maggie Schultz, Johnny Floyd, and Evelyn Hollenshead. Lauren has performed the lead role of Abby Jones in the play *Lay Your Comfort Down* and she co-directed the controversial cast of *The Vagina Monologues 2006 Colorful Production*. Lauren, who believes that it is her time to fly, is a founding member of the performance poetry troupe Ann Arbor Wordworks and a three-time member of the UM Poetry Slam Team.

DANGEROUS MIRRORS
ABOUT INSOMNIA, FOR MY MOTHER
SAILOR J

WHEN I CAME home last night it was 5:38AM and you were on the couch, awake. The door was open to the summer air and I stumbled in, sweaty from a bicycle ride, slightly drunk and trying to hide it. You were watching the Discovery Channel and said you couldn't sleep.

You reminded me recently that even when I was small I had trouble sleeping. Even as a baby, I'd cry and scream and act distracted. I remember being told to count myself to sleep, counting easily to seven thousand still awake, my closed eyes just a veil between me and my numbers and the huge world outside that started in my bedroom, at the pale windowpane. I remember thinking myself in circles so hard I'd bring myself to tears and come into your room, sobbing, hours after bedtime, afraid of some concept I'd concocted. Afraid about some lie I'd told, or that I'd never have enough time in a day.

It seems sometimes to hit you—this same circularness, a grinding grating fear of the inability to survive, or continue, or move. I wonder if this is something you passed on to me, sometimes. Insomnia.

They seem to be of a different nature—the thing that keeps me up at night and the thing that wakes you. You used to say you got a ringing in your ears so loud you'd wake yourself up with it. This turned out to be some kind of sinus infection that the doctors took care of. Lately I've been waking up itching. Pestering the boy next to me for a scratch, and finding myself wide awake, driven to distraction by the early grey light outside the window, the feeling of skin, the newness of every moment.

You are getting older. You talk about headaches and you hold back tears artfully—yesterday it was in the kitchen, and you were frowning over the First Aid kit, sorting bandaids, choking on words. I wonder if you cry when you awaken, jolted by the steady ache that seems to float around you. I wonder if you are reminded of similar times when you were young, or if it is a condition of your age and experience, that you know disappointment so deeply you can't fall back asleep. I wondered, last night, if you'd just noticed that I hadn't come in, and stayed up worrying about me. You've told me before that many of your nights have gone to that; worrying about me.

Where your insomnia seems to stem from some deep-seated pain, an ache that moves you, mine seems still to be based in wonder. I can't get enough of the world, even when the sights are gory and raw and the boy next to me sleeps mumbling sad sounding things and everyone's parched histories seem to be crumbling around us. These recent summer thunderstorms sound to me like something huge, crumbling. Warm rain at night and warm skin radiating and piles and stacks and clogged passageways of words and texts are the things I fixate on. This is an ecstatic state of alive-ness, insomnia, wise to the pain and joy that we spend our waking hours balancing. This is not the first summer I've spent skating across humid skies to the low points, and rising through long hot nights to the highs.

One time, I remember catching you crying, and catching my breath to ask you, really, what's wrong? You were in that same place, on the couch by the door, and in that same delinquent way I had just walked in, backpack on, feeling young and strange and suddenly so much more solid than you. I could feel my feet in my boots planted on the ground. I must have been fifteen, trying desperately to understand you through screaming arguments and striking similarities and curfews and your deep misunderstanding of me. I said something like, "What makes you so sad all the time?"

"Oh, everything." I remember having to push. What everything? Which things? Your voice was sticky and weak as you started to tell me. The world, you said, the way it's set up and the way it's killing itself off. The things you read in the news, the sense of helplessness you have, the lack of change you see in a lifetime. I started to try to articulate this feeling I had started to have—that all people who make sense, and see the world as it is, get halfway sad. I tried to tell you it was normal, it only makes sense to feel this way, Mom. Next you said, "You. You are one of the things that makes me sad."

What could I say to that? I couldn't empathize. I was not any more or less sad than I have been, or will be. I can see that I am at the mercy, like so many of us, of pain and heartbreak and hopelessness in the world now. These things can overcome you, keep you awake at night, destroy you even. Maybe these are things you've felt, that you don't want to tell me about. Huge dangerous things you don't want me to know. Maybe the world itself is what you are trying to protect me from.

This is being alive. These are the pains of growing, and seeing the world go round and round and seem to fall apart, but never change. These are the pains of leaving things undone, and never finding a chance to try again. I wonder if at your age I will share the same resolve, the same unwillingness to be vulnerable, the same inability to see beauty and hope where it does still lie.

I don't know what I said to you, that day when you looked up from the couch, tired in your eyes, and told me why you were sad. I understood. Last night as I stumbled up the stairs to bed I felt that you had stayed awake for me, and this morning you told me that you fell asleep, there on the couch with the front door wide open, shortly after I got back. I understand you now, even as we stand at more than arm's length, sharing the pot of coffee in the morning, and I talk incessantly, flipping through the newspapers on the kitchen table, while you listen nervously, as if you're expecting something flammable to come out of my mouth and ignite between us. Sometimes I think we can't look each other in the eyes because we can't stand to see the same things, written so differently across these dangerous mirrors we carry ourselves behind.

I don't know if I will ever make you happy, ever come home early, ever embody the fixing of all the things you feel went wrong. I know, in fact, that I won't. No one is without hang-ups. I don't know if I will ever be like you, or if I'll step differently through this labyrinth of lifelike messes under a stunning sky. I don't know what we will ever find to have in common if not the passion that keeps us awake at night. I hope, if anything, that if you stay awake nights waiting, it won't be for me for too many more years. Maybe we can wait mutually—for change, maybe, and wait through the long stretch until sunrise, from our opposite sides of the country. I can hope, at least, that if I can't sleep it is for a reason that transgresses the walls of my eyes and rises like heat past the walls of the bedrooms I sit staring awake in. I hope for you too—that some of these nights awake will be spent in the sky, seeing the world this way, renewed by each day passing.

Sailor J is the 2000 Ann Arbor Youth Poetry Slam Champion and a two-time member of the Ann Arbor Youth Poetry Slam Team, including the 2001 National Youth Poetry Slam Champion Ann Arbor squad. Sailor has performed with such luminaries as Alix Olsen and the performance poetry troupe Sister Spit. He has worked as a sex education presenter and as a community organizer. He founded both the Rebel Grrls and Riot Youth programs at The Neutral Zone and has published several chapbooks of poetry, stories, and essays. He is also a talented musician and actor.

OPEN LETTER TO THE MICHIGAN PRISON SYSTEM

FOR BRANDON GATSON, WHO WROTE HIMSELF OUT OF #381814 & INTO FREEDOM

MOLLY RAYNOR

When you enter JMF,
You enter through a metal detector first.
They gotta know you're not coming with weapons.

Next, you walk quick through the courtyard—
A sea of orange jumpsuits and cigarette smoke
laughter and cat calls, running laps, playing ball
there is a rhythm to it, men lifting, pushing weights
thick arms rising and falling, like this is a cotton field or a factory,
muscles tearing and mending
hardening is an art
the metal starts on the outside and works its way in
from barbed wire to cell bars to bar bells through rough skin
until it reaches every muscle, every tendon
until you become part of the machine
#984713
hardening is an art
closing is the key
which makes opening feel like birth,
raw and red, the deepest pain,
which makes dreaming feel like danger
that goes deeper than a shank can cut,
to that soft spot, encased in cold iron,
untouched for so long,
see, hardening is an art
but opening is far harder

my heart is a metal detector.

It was a line one of the men wrote in my first workshop there
It is a line that I carry deep to help me remember
The men who refuse to be reduced
Eastside, Meachy, G, Savage, Spice, Edward, L, Richard, Henry X, Marvin, Zeek,
Two years at JMF taught me the sharpest blade of poetry

the last night there left me with scars of my own doing
Sixty bodies packed into one room to hear these men read
inmates mingled with Ann Arborites, all moved to their feet by the writing,
thick air sliced like lightning and lifted with laughter

each mouth fully loaded with thirty-two teeth and a tongue ready trigger
we fired
#765284

I remember
The hands of the blond, blue-eyed guard who grabbed me
They were heavy, tired
Like what you doin' here, girl
Why you busting my routine
I'm just part of the machine but I gotta keep it going
They were rough on my shoulder as she shoved me out the door
And locked them in behind us, caged poets seething
Eastside banged the window and yelled in disbelief
G just raised a fist and laughed

#459583
My final goodbye left them
Pressed up against glass
Clawing at the memory of freedom
As we, the free, fled
My face full of tears
Eyes red with apology
For not having more power
Not being more than a weekly visit
More than glitch in the system

And when you saw me, woman,
Me, still branded by your hand,
Me, the damn glitch, the li'l bitch who'd never leave
Teary-eyed, crossing courtyard
You grinned to yourself and grimmed me hard,
Pulled me aside and growled,
"Girl, don't you know, you not s'posed to cry in prison"

No, you're supposed to die in prison
#931260
Supposed to shut down slow
Go cold, broken furnace,
Go hard, broken hearted,
You are supposed to break in prison
Lift weights in prison
better bulk up cause you don't wanna be
scrawny in the shower, everything is power,
#945382
you're supposed to kill in prison,
Whatever it takes to get him before you get got,
And if you're gonna go *you* better flip the switch,

Be your own death row so when they find you in the morning
you are one less black man for them to lynch and laugh at,
#732918
You are supposed to forget in prison,
How to feel, how to touch, how to flower
Forget your family, your man, your woman, your passion,
Forget the trees, the streets, the sun, everything is power,
Go numb, go dumb, boy, bend over, bitch,
Yes, there are many ways to do it,
but the lesson is the same,
#563439
hardening is an art
but opening is far harder
you are supposed to die
but you never, ever cry in prison.

So what happens when you pick up a pencil
And decide to write a poem.
What happens when ten black men and two white women
Practice the art of opening in prison
dream dangerous, deeper than a shank can cut,
what happens when the metal melts,
when tiny bits of the machine malfunction,
what happens? Number 8-5-2-eh, 5-2-eh
the official accusation claimed I said "I love you" to an inmate
you're not supposed to love in prison, live in prison, give in prison
what happens? Number 6-8-3, eh, 8-3
The white women get banned and black men get segregated to solitary
Their sentences lengthened, while I walk free
And now I wonder if it's more hurtful in the end
To flaunt freedom in front of caged men

Dear Michigan prison system,
#52-eh,
you are the bitter taste of iron in the back of my throat, fading with distance.
But the men you hold captive don't need me to be dangerous,
#17-eh
Remember Haiti, remember Harriet,
The slave *will* uprise
You will realize
The hardest weapon of all is not a whip or a gun
It is the tongue, taut trigger
It is the muscle that tears and grows back stronger
It is the heart when it speaks offbeat
I'm #6-8-3-eh, 83-eh, 83
no . . . my name is G, my name is Eastside, my name is Meach,
This name, your darkest nightmare, my brightest dream

This poem a mine ready to take you in your sleep
A loose bolt in your machine that always worked before
Now see, *my heart is a metal detector*
And I'm not letting you through no more

MY MOTHER'S GARDEN

flow·er n
1. a colored, sometimes scented, part of a plant that contains its reproductive
organs.

I don't remember the flowers
my mother planted in her garden,
But rather the wild ones
That popped from cracks and creases of our yard.

I remember her clipping roses in June.
They were peach and crimson,
crawling toward my bedroom window.

I remember what she told me
The summer before I left for college—
There is sensuality in the mundane
 a plate of gorgeous food
A fresh bouquet

Some flowers could not be gathered.
Before the pears fell clumsy from our tree out back
The pear blossom fell like feathers, petal by petal,
blanketing the mud and new grass.
When a strong wind came
I'd lean against the tree and let the storm swallow me.

The peonies came later.
Pink and chubby,
I used to watch the ants that lived in them.
Hot, red, shining with anger or desire.
I used to think about their sting.

Behind the garage,
Under the shade of the hung canoe,

Framed by paint, yellow and cracking,
There was a patch of rubarb.

My secret place, I'd sneak there,
Eight years old and sit cross-legged,
A piece of rubarb held in one hand, firm.

I'd peel the layers from its stem,
Red bleeding into green,
And press my thumb into the
Fleshy pink that tasted bittersweet.
I would pull my thumb away—
wet, familiar.

My mother told me.
She saw her own reflection
Bending to pick a peonie,
Reaching to clip a rose.
She'd smile, cheeks a deep pink,
flushed in her finding.

My mother taught me.
About flowers and food and men and myself.
Every night before dinner,
She asked us our daily blessings.
We couldn't eat until we wrote
A poem into the air:

Late for school I dropped my keys
and when I crouched
to fetch them, flustered,
I found something else—
Lillies of the valley,
lined along the gutter,
in the shadow of our house,
arching sweet into themselves

Lilies of the valley
like necks of women
bent in love

Molly Zipora Pershin Feigele Raynor likes people to know that she has five names because it makes her feel cool. The first story she ever wrote, saved by her nostalgic mother, goes like this: "Once upon a time, there was a sad, sad, little orphan girl. She was such an orphan that her parents died before she was even born!" See, she's deep like that. Molly, a founding member of the performance poetry troupe Ann Arbor Wordworks, a cast member of the play *Lay Your Comfort Down*, and co-director of *The Vagina Monologues 2006 Colorful Production*, is fond of doodling, *The Dave Chapelle Show*, teaching poetry in prisons and youth "correctional facilities," her thumb-ring from little Tibet, and wolves. Oh yea, and she super-duper-likes chocolate peanut butter chunk ice cream, although she culturally identifies more with white russian fudge. Because she's just deep like that.

ROXANNE RYDER
LAURA PERSHIN RAYNOR

ROXANNE RYDER ALWAYS dressed in black with the tightest skirt I'd ever seen and she sat right next to me in my seventh-grade public speaking class. When the morning sun shone through the dirty classroom window it lit up her strawberry blonde beehive hairdo and she glowed. She had a tiny freckled face under all that hair and thick black liner around her blue eyes. Roxanne Ryder was exotic. She was Catholic, a cream puff surrounded by all the dark haired Jewish kids in the class. I knew on the first day of class that I wanted Roxanne Ryder to be my friend because her smile never went beyond a smirk and that smirk told me that she knew many things about the world and I knew nothing.

Roxanne did the same thing every morning before class began. She took a piece of Beechnut Chewing Gum out of her front pocket, unwrapped it, rolled it like a cigarette, and popped it in her mouth even though gum chewing was strictly prohibited at Robert Frost Junior High. Then she reached into her back pocket and pulled out a very futuristic looking foil packet of ketchup from the new joint that had opened up on Greenfield Road called Burger King. Roxanne sat there, rubbing her thumb over the packet like a lucky stone or a rabbit's foot. I knew she was smart because those packets never once exploded in her pocket no matter how hot it got in the classroom that spring. Even though I sat next to Roxanne Ryder every day that year she did not speak to me until the first week of May. That's when our very dramatic public speaking teacher, Mr. Silverman, who directed the school plays, announced to the class that we had until the end of the week to prepare a three-minute speech on any subject.

"Don't bother with dull things like country reports or essays on the presidents. Here's your opportunity to be heard! Make it topical!" We didn't know what that meant. "Make it exciting! Make it groovy! Whoever has the best speech and gets the loudest applause from their classmates, wins the honor of announcing the lunch menu, which has never been done by a student, over the public address system in the principal's office the following week. Now that's the true test of public speaking—making school lunch sound good enough to eat!" Mr. Silverman laughed at his own joke while we all sat there, squirming, dreading the assignment.

On my way home from school that day it came to me, a brilliant idea, something new and exciting! I could do a speech on the miracles of bleeding madras! My favorite shirt from sixth grade was a bleeder. My mother had grumbled about how many pairs of my father's underwear had come out with purple splotches when she washed them with that shirt by mistake. I could even wear the shirt as I talked about this amazing fabric. But when I looked up "bleeding madras" in the 1964 *World Book Encyclopedia* at my house I was shocked and dismayed to find out there was no information. There was only one thing to do. I walked to Suzanne's Stitch and Sew, an old fabric store where my mom let me pick out material for a new dress every year. I interviewed Suzanne. She was also a bleeding madras fan and she loved to talk. She was thrilled with my speech idea. She even gave me a free yard of the magic cloth so I could hold it up in the classroom.

When I performed my speech for my parents the next night after dinner they laughed and clapped and my mother said she especially liked my beginning sentence, "What would the world be like without color?" My father just chuckled and shook his head. The next day, when I stood up in front of the class, my mouth was so dry I could barely speak. I was afraid my madras shirt would start bleeding right then and there because I was sweating so much. I took a deep breath and said "My speech is called Born to Run—the Miracles of Bleeding Madras." As I talked I noticed that my classmates were actually listening and I warmed up a little. I held up the yard of cloth and sprayed water on it, and I said with confidence, "See how it bleeds now," and everyone was quiet as they watched the colors begin to blend and change. That day for the first time in my life my classmates clapped and even cheered a little for me.

At the end of the hour Mr. Silverman proclaimed that Laura Pershin had the "grooviest speech" and would be announcing the lunch menu on Thursday, May 18 at 8:30AM. As I sat there beaming, something surprising happened. Roxanne Ryder turned to me and smirked in my direction. She played with the wrist sized hoop earring on her right ear, rubbed the ketchup packet with her left hand and said, "Okay, we'll have to work a little with you before next week. Can you come to my house after school today? Meet me at the tether ball."

All day I was dying of curiosity. What did she mean "work on me?" When I met Roxanne after school I could tell she had a moment's hesitation. She looked me up and down and said, "A visit to the principal's office when you're not in trouble—that's pretty cool. Got any money?"

"No, why?" She shrugged and said, "I told you we've gotta work on you for your big day. You gotta look good. We need to stop at Ben Franklin's. You can owe me."

We walked the ten blocks to Ben Franklin's Five and Dime while Roxanne whistled Rolling Stone songs the whole way and snapped her Beechnut gum like an exclamation point at the very end. When we walked in the cool musty store, we passed right by the pink Barbie section to the aisle where the dusty lipsticks were displayed. Roxanne picked up one after another, looking at me with her head cocked and biting her cheek, until she found one called Sugar Frost. She marched up to the cash register, bought it, and handed it to me. "Now we'll work on you at my place."

Roxanne lived right near the store. Her house was dark and small and smelled like a combination of smoke and fried potatoes. We walked into the kitchen where Roxanne's grandmother was standing near the sink, licking green stamps and putting them into a little book. I just stared up at her. She was tall and dark with big hands and long black hair with gray streaks and she looked like Natasha from the Rocky and Bullwinkle show. Every time she stuck a green stamp into the book, her silver bracelets clinked together making a musical sound. Roxanne surprised me by walking up to her grandmother, standing on her tip toes, and planting a noisy kiss on her cheek. Her grandmother smirked, hugged her close, and then nodded in my direction.

As Roxanne grabbed a couple of Twinkies and led me down the hall, she said, "My grandma doesn't sit down—ever. I mean ever. You want to know why?" It wasn't a question. Roxanne kept talking. "My grandma was in the camps—you know, the ones your people went to in Poland? She was in the camps because they said she was a gypsy." Roxanne pointed to her enormous hoop earrings. "These are hers. Anyway, the Nazis made her stand still for a long, long time in the cold and they said if she fell or sat down they would shoot her. She never fell and she never sat down again. She lays down a lot though."

We walked into the bedroom that Roxanne shared with her brother who was two years younger than us. His side of the room was a mess, with dirty socks and GI Joes laying on the floor but Roxanne's side was neat. There was a huge poster of Mic Jagger over Roxanne's bed and frilly pink curtains on the window. The few items hanging in her closet were black except for one powder blue dress, the same color as her eyes. She reached into her closet and pulled out a ouiji board. We sat on the bed and she said, "Now concentrate—close your eyes."

We put our fingers on the triangle, and she said, "Lighten up—you are so clunky!" Then she said slowly, "Will Laura succeed in her goal this month? Will she pull off announcing the menu?" I tried to remain very quiet and still and keep my fingers lightly on the triangle and could feel it slowly moving to the other side of the board. "Look," she said and I opened my eyes to see the dial pointing to YES. "Okay, now that I know it's worth my time," and she picked up her eyeliner.

When I left Roxanne's house that afternoon my face was covered with makeup. I had thick black liner around my eyes and I carried a paper sack with eye makeup and lipstick and clear instructions as to how to apply it on the morning of the big day. In another paper sack was a four-inch-wide white belt, to be worn on the hips, and white fishnet pantyhose that were three sizes too small for me.

One week later, on the day that I, Laura Pershin, would announce the lunch menu over the PA system, I walked into Robert Frost Junior High School in a sleeveless polyester herringbone mini dress. Roxanne Ryder's huge belt, that was supposed to lay seductively over my hips, was squeezing my stomach. The fishnet pantyhose never made it up to my waist which meant that the crotch was almost at my knees so I walked a little funny but my classmates were too amazed by my face to notice. I had applied my makeup just as Roxanne instructed so that my eyelids looked slightly bruised and my eyes were surrounded by a thick black line and my lips were white and shiny. I was ready.

I walked into the principal's office, the school secretary looking me up and down with a "what happened to you?" expression on her face. "Good morning, young lady," said our principal who had never learned any of the good kids names. "Sit right here."

I sat in front of a microphone that was black and as big and round as a softball. "Just press this button and keep it pressed the whole time you are speaking—here's the menu." My heart was thumping so hard I was sure the whole school would hear it. I wished I had one of Roxanne's ketchup packets to rub and calm myself down, but this was it, my big moment. I pressed the button, leaned in and read that day's menu in the lowest, sexiest voice I could muster—the voice of a confident girl who wore one pound of eye makeup and had "kiss me" lips, the color of milk.

"Good morning, Robert Frost students. Today, for lunch, we will have a selection of: hot dogs on a soft bun or Johnnie Marizetti with tater-tots and peach cobbler for dessert. There is a choice of white milk or chocolate. Enjoy your meal." That was my unique ending that I had practiced in front of the mirror. "Enjoy your meal."

"Very fine job young lady—you may return to class now."

When I waddled into English class late, my fishnet stockings falling down almost below my mini dress, Michael Dugan, the most popular boy in the seventh grade class said, "Hey—good goin', Pershin," and clapped his hands slowly as I shuffled to my seat. I was close to fainting from happiness as I sat down and then I saw Roxanne Ryder standing in the doorway of the classroom smirking in my direction.

That was the last time Roxanne Ryder ever looked at me. In public speaking class, when I asked if I could come over to her house sometime to return her belt and fishnet pantyhose, that I had totally stretched out, she just stared out of the window. I said, "I have another question for the ouiji board—like, will I maybe be a public speaker someday when I grow up?" She just shrugged and turned away.

Two days later, when I walked to her house and rang the doorbell no one answered. When I looked through the front window I saw her grandmother in the living room, standing in front of the TV, watching *As the World Turns*. I left the fishnets, belt, and makeup in the bag on the front porch and walked home thinking about what it felt like to share a ouiji board with Roxanne, thinking that even her grandmother knew that Roxanne never wanted to see me again.

School ended a few weeks later. Roxanne and I never talked again. But because our last names were close in the alphabet we are frozen in time next to each other in the 1967 Robert Frost Junior High School yearbook. I'm smiling with big dimples showing, in my peter pan collar and cardigan sweater, looking twelve years old. Roxanne, in her black turtle neck helenka and white lipstick, looks like a woman. She is smirking into eternity.

Besides the beehive blonde in her seventh grade class, **Laura Pershin Raynor** was most fascinated by the outrageous characters in her own family. She writes extravagant versions of tales from her family history. Laura tells her stories at festivals around the country but her home is in the library in Ann Arbor, Michigan where she tells stories as the children's librarian to enthusiastic listeners every week.

PAST, PRESENT, ELSEWHERE
EILEEN POLLACK

BARBARIANS WERE CHURNING the farms into mud, polluting our wells. I had to escape.

This was 1969. I was thirteen years old, hiding in the basement. The frayed plastic webbing of my father's green lounge chair tickled my legs, which were only half-shaped—curved here, blockish there. A photo from *Life* was taped to the window: the earth from the porthole of Apollo 11. The light from behind made the earth luminescent and nearly 3-D. It stared down upon me, a cloudy blue eye.

The hot-water heater kindled itself in the basement's black heart. "We have lift-off," I said. "We have separation," and I could feel gravity slipping away.

Then the heater stopped roaring.

"We have engine malfunction"—my voice stony calm—"I repeat, engine failure." I arose from the lounge chair, swimming my arms. With my ear to the tank, which was warm as a chest, I heard: *tickticktick* sigh, *tickticktick* slosh, like the slosh of a stomach. I rubbed the tank, soothed it. The tank purred. Then: BROOSH.

"Thank God," Houston said. "The experts were stumped. How did you fix it?"

Though I was too old to be playing such games, the lounge chair seemed to beckon as a first love might do. Other girls had crushes on Dylan, Mick Jagger, but these men seemed dangerous. I dreamed of Neil Armstrong in his white padded suit. We'd be bounding through the vacuum of an unexplored planet when a meteor would sizzle through the sky toward his head. I would push him to safety and be crushed in his place. As he carried me tenderly back to the ship I would smile at him weakly, but the pain would win out and . . .

"Judith, are you down there?"

My parents were standing at the top of the stairs; the door to the kitchen was open behind them so a shaft of gold light cut through the murk. This made me feel lonely, as a small fish must feel lonely in the shadowy depths.

"I'm thinking," I said. "Can't a person find anywhere in this whole house to think?"

Ordinarily my parents would have flinched at that word. Because I was smart and obviously destined to travel much farther from Bethel than they had, they made the mistake of treating me as though I were older and braver and needed no help understanding the world. But this time my mother wanted to know: Was anything wrong? Was I feeling . . . unwell? She whispered to my father, and since they were both timid and small they looked then like children daring each other to venture downstairs.

"It isn't that!" I said, and wished for a blanket to cover my body, which stretched out before me with its landscape of breasts, rib cage, belly, pelvis, and knees.

All week the paper had been lurid with photos of the barbarians who'd overrun our town—sunbathing on car hoods, dancing to music at this "festival" of theirs—but an inky strip covered each interesting part, like a gag on a mouth. I scraped at those boxes, even turned the page over to see from the other side what was masked on the front. I felt the reporters had found out my future and printed it here, but blotted the facts I most wanted to know. At the same time I wished those bodies had been blackened with ink; the editors were publishing my most shameful secret with only this slight disguise of my features, and the secret was this: that I wasn't destined to leap on the moon but to grovel in mud.

I took out a book from under my chair. "I'm reading," I said.

"You'll ruin your eyes, sweetheart," my father clucked sadly. "If you'd only take that paper off the window . . ."

"That's not just some 'paper.' That's our planet. That's Earth. Don't you know anything?"

My father retreated, noiseless as the dust motes that chased around his head. My father was a milkman; he woke up at three and was so schooled in silence that floorboards wouldn't whimper under his feet, doorjambs wouldn't click.

"We're leaving the house." My mother moved down a few steps, as though the stairs were a seesaw and she had to balance her husband's retreat. "Some of us are going to try to get food to those poor hungry children."

Two days before, when the roads were still open, she'd made her weekly shopping trip to Monticello (the only stores in Bethel sold beef jerky, beer, and Eskimo pies) and she'd found the streets jumbled with barbarians foraging for something to eat.

"I even saw people I know selling water. From their hoses!" she said. "At a dollar a glass!"

It surprised me that anyone would think to sell water. I still regarded water, air, food and land, even gas for the car, as the barest supplies that God could hand out so all human beings could make do on Earth, the way that a teacher would supply every student with pencils and paper on the first day of class. But my mother's condemnation seemed far too harsh.

"Do you blame them?" I asked. "I wouldn't let those animals drink from our *hose*."

This clearly disturbed her. My mother was plump, with a plump olive face, and her moods were as easy to read as a child's. when she was disturbed, everything drooped—her hair, cheeks and bosom. Even her ankle socks seemed to droop. "I know they look strange . . . but I couldn't help but think they might be my own daughter and wouldn't I want somebody else's mother to feed her?"

I was sick with the insult. "If they were too stupid to bring enough food you should let them go hungry."

"Well, foolish or not," my mother admitted, "I saw this young woman . . . she was seven months pregnant . . . she couldn't find her husband and he had the money . . ."

"Don't tell me you gave this woman our groceries!" I would have been embarrassed to be so naive, but my mother wore her innocence as proudly as she'd wear a suit of bright armor; if she thought well of everyone, this would deflect all ugly intentions and no one would hurt her.

"Only the bread," she told me. "And cheese. She didn't want the chicken, it was too hard to cook."

And so we had eaten our Friday-night supper without any challah, sucking our chicken bones to amplified shrieks—"Give me an *F!* Give me a *U!*"—as though Satan himself were holding a pep rally just down the road.

After dessert we turned on the news, and we saw on the screen not an invasion of a faraway hamlet, but our own town this night, not a mob of barbarians screaming outside the Pentagon, but outside our house. On the black-and-white set, even the film taken earlier that day was lifeless as ash, so it seemed these intruders had stolen the color from the land near our home. Then the newscast went live and the cameras flew over the field near the stage, which looked like a pond writhing with newts in the beam from a flashlight, and the chop of the rotors over our roof was the same *chop-chop-chop* as from the TV. These were our roofs, our fields, the mob down the road, and my insides went cold with the helplessness of watching yourself in a dream while you drop from a cliff.

On Saturday my parents walked to the synagogue, pretending they saw nothing amiss, as Lot and his wife must have tried to look casual as they picked their way through the outskirts of Sodom. And after the service they'd found out how bad the emergency was—not a few hungry kids, but a few hundred thousand. The people in charge of the festival hadn't prepared for such crowds. All the highways were choked. No food could get through. No one had wanted these young people here, but seeing they *were* here . . .

So now, Sunday morning, my father and the other deliverymen at Yasgur's were planning to carry milk to the hordes, while my mother would help the Ladies Hadassah spread tuna on white bread, which nuns from the convent would deliver on foot.

"Great," I said, "fine, go feed the enemy, only leave me alone."

"Well, if you're sure," and I heard the stairs sigh, watched the light disappear.

I was cruel to my parents and I've lived to regret this, but then I felt justified, as though I were the parent, yanking the arms of a daughter and son who insisted on watching a worm on the ground while a yellow-haired comet blazed through the sky. Just four weeks before, while I'd been transfixed by two men in white leaping and landing with infinite grace on the moon—on the *moon*—my mother had wandered in from the kitchen, rubbing a glass. "Judith," she said, "this is historic," but she hadn't stopped rubbing that glass with her cloth, and my father kept saying, "Such brave men these are," shaking his head in a way that implied "not brave but foolish," while I felt the Messiah had announced the new kingdom: we were no longer animals whose feet had to stick in the muck of the earth, we could leap on the moon, anything was possible. But how could I argue with people who preferred a lifetime in orbit around this small town—delivering milk, shopping and cooking and washing the pots—to a flight to the moon?

That night as I lay on my back in our yard, plotting my course by connecting the stars, I whispered: "I'm coming." And the next day I bicycled up and down hills to Monticello and took out some books about space travel, asteroids, gravity, light. I didn't understand a word that I read but I felt their mere presence would help me become an astronaut sooner: I could stack these thick books, climb on top, brush the stars.

Then a boy I knew, Steven, informed me that astronauts had to be men, in perfect condition, with 20/20 eyesight so their glasses wouldn't float from their faces or break at critical times. After that I spent hours chinning myself from the beams in the basement until my arms grew as muscular as any boy's, though I later found out no boy would have felt that fullness and throb as he pulled himself up, thighs pressed, legs crossed. I did twenty push-ups, palms damp on the floor, jumped rope, *slap, slap, slap.* I spun in a circle so I *would not* throw up when tested for the job in that bucket in Houston. And I strengthened my sight by taking off my glasses, lifting a corner of the photo on the window and straining to read the signs on the farm stand in the Dwyers' front yard.

"Sweet corn," I said, though I knew I was reading from common sense—what else would the Dwyers be advertising at this time of year? I was squinting to make out the next line of print—tomatoes? peas? melons?—when an ambulance pulled up and Steven jumped out. He trotted up our drive like an overwound toy. He was always so scrubbed he appeared to be wearing a doctor's white coat even when dressed in corduroy trousers and a polo shirt for school; now that he actually was wearing a lab coat (it hung past his knees) he was blindingly clean.

Of everyone I knew only Steven had dreams as intense as my own, and this must have been the reason I'd let him lead me one night to the Little League field behind the Jewish cemetery and why I'd confided what others would have mocked, pointing to illustrate at the pulsing full moon. That's when he said that astronauts weren't allowed to wear glasses, and he lifted off mine, leaned down, kissed my cheek where it merged with my nose, and told me his dream of mapping each neuron and cell in the brain so he could determine the tangles and gaps that made people ill, as his mother was ill. Using his thumb, he traced the long nerve from my toes to my thigh, and I knew he was using his dream as a reason to touch me this way, but right then the moon seemed very far-off, a circle of ice, and his fingers were warm.

"You're cold," Steven said. "It's like you're not here."

And even as I lay there I thought this was true. I regarded my body as some sort of spaceship that workmen were building and I wasn't yet sure I could trust their designs, things might go wrong—already I'd witnessed that leaking of blood—so I hadn't decided if I should move in. I saw myself lying on the bleachers near Steven, long, narrow, stiff, with an angular chin, eyes pale as slugs with my glasses removed.

"Even your hair is cold," Steven said as his hand fell away.

Now he bent to my window, and his face gleamed behind the earth like a bulb.

"You've got to come quick. The kids at the concert are really getting hurt.

They're all on bad trips. Someone called up my father and asked him to come."

Steven's father was a surgeon, a swaggering man though five foot two. Dr. Rock ran the hospital as if any question of his authority would be punished by traction, so no one objected when he let his son Steven take blood from patients, give shots, and stitch wounds, though Steven had only just turned fifteen.

"I'll be his assistant," Steven said now, "and you can help me. But you have to hurry up. It took us all morning just to get this far and we still have the hardest half-mile to go. We can't leave the ambulance, it's full of supplies."

"How could you?" I said. "They're our enemies, remember? These people think you can cure a disease by rubbing a certain part of your foot! They don't like machines. They don't like *computers*. You can't reach the moon without a computer! If they want to louse up their minds with those drugs, why don't you let them?"

His expression was blank, as though he had never heard this before, and I realized he hadn't; I'd been the one who'd done all the talking and he'd only nodded to humor this girl he wanted to kiss.

"It's a great chance to practice. Maybe I'll get to help my dad operate." The ambulance whined. "Sure you won't come?"

I shook my head no.

"Well, if you do, he said we'd be working in some kind of tent." And he trotted away.

With Steven's departure the cellar seemed twice as dim as before. I lay on the lounge chair and suddenly felt chilled, though the air was so heavy I felt I was lying smothered beneath a big, musty cow. With my book on my chest I daydreamed I'd left this planet behind—it was charred and defiled, and I was the last civilized being, in a ship so advanced that I would lack nothing, except somewhere to land, someone to greet me when I returned.

"Guess no one's home." A voice from outside, or maybe a dream.

"Hey, trick or treat!" A reedy voice, singsong. "Give us some food or we'll give you a trick."

"Shit, man, I'm hungry." This voice was deep, its edges were tough. "Can't you just smell that food? Bourgeois fuckin' pigs, hiding in the dark and stuffing their faces while the people are eating berries and shit. Let's liberate the food. Food for the people!"

And I charged up the stairs the way that a sleeper will bolt from her bed swinging her arms to ward off a dream before she wakes up and knows where she is, so I found myself standing with nothing but a book and a flimsy screen door protecting me from three starving barbarians.

The smallest was scraggly, with a beard like a goat's. He was shirtless, in cut-offs and small muddy sneakers. The second was a black man with a square-cut black beard in a dozen thin braids, each laced with gold. The biggest barbarian was shaggy, unkempt, but even in my fear I could sense something sweet and harmless about him, a circus bear fed on popcorn and nuts. He had on a jump suit; the patch on the chest was embroidered with RUFE. His feet were enormous and hair sprouted from his toe joints.

"Jesus, we scared her," the goat-boy was saying. "We didn't mean to scare you.

Jesus, we'd never . . . We were kidding around. Pretending to be these tough guys, you know?"

The black one said, "Shit. We just need a phone. Fitz here, Fitzgibbon"—he pointed to the goat-boy—"was on his way home when we shanghaied him here. His poor momma must be shitless by now so we thought he could call."

"And then we smelled food," the goat-boat said, wistful. "We thought maybe your parents would give us some food."

I kept the door locked, my book poised to strike. Who'd believe a barbarian cared if his mother knew where he was? But they did seem upset, as though the Three Stooges had realized their slapstick had really hurt someone. I hadn't had time to put on my glasses and this made them blurry, less capable of harm.

"Well, then, come on," the bearish one said. "Can't you see that we've frightened her out of her gourd?" His accent was Southern, his tongue thick and slow as a bear's tongue would be. It struck me as right that a bear should be Southern—I suppose that the bears in some Walt Disney movie had spoken like this, and bears were slow-witted and crude in a way I'd grown up thinking Southern men were. But I couldn't figure out . . . Didn't Southern men hate black men? Didn't they hang them from trees?

The bear swiped his friend's arm and I almost expected to see bloody claw marks. "Imagine just can't you if some big ugly fella with braids in his beard showed up at *your* door? You figure your sister should welcome him in?"

"Braids? Hey, I . . . Shit." He touched his beard. "Shit. There was this girl, and she asked if she couldn't put braids in my beard, and I said why not, it would help kill the time. Just a game man, you know? Don't you ever play games? Don't you ever dress up in your momma's high heels?"

This was too much to tolerate. "I have better things to do."

"Can see that," the bear said. He narrowed his eyes and recited the title of the book I was holding. "*Gravitational Theory*. That's awful heavy reading for someone your age."

"How would *you* know?" I asked.

"Sure he knows," chimed the goat-boy. "At Princeton they call him the Astrophys Whiz."

This didn't take me in. None of the astronauts *I'd* ever seen would walk around barefoot, though I had seen Neil Armstrong wearing a jump suit.

"Don't let the hair fool you." The goat-boy was grinning. "I mean, think of Einstein. Now *he* was a mess."

"And you two?" I sneered. "I guess you're both Einsteins?"

"Jesus no," said the goat-boy. "Do you think we'd do anything as practical as that? Leon here"—he pointed—"when Leon grows up he's going to be a pure mathematician."

"Pure as the snow! Pure as the rain!" Leon crossed his white t-shirt. "And Fitz here's a classicist," though I had no idea what a classicist was. "Fitz, do your shit, man. Show her how useless a classicist is."

And the goat-boy threw back his long, skinny neck and recited—no, sang—a poem in a language I didn't understand, though I did feel the poetry, like the gallop of horses, and the goat-boy kept singing until I was hypnotized and let down my book.

"Sorry to have troubled you." The bear turned to leave. "We'll just go next door."

"Oh no," I said quickly, "the Dwyers have Dobermans and old Mr. Dwyer said he'd turn the dogs loose." I stopped there, ashamed to remember that I had once been in favor of old Mr. Dwyer siccing his dogs on any barbarian who came near his farm. "You can use the phone here."

"You're sure of that?" the bear said. "If you'd rather we didn't . . ."

Suddenly I felt my bravery in question: he thought I was scared!

"All right, if you're sure. Fitz can go in, and Leon and me, we'll stay on the porch."

The goat-boy pawed his sneakers to scrape off the mud. If he meant to slice me open and paint the walls red he wouldn't be so careful to clean off his shoes. I lifted the latch.

"It's a big house," he said as we walked through the living room. "I grew up in the city, we just had two rooms."

We got to the kitchen and I watched him dial 0.

"Yes, thank you, ma'am, I'd like to place a call, long-distance, collect, to Mrs. Anne Fitzgibbon from her son Timothy."

When his mother got on I could tell she'd been crazy fright where he was.

"Yes, Mom, I'm sure, Mom, I really didn't mean to give you such grief but this was my first chance to get to a phone." He tried to assure her that he was all right, getting plenty to eat, so his words made me feel like a kidnapper who had treated him badly and forced him to lie to his mother at gunpoint.

He hung up the phone. "What a wonderful smell." He sniffed with his mouth. "I'll bet you had chicken. I smell pickles and potatoes . . . I even smell your mother."

"I don't smell anything." I was horrified that anyone should say our house smelled; most of our neighbors wore the odor of their barnyards like ratty old coats they couldn't stand to part with but my family took pride in how often we bathed, how the kitchen floor shone.

The goat-boy said, "A person can't smell her own house. You need an outsider. Someone who's trained. Archaeology, see? When you dig up some ruins you have to be able to sniff out the food the people once ate there, what sort of clothes and perfumes they wore, how they treated their slaves."

I knew he was lying, but I believed him enough to feel sad that no one would stand here and sniff and know I had lived. And I nearly believed he could sniff out my future, as he'd sniffed out the past. I wanted to ask: Would I go to the moon? Or would the barbarians destroy the world first?

We'd reached the front door. Leon and the bear stood up and stretched.

"I could make you some sandwiches."

"Oh, we don't want to bother—"

"No, it's okay. You just stay here."

I ran to the kitchen. We didn't have much food but I found a few slices of stale pumpernickel . . . a jar of peanut butter . . . and honey. A bear would like honey, I thought, so I spread that on too.

The barbarians stuffed their mouths with these sandwiches, then they couldn't say a word.

"W-w-w-w," moaned Leon, "w-water," and I thought of the hose, but I ran off and got them glasses of milk.

"Ahh," said the goat-boy. He lifted his glass. "Milk fit for gods." And I had to laugh because he and Leon had milky white rings encircling their mouths—they didn't look like gods but surprised little boys. The two seemed offended, but they glanced at each other and swiped at their mouths with the backs of their hands.

"I don't suppose you'd know a place we could wash at?" The bearish one stood and yanked down his jump suit, where it caught in his crotch. "Some swimming hole nearby?"

"Yeah," Leon said, "I sure as shit could go for a swim."

"There's a pond," I said, happy to have the right answer, though sorry to think they would soon leave my porch.

Leon wrinkled his nose. "Not some little cow pond covered with green shit and pissed in by a half-million hippies like the cow pond back there?"

"No, this one's big, and the water's really clean." I flushed with the arrogance of access to places that strangers couldn't find. Then I realized these strangers wouldn't be able to find the pond without me. "I could show you," I said, then wished that I hadn't.

"That would be awful nice," the bear said, and smiled. "Then you and I can talk about gravity. That is, if you want."

"Just a minute," I said, and ran to the cellar to put on my glasses, so when I came back I saw all three clearly, their pimples and dirt, the pores where the beard hairs poked through their skin, and this made them seem less frightening, and more.

"Follow me," I said. And I led our parade down a trail through the woods—it seemed the cool air had fled the other barbarians and was trembling here beneath this camouflage of leaves. The trail passed a tractor whose tires had been used for archery practice. I felt someone draw the metallic tip of one of those arrows down my neck, down my spine, but I turned and saw no one except for the goat-boy, who was sniffing the air and skipping a little, and the other two behind him.

When we got to the pond I heard Leon whistle.

"Shit, look at that. In Newark, man . . . shit."

I didn't understand. This was only the pond down the road from my house. Then I saw it as a boy from a city might see it, and if I'd accused the barbarians of stealing the color from Bethel, they gave it back doubly, once right-side up and again upside down. Every orange salamander and blue darning-needle signaled me like some code from beyond.

The goat-boy and Leon stripped to their undershorts, then dove in long arcs, came up again and started to race, one heavy black arm and one scrawny pale arm rising and falling, the gold-threaded braids of Leon's beard floating out from his chin like some intricate lure.

"Hmm, I'm afraid . . . " The bearish one was fiddling with the zipper on his jump suit.

"Afraid of the water?" I asked.

"No, afraid I don't have any underwear."

"I won't look," I promised, though I found when he started to pull down his zipper I couldn't turn away. As he stepped from the jump suit I expected to see a heavy black rectangle blocking his crotch. Instead, what I saw was my first naked man, layered in fur so he seemed like an animal, a burly brown bear, and poking from the pouch that hung between his legs was a separate little animal—a baby, a pet, like a baby kangaroo peeking out shyly and waving its arm. And what I felt then wasn't love at first sight, but my first sight of love, of what it could mean to love someone else, a stranger, not family, and how risky this was, loving a pitifully weak, naked man.

He clumsily paddled out a few yards, furry bum in the air.

"Don't you want to come in? Water's just right."

I shook my head no. "I don't have a suit," though this was ridiculous—neither did he. And the way that he looked at my body just then made me want to disclaim it: "That body's not mine, I haven't moved in." But I knew that I had, though I didn't feel at home yet, its corners still dark, its workings mysterious.

He was standing in the shallows up to his waist, slapping the water as a bear tries to slap a fish onto shore. This made the reflections of the trees and sky shimmer, then shatter to fragments of green, blue, and white, which were fragmented further by the drops on my glasses.

The goat-boy and Leon dragged themselves, dripping, onto the rocks to warm in the sun. "Man, don't those lizards have the right idea?" And they both fell asleep.

Grumbling because the stones cut his feet, the bear hobbled through the shallows. He sprawled by my side, draping his jump suit over his thighs.

"I'm lying here naked and you don't know my name." He held out a paw. "Meyer Rabinowitz. Pleased to meet you."

"Not Rufe?"

"Rufe? Oh yeah, this." He plucked at the jump suit. "Guess somewheres outside Atlanta, Georgia, a fella named Rufe is pumping gas naked."

"You're Jewish. And Southern." None of our relatives lived farther south than Paramus, New Jersey.

"If your mind can't stretch over those two categories, you'll never be a physicist. You've got to be able to imagine a thing"—the word came out *thang*—"being two thangs at once."

"A physicist? Who said I'd want to be that? Is that what you are? I thought they said you were some kind of astronaut."

"That's all right," he said. "Even my mother can't keep it straight. The difference is this: an astronaut goes up there, flying in space, but an astrophysicist only *thinks* about going, what the trip would be like."

"You never leave Earth?"

"A fat guy like me? Besides, I got asthma."

I was very disappointed, but glad that I hadn't really believed this was a man who could pass NASA's test. "It doesn't make sense. I don't understand how you think about space. What do you think about?"

"For now I just think about whatever my professors tell me to think about. But later . . . I mean, when I'm out on my own . . ." He leaned forward, excited, and his jump suit slipped a little, exposing his navel; its pattern resembled the continents and oceans dividing the earth. "What I'd really like to think about is what it's like living in higher dimensions."

I'd been fooled after all. "You're not talking science. You're talking the way the barbarians talk."

"Barbarians?" I waved my hand toward the dairy. He wagged his head, laughing. "That what you call them? How come 'barbarians'?"

"We learned it in school. The barbarians came down and took over Europe and except for the monks there, nobody read. They kept alive science while the vandals outside their caves pillaged and sacked."

"That what you think? You're really afraid of those hippies out there? You're an awful strange kid." I should have felt strange then. I'd felt strange all my life. I'd had the premonition I would never have allies, except false ones like Steven. But now I could see I was part of a team, and though our team, the monks, might be greatly outnumbered, I wouldn't have to fight the barbarians alone.

"Guess I'd better tell you about higher dimensions, in case it's all up to you." He slid down the rock; his toe stirred the pond. "It's this way," he said. "Suppose you had left a note for your parents: 'I went for a swim, and if you come looking here's where I'll be.'"

The example seemed ominous. Was he trying to say that I had been foolish not to leave such a note?

"Well, you'd need three dimensions to say where you were, three dimensions in *space*. And you'd have to let them know *when* you would be here or they'd miss you entirely. You and your parents would pass through each other in space-time, now wouldn't you?"

I guessed that we would and this made me feel sad, like Dorothy in Oz when she'd seen Auntie Em in the witch's glass ball and called out her name, "Auntie Em, Auntie Em," but hadn't been able to make her aunt hear.

"It's like this," he said, using a stone to draw on the rock the way little girls draw boards for hopscotch. When he finished I saw two ice cream cones with their pointy ends touching.

"See this point here?" Meyer placed his finger where the ice cream cones met. "That's us, here and now. And all this up here"—rubbing his finger on the right-side-up cone—"that's our future, okay? All the places and times we'd be able to reach moving at any speed slower than light. Because no one can ever go faster than light. You must have read that."

Although I had read this, the equations that proved it were a dense drape of lace I could not peer through to the reasons beyond, and so, in my ignorance, I was free to believe that once I got up there I'd show they were wrong, my rocket would tear that paper-thin curtain, that barrier of light.

I nodded. "I read it."

"But you think maybe somehow *you'll* find a way to go faster than light?"

I shrugged. I didn't want him to think I was boasting.

He snorted. "Okay. Everyone thinks that. But you'll find out you're wrong. This is the only future you'll have. And this cone back here, this cone's our past. And all of this other stuff, outside the cones, all this is elsewhere."

"Elsewhere?" I said.

"Sure," Meyer said. "Out here is elsewhere, the places you and I can't ever reach, can't ever have been, because even if we traveled fast as a light beam all our born days, that's far as we'd get."

I still felt defiant. "How do they know?"

"Because there are limits. Who knows, maybe angels can live out in elsewhere, but people can only live in the past, or the future, or now." He seemed to be thinking aloud for my benefit and this eased the frustration of having to travel slower than light. "Animals, I suppose, can just live in now, we're ahead of them there. People at least can imagine what it's like to live out in elsewhere. At least we have that."

I was going to ask him to help me imagine what elsewhere was like, but a cough tore the stillness. The goat-boy and Leon had awakened, I saw, and were passing a cigarette back and forth, back and forth. I was stunned by this intimacy. Then something—the smell, like some bittersweet flower, or the curve of their cheeks as they sucked at the smoke—shocked me the way that seeing a movie star in person can shock.

"But they're smart guys!" I said. "Leon knows math."

He shrugged his big shoulders. "Smart guys do dumb thangs. Leon thinks it helps him visualize thangs like imaginary numbers. And Fitz, well, he likes it, he can't seem to stop."

I suddenly glimpsed the future and it had no Fitz in it. His mother was weeping, haunting this rock and weeping for a son who had killed himself smoking too much marijuana.

"Why are you here?" I asked Meyer brusquely.

"You mean, why are the three of us here at this pond?"

"No, I mean all of you. Why did you come?"

"Me? I don't know. The music, I suppose. I needed a rest before the next term. I like the outdoors. And I figure it's good to pack in as many thangs as you can before you're too old. Some of them, like Fitz, they came for the ride. And a few of them were hoping to find somethang . . . big. I guess they found that. Somethang big, somethang pure. You know what you see when you look at the moon? You think it's all right to spend your whole life trying to get there, it's so big and pure? That's how they feel. They don't even see the mud that they're sitting in. They found somethang pure."

"Does that mean they'll *stay*?"

He laughed. "I don't think so. No matter how stoned you are, you can't ignore the mud and the stink and the hunger for more than a while. Not if you're human. You can't live in elsewhere, you can't live in space, you can't live in squalor much more than a week."

My relief didn't last long; he asked me politely if I'd please turn my head, and when I looked back he was standing and dressed.

"Hey, don't y'all think we should go?" he shouted to the others. "Don't want to miss Hendrix. That's why I came." Then he turned back to me. "You've been very kind." He held out his hands and lifted me up. "Don't look so glum. World's not so big. We could meet again."

I wanted to set a place and a time, all four dimensions, so I'd know he'd be waiting and the years wouldn't feel long. Before I could say this, Leon had bowed and the goat-boy had kissed the back of my hand and all three had left.

I must have found my way back to the house, lain brooding on my lounge chair, but no events marked the passage of time so those hours are lost. I only remember when my parents returned. I heard noise in the kitchen and went up to join them.

"I've a mind to press charges!" My father was rifling the drawer by the sink. "The cowards!" he said. He took out the Band-Aids and slammed the drawer shut. This noise from my father was as shocking as speech from a mute would have been. He handed the box of Band-Aids to my mother, who was slumped on a stool, and that's when I noticed her checked blouse was ripped. A safety pin held the pieces together but a slice of bright pink brassiere still winked through.

"How did you do that?"

"There's no need to tell her," he cautioned my mother. "The son's in her class."

"It was someone I know?" Why would anyone I know rip my mother's checked blouse?

She applied a small Band-Aid to a scratch on her wrist. "Oh it's nothing," she said, though she'd never drooped so badly—her anklets had vanished into her shoes. "We ran into old Mr. Dwyer in town, and he and a few of the neighbors are furious that we'd try to help—"

My *father* was furious. "If they don't want to buy Max's milk anymore, that's their prerogative. But ripping a blouse! Scratching a woman who tries to do good!"

Since my father spent his days delivering milk and was so smooth and pale, I'd always half-thought his essence was milk, which I guess meant untroubled, innocent, clean, but his face was so streaked and his features so clouded I couldn't help but think of the milk behind the dairy that was left to be dumped, it was tainted or sour.

My mother was holding her hands to her blouse, hanging her head. "It was partly my fault. When I pushed him away my arm caught his buckle."

I tied to imagine my mother wrestling with old Mr. Dwyer—he was only an inch or two taller than she was, and quite a bit plumper.

"And blaming the Jews! To say Max is a kike who rented his land to Communists because he can't resist money!" He had always assumed that since he was privileged to open the boxes on his neighbors' back stoops and decipher the notes they'd left him inside ("Judd has an ulcer . . ." "Can't pay this week . . ." "Miscarriage . . ." "Transfer . . ."), because they allowed him to see them in curlers and torn robes or long johns he knew who they were.

"If that farmer wants a lesson in manners," he said, "he should look at those kids. Who would expect they would be so polite? Look what they gave, for a few quarts of milk." He pulled a feather from his pocket; in a crate by the door were a string of purple beads, a collection of hats of all sorts and shapes, a broken guitar, a bouquet of weeds in a ponytail wrapper, a freshly whittled flute, and a cookbook whose recipes were blessed by a man whose mustache and nose made him resemble my grandfather Morris. "So maybe they don't act like people like us. The young men don't mind if their girlfriends show off their bodies in public—not to say the girls have bodies to shame them. Such big, healthy girls!" And his face made me think he was seeing them now, those big, naked girls.

"And the little ones." My mother refastened the pin so it hid the pink bra. (Why had she bought it? Her others were white.) "In town they were saying the diseases are dreadful—they can't get the pumps in to drain out the toilets."

My father joined in. "If a fire breaks out . . ."

"I guess I should open a can of soup for dinner." My mother didn't move. "But I'd feel guilty eating with those poor hungry children . . . and sleeping tonight on a bed with clean sheets . . ."

That was it! I'd invite them to sleep in our house, in cots in my room.

I left my parents sitting on the floor in the kitchen, sifting through the relics they'd acquired that day, and I almost wish I hadn't—my father was never so silent again, my mother drooped much more often, it seemed. And though their confrontation with old Mr. Dwyer only began a chain of events that made them feel less and less part of the town, I blame this beginning for their decision many years later to do what they'd said they never would do: they moved away from Bethel when my father retired. And then they kept moving, trying new places—they even bought a camper, lived in that for a year—as if once they'd been knocked from their tiny fixed orbits, they wobbled, unrestrained, all over the country: first Florida, then Phoenix, then Houston near me (I was glad when they left, afraid they'd find out I wasn't as smart as they'd once thought, wasn't destined for greatness; the machines made my job seem more impressive than it actually was). They still tried to see only the best in the people they met, even if this meant they had to move on before seeing the worst. And whenever I got a postcard from someplace like L.A. or Reno, I feared for their innocence as once I had scorned it, and I was impatient with their wanderings as I had once been impatient with their unchanging lives. Because even though I didn't want to go home to Bethel, I felt they should be there in case that I did; I felt I'd gone swimming and they'd stolen the shore.

It was five when I left them. The day had been clear, but now, as I walked, two thin black clouds swirled through the sky like a helicopter's rotors slicing the sun. In the shadows of a corn field I made out two men, one holding his fly, the patter of his urine spraying the stalks, the other man squatting with his pants to his knees. When the wind came I thought it was bringing their smell, but as I walked on, the air thickened with the odor of three-day-old garbage and I had to pull the neck of my jersey over my nose to inhale the fresh breeze captured in the fabric days before on the line. How could they stand it? But then I remembered what the goat-boy had said about people not being able to smell their own smell, and what Meyer had told me about people who wanted so badly to think they'd found something pure that they wouldn't smell its smell, at least for a while.

The sky was gray-black and the winds had picked up so they swirled bits of litter over my head. I heard human howls and grunts from the woods, saw flames here and there, and I almost turned back—the trucks wouldn't get through and we all would be burned. But then I saw faces bobbing over the flames like yellow balloons and I realized these people were cooking their dinners, what little they had, though how could they eat with so many flies? These rose from the mud with each step I took, settled on my eyelids, trapped themselves in my ears. I could hear trees and wires snapping like whips, and the throb of the music—I couldn't hear the words—and thunder, in the distance, and the helicopters grinding over our heads.

And though I brag now about having grown up there, having been in that crowd when I was thirteen, the truth is I only remember my terror, my wish to escape. I wandered those fields I'd known all my life, picking my way among feet, heads, and limbs. I stepped over bodies face-down in the mud, and I knew it was hopeless, I'd never find Meyer or the goat-boy or Leon.

I saw a big tent. I went in and stood. A woman in a uniform came up and said: "Honey, are you in there? What did you take?" snapping her fingers in front of my eyes.

"No time for that, just get her a blanket." Dr. Rock, rushing by, glanced at my face without recognition. "These fucking asshole parents ought to be shot, exposing a kid to something like this."

The nurse took my arm but I shook her off. I saw Steven kneeling by a female barbarian, swabbing a cut. He was still shining white but the whiteness was stained, which unsettled me as much as seeing a statue spattered with blood. His eyes weren't focused, so it took him a while to see that I'd come.

"You're too late," he said. "This woman had a baby . . . and this other one, she had . . . My father said some butcher must have done a bad job but I'm not really sure . . . And this kid, he was sleeping, and some jerk on a tractor thought the sleeping bag was empty. . . . And this one diabetic who didn't bring her insulin, she went into shock. What jerks! I mean, coming to someplace like this and you don't bring your medicine? And these guys on bad trips, one had this knife and he came at my father—"

"Goddamn it, Steven, get your ass over here!"

Steven obeyed, leaving me at the edge of the tent. The wind ripped right through, blowing gauze pads from carts rattling bottles. The canvas roof billowed and the center pole shook so I went back outside, out in the rain, which tore at my skin. A dozen barbarians were stomping and sliding and splashing one another but everyone else was huddled together close to the ground, holding garbage bags, sleeping bags, parkas, and blankets over their heads; in the half-light it seemed the ground itself shook.

"Hey, come on in."

Slowly I knelt and took shelter under a huge plastic tarp. It was humid and dark, body to body. Someone put an arm over my shoulder and we started to sway; people were chanting "no rain, no rain" as though this were a spell to make the rain stop. We were so many people so close together I had the sensation of losing my boundaries—the wind had stripped off the walls of the house that I had moved into only that day, and I had trouble telling where my own body ended and the others began.

This scared me so much I said half-aloud: "I'm not far from home. I've been here before." And I pictured the field the way I had seen it thousands of times, the green and gold pasture with its intricate shading and texture of weeds, clover, alfalfa, a great green bowl rising to a rim where it met a blue sky with clouds like the blue-and-white china in my mother's glass cabinet, and the land beyond that, with its swells and depressions, so a tractor would sink and disappear a moment, then float back to view.

I tried to imagine the scent of fresh hay warmed by the sun, but the stench of the present brought me back to this place. I was stuck in this time and would never get out. We would die in this place, buried in mud, so that years in the future, archaeologists would stand here and see only dirt, though they might sniff our presence under the earth and know we had lived, know we had once been huddled together under this tarp chanting "no rain, no rain" as if we believed that we could get elsewhere simply by wishing as hard as we could.

Eileen Pollack is the author of a collection of stories, *The Rabbi in the Attic*, a novel, *Paradise, New York*, and a work of creative nonfiction, *Woman Walking Ahead: In Search of Catherine Weldon and Sitting Bull*. She is co-director of the MFA Program in Creative Writing at the University of Michigan in Ann Arbor. A new collection of stories, *In the Mouth*, is forthcoming from Four Way Books.

WHAT I'VE BEEN TOLD WITH REGARD TO THE PIANIST

ELIZABETH ELLEN

HE'S 6'1".

His wife is a nurse.

He has a son three years younger than me.

He sits in on Tuesdays and Thursdays at the Lion's Den on South Main, which is where Mom ran into him. They'd gone to school together, years before. He's two years older than she is. He's the same age as my uncle. He and his wife split up a long time ago. They split up before Mom ran into him.

On the way to school we stop for donuts and she tells me that he used to be a heroin addict. "He moved out west and sold his body to men to pay for his habit," she says and I picture Samuel standing on some street corner in a flat, western town I've never been to waiting for the highest bidder to come and claim their prize, to fold their dirty bills into his clenched fists. "He took their appendages into his mouth and let them do whatever they wanted to with his," she adds, pulling a maple-frosted from the bag between us and breaking it gently in two with the same strong hands that chop our wood and build our fires. She dunks each half twice into her mug then shoves them whole into her mouth while I watch, wondering about the current state of Sam's appendage and the cleanliness of my mother's mouth.

"After seven years he moved back here," she tells me as we climb into the truck for a second time this morning, the remains of our breakfast tossed onto the dash in a rolled up sack with pink and brown lettering. "He told me that's how long it takes to lose your taste for the stuff. He said that if you can manage to stay alive that long, you walk away a free man."

At school I think about that, about the possibility of outlasting a desire once so strong a person was willing to soil every orifice of their body in order to fulfill it, and wonder why it isn't the same with the gins and tonics and scotches and sodas that litter our living room in the evening hours after I've gone to bed. I think of how my mother's skin glistens in the morning sunlight as the alcohol rises to the surface, seeping through her pores. I think of becoming intoxicated in her goodbye kisses, of looking back over my shoulder and waving as I stumble up the steps to school with children whose mothers smell only of Folgers and Marlboros and who protect them with the withholding of truths and the telling of lies.

My mother and I are in a near-constant state of fluctuation. We move annually from one rented farmhouse to the next while the men we know rotate in and out of our lives like the cats and dogs she brings home for me and then gives away. After the men have gone, and sometimes before they've left, she confesses to me their sins, lists for me their strengths and weaknesses:

"Larry's penis was long and thin, like a pencil, like he was writing sonnets inside of me; Dusty's is uncircumcised, which took some getting used to; Michael wasn't that large but he made up for it in other ways; Henry only has one testicle. People say it's on account of a woman, that she cut the other one off, but the truth is, it never descended; Russell's is enormous, almost too big, really; your father was only comfortable doing it in the missionary position; Samuel's is long and lean like the rest of him, just like you'd imagine it to be."

There is a lot for me to remember and even more for me to forget. There have been three husbands and many more lovers. There have been ditch diggers and bartenders, tool and dye workers and cemetery caretakers, raquetball players and soul singers. Russell taught karate at the Y and for the six months he lived with us I got free lessons on Wednesday nights. Dusty worked at the dairy and brought home fresh bottles of milk on Mondays and gallons of ice cream on Saturdays. My last stepfather drove a tow truck during the day and sold pot at night. There was a party in our living room every weekend when he was here.

Samuel is a pianist.

On our way to the library she tells me he was a child prodigy and I wonder why she didn't tell me this before. "When Sam was seventeen he was accepted into Julliard where people like Superman and Mork went to school. He could be playing Lincoln Center right now," she says, trailing off. She lights a cigarette and dials in the classical station on the radio. Since Sam moved in we've been listening to Keith Jarrett and the other jazz pianists he tells her about. Our record collection expands each time she brings someone new home. Michael liked Steely Dan and The Eagles. Larry played Ray Charles all night and James Brown all day. My mother likes whatever they like. This week she likes Keith Jarrett.

The day he moved in she neglected to mention anything about it to me. I walked into the house after school, expecting to find it empty as usual, and found instead a baby grand in the dining room. Samuel was bent over it, his back to me, too engrossed in the pounding of keys to notice my intrusion. I stood for some time in the doorway, my book bag slung over my shoulder, watching this man I did not know, watching his head jerk up and down and back and forth, as though in an epileptic fit, not so much playing the piano as attacking it. It was only when he stopped to retrieve his sack of tobacco from the windowsill beside me that he saw me and called to me by name.

He looks nothing like the others she has brought home. He bears little resemblance to the lumberjacks and plumbers who sit nightly at the bar where she works, watching as she bends and straightens, filling their glasses and letting them take turns lighting her cigarettes; or the ones who come in on their lunch hours just to hear her say their names. He's tall and lanky and looks like he could stand a good meal. His hair is sandy and thinning and reaches the back of his collar, and his mustache is thick and wiry. He dresses in worn corduroys and elbow-patched cardigans and I think he looks more like a professor or a poet than a junkie or a failed prodigy. And when he speaks he uses words I've never heard before, words like fabricated

163

and Kafkaesque, and I have to look them up or ask my mother what they mean.

"By age five he was composing his own music," my mother says proudly, as though he were her child rather than her lover, as though she had anything to do with it, and I think of her mother, my grandmother, telling me of my mother's early acceptance into Northwestern.

And later in the evening, as I lay in my bed feeling the vibrations of a Schubert symphony rattling the floorboards and windows of my room, I think of the yellowing sheets of paper under my mother's bed and the lines of poetry jotted onto them in her careful hand.

At school we're working with clay. Mr. Hoffman, our art teacher, says it's up to us to decide what to make. He shows us the objects he's made in the past: bowls, vases, pencil holders. He says these are just examples. He says that really, the possibilities are endless. I roll the ball of clay I've been given around in my hand and stare out the window. It's late November and there is no snow on the ground. Both the sky and earth are dark and it's nearly impossible to tell where one ends and the other begins. The clay is wet and cold and feels good pressed against my cheek and in my hand. I watch Julie. In her hands is a sickly giraffe. I wonder why she made it so thin. Its elongated neck can barely support its head. I stare too long. She turns her eyes to meet mine and I quickly look away. I stare back down at the gray matter in my hand. Mr. Hoffman told us when he handed out our clay that these would make excellent Christmas presents. He said to think of someone special before we begin. So I think of my mother. But as I'm thinking of her I start thinking of Samuel too. I set the ball on the table and with the knife I've been given, divide it in two.

Heather rides the bus home with me. She says she wants to meet Samuel. She says she's never seen a pianist or a heroin addict before and she wants to see Samuel before it's too late. "But he's not addicted to heroin anymore," I remind her, but she doesn't answer, she's too busy concocting images in her head.

He's not there when we get home. The house is silent and his car is gone. Heather sits at the kitchen table lighting my mother's cigarette butts while I make snacks to take upstairs. We sit on my bedroom floor watching TV and eating. Heather listens for cars. When she hears one she jumps to her feet.

"It's him!" she says, watching Samuel from my window. "Come on!"

But I don't stand. I stay where I am, watching *General Hospital* and breaking graham crackers into bite sized pieces.

"Not yet," I say. "He's not the elephant man. Jeez."

An hour later, just before her father comes to pick her up, we sneak silently down the stairs. We pirouette across the living room floor and peek our heads around the dining room wall. The room is smoke-filled and dark and Samuel is barely visible within the candle's flickering flame.

Heather watches with a hand covering her pink mouth, an attempt at containing the giggles that convulse her body in rhythm with his. I watch alongside her, wondering why he's here in our house, being made a fool of by little girls, instead of in a concert hall before an appreciate audience.

"Come on," I say, tugging on Heather's sleeve. "You've seen him and your father will be here any minute."

After she's gone Sam sits at the kitchen table making red marks on an essay I have to finish for English while I open cans of tuna and boil noodles. I want to apologize for Heather, for the way she looked at him, but I stop myself. When she left she shook his hand and smiled at him real big like she meant it and he probably thought she did.

I set the table for two and sit down next to him. He asks me to pass the salt and I ask him what he thinks of my essay and this is how it goes and it feels okay.

The house is silent except for their voices. The dog she found on the side of the road is asleep beside me. I lift my head to look at the clock. It says 12:39. I have to be up at 5:30 in order to make the bus. I should have been asleep three hours ago.

I slip down the stairs without making a sound. I pass their bedroom on my way to the bathroom. On the way back I see that their door is ajar. I stop on the first step. The heels of my feet dangle in midair and my right hand grips tightly to the railing. I could hover here all night. I could hover here forever.

Her bedroom flickers with light and I want to run into it. In between men she allows me into her bed. She says she doesn't like sleeping alone. I crane my neck to hear what they're saying but their voices are overpowered by the music on her radio and the ice swimming feverishly in their glasses.

In the morning I will ask her what it is they do in her bed all night and she will tell me that they read. "But I hear you talking," I will say. "I hear your voices beneath me all night long."

"We're reading aloud to each other," she will tell me, blowing smoke from her nose like the bad girl in a movie I once watched. "We read passages from *Tropic of Cancer* and *A Spy in the House of Love*. Samuel gave them to me. He says they will help me with my poetry. He says I should keep writing."

My mother will tell me these things in the morning as she walks from the bathroom to the kitchen, naked and smoking. She will talk to me as I wipe the crumbs and smears of grape jelly from the counter and she stands in front of our fridge, drinking juice from the pitcher. She will kiss me goodbye and pitter-patter back to her bed with the pianist while I walk down our drive singing to myself and wondering if it will ever snow.

Christmas morning we sit in a circle in front of the wood burner with mugs of warm tea and Samuel opens my present first. He unwraps it carefully, as though it's been handed to him by an angel or a new lover, and I turn away embarrassed by my rudimentary creation. I have made men presents before: pictures of rainbows and the families that live beneath them, lopsided bookends, and needlepoint pillows. I have given these presents without reddening my cheeks or staring uncomfortably at my feet.

Samuel pulls my ceramic ashtray from the tissue inside the box and holds it up for my mother to see. She smiles and nods and holds her cigarette out as if to ash and he pulls it back away.

"It's so beautiful it's almost a shame to dirty it," he says, turning it over in his hands, fingering the indentations of my initials on its underbelly. "Would you mind if I use it?"

I can feel his eyes on me. I can no longer avoid them. I lift my gaze to meet his.

"Yes," I say. "I mean, no. I don't mind at all."

"Great," he says, lifting his pouch of tobacco from his pocket and pouring it into a pile on the coffee table beside his tea. "Go ahead and open mine," he tells me, nodding at a flat, square box leaning against the tree. It is wrapped in the Sunday comics and has my name written across it in red felt tip. I want to take it to my room and open it where no one can see me. I don't want my reaction to disappoint him. I open it carefully. I peel back one corner and then another and soon Michael Jackson is smiling at me in a white suit. I'm so excited I forget all about monitoring my reaction. I run to the stereo. I tear off the cellophane. I place the record on our player and lower the needle slowly down onto it and Vincent Price narrates the rest of our Christmas.

It's a Friday night in the middle of January and she's working late again. She works weekends whenever she can because that's when she makes the most tips. She brings them home, stuffed deep down in her purse, and in the morning we spill them out onto her bed and separate them into piles of quarters and nickels and dimes and dollars.

Tonight she's busy and barely has time to talk to us. I watch her from our booth as I eat my fries and grilled cheese. She's pacing up and down behind the bar and I hope she's making good tips. Sam pushes his plate to the end of the table and lights a cigarette. Then he looks at me like he's got something to say and I take a bite of my sandwich before he says it.

"Listen, maybe we could do something tonight. See a movie or something. Before we go home."

My mouth's full so I think about this for a minute while I chew. I glance back at the bar and Mom looks at me and gives me a little wave. I lift my hand to wave back but she's already busy talking to one of her regulars again and doesn't notice. I rest my hand back in my lap.

"Sure," I say, wiping my mouth with a paper napkin. "I guess."

"Well, we don't have to. I just thought it might be fun, instead of just going home and watching TV."

"Yeah." I look again at my mother, wondering if he's already asked her about this.

"Great then. So what do you want to see?"

"I don't know," I say. We haven't been to the movies since he moved in.

"You like Paul Newman?" he asks and I can tell he's hoping that I do. My grandmother likes Paul Newman. I've seen *Cool Hand Luke*. I laughed when he ate the fifty eggs.

"Sure."

"Cool. There's this movie called *The Verdict* with him in it that I've been wanting to see . . . "

"Doesn't Mom want to see it?"

"I don't know. We haven't talked about it yet. But I don't mind seeing it twice."

"What's it rated?"

"Oh. I honestly have no idea. But if it's R we can say I'm your guardian. You could be my daughter. They'll never know."

I nod my head and think about his son. I wonder where he is tonight and if he's ever been to an R-rated movie. This will be my first. I think I should ask Mom if it's okay.

"Hey, I've got a couple quarters. How 'bout we play a game or two before we go," Sam says. When he smiles I can see his chipped tooth. It's sharp like a dagger.

He leaves money on the table for the waitress and puts his hand on the small of my back as we walk to the backroom where the pool table and video games are. Mom likes Galaxia. She's really good at it. She plays it on her breaks and when it's slow. On the days she works, she always has the high score. Sam drops two quarters into Asteroids and waves his hand toward the machine indicating that I should go first. I take a deep breath and stand at attention. I suck at Asteroids. Within ten seconds I'm dead.

On the way to the movie Sam stops to get gas. He runs in to pay and on the way back out, before he fills his tank, he knocks on my window and hands me three dollar bills.

"Here," he says. "Buy yourself some candy. It's a rip off at the theatre. I always buy mine beforehand."

I walk into the filling station and stand in the candy aisle for five minutes like I'm picking out my engagement ring instead of a chocolate bar. I'm not allowed to eat things like Twinkies or Pop Tarts or Fun Dip. For dessert Mom scoops spoon- fuls of homemade yogurt into a dish and drizzles it with orange juice concentrate. "White sugar is the worst thing you can eat," she tells me. "White sugar is like poison to your body."

"Can't find anything?"

I spin around on my heels. Sam is standing behind me with a Marathon bar in one hand and a can of grape soda in the other. I grab a Reese's and an Orange Crush and take them to the counter.

"Good choice," Sam says as we slide into the car and stuff our pockets with our loot.

The movie is long and sad and halfway through I've already eaten all my candy and finished my can of pop. My eyes are heavy and I close them for a second or two and then squirm in my seat. I lean to the side and rest my cheek on my fist and close my eyes again. When I open them the credits are rolling and people are standing at their seats and picking up their empty cups and buckets.

"Man, that was bleak but beautiful and so well written," Sam says and when he says this I look up at him and I can see that his eyes are damp and red-rimmed like mine were when Mom took me to see *Kramer Vs. Kramer*. "Newman deserves an Oscar for that. Did you like it?"

"Yeah," I say. "But it was really sad."

"I hope you're not disappointed," Sam says, pulling his coat over his shoulders then helping me with mine.

I shake my head. "I'm not. I really liked it. I like sad movies."

"Good," Sam says, his hand on the small of my back again.

Outside the parking lot looks like the inside of a snow globe and every car looks the same. The pavement is slick and I stumble and have to hold out my arms like a tightrope walker to steady myself. Sam walks up next to me and takes my hand and we walk the rest of the way together and I don't fall or stumble again.

It's 11:30 when we get home but he doesn't say anything about going to bed so I put the kettle on and make us tea while he carries in wood and throws it on the fire.

He sits on the couch and I stand with my back pressed against the wood burner until it's too hot and I can't stand it anymore and then I sit down on the couch across from him. We sip our tea and he rolls a cigarette while I glance at the comics in *The New Yorker* because it's the only thing within reach.

"What's your favorite movie?" he says finally, breaking the silence and lighting the end of his cigarette and I set the magazine down on my lap and squint my eyes to indicate that I'm thinking and after a few seconds have passed I say, "I don't know . . . E.T.?" because I always begin every answer with "I don't know" even when I do.

"You know, I haven't seen that yet. But I want to. I wanted to take my—"

I hold my breath, thinking he's going to talk about his kid for once, but before he can finish his sentence, my mother's headlights illuminate the window behind him and I jump from the couch. I scurry up the stairs to hide like a puppy that has soiled the carpet even though I'm not sure that I've done anything wrong.

"Hey, baby," I hear her call as she sets her keys down on the table. "Man, what a night. I'm shot."

"Yeah?" he answers. "Come here then and I'll give you a rubdown."

I fall asleep listening to their faraway voices. I listen to the animation and urgency in hers and the calm, soothing tone of his. I'm not sure what it feels like to have a father but I'm guessing it's not too different from this.

In February I come home from school and Sam's car is gone and one I've never seen before is parked in its spot beside my mother's. It's a green Nova with Florida plates and I try to remember who we know in Florida.

I set my book bag down on the kitchen table and pour myself a glass of water. I can hear my mother laughing in the living room. I walk through the dining room with the glass still in my hand. My mother and a woman I've never seen before are on the couch. Each of them has a glass of wine in her hand and Stevie Nicks is playing on our turntable.

"There you are, sweetie," my mother says. "We were just talking about you.

Honey, this is Mickey. She's a good friend of mine."

I say hi and nice to meet you, too and then I walk back to the kitchen and make myself some toast and wonder where Samuel is and why he's not here.

Two nights later I wake up to a fight. I hear crying and pleading and then I hear what sounds like a slab of meat being thrown against our front door. I look outside. Sam's car is parked in its usual spot. I listen from my perch at the top of the steps to more pleadings and apologies and sobbing of indistinguishable gender. I pull my arms inside my nightgown and wrap them around my body to stop my shivering.

After a while when the voices have quieted and the sobs have been contained, I crawl back into my bed. My body is still shaking and I pull my blankets up to my chin and wait for warmth. As I feel myself drifting back into sleep I think I can hear the faint sounds of a melancholy symphony from outside my window. I want to rise, to look down at the field below and the woods beyond, but I am already too far gone and before I know it is morning and I am unable to distinguish what was real and what I imagined.

She's moved her bed upstairs into the room across from mine, though she swears she is not afraid. She calls me into the room and lifts the covers to me and I slide my body beneath them and toward her. We sit in the dark with our backs resting against the wall and the dog at our feet. An ax leans against the mattress, beneath her fingertips, and it feels like we're waiting for a bear or a monster to enter her room and tear us to shreds.

"I asked him to move out," she answers though I haven't asked a question. "Last night. Things just weren't working out."

She pauses, as though waiting for me to say something, but I don't have anything to say.

"He's probably on his way here now. Smoke just called to let me know that Sam left the bar a couple minutes ago. He said he was pretty drunk."

She lights another cigarette and takes a drink from her glass. The dog whines in his sleep. His paws tread air and I wonder how much longer before we have to move again.

"It's funny. He took a shot at his first wife once. They'd been drinking all night. Lucky for them both, the man has terrible aim."

She leans her head back and closes her eyes and takes another drag off her cigarette. She laughs without opening her mouth.

"You can never be too careful with men," she says. "Which is different than being afraid, okay? Even the most peaceful of men, even Gandhi himself, are capable of ordinary violence when a woman stops loving them the way they want to be loved, the way they believe themselves entitled to be loved, especially if he's drunk on cheap whiskey."

The dog sits up first. He sits and cocks his head and looks around and we sit up too. A car is crawling down our drive. The dog barks and my mother grabs him and pulls him between us. She holds his head under her arm as the car door slams and footsteps are heard on our porch. I've seen my mother decapitate a turkey on

Thanksgiving. I've felt her hands wrapped around my neck when I've talked back. I tell myself I'm not afraid.

Samuel knocks on the door. "Julia! Julia, open up! I know you're in there." His voice is high-pitched and frantic, barely recognizable. He calls her name again; he screams it over and over through the glass. He pounds both fists on the door. He does all the things men in movies do to make their wrath known to the women who have wronged them while we do what women in movies do when the men who once professed to love them suddenly want to kill them: we don't move, we stay silent and wait for him to go away. Eventually, he does.

When we can no longer hear the familiar hum of his engine, she lights a candle and opens a book. I turn on my side and stick my nose under her arm where the dog's was and when I wake up it is morning, it's after eight and I've missed my bus.

We're on our way to dinner when she tells me that she's heard he's left town. "Smoke said Sam stopped in last night to say goodbye. He said he mentioned something about heading back out west." She says this as casually as she mentions the forecast and my throat tightens and I have to swallow real hard.

For six weeks the piano sat in our dining room, waiting, like a packed suitcase or a bundled child. I'd pass by it after school and on my way to the kitchen. I'd sit on the bench and trace my initials in the dust with my fingertips. When Mickey moved in she started using it for storage. She piled her sheets and towels and clothes on top of it and stacked her record collection on the bench.

She took to borrowing the ashtray I'd made him as well. I'd find it on the edge of the tub after she'd had a bath and in the kitchen after dinner. Each time I'd wash and dry it and set it back on the piano next to his music. A week after she moved in, after finding it in her bedroom after school, I wrote SAM on a piece of paper and taped it across the top.

The next day both the ashtray and the piano were gone.

"I hope wherever he goes, he keeps playing," my mother says, as though he has a choice. "You know what they say: musicians make great lovers."

I laugh and roll my eyes, knowing this is probably something she's read on a bumper sticker or on the cover of a magazine at the grocery store.

"It's true," she says. "Samuel had very strong and agile fingers."

I've stopped laughing. I'm already thinking of something else.

"Hey, Mom," I begin. "Today Mr. Lowry told us that our cells are constantly replacing themselves. He said that about every seven years we are completely new people."

"That's interesting," she says, changing the dial on the radio. We haven't listened to the classical station in weeks. "Hey, did I tell you that Mickey is an archer? She wants to take us both out shooting sometime."

Mom parks the car next to Mickey's and we walk inside. Mickey's in the back playing a video game and I stare at her fingers as I watch. They are thick and callused and I wonder where they've been. She's playing a game I've never seen before. Galaxia and Space Invaders are gone.

....

"I can't believe it's snowing in March," my mother says as we pull down our drive.

She waits outside for Mickey. I can see her car turning in as I walk into the house. The fire has died out and it's freezing. I can see my breath. I go into the kitchen and make a cup of tea. I watch Mom and Mickey from the window. They're taking turns with the ax. They're laughing and having a good time. I carry my tea into the dining room and open the record player. I look through Mom's albums. All the way at the back I find Keith Jarrett. I put on *The Koln Concert*, Sam's favorite. I lie in the middle of the rug, boxed in by the grooves etched into it from the piano's feet, the only remaining evidence of Samuel's existence in our lives. I close my eyes and think about being a different person in seven years. I think about all of us being different people: me, Mom, Sam, Mickey. I wonder if we'll love the same people or brand new ones. I wonder if we'll remember or if the heart has a memory all its own.

They say he moved to Oregon.

He's got a sister out there. A niece. A nephew.

They say he plays piano in a bar in Portland, but no one really knows for sure. You hear things and sometimes they're true and sometimes they're not.

He's 6'1".

He used to be a heroin addict.

Elizabeth Ellen does not have an M.F.A. In fact, she dropped out of college after only her second year. But, she reads a lot. She hopes this counts for something.

SUPERBOY DOES NOT LOVE DUO DAMSEL

RAY MCDANIEL

I've come to you
just to see you do
what I know you'll do

which is leave her even though
it will look as if she is leaving you
and I know that and so does Claude Raines

and maybe Conrad Veidt
but not everyone in *Casablanca*
mixed-up crowd and a few crickets

anyway this girls I'm with
two mono-twins
in the backseat of Pa's car

she's spooky, these two,
well she wants to see some
gothic space movie

living intestines and dead intestines
but I want to see you
just like you wanted that same old song

even though it was no darn good—

I've spent all day in the future-pool
chemical stink and age
for skin less than steel

these girls finish each other's sentences
'gosh I'd like a root beer?'
I'm ganged up and outnumbered

when one of her slides
from the inflatable dolphin
and says she thinks I am keen

a weak solution
of Halloween payday & rust
but for just a second

I think it is the other
whose lips are moving
anyways I know

every word to this movie
except what the Nazis say
and the boring bits in Paris

but yes to the airport scene
and all the banter and I'm asking you
how can you be so sure

about what you don't want

Due to an industrial accident involving experimental pan-dimensional energies, **Raymond McDaniel** is not now, nor has he ever been. This didn't stop him from writing a book, though. It's called *Murder*.

HEADLESS AND BLUE
STEVE AMICK

SOMETHING JUST WASN'T right with The Headless Horseman. For one thing, it was getting a bit dull. Year in, year out, it was the same old same old. *Ugh*, he thought, *here we go again . . .*

He stood in his kitchen, contemplating the Post-It he'd left for himself on the refrigerator, overwhelmed by the timelessness of the thing; the melancholy of deja vu. The note read:

From the desk of *The Headless Horseman . . .*

To do:
- *pick up black cloak from cleaners*

- *buy pumpkin / carve jack o' lantern*

- *groom horse*

- *find victim / chase / collect head*

It could pretty much be any other year, it was now so routine. He could do this in his sleep.

But he wondered if it was something else making him blue; something more personal. Maybe—just maybe—he was starting to dread Halloween because of how he felt about himself, not The Night itself or the grisly work involved. It was hard to admit, but if he were to be truly honest, he'd have to confess he just wasn't all that thrilled with his personal appearance. Oprah had just done a show on that, called "Loving Your Looks." Experts came on and talked about how it was getting increasingly difficult, in our aesthetically-obsessed, have-it-all culture, to feel good about oneself without rushing off to the cosmetic surgeon. And it had struck a chord with him. More than once, feeling low and sort of ugly, he had considered consulting one, though he wasn't completely certain even a cosmetic surgeon could do much for headlessness. He'd made a few exploratory phone calls, just to see what the possibilities were, but most of them said right up front he pretty much needed something in the way of a head to give them a good foundation on which to build.

But he told himself it wasn't *that*—it wasn't him. It was just the drudgery. Had to be. After all, to be cursed to walk the earth for all eternity was one thing, but to be sentenced to a hick town like Sleepy Hollow? Please. Maybe if he could haunt a bridge somewhere hip and happening—like Portland or Seattle maybe. But Sleepy Hollow—you could pull a Rip Van Winkle and not miss a thing. Last big thing that happened around here was the Blockbuster Video opening. There was a parade.

But still, he had to admit, the whole headless thing *was* getting a little depressing. It was starting to affect everything. He couldn't even make a trip to the mall without people pointing and whispering. To get there, he had to take the bus—the headlessness problem having impeded his qualifying for a drivers' license—and invariably a few tough guys would get confrontational, calling him a monster and lumping him in with Jeffrey Dahmer and Ed Gein and Ted Bundy. Which was totally unfair. Those guys were sickos. He, on the other hand, was part of a long-established folk tradition. He served the community, for Christ's sake. Gave the place color, civic pride. The least he expected was to be able to go buy a shirt at the Gap without some bully calling him names and getting him down about himself.

Even so, he thought, one must carry on.

It was one of the unforeseen disadvantages to living in a condo community—these xeroxed flyers the management shoved under his door, cheerfully announcing some dreadful forced fun down at the clubhouse. This one, printed on a candycorn orange with cheesy silhouette icons of high-backed cats and bats in flight, announced that there were would be a Singles Mixer the following night. *Pre-Halloween* was the excuse. It figured: the non-loser people—the families and kids—would get the clubhouse on The Night, while the singles got the leftovers, the mid-week party.

He could see it now—the pointless circling and minglely chit-chat ("Oh, hey. You're that headless guy, right? The one in 12B?"); the staking out a place by the chip dip, trying like hell to blend in. And the horrendous costumes!—squash-shaped men as Zorro, women in bunny suits marred by thick eyeglasses that all but screamed computer nerd. The idea of attending was loathsome.

But he knew he must. As awkward as those things were, there was always the off-chance that this might just be the thing to put some zing in his step. Perhaps he just needed to meet some new people, make a few friends. Or possibly even some lovely lady would appear like an apparition in the mist—someone understanding and down-to-earth enough to accept that he just happened to be "cranially challenged." Someone who thought, *So, no head? No big deal.*

He noticed it said *Costumes optional.* He would forgo the cloak.

The party was going pretty much as he'd anticipated. So far he'd met two insurance salesmen (maritime and commercial), a producer of infomercials, three computer software designers, two telemarketers, a self-proclaimed inventor, and a corporate lawyer who worked for a large dog food concern. Each one called him *Dude* or *Pal* or *Bud.* The few women there called him *Doll.* All of them had their own websites and they insisted he check them out.

It was all he could do to fight back the urge to just collect his head now—do it early this year. Any one of these losers would do. They kept trying to get him to come bob for apples, but he desisted, thinking, *Jesus—do I* look *physically capable of bobbing for apples?*

At first he was puzzled: why were these people being so warm to him? It wasn't quite the reaction he was used to. Why weren't they cowering and pointing, waving Bibles and Crucifixes? Why weren't they hurling spittle-flecked insults and fecal matter?

It wasn't long before it dawned on him. The *feng shui* chick was scribbling her website address on a pumpkin-shaped napkin (www.couchangle.com), and he almost reeled with the realization: *These people have worse lives than me.*

Every single one of them.

And then in walked the headhunter.

Her name was Tina and she was an executive recruiter. "A headhunter," she said.

She told him she was new to the building. She had to be brand-new, he thought. Anyone that beautiful, you notice pretty fast.

He loved the way she kept her gaze steady and didn't look away; didn't seem thrown by the empty abyss beneath his collar, his lack of head. She laughed at his jokes, she smelled of peaches, she told him he was obviously too talented to be doing what he was doing.

They talked for almost ten minutes. When she started to excuse herself to go have a smoke, he did something he rarely ever did. He gave her his card.

"Thanks," she said. "I'll call you. We'll have lunch. I'm sure we can figure out another line of work for you." He watched her remove a blood red Gucci card case and slip it inside. She shook hands with him and smiled as if they shared a secret.

For several minutes, he just stood there by the punch bowl, watching the dry ice fog and bubble, feeling damn glad he'd come. At the most, he might have a new career soon; at the very least, he would be having lunch with a vibrant, beautiful young woman.

He wondered if anyone could tell he was beaming.

It was time to leave. Anything after that would be anticlimactic. Outside, crossing the parking lot, he saw a small crumpled business card; his.

Back in his apartment, The Headless Horseman emptied his pockets into the trash: scribbled-on party napkins and a toy jack-o-lantern that made a flatulent noise when squeezed—third prize for his "costume." (The judges had seemed impressed by his headlessness, but felt the Eddie Bauer pullover "detracted.") It was almost 1:00AM. He'd only planned on staying a half hour. Why on earth had he wasted his time at such a desperate gathering? After all, much preparation lay ahead.

Checking the calendar hanging over the sink, he saw now that he had only a little less than a week in which to find and polish his long black boots and oil his saddle and get his nefarious laugh back to snuff. He'd have to drink a lot of honey tea and grind through his vocal exercises a couple hours ever day. *Better pick up some zinc lozenges too*—he added that to the Post-It reminder. He tried not to think of the woman, Tina; her lovely neck.

Christ Almighty, he thought, what a life . . .

With a sigh, the Headless Horseman flipped up the calendar to the next month. Soon it would be Thanksgiving and he could go visit his sister down in Florida and start to try to forget it all for another year.

Steve Amick, born in Ann Arbor in 1964, has never been beheaded. His first novel, *The Lake, The River & The Other Lake*, was a 2006 Michigan Notable Book and a *Washington Post* Best Book of the Year. He has also been a singer/songwriter, playwright, artist, copywriter, and college instructor, but never a maniacal killer. His work has mysteriously appeared in *McSweeney's*, *Playboy*, *Story*, *The Southern Review*, *The New England Review*, *The New York Times*, the anthology *The Sound of Writing*, and on NPR. His CD of original music, *There's always pie . . .*, contains more goofy tales of heartbreak. He has, at times, been very lonely, but not since meeting his wife, Sharyl. The pumpkin (*Cucurbita pepo*) is a member of the squash family. Visit his website, *steve-amick.com*.

BUTTER KNIVES
ERICA ROSBE

WASHINGTON, 18, *sits in the driveway, flicking the tab of his beer can.*
NELLY, 17, *enters. She attempts to go around Washington, but he stands in front of her.*

WASHINGTON
Wanna hear a good retard joke?
NELLY
I don't believe in retard jokes.
WASHINGTON
My brother's retarded.
NELLY
No he's not.
WASHINGTON
He could be. I could have a retarded brother. Moral. Good. Dealing with hardship in my own living room. I could be that.
NELLY
Washington—
WASHINGTON
Wanna smoke?
NELLY
Please—
WASHINGTON
Jack has some inside.
NELLY
I'm pressing charges.
WASHINGTON
He said I could smoke half.
NELLY
I am.
WASHINGTON
Fuck you are. About last weekend?
NELLY
I will.
WASHINGTON
You didn't think for a second that we would—
NELLY
How do you know what I thought?

WASHINGTON

Everybody plays with knives.

NELLY

Butter.

WAHINGTON

What?

NELLY

Butter knives. Dull knives. You guys play with switchblades.

WASHINGTON

It was fun. (*introducing imaginary brother*) Nelly, this is my brother, Gregory.

NELLY

Stop it.

WASHINGTON

Sure, he's a little slow, but I love him.

NELLY

Listen.

WASHINGTON

Because I'm like that. I just love. I give it away for free.

NELLY

I was scared, okay? You guys scared me.

WASHINGTON

So why'd you come here tonight? If you're so scared of us.

NELLY

Peggy.

WASHINGTON

So?

NELLY

I'm sleeping at her house. She wanted to see Pool.

WASHINGTON

She wants him?

NELLY

I guess, I dunno. She didn't say.

WASHINGTON

So you casually drop by the home of the people you want to take to court?

NELLY

She drove.

WASHINGTON

Doesn't look good, Nelly, doesn't look believable.

NELLY

I wanted to wait in the car.

WASHINGTON

Do you believe her, Greg?

NELLY

It was too cold.

WASHINGTON
Greg doesn't believe you.
NELLY
Stop.
WASHINGTON
You were laughing. We have you laughing on the tape.
NELLY
I laugh when I'm nervous.
WASHINGTON
You know that show with the people who jump into tanks of snakes? The bungee jumping, you know, celebrities wrestling lions and stuff?
NELLY
I don't watch TV.
WASHINGTON
Fuck is that, I don't watch TV. You do. Everyone does. Last night on that show we saw this guy's arm pop in half. Arm wrestling, and pop, slip . . . bone coming out of the arm, like, the actual bone, white. So much pressure and then just snap—
NELLY
Look, I know it wasn't your idea—
WASHINGTON
Snap.
NELLY
—you just go along with Jack.
WASHINGTON
Fuck you.
NELLY
I'm saying—
WASHINGTON
It was my idea.
NELLY
You couldn't come up with something so horrid—
WASHINGTON
Well I did.
NELLY
Then you're sick.
WASHINGTON
Hey. It wasn't real.
NELLY
It felt real.
WASHINGTON (*smiling*)
I know.
NELLY
You know.

WASHINGTON

Jack's face in the back of the van, with the knife. That smile.

NELLY

Jack's creepy. I hate it when he smiles.

WASHINGTON

It was like, what if it slipped, you know?

NELLY

That's my neck you're talking about.

WASHINGTON

Yes. Yes it is.

NELLY

You talk about this so calmly.

WASHINGTON

Why shouldn't I? I am calm. I'm just talking. We're just talking. There's nothing at stake or anything. No one's dangling over a cliff. Just talk. Rumination. Late night rumination on the rooftops of our receding adolescence . . .

NELLY

We're in a driveway.

WASHINGTON

Say something happened. Knife slipped, or the gag had rat poison on it, or you had asthma, heart stopped, you've seen it happen in movies, all that, say something did happen—

NELLY

I should really get Peggy—

WASHINGTON

Do we admit defeat, bumbling butterfinger kids—prank gone wrong! we thought we were immortal! hands caught in the cookie jar—Mom, don't send me to jail! Do we become the kids who fucked up royally, waited a bit too long to say the punchline in their little joke so it flipped right around on them? Or.

NELLY

Or what?

WASHINGTON

Option two: we Assume Responsibility for what we started. See it through to the end.

NELLY

Become actual murderers?

WASHINGTON

Because that's what we meant to do all along.

NELLY

But you didn't mean to. The purpose was the joke, right?

WASHINGTON

Right.

NELLY

It would've been a mistake.

WASHINGTON

> There are no mistakes.

NELLY

> What does that mean? No, what does that mean? I slipped on ice this morning. That was a mistake. I didn't want to fall.

WASHINGTON

> And I didn't want to slit your throat, but what if?

NELLY

> Stop it! Washington. Stop it.

WASHINGTON

> What's worse than being in jail for an accident?

NELLY

> So you'd rather be a psycho?

WASHINGTON

> We forgive the psycho because he's interesting. Plus, his brother's retarded.

NELLY

> I wouldn't.

WASHINGTON

> What?

NELLY

> I wouldn't forgive him. You. I wouldn't forgive you.

WASHINGTON

> Well obviously, Nelly. You'd be dead. Doornail dead.

NELLY

> How can you even talk about this like it, like . . .

WASHINGTON

> We're doing it again.

NELLY

> Not if I call the police first.

WASHINGTON

> Christ, we're not killing her. We're not, like, raping her. It's a joke.

NELLY

> It's not funny.

WASHINGTON

> It'll probably be the most exciting thing that ever happens to her.

NELLY (*dialing*)

> Look. 9-1-1.

> > WASHINGTON *grabs the phone from her.*

NELLY

> They'll search the house. They'll find the tape. You'll go down. Down!

WASHINGTON (*laughing*)

> Down, down . . . !!! What the fuck, Nelly?

NELLY

> It was kidnapping. You had a knife. It was attempted murder. It was serious.

WASHINGTON *takes the switchblade out of his pocket. In slow motion he brings it toward* NELLY.

WASHINGTON

So this is attempted murder?

NELLY

Put it away.

WASHINGTON

Take it from me.

NELLY

No.

WASHINGTON

Take it.

NELLY

I don't want it.

WASHINGTON *moves the knife around, getting it a bit too close to her.*

NELLY

Stop!

WASHINGTON

Then take it.

NELLY *snatches it from him.*

WASHINGTON

There. Now you don't have to fear for your life. Maybe I have to fear for mine. You have a knife.

NELLY

Just don't do it again.

WASHINGTON

Maybe Peggy is better at taking a joke.

NELLY

Peggy? You're doing Peggy?

WASHINGTON

What are you, better than her?

NELLY

I didn't say that.

WASHINGTON

No. You just got incredibly offended that we would put you in the same category.

NELLY

It's just she's . . . well, harmless . . . nice. And—

WASHINGTON

And what?

NELLY

She couldn't handle it. It was serious.

WASHINGTON

Nothing's serious.

NELLY

This was.

WASHINGTON

Why? Because your heart was racing? Because you peed your pants?

NELLY

Because—

WASHINGTON

You saw our faces and you saw that knife and you had a whole half hour in the van to think maybe we're not as harmless as you always pegged us, maybe there's something dark and relentless inside us that makes it okay to do what you're afraid we're going to do to you?

NELLY

I don't like jokes where someone doesn't know the rules.

WASHINGTON

She speaks as if she's never hid in a closet waiting to jump out.

NELLY

There is a big difference.

WASHINGTON

Not when it's distilled.

NELLY

Jack said I was going to die and you said, "You better pray coz God's the only one who can save you now."

WASHINGTON

I know. I remember.

NELLY

You said that while Jack had the knife and Pool shoveled dirt on me, right on me, and it would've been so fucking funny that you said that coz it was so cheesy and cliché and straight out of the third Batman movie, but you said that and I started praying out loud, saying, "Please God help me . . . " and I don't even believe in God, I'm agnostic—

WASHINGTON

Atheist.

NELLY

Whatever. You said that and there I was on the side of Scio Church Road in some hole praying to God and I've got one shoe on and I can't remember what happened to the other one and there's never been a time in my life when—

WASHINGTON

Calm down.

NELLY

—I have lost something as vital as a shoe and not even remembered where it went. And I'm trying to pray to God just because it seems a little better than praying that the fucking police are just going to be happening by this road at this exact moment but all I can think about is shoe, shoe, SHOE, and I pee. (*pause*) And then you're all laughing. And I'm laughing too because I laugh when I'm nervous and it's very very funny to me at that moment that you guys did that and that I'm not going to die. It's funny and I ask about my shoe and haha, you retards, you suck, bring me home, I wanna take a shower. I've got dirt in my hair, no I don't wanna watch the video of me screaming take me home now, okay? Am I like her? Like Peggy?

WASHINGTON

We have different criteria for each victim.

NELLY

Did you think that last weekend would be the most exciting thing that ever happened to me?

WASHINGTON

You were supposed to be changed by the experience, come out of it more aware. A wake up call.

NELLY

I'm awake. I've been awake! I'm not like her.

WASHINGTON

You just sit around, drinking but not enough to get sloppy, coming here because it's not your house so you feel like you're going out, doing something, so in school on Monday someone will ask you about your weekend and you'll say it was all right before you even remember what it consisted of because if you don't remember it being horrible it might've been fun.

NELLY

Last weekend I remembered.

WASHINGTON

I bet.

    NELLY *swings the knife through the air.*

WASHINGTON

Well, look at you!

NELLY

I want to help with Peggy.

WASHINGTON

No you don't.

NELLY

Don't patronize me. Don't patronize me. Stop smiling.

    He doesn't. She brings the knife closer. He does.

NELLY

I want to wear black.

WASHINGTON

I'd have to ask Jack.

NELLY

I thought it was your idea.

WASHINGTON

I don't know if you—

NELLY

I want to be the one holding the knife.

WASHINGTON

We might not do it tonight.

NELLY

Yes. We will do it. Tonight.

WASHINGTON

Okay.

NELLY

I'll get her out here in fifteen minutes. Be ready.

NELLY *goes inside.* WASHINGTON *waits.*

(END)

Erica Rosbe is a proud Ann Arbor native and Pioneer High graduate, where she wrote with the then-fledgling VOLUME Poetry Project. She received her BFA from NYU in Dramatic Writing in 2005 and upon graduation taught high school students at Interlochen Arts Camp in Traverse City. Erica's plays have been performed in New York and Michigan, but she currently writes for video games with Longtail Studios and lives in Brooklyn. She misses Sleeping Bear Dunes, the meat platter from the Blue Nile restaurant, and wading in the Huron River.

CHRISTINE HUME

WALK DOWN A windy pike with an aviary unkeeping ashes. Pose as a Chinese princess swept here by a series of shipwrecks and captivities. Even if you've never seen a dead person before, your body will know what to do. Come home smelling of your husband's smoke. Cry easily and overlook the danger in crying below zero. In-between, note an inexplicable ocean. Nothing can take its place in the human mind. A forgotten name always moves fitfully. Sweep pine until you think of how often there is no-mind so that any minute is not. Neglect to tell the children when it's night. This one looks like a constellation, but you remember by accident. Do not expect to be rewarded. Or to be a river. The mind is awake because it's weightless. The mind is trying to be lesser than an exit. Garner some ideas from a cheap video anyway. Dismiss loud haunts of whirling moths. Court miniature electricities like static and friction. Creep under the tundra until you find an unlikely place to burn. Insist that there has only been one fire and its history of ten million airs and a second. Enfold the pass. Fog over like an oil field. There is no chorus in the human mind. Speak of only land and no yard for which it stands. Herringbone up the hill and wait with the others for a vaguely metaphysical event. Because someone must be filming you on a day like today. On napkins in bars, re-draw the human nervous system. Break habit with aerial views. Age the land by freezing animals in it. Nonetheless, the failure of recollection is a common experience. Arrange decals on a luggage set. Leave a quote on the kitchen table, we are so sorry, but you are no longer possible here. We have elected you to be a whale's mouth on its forehead. Smell salt like the inside of a mouth and go down on it. The human mind also is a mouth worshiping a moderately sized stone. The land is flat from when you wander, but he had already slipped off. It's human nature to be arch or arched against. Admire what's sprung lately from your brow. Repeatedly call the air sky; think empty but for ether. Do not fall away in the absence. Keep falling until the mind can strike. Suit yourself as something holy and sit for it. By the fire, your parka begins to reveal its urine-curing. Invent a talk town in a bubble full of room temperature. Come in with your notions and integrities. Shatter not only the yard-arms, trigger a herd. Be bound to listen because the miles stretch out on tracks. Come back as a little black dot, an unincorporated capital. Keep going past pluperfect. In your dark suit, ticking.

Christine Hume is the author of *Musca Domestica* and *Alaskaphrenia*; she is an associate professor of English at Eastern Michigan University.

HAPPY

DEAN BAKOPOULOS

WHEN HE WAS TWENTY-NINE years old, Charlie Pappas left Vermont and moved back to Detroit after suffering from what—in a more innocent, big-band-playing, hat-wearing era—would have been called a crack-up.

The many factors leading to the crack-up included Charlie's disillusionment with teaching in private schools, a tendency to self-medicate with six packs of Blatz, and his fiancée Jana's affair with a prominent sculptor named Harris Mills. One day, a little drunk on after-school martinis, Charlie was searching for the checkbook in Jana's backpack. There, he discovered a note that said: *Jana, I know we were meant to be together, because after we make love, I dream of God and his angels, and they are dancing and they are made out of the most beautiful clay.*

He waited for her all night. She often worked late in the studio and sometimes came home after Charlie had fallen asleep. That night, however, Jana did not come home at all. It was if she sensed that Charlie had discovered the note.

Charlie finished a case of Blatz; he stayed awake, watching the darkness slip out of the sky.

In the morning, Charlie crumpled to the floor in the middle of teaching a lesson on the Transcendentalists. He began to whimper, then turned on his stomach, slowly and softly pounding his head against the tile floor, murmuring, *There is no Oversoul, there is no Oversoul, there is no Oversoul.*

The children in his class, sensitive, wholly tolerant, and intellectually gifted offspring of wealthy ex-hippies, ex-activists, and ex-organic farmers, sat in silence for a moment, and then, led by Skye Nelson and Prairie Masterson, they joined Charlie in his mantra. Some students even tapped their foreheads on their desks, so that, minutes later, when the headmaster arrived in the doorway, he found the tenth grade American literature class tapping their heads on desks and denying the Oversoul in unison.

And there was Charlie, twitching on the floor.

Charlie arrived in Detroit during a May that was still damp with the last chill of winter, carrying all his belongings in a duffel bag. His father, Jimmy Pappas (The Restaurant Supply King), to whom he had not spoken in three or four months, picked him up at the airport. Charlie had spent very little time with Jimmy since the age of twelve, but his father had money and a house, and Charlie did not. On the way home from the airport, Jimmy Pappas's driver, a college student named Ray, talked more than Charlie did. There was not much to catch up on between father and son; they barely knew each other anymore.

Charlie moved into his father's five-bedroom, three-bathroom home in Elk

Ridge, a ridge-less, elk-less subdivision in Livonia. Now that Charlie felt himself without options, he figured it was time to accept his father's invitation to visit. Jimmy had been sober almost two years. Ever since Jimmy had gotten out of his six weeks in rehab, he'd been asking Charlie, his only child, to come home for a visit.

The first night of the visit, just before bed, Charlie looked at his father's bare white skin and noticed the small black band around his ankle. His father was still under house arrest for four drunk driving convictions. He had to wear an electronic tether to prove to the police that he was home by dinnertime each evening. There was a whole year left on his sentence, but he'd avoided prison and was allowed to keep working. Jimmy had a lot of friends.

Charlie looked at the red light of the tether as he followed Jimmy up the stairs and down the hallway. Jimmy flipped on the light to the room at the far end of the house.

"See, you've got your own can," Jimmy said, showing Charlie to a white-carpeted guest room. "You can't beat that."

There was something poetic in convalescing in his estranged father's guest room, spending the summer largely in the climate-controlled indoors, reading novels from the public library, and watching documentaries on PBS. He felt a bit like an eccentric, weak poet in an E.M. Forster novel, and for weeks he shuffled around as if he were a bastard cousin in a Merchant & Ivory film, grimacing and trembling, exaggerating his mood swings for dramatic effect. He had lost weight, had gone from slim to skinny. His father allowed him his space, cooked egg-white omelets for him on weekend mornings, and brought bland meals heavy with starches to his room.

Sometimes Jimmy would ask questions: "Do you think you might want to call your mother?" or "Do you want to tell me what happened with Jana?"

Charlie would always shake his head. "I'm not ready," he'd say. "Not yet."

Some afternoons while his father was at work, Charlie walked to the corner Rite-Aid and bought Canadian Club whiskey and magazines. Charlie hid the whiskey in his sock drawer. He was happy for his sober father, and did not want to tempt him. He'd skip home from the store, holding a brown bag. He'd read Blake before bed, sipping from the whiskey, and all night he dreamt of angels and tigers and flames, and, of course, sometimes, Jana.

Jana would call every week, and Charlie kept refusing her calls. Charlie did not know how she had found him there, since his family should rationally have been the last place he turned to in times of emotional crisis. Charlie suspected that Jimmy had called Jana, just to let her know Charlie was okay.

"She really wants to talk to you," his father would say. "She wants to hear that you're okay."

"Tell her I'm dead," Charlie said. He raised his voice and made himself sound woeful and breathless, hoping Jana would hear him on the other end. "I've withered away and disappeared. Tell her I no longer exist!"

"I'll tell her," his father would say.

Charlie would bury his face in his pillow. From down the hall, he could hear his father's voice: "He's in the can, honey. Can he call you back?"

Charlie had been in his father's house that whole summer, but he'd spent it largely locked in his room, and it wasn't until August that certain things about his father really began to sink in: Jimmy Pappas was not just thinner than Charlie remembered, he was trim. The decades of drinking had melted off his body like wax. Jimmy was only 5'7", three inches shorter than Charlie, but had always been bigger, sturdier. Jimmy was once a man with big shoulders, a barrel chest, and a gut like a beer keg. Charlie figured that his father's waist was now maybe six inches slimmer, and his chest and shoulders less like massive slabs of meat than they once were. He also had stopped dying his thick and wavy black hair, which had now gone completely gray. And Jimmy wasn't smoking; he was barely even swearing. Charlie, at first, imagined this was just a sign of old age. His father was sixty now, and had begun living with a little less day-to-day intensity, letting the vices of youth and middle age fade into the acceptable, lovable eccentricities of an old man. But one morning in late August, Charlie awoke and heard his father singing "The Old Rugged Cross" in the shower across the hall. Charlie got up, showered and dressed, and came downstairs just after dawn (his earliest rising yet) and found his father eating a bowl of Fiber Madness cereal and reading the Bible.

"Pop?" Charlie said, walking into the kitchen. "Is that what I think it is?"

"Yeah, bran flakes," he said. "Have to keep an eye on the old ticker."

"I mean the book," Charlie said. "Is that . . . "

"The unadulterated Word of God?" Jimmy said. "That it is."

Jimmy pulled up the leg of his khakis to reveal the black, plastic band with a small box, the size of a pager on his inner ankle. He tapped the device.

"This is what saved my life," Jimmy said. "Getting this sumbitch on my ankle."

Jimmy had, thankfully, lost his driver's license after the arrest, and for the last year had to hire Ray, the college student, to drive him on his sales calls. He now attended AA meetings at least five days a week. But Charlie already knew all of this. What Charlie was just learning was that Jimmy had also left the Greek Orthodox church, more a social club than a place of worship, and now attended New Promise Evangelical Free, a giant suburban church where Jimmy became involved in a group known as the Covenant Men.

"That fourth accident," Jimmy said. "You know, I ended up on the lawn of Stevenson High School, your alma mater, crashed into the statue of the giant Spartan, and right then and there, I said, 'Pappas, you've fought your last battle.'

"I had a bottle of vodka left," Jimmy said. "And I sat there sucking it down, knowing it was the last drink I'd ever take. I waited for the cops to come, and when the first officer responded to the scene, he poked his head in the window, saw me, drunk, with a bloody nose, and he said, 'Sir, do you know Jesus Christ as a personal Lord and Savior?'"

"You were converted by a cop?" Charlie said. "Can they do that?"

"The Spirit just moved him," Jimmy said.

"How could you keep this from me? You never told me you'd been born again."

Really, though, it all made sense. His father was more sensitive, more earnest than ever before. Charlie felt like he was living with some rich, gay uncle.

"I had a vision," he said. "I wanted you to work on your problems before you had to listen to mine."

"Jesus Christ," Charlie said.

"Amen," Jimmy said.

Jimmy shoveled a spoonful of bran flakes into his mouth.

"Son," he said, milk dribbling down his chin. "I want you to come and work for me. I know you've had a rough go of it lately, but you need to get back in the game, get back on the horse. Let go and let God."

Charlie was twenty-nine, homeless, broke, and out of options. So he said yes.

"One day at a time, son," Jimmy said. "Easy does it."

Jimmy went to give his son a long hug. Charlie kept his arms at his sides.

"You start tomorrow," Jimmy said. "Shave. Wear a clean shirt."

The next morning, Charlie woke up, shaved, put on a blue oxford, and began working as his father's driver. Ray was demoted back to warehouse picker, and from that moment on he would look at Charlie with sharp glares of resentment and scorn. "Ignore him," Jimmy said. "He was a lousy driver and talked too much. I was about to can him anyway."

Jimmy called Charlie a "sales assistant," but Charlie's duties were obviously those of a chauffeur. He would shuttle his father from one appointment to the next. He would make eleven dollars an hour, two dollars more than Ray had been paid.

His father, always the salesman, put a lovely spin on things: "Jimmy Pappas, the Restaurant Supply King," he said, "has found an heir to the kingdom."

"Let's not get ahead of ourselves," Charlie said. "I am, technically, a professional educator."

"I know," Jimmy said. "One day at a time."

After a few weeks of work, Charlie was feeling better. By Labor Day, he was able to dress, comb his hair, and speak in complete sentences about his ex-fiancée without crying. He'd cut back on his drinking, no longer hiding Canadian Club in his sock drawer. In fact, while sitting with Jimmy in those court-ordered nightly AA meetings, Charlie slowly began to have the realization that he was not really an alcoholic at all. Charlie only made himself drink out of sadness and boredom; he'd almost quit drinking entirely, without any withdrawal or effort. It almost depressed him—all of that drinking, and still, he'd failed to become an alcoholic. He was a fraud; he'd been faking alcoholism. He quit going into the meetings with his father, and instead waited in the car, listening to *All Things Considered* like any normal, sober citizen.

Jana continued to call. She'd been working as a development officer at an arts colony when she'd met Harris Mills. Charlie liked to believe that she had had enough of passion; she was calling because she craved the comfort of Charlie. He imagined going back to her, maybe after a brief fling with a Hooter's waitress, and for the rest of his life having a moral upper-hand in their relationship. But no, he knew, they would not get back together: soon, he would have to return one of her calls and discuss the details of their break-up— who got their jointly owned assets, what to do with the engagement ring, the Volvo, the tandem bicycle. They had lived together for almost seven years and this break-up would not be easy. It would have logistics.

But before he dealt with Jana, Charlie wanted to visit his mother. He had not called her all summer, because he was not sure he was in any condition for such a meeting, but now he was ready to see her. One day at a time, he thought. He wondered if she knew he was in town.

One morning, after dropping off his father at the Restaurant Supply King warehouse in Wyandotte, Charlie drove down Jefferson Avenue, past abandoned homes with plywooded windows, abandoned cars without wheels or windshields, abandoned factories, warehouses, storefronts. It was easy to imagine that somewhere, amid the wreckage of abandoned industry, there were hundreds of aimless, abandoned children, mouths ajar, clamoring for attention.

His mother, like his father, was a drunk—but she was a drunk without money, and thus her life was more reckless and riskier than any life Jimmy Pappas had ever lived. Jimmy always had money; Mary had not.

Jimmy and Mary divorced when Charlie was ten, right after Jimmy's first arrest, a DUI that discovered him driving naked with a real estate agent named Tina.

His father moved to an apartment downriver, near the Restaurant Supply King warehouse. Charlie lived with his mother, who was furiously upbeat and struggled to be sober. She was a painter, and after the divorce she shifted to painting landscapes and bland nature scenes because she could sell them for inflated prices at craft shows. She remained that way—a hard working, housekeeping, rock-solid Mom—until Charlie went to high school. After that she entered a string of gradually worsening relationships—an alcoholic professor, a violent truck driver, a homicidal chef—and began painting in the abstract. She accelerated her social drinking and lost her job at Wayne State University, where she had been teaching studio art as an adjunct. By the time Charlie started his first year of college in Ann Arbor, his mother had lost the house and had moved back to Detroit, where she lived in the small ranch that had once been her childhood home.

While he was in college in Ann Arbor, Charlie fell into the pattern of bringing his mother nutritious groceries and maintaining the modest house. When he moved to Vermont, he began to give up on her, slowly. He wrote letters, called every other Sunday, and visited when he was in town, which was (deliberately) rare. His mother had been living with a security guard named Frank Geary, but just before his crack-up, Charlie had learned that Frank Geary had moved to Alaska with most of the contents of his mother's modest savings account. He knew his worrying about his mother was another factor in his crack-up episode.

He pounded on the door. "Mom," he said. "It's me, Charlie."

He waited for a moment.

From the small house next door, a dark, bearded man dressed in white pants and a black shirt emerged. "What do you want?" he said, his voice thick with a Middle Eastern accent. "What are you looking for?"

"My mother lives here," Charlie said.

"Oh, of course," the man said. "I recognize you from the pictures now, from up close."

"I'm Charlie," he said.

"Sam Alireza," the man said. "I am the neighbor of your mother."

Standing in the front yard, Charlie learned that Sam was from Yemen, and lived next door with his two bothers. Sam was trying to earn enough money to bring the rest of his family to the US. He owned a dollar store on Warren Avenue called Dolla-Palooza.

"My brothers and I help your mother out sometime," Sam said. "She, you know, she sometime drinks too much wine."

"I know," Charlie said.

"I help her sometime. I check on her some days, take her for groceries. She is a nice woman. Very pretty, used to be, right?" Sam said. "She talks very nice about you."

"She does? That's nice," Charlie said. "I just moved back to the area. I've been trying to call her."

"Yes," Sam said. "You've been in Vermont."

Charlie took out one of the new business cards his father had printed for him the week before. On it was his new cell phone number. Seeing his name embossed on cardstock, a slew of printed digits beneath it, suddenly made Charlie feel powerful.

"Well, Sam, if my mother ever needs anything, my phone number is on this card," Charlie said. Sam studied the card and slipped it into his pocket. Charlie was feeling territorial. It's my wreck of a drunk of a mother, he thought. I'll take care of her, pal. You get your ass back to Dolla-Palooza.

"Do you want a house key?" Sam said. "I can let you in."

"I appreciate you taking care of my mother so well," Charlie said.

"It's what neighbors are for," Sam said. "Besides, your mother she's been very good to us. She gave us a car. She couldn't drive it anymore."

Sam waved to the Ford Tempo in his driveway.

"She gives my little brother, Ali, a little money when he cuts her grass and shovels her snow," Sam said.

Sam went inside his own house for the key to Charlie's mother's front door. Charlie did not know how he felt about this, a neighbor he had never met, with keys to his mother's home.

They found her on the floor in nothing but a slip. Sam apologized and back-pedaled his way out of the house, whispering, "I think she is drunk."

Charlie considered fleeing with Sam, but then he saw his mother stir. She pushed her face off of the carpet, and looked at him.

"Charlie?" she said.

"Mom?" he said.

"Oh my God," she said. She managed to stand and hug him, and then backed away, put her hands on her sides and smoothed down her slip, realizing she was barely dressed.

"My God, you look terrible," she said. "What's wrong?"

"You look great," he said.

"Oh, God, I know, sorry. I was up all night, and just couldn't sleep. Back problems. I finally just stretched out on the floor, hoping to get rid of the pain. I took some Tylenol PM and it worked. I was out like a light."

She excused herself and went into the bedroom. "Help yourself to a Coke or something," she said. "I think there's some in the fridge."

The fridge was empty except for beer, a box of wine, and condiments. He opened the freezer, and found nothing but a tub of ice and two gallon bottles of vodka.

His mother came back to the room in a gray t-shirt and jeans.

"I called you a few times this summer," his mother said. "I never got an answer."

"I've been traveling," he said.

His mother had once been radiant, full of intellect and verve, and, even when he was a small boy at social events, he could tell that the men in the room wanted to be near his mother. They gathered around her, laughed at her jokes with great enthusiasm, helped her with her coat, admired her dresses, called Jimmy Pappas a lucky son of a bitch.

Jana reminded him of that, in some ways. Jana had always been the most beloved of the women in the room, and Charlie also felt as if people were muttering behind his back, Why is she with him?

Jana had fine, black hair, which she wore long, a small face with delicate cheekbones and a delicate chin, aqua blue eyes. Jimmy, when he met her for the first time, said, "Christ, Chuckie, she looks just like your mother."

When Charlie met Jana, it was in his last semester of college. An English major, he enrolled in Drawing 101 because he imagined it to be easy, or at least, to be free of required reading. His teacher was a graduate student named Teddy who wore oversized tweed coats and had a painfully wispy red beard. Charlie was one of the only men in the class, and Teddy didn't seem to like him.

After only a week of class, Teddy said to Charlie, "You have a tendency to depress people, Mr. Pappas. People have been complaining. Your sullen mood makes it hard for them to work."

On the day they were to try their hands at figure drawing, Jana entered the art room, shed her robe, and stood, completely naked in front of Charlie. His instant erection proved to him that he didn't have the mind of an artist at all, but rather the temperament of a Greek from Detroit.

His hands were paralyzed. He couldn't draw the woman in the room. At the end of class, Teddy stood behind Charlie and said, "Pappas spent the whole hour staring at the model, but there's not one mark on the paper."

The class laughed as they gathered their supplies, Teddy smirked in Charlie's face, and Jana, on the platform in the middle of the room, put on her robe, and frowned. Barefoot, she walked right up to Teddy and said, "Last time I work in your class, fuckstick. That was completely inappropriate."

Charlie found himself at the bus stop with her a few minutes later and stammered an apology. "I'm not a very good artist," he said. "My mother is one, though."

Jana smiled and nodded.

"It wasn't like I was just staring at you," he said. "Not like Teddy implied. I'm not some kind of sicko."

"Teddy's a fuckstick," she said. "But you were. Staring, I mean. That's not cool in an art studio, ogling the model."

A bus was coming and Charlie decided he was in love. He went for broke. "Everytime I went to put a mark on the page," he said, "I couldn't. It was too overwhelming, the idea of catching any sliver of your beauty. I couldn't do you justice."

"Please," she said. The bus came by and she got on. It was not his bus, but he followed her. Maybe he was a sicko.

"Could we have coffee?" he asked her.

"I don't know," she said.

Three weeks later, he found her again at a small graduation dinner party hosted by a mutual friend. The mutual friend assured Jana that Charlie wasn't a freak. (Later, Jana had said, she liked Charlie's looks so much—the olive skin and black hair of a Greek, with the blue eyes and slender frame from his mother's Ukrainian side—that she'd have dated him even if he had turned out to be a freak.)

At the end of the evening, Jana came up to Charlie and said, "I'll give you another chance."

"At what?" he said.

"At dealing with my beauty," she said.

It was already October. Charlie had settled into a comfortable routine. In the morning, he would drive his father from client to client, and then after lunch, he'd drop him at the office in Wyandotte and head over to visit his mother. He began buying his mother art supplies, helping her clean and organize the chaos of her basement studio, intent on helping her paint again. He'd been a bad son. He'd neglected her. She needed his help.

Though most business could be conducted via phone, fax, or e-mail—who really needs a saleman to sell plastic soup spoons and mint toothpicks?—Jimmy Pappas preferred to call on most of his clients in person.

"A firm handshake, a warm smile, a look square in the eye," Jimmy said that morning, "is the difference between a carton of toothpicks and a whole crate of them."

A gray sky and Jimmy was quiet. Jimmy had felt a burning need to go to an AA meeting that morning, so Charlie had to take him. Now they were behind schedule. Jimmy sat in the passenger seat, depressed and grim, looking over his order sheets, occasionally scratching the area of his ankle that was covered by the tether. Charlie's new cell phone rang, which it almost never did, and, because Jefferson Avenue was, as always, completely free of traffic, it was easy for Charlie to answer the call.

"Charlie," a thick-accented voice said. "This is Sam Alireza."

"Who's that?" Charlie said.

"Sam. Your mother's neighbor."

"Hey, Sam. What's wrong?" Charlie asked, though he already guessed at it.

"Your mother fell."

"She fell?"

"She's fine. She's okay, really."

"Can I talk to her?" Charlie said.

Charlie gripped the wheel tighter, glared in his rearview at an old LTD that had come out of nowhere and was tailgating him. What if he was in Vermont, he wondered? What would she do then? Who would Sam call?

"No, no, she not know I call you. She went inside. I found her. She was bleeding. I tried to call the ambulance, but she says she's fine."

"Thanks, Sam. I'll be right over."

"Okay," he said. "Don't tell her I called, okay?"

"No, Sam, I won't."

Charlie hung up the phone. Jimmy turned the radio back on and looked down at his orders.

"We need to make a detour, Dad."

"A detour? I'm on a schedule today, Bub."

"Tough shit, Dad," Charlie said. "I have a driver's license, and you don't."

When Charlie pulled into his mother's driveway, Jimmy looked at the small red brick ranch, the same house where he picked her up for a first date thirty years ago.

"I can't believe she's back in this old place," he said.

"Well, she is," Charlie said.

"Is the neighborhood safe? It's full of Arabs."

"You coming in?" Charlie said.

"What do you think?" Jimmy said.

"Fine. Stay out here."

It took his mother a few minutes to come to the door. Charlie could hear her coughing and sneezing, which for some reason she did anytime she was drunk, and when she opened the door she looked dazed, a trickle of blood running down her forehead.

"What?" she said.

"Open the door," Charlie said. "Now."

In the light of the kitchen, Charlie cleaned his mother's head wound with damp paper towels and a little hydrogen peroxide before realizing that the gash was worse than he thought. She'd definitely need stitches.

"How much did you have to drink?" Charlie said

"One beer," she said. "The steps were slick. I just fell."

"The day is dry as bone."

"Then I tripped on something. A stick."

"You need to come with me to the hospital," Charlie said. "You need stitches."

"I do not," she said, but her face was worried and her defiance half-hearted. She knew she had messed up, and could not get out this mess alone.

On the counter, six empty beer cans were stacked on the cutting board. Charlie went and touched them, one by one. "Where's your coat?" he said.

"Wherever I left it," she said.

Charlie helped her with her coat, helped her with the buttons, and then led her to the car. Midway down the driveway, she stopped. "Who the hell is in the car?" she said.

"Nobody," Charlie said, and tugged on her arm. "Don't piss me off, Mom. I'm all you have left."

"Not true," she said. "You just like thinking that."

They got in the car, closed doors, buckled seat belts. Jimmy had turned off the radio.

"Dad? Mom?" Charlie said. "Jimmy Pappas? Mary Olszewski Pappas? I believe you two know each other, right?"

"I can't believe this," Mary said.

"We've met," Jimmy said, winking. "Hello, Mary."

Jimmy said you couldn't trust the hospitals in Detroit, because the emergency rooms would be full of real traumas—shootings, stabbings, overdoses. He had Charlie drive out to St. Mary's in Livonia. On the way, Jimmy busied himself by taking out his cell phone and rescheduling the day's appointments. "Family emergency," he told client after client.

In the backseat, Mary huffed and sighed.

"I don't need any goddamn stitches," she said, as more blood worked its way down her forehead. Jimmy handed her a clean handkerchief and said nothing.

At the hospital, Jimmy did all the talking. He talked to the nurse on duty, explaining the situation, helping his ex-wife fill out forms. He flagged down a doctor after they'd been waiting nearly an hour. The doctor, about the same age as Charlie, seemed to know Jimmy. The two men shook hands, and Jimmy mumbled something in the doctor's ear.

The doctor gave Mary three stitches and then presented a short lecture on drinking too much. He handed Charlie some pamphlets, *The Alcoholic in Your Life* and *When Someone You Love Can't Stop Drinking*. Charlie pictured a frantic family gathered around a man that was chained to a sink, his mouth fixed on the faucet. He smirked at his own joke. The doctor scribbled some notes in a file folder and frowned.

"You might want to consider getting your mother into a treatment program," he said to Charlie.

"That's a good idea," Jimmy said. "We hadn't thought of that, doc. Thanks."

The doctor shrugged and left the room.

"Fuck you very much, Dr. Asshole," Jimmy said. The born-again Jimmy would resort to swearing, Charlie guessed, if it would make his ex-wife laugh.

It worked. For the first time all day, Mary laughed, holding a hand up to her newly stitched forehead.

"Thanks, Jimmy," she said.

. . . .

Charlie and Jimmy walked Mary to the door. Jimmy turned on the TV for her, and Charlie fluffed a pillow.

"You'll be okay?" Charlie asked.

"I know how to flip channels," Mary said.

"Are you dizzy at all? The doctor says you may be dizzy," Jimmy said.

"I've been dizzy for the last five years," she said. She was still a pretty woman, Charlie thought, her hair still black with a few strands of silver, her blue eyes, despite their weariness, a dazzling blue. Her skin, olive-toned, but perhaps, Charlie thought, it was now simply jaundiced. I've pickled myself, she said to him once, and now I don't age. She was thin because she never ate more than a few meals a week. The slurring, wrecked voice, the snorting chuckles, seemed out of place with her graceful features, and the cut on her forehead stood out like a signal that the worst was yet to come. She slumped on the couch, took off her sneakers and socks, undid the button on her black jeans.

Charlie could see Jimmy scanning Mary's current life, the stray cups and plates on the end tables, tubes of paint and brushes everywhere, cobwebs in the corners, walls with crooked pictures.

"Take care, now," Jimmy said and turned to go.

Charlie went out the door a few minutes later, his mother, sober now, calling after him: "Don't be mad," she said. "Thank you, Charlie."

In the car, Jimmy said nothing until they were a few miles down the road.

"I had no idea," he said, "that it was this bad."

Before they turned for home, Jimmy said, "Maybe we can make the five o'clock meeting, son? I think it's a two-meeting day."

That night, exhausted and weary, Charlie fell into bed before dinner. Around eight, he heard the phone ring, heard his father answer it.

"Hi, Jana," he said. "I'm fine, thanks. Well, he's here," his father said. "But he's had a rough day. I don't think it's a good day to be talking to him."

"No," he said. "I think he just needs to sleep."

Charlie drifted back into sleep, and, in and out of dreams for the next hour, he heard his father talking in a low voice. Could he still be talking to Jana? What could he possibly be saying to her? They'd only met a few times, brief occasions, and if Charlie had remembered correctly, Jimmy had been drunk every time.

Later, around ten, Charlie woke up to find his father standing in the doorway to the bedroom.

"Chuckie," Jimmy said, leaning against the doorjamb. His tether stuck out from his pajama bottoms like some mechanical tumor. "Chuckie, did I do that to your mother?"

Charlie realized something: It's the question he'd been waiting years for his father to ask. His mind raced to fights in the kitchen, to Jimmy's tendency to disappear for long weekends, Jimmy's failure to make school plays and soccer games, Jimmy, and his booze and his business and his women.

"Yeah, Dad. That was you," he said, though he didn't believe it. "That was all you."

Jimmy nodded and looked at the ground. "Okay, son," he said. "That's fair. I accept that."

That autumn was heavy with early frosts and clear nights, nights too cold for clouds. The skies speckled with stars. In the evenings, Charlie would read the stories of Cheever by the gas fireplace and drink tea. Charlie had fallen in love with Cheever, all that gin and sadness, gin and sadness. It stirred him; he longed to meet a woman who was also stirred by Cheever. It was the first he'd thought of the possibility of another woman since he'd left Jana.

One night, Jimmy, unable to exit through the front door for fear of setting off his tether, hung his head out of the living room window.

"Would you look up at all these goddamn stars," he said. "Points as sharp as daggers, I bet."

"Actually, they're giant balls of gas," Charlie said. "They don't have points."

"What's your point?" Jimmy said.

"My point is that the common representation of a star with five points is not the same thing as one of the celestial beings you so admire."

The window was still open, and the air was filling with a crisp chill. Charlie buttoned another button on his thick flannel.

"You know what, Chuckie?" Jimmy said. His face reddened, and tiny blue veins seemed to pulse on his cheeks and nose. "You know what? Sometimes I'm so fucking glad I'm not you."

"How's that?" Charlie said.

"You don't know how to have any joy in your life, do you?"

"I do, Dad. I'm just in a really weird place right now." Charlie didn't want to hear this, his chronic fuck-up of a father offering his hard earned wisdom. Charlie looked at the floor.

"What the hell are you talking about?" Jimmy said. "You're in Livonia, in your old man's living room."

"I mean it, Dad. You don't get where I'm at."

"I get that you have a beautiful woman who is dying to talk to you, who wants you to come home, and you can't even answer her phone calls."

"What do you know?" Charlie said. "She cheated on me."

"People fuck other people, Chuckie. Then people say they're sorry. They make up; they're still in love. Or they split up for good, and they spend the rest of their lives a little heartbroken, but still breathing. And they start fucking someone new. That's life, Chuckie. You can't sit around in limbo all day. You know, if you want, pick up the phone and tell Jana to go jump in a lake, tell her you never want to see her again."

"My father the philosopher," Charlie said.

"I've taken my hits. I've licked my wounds. I know some things."

Jimmy shut the window and left the room.

Charlie closed the Cheever, folded his arms on the couch, thought of Jana. He could call her now, announce that he was coming home, and be done with all of this. Maybe they could reconcile, and he'd build the kind of life he once imagined he would build for himself in Vermont—quiet and peaceful, full of beauty, full of art and philosophy and every fine thing a fine home should have. He could quit chauffeuring the Restaurant Supply King to and fro; he could quit having to see his mother in the sad chapters of what had become a quiet, desperate life. Vermont would be covered in snow within weeks, and he could hide there in the mountains and go after his old life with passion and vengeance.

The weeks ahead were somber ones. Charlie still drove his father in the mornings and visited his mother whenever he had free afternoons. His father seemed quieter, less enthusiastic than he had once been about their partnership. His visits with his mother were brief, he would go somewhere with her, to the bank or the grocery store or to the mall, and then he'd be gone.

By the first of November, the gold and red leaves had been erased from the trees. The air turned relentless with its wind and its gray dampness, and suddenly, one morning, the trees had bare black branches slick with frost and mist and looked like the skeletons of obsolete machines.

One morning, a Wednesday, Charlie agreed to go with Jimmy to a Covenant Men prayer breakfast at church, where he sat with his father and listened to ex-football coaches, broke businessmen, and former city council members recount how Jesus had freed them from shackles of adultery, alcohol, and pornography. Charlie was not buying into it, but it fascinated him. It amused him. He found something endearing in everyone in the room. He longed for a conversion, but knew conversions never came when one is dying to change course. They come only when you think you're happy, and Charlie was not yet delusional.

Afterward, Jimmy suggested that instead of the usual morning rounds, they'd go and visit Mary. He was holding a box of leftover donuts.

"Why?" Charlie said. "She's probably still passed out from a night of drinking."

"Don't talk about your mother like that," Jimmy said. "Besides, I want to bring her these donuts. They're very good."

Charlie humored him. Jimmy also stopped at the Beirut Bakery and bought her a couple of loaves of dark rye. "Her favorite," he said.

They had to knock for five minutes before Mary answered the door in her robe. "What the hell?" she said.

"Red Cross," Jimmy said. "Care package."

Mary opened the door. Jimmy handed her his gifts.

"Uh, we can't stay," he said. "Uh, Charlie wanted to bring you this stuff for breakfast. And, uh, I wanted to invite you to Thanksgiving next week."

Charlie looked at his mother and nodded. What else could he do?

"That's sweet of you boys. I'll check my calendar. I'll let you know."

There was silence. Mary set the box of donuts and the bread on the coffee table. She held the top of her robe closed.

"I've got to get this house clean today," she said. "I've been so busy. It's a wreck."

"We wouldn't notice a dirty house," Jimmy said. "A couple of bachelors like us? Well, okay, Mary, sweetheart, we got to run. Keep the family business going."

Charlie nodded again. When he got in the car, he was about to say something, but he wasn't sure what to say. Before Charlie could speak, Jimmy put up his hand.

"It's my house," Jimmy said. "I don't need to explain a freakin' thing to you."

The day before Thanksgiving, winter gave way to a warm, yellow morning with wind barely strong enough to push a few dried leaves along the pavement. Charlie woke up a little after eight in the morning to the sound of his father vacuuming. Charlie got out of bed and went down the stairs. Jimmy was in boxer shorts, an undershirt, and black socks. His legs were thin and white and nearly hairless, and his arms no longer pulsed with definition. He was struggling with the vacuum on the steps, without his clothes, his thinning hair flopped over his forehead beaded with sweat.

My God, Charlie thought, he's just an old man.

"Morning, Dad," Charlie hollered over the vacuum cleaner.

His father hit the power switch and the machine coughed itself quiet. "Hey," he said. "Sorry I had to wake you. I've been up for two hours, and couldn't wait anymore."

"No, that's fine," Charlie said. He smiled. He wanted suddenly to be cheerful and full of youth and energy. "I'll get dressed and give you a hand."

"There's coffee," Jimmy said.

In the shower, Charlie began to believe that his father was trying for something specific here, with this Thanksgiving. What if his mother would be so moved by the invitation, what if she would be so impressed by the new Jimmy Pappas and his giant, clean new house that she would decide to go on the wagon herself. Charlie pictured his mother and father saying their morning affirmations together, exercising at some sterile suburban health club in matching his & her sweat suits, then, after breakfast at Big Boy, walking arm in arm into an AA meeting.

Is it true, Charlie wondered, that children of divorce never quite come to terms with the end of their parents' marriage? Do they always, in their heart of hearts, believe that reconciliation and reunion are possible?

Down in the kitchen, Charlie whistled as he poured his coffee.

"You're in a better mood," his father said.

"I am," Charlie said.

"You're glad that your mother is coming over?"

"I am," he said. "Yes."

They spent the morning with the *Today* show on the television, dusting the furniture, washing the floors, cleaning sinks and toilets.

"I hope she notices all our hard work," Charlie said. Now, not only was he feeling like some naïve, hopeful kid, he was sounding like one.

They ate an early lunch of tuna salad on wheat garnished with fat-free corn chips and then they went shopping. His father insisted on a twenty-pound turkey at the grocery store; he bought a cartload of food, enough for a family of twelve or more.

. . . .

Late that night, after they'd cleaned every room in the house, prepped much of the food for the next day's meal, and called Mary to confirm the invitation (Jimmy was sending a cab), they sat in the family room, watching television. A van pulled into the driveway.

Charlie stood up and went to the door. The sign on the side door of the van read A-1 Airport Transport.

"Don't say anything," Jimmy said. "Like I said, it's my freaking house."

Jana was wearing a long charcoal coat, black leather boots, black gloves. She pulled a small suitcase behind her. In her absence, Charlie had detested her, loathed her, wished danger and despair on her person. Seeing her coming toward the door in a dim flood of porch light, he loved her again.

"Hey," Jana said.

"Jana," Charlie said. "Jana."

"Charlie," she said. "I'm sorry."

"About what?" he said.

She looked at him crooked.

"Oh, oh that?" Charlie said. "I'd almost forgotten."

"Happy Thanksgiving," she said.

"Right," he said.

Jimmy shook Jana's hand, invited her inside. It was not how Charlie had pictured such a reunion at all. He'd rehearsed cold lines and steel-eyed stares. But he had not had anytime to prepare, and he moved along with his whims. He hugged her.

"Is this you, Dad? Did you do this?" Charlie said, when he finally was able to let go.

Jimmy said, "Big freaking day tomorrow. I'm turning in."

Then they were alone in the kitchen; Charlie came up behind her and kissed her neck.

"There's a double bed in my room," Charlie said.

"And you'd have your own can," Jimmy called from the top of the stairs. "It's nice."

They'd been in love a long time, Charlie thought. They could talk in the morning. He didn't know what Jana was thinking. She had grown quiet. Maybe he didn't want to know what she was thinking.

He led her up the stairs. "We should talk," Jana said. "Don't you think this is a little odd? I should sleep in another room."

"Jana," Charlie said. "I loved you for seven years. So we've been apart for a few months, so what?"

"A lot has happened," Jana said. She was whispering.

"I haven't had sex in a long time," Charlie whispered back.

Jana did not smile, not at first, but then she laughed. "I can't believe you," she said. "But you look good. And it's been a long time for me too."

"It has?" Charlie said. He couldn't help beaming.

She nodded and kissed his lips.

"We can talk tomorrow," he said and took her hand.

Right now, he just wanted to lie in bed and be glad that she was there. He had no rage in him, he felt like a child who had thrown a tantrum and had finally come out of his room for dinner. He felt embarrassed by everything, the affair, his breakdown, how he would not come to the phone.

"I thought you hated me," she said.

"I did," he said. "Until I saw you again. I had planned to be mad."

"Did you know your father invited me?" she said. "He sent me the money for a ticket."

"No idea," he said.

"Does this mean you want to get back together?" she said. "Because, I don't know. This is still very odd, too fast."

"Jana, I want to be with you here, just for now. That's all I want. We might die tomorrow. Let's just be together tonight."

They went into the bedroom and closed the door. She touched his face and whispered to him. "Fine," she said. "I'd like that."

"Are you okay?" he asked.

"I'm fine," she said, taking off her skirt and folding it on a chair. "I've just been traveling all day. You're right. We can talk tomorrow."

"I missed you so much," he said.

The next morning, snow flurries. Charlie awoke to a window filled with gray light and downy white fuzz floating in the sky. It felt divine. Suddenly, Charlie understood his father's cheerfulness, understood what it felt like to have another chance. *One day a time. Easy does it. Let go and let God.* His father's petty maxims somehow seemed wise and full of truth. He nudged Jana.

She seemed to take a few minutes to figure out where she was, and then she sat up in bed, pulling the sheet over her breasts.

"Look," Charlie said. "Snow."

"Oh boy," Jana said. And then she buried her face in her pillow.

They showered together in silence, as familiar as if there had been no five-month hiatus in their morning rituals. She sat on the toilet and peed as he brushed his teeth. They picked up their intimacy with ease.

Dressed and with wet hair, they went downstairs. Jimmy Pappas was brushing melted butter on the spanokopita, about to put it in the oven.

"Good morning, you two," he called and Charlie couldn't help blushing. Jana looked annoyed and exhausted.

"Everything okay, Jimmy?" Jana said.

"Great, great. I've got a taxi picking up your mother around one, we should eat by three, and you don't have to lift a finger."

Jana looked at Charlie and mouthed the words, *Your mother?* Charlie had, of course, told her everything about his parents.

Charlie picked at some carrots that Jimmy was chopping.

"I did forget one thing," Jimmy said. "Cranberries."

"We'll go get some," Charlie said.

"If you don't mind," Jimmy said.

"That's fine," Jana said.

They kissed in the car, a long, slow kiss that Charlie wanted to last longer. Jana pulled away. "Cranberries," she said.

In the store, Charlie wanted to buy canned cranberries, but Jana insisted on fresh.

"Fresh is too much trouble," Charlie said. "I want canned ones. Open and eat."

"Buy fresh," she said. "I can prep them myself. I'll need some sugar and some oranges too."

The express check-out was crowded with men standing in line, all holding single items—butter, canned pumpkin, or bread crumbs. Charlie flipped through a men's magazine. He found an article that said, "How do you know when she's cheating?"

He laughed, and showed the article to Jana. "Wish I had seen that article a long time ago," he said.

Jana walked out of the store, leaving Charlie standing in line.

He paid for the groceries and found her in the parking lot, standing next to the car.

"What was that?" Jana said.

"A joke," Charlie said.

"Not funny," Jana said.

"A little levity, that's all," he said.

"You know, I didn't come here to fuck you. I came here to settle things once and for all, to see what remained."

"I know," Charlie said. "I was wrong. It's weird. I'm adjusting. You had time to adjust. You prepared yourself for this. I was taken by surprise."

She wouldn't look at him. He set the groceries in the backseat.

"That's fair," she said. "Okay."

And then, when they were back in the car, the heater on, she told Charlie something she'd been waiting to tell him.

"Last night," she said. "It's just that I may have given you the wrong idea. I'm not saying it was bad, but I'm also not sure we should get back together."

"Why are you here then?"

"Your father, he begged me. He said that you needed closure. He said you were suicidal, he worried for your life. I didn't want you to die. I think he was exaggerating though. You seem fine."

Charlie felt his insides crumple, his organs deflating.

"Are you still with the sculptor?"

"No."

"Really?"

"He left," she said.

"So what was last night?" he asked. "I don't get it."

"It was closure, Charlie. I guess that's what it was. It was nice."

"It felt nice? Or it was a nice thing to do?"

"Both," she said. She touched his arm. "Oh, Charlie."

They drove back from the store in silence: Charlie with windshield wipers on although there was no rain, Jana looking at the package of cranberries in her hands.

"Hey, can we do one thing?" Charlie said, as they pulled into his father's driveway. "Can we deal with this later? Can we wait until tomorrow to tell my father? Could we just make sure he has a nice Thanksgiving? I mean, he's been very nice to me and . . . "

"Of course," Jana said. "Of course. I'm a human being, Charlie. I'm not some kind of monster."

"Whatever," Charlie said.

They turned on the Lions' game at noon, which helped to keep the conversation to a minimum. Jana seemed overly interested in the game, Charlie pretended to be concerned about the Lions losing, and Jimmy chattered incessantly while he cooked, about Greek men, and their ability to cook without recipes.

"We make love without manuals too," he said.

Around one-thirty, Mary arrived at the door, shaky and pale, but with clean hair and perfume and a long-sleeved black dress Charlie recognized from years before. She had dyed her hair, Charlie noticed. There was no gray. She smiled when she saw Jana. "This is so nice," she said. "To see the two of you together."

"Mary, how are you?" Jana said.

Jana embraced Mary. Mary appeared startled. Charlie's stomach turned under the weight of the fraudulent pleasantness in the air. He felt hot.

"Mary, you look radiant," Jimmy said, his voice booming. "A sight for sore eyes, welcome, welcome!"

He wiped his hands on his apron, gave his ex-wife a half-hug and kissed her on the cheek. Mary's hands remained at her sides. Jimmy almost knocked her over. She did look good, Charlie thought. She was trying. Jimmy was always barreling into people, hugging them without warning.

Jana seemed too practiced at insincere conversation, Charlie thought. He had always thought so, and now he was convinced. Jana engaged everyone in conversation, talking to Mary about painting, talking to Jimmy about the art of salesmanship, even getting Charlie to talk about his love of teaching, which was non-existent. Jana punctuated the talking with spurts of high, delirious laughter. Her cheeks seemed flushed red with the effort. Jimmy left the room to check on the turkey.

"So, Mary," Jana said, "What do you do with yourself during the day? Are you teaching? Or do you just paint, paint, paint all day?"

"Jesus Christ," Charlie said. Jana knew Mary was a drunk who could barely hold a brush most days.

"Well, I'm between things," Mary said. And then her voice went up a few decibels, just loud enough so Jimmy could hear her in the kitchen, where he was basting the turkey. "My boyfriend, Frank, he's up in Alaska right now, looking for a place for us to live. He'll send for me soon, I'll sell the house, and then I'll go up there with him and paint some landscapes I've never seen before. Frank is very supportive of my work."

In the kitchen, there was the shattering of glass.

"Are you okay?" Mary called. "Jimmy?"

"Everything is fine," Jimmy said, walking into the room wiping his hands on a towel.

"Good," Mary said.

"You know, this is so nice," Jimmy said. "Maybe we should all move in here and it could be like this all the time. One big, happy family."

Everyone burst out in delirious laughter, even though everyone, Charlie thought, knew that Jimmy Pappas was dead serious.

The Lions lost, the turkey was done, and a little after three they sat down for dinner. Mary had a flask in her purse, and had gone off to the bathroom every twenty minutes or so for a hit. She was not drunk, but there was some color in her face and her hands had stopped shaking.

Jimmy said grace, a long rambling prayer that thanked the giver of all good gifts, especially the Lamb of God, Jesus Christ.

"Cheers," Charlie said. "Here, here." He lifted his water glass for a toast.

"Um, is there any wine?" Mary said.

"That'd be nice," Jana said. Charlie knew her stamina was leaving her. She would need alcohol to get through the rest of the afternoon.

"My father is a recovered alcoholic," Charlie said. "Goddamn, people."

"So," Mary said. "We're not."

Charlie wanted a drink as bad as anybody. In fact, the whole table seemed terrified of getting through dinner without anything to drink.

"I could run out and get some wine," Jana said. "I mean, that would be easy to do."

"Yes, great," Mary said.

"I'd rather we didn't," Jimmy said. "You know, I'm still in the early steps of the program. Lead us not into temptation, you know."

"People, I think we can have dinner without wine," Charlie said.

"Oh, I almost forgot. I got Vernor's," Jimmy said. "I'll get out the Vernor's. It's just ginger ale, Jana, but it'll knock your socks off. It's a Detroit delicacy."

"I've had it," Jana said. "In college."

"I'd prefer wine. Or beer? If you have beer," Mary said, "that would be fine."

"Yeah, beer sounds good," Jana said.

Charlie glared at his mother, who shrugged, and then at Jana, who glared back.

Jimmy came back to the table with four frosted mugs of Vernor's. He remained standing and raised his glass.

"We should all say what we're thankful for," Jimmy said.

Nobody agreed aloud, but Jimmy was determined. "Jana, you go first."

"My art," she said, keeping things generic. "For good friends."

"For my boyfriend Frank and our new life in Alaska," Mary said. "I'm so thankful for Frank."

Charlie watched Jimmy's smile waver. "Besides Frank," Jimmy said.

"What else besides Frank?"

"This is sad," Mary said.

"For Jana," Charlie said, going next, keeping the thankful train on the tracks. "Yes, for Jana. Jana, Jana, Jana! And for my family."

"That's so sweet," Mary said.

"Isn't it?" Jana said. "Except we're not getting back together."

"What?" Jimmy said.

"We're not getting back together," she said.

"Fine," Jimmy said. He took a note card from his shirt pocket. He cleared his throat. "I am thankful for second chances. There is a woman I met over thirty years ago, who I never treated the way she deserved, but, by the power of Jesus, I want to ask her forgiveness."

"Pathetic," Mary said.

Jana slumped down in her chair.

"Let him finish," Charlie said.

"He's a fool," Jana whispered. "Mary doesn't love him."

"I love Frank," Mary said.

"Frank left you," Charlie said. "Face it. He's gone."

"And your wife left you," Mary said. "How much did he pay you, Jana? Isn't that just like Jimmy? He paid you, didn't he? Paid you to fake happiness for awhile?"

Jana put her hand over her eyes.

"What, I'd say it's worth at least a grand or two?" Mary said.

"Did he pay you for the ticket?" Charlie asked. "Or did you make money on this. Is this a job? How much?"

"Charlie, what do you think I am, some kind of whore?"

Mary snorted. Charlie pounded a fist on the table.

"I need to call a cab," Jana said.

And as the shouting grew louder, Jimmy Pappas ran from the table, down the basement steps, and there was the sound of wood being split into pieces. They sat at the table; nobody said anything. Charlie started serving food.

"He'll be okay in a minute," he said. "He just needs to cool down."

After Charlie had heaped everybody's plate with food, Jimmy called to him from the basement. "Chuckie, come down here."

Charlie stood up from the table. He picked up a piece of white meat, and chewed it.

"Nobody leaves," Charlie said.

"Be careful," Jana said. "He might have a gun."

"He won't hurt anybody," Mary said. "Not Jimmy."

"Charlie," Jana said.

"You guys keep eating," he said. "I'll be right back."

"Chuckie, please," Jimmy called from the basement.

Charlie was picturing his father holding a pistol to his head, but found his father standing in the space beneath the stairs, looking at a large wooden crate that was nailed shut. He'd already pried one of the front panels off of the crate, but there was another panel underneath it.

"Son, the day I quit drinking," Jimmy said, "I came home and I spilled every drop of liquor I had down the sink. I was shaking the whole time. I felt like I was going deaf and blind. I was sick. No fooling, I even licked the sink out of regret after I'd gotten rid of all the booze."

Charlie nodded. He heard Mary and Jana coming down the stairs, and he felt them stop and stand behind him, but he didn't turn toward them at all. Jimmy kept on talking.

"But in this crate," Jimmy said, "in here, there are forty-eight bottles of wine. The last batch my father—your *Papou*—ever made. He wanted me to save them until your wedding day. It was his dying wish. He loved making this wine, and he thought it might help him be present in some way at your wedding."

"I see," Charlie said.

"You were the only one to carry on the family name," he said. "The only male grandson he had."

"I know it," Charlie said.

"This crate is nailed shut, and with God's help, I never tore it open, even at my lowest point."

"Well, Dad. It doesn't look like I'll be getting married anytime soon. Let's go upstairs."

"That's okay, son. Maybe you and Jana will get back together and marry. Maybe you won't. I just want you to know there is some happiness in life, and it's always there, lurking in the darkest corners, waiting to be set free."

Charlie nodded. He didn't know what else to do.

"Come on, Dad."

"That's all I want for you, son," Jimmy said. "Happiness. A nice, peaceful life."

Charlie turned back to see his mother rolling her eyes. Jana started to go back up the steps. Then Charlie followed her. "Mom and Dad, enough is enough. We might as well eat. There's all that food that Dad made."

Jana and Charlie sat back down at the table, waiting for Mary and Jimmy. "He won't do it, he won't open the wine, he's bluffing," Charlie said.

And then, suddenly, there was a sound that sounded like a hole being punched into a wall, and Charlie turned around. Then he heard Mary yell, "Atta boy!" and Jimmy could be heard huffing and stomping his way up the stairs. He reappeared, suddenly drenched in sweat; in each hand he held two bottles of his father's homemade wine.

"You're right, everyone, we need to drink!"

Mary was behind him, an open bottle already tilted toward the ceiling.

Charlie almost stood and wrestled his father to the ground. But he could not move, he had no idea what to do next. Jana clucked with concern, and looked at him, raising her eyebrows.

"That's the holiday spirit!" his mother said, and Jimmy and Jana laughed. Charlie just watched his father take the corkscrew to those long-saved bottles of wine, and did not move. His mother rummaged through the cabinets for wine glasses, which were hidden on a top shelf behind the flour and sugar. She took the glasses from the cabinet and brought them to the table.

"There's more where this came from," Jimmy said, he handed each person a bottle of wine. "The best wine in all of Greece!"

Then he drank half of his down in one wild, frantic gulp. Charlie and Jana looked at each other, shrugged, and then filled their glasses.

By the time dinner was over, the house had the warm, affectionate glow that can only envelop a house full of drunks. Everyone was touchy and feely, stumbling about the house. Twelve bottles of wine had been opened. Charlie and Jana had already snuck off to the bedroom once, taking pumpkin pie upstairs with them, but instead of sharing the dessert, they found themselves falling into bed, and making drunk, quiet love. Jana fell asleep in bed, her skirt still pushed up around her waist, her blouse unbuttoned, her bra open. She was snoring. Charlie helped her out of her clothes, knowing nothing was different, knowing the intimacy was as empty as any other intimacy. Tomorrow, she would leave him. He would not see her again. He felt sick. He wondered if he could get his father to an AA meeting that night. He knew they stayed open all the time on holidays. Maybe all four of them could go to the meeting. They could throw open the door and bellow, "Happy Drunks-giving!" as they took their seats.

Charlie went down to the kitchen. His mouth was dry. His body ached. He heard his parents' voices, and he walked slowly and softly, trying to hear what they were saying. What could they possibly have to say? He stood in the doorway to the kitchen, and saw his mother and father sitting at the table covered in half-empty serving bowls, dirty dishes, and empty bottles of wine. They were slouched in their chairs, eyes half-shut, talking in inaudible, hoarse voices. To Charlie, it was apparent—there would be no reconnections, no second chances, no renewals or rebirths that would come out of that blurry, wine-soaked haze. But then he looked at Jimmy, who was reaching across the table to touch Mary's hand, and Charlie saw that his mother was leaning in close to his father, as if she expected to hear some profound secret. Mary sat up, and her eyes brightened. She smiled. Jimmy said something to her, and then Charlie saw that his mother was laughing; she was laughing and tossing her hair.

Detroit-area native and University of Michigan alum **Dean Bakopoulos'** first novel, *Please Don't Come Back from the Moon*, was a *New York Times* Notable Book in 2005, as well as a Michigan Notable Book and a New York Public Library "Book to Remember." His second novel, *Harmony*, will be published by Harcourt in the fall of 2007. The recipient of a 2006 National Endowment for the Arts fellowship, he lives in Mineral Point, Wisconsin, with his wife and daughter and is the executive director of the Wisconsin Humanities Council.

THE SISTERS GODHELPUS

THOMAS LYNCH

MY SISTER BRIGID'S yellow lab bitch Baxter was put to death last Monday. What can be said of such proceedings? That every dog has its day? The following from my sister's partner Kathy tells the tale.

It is with a heavy heart that I write this e-mail to notify family of the death of Baxter Bailey (11 1/2 years old) on Monday, July 14th. Kidney failure. She was buried in a deserved spot, at Mullett Lake. She is survived by her sister, Bogey Bear (who is a little lost as to what has transpired) and her mother/best friend/companion—Brigid. A brief ceremony will be held the weekend of the 25th on Mullett Lake.

Whether you loved her, feared her, or were entertained by her, she will never be forgotten. Long live her memory.

Kathy

In receipt of which I replied:

Dear Kathy and B,

Thanks for the sad and tidy news. I will not pretend to have admired the deceased. She was, however, a walking (more lately hobbled) example of the power of love. She was not bright, not lovely, less communicative than most mum plants, and drugged into a stupor for most of her life. But here is the mystery—the glorious mystery—that a woman as bright and lovely, articulate and sober as our B loved her, loved her unambiguously. For a man of my own limitations (and they are legion) the love B showed to Baxter was a reminder of the lovability of all God's creatures—even me. In that sense she was a constant beacon of faith and hope and love. If this is what they call the Dog's Life, I say more of it is the thing we need.

You and B will be in my prayers for a brief if deserved bereavement.

Love & Blessings,
T

PS: Pat and I will get the stone and willn't stint.

It was a hasty but heartfelt sentiment, managed between the usual mélange of mortuary, literary, and family duties. I meant only comfort by it. And though we get the headstones at wholesale, the gesture was genuine.

Part of the comeuppance for calling our small chain of funeral homes Lynch & Sons is that the daughters—our sisters—control the purse. Three of my father's six sons, I among them, went off to mortuary school and got licensed, years ago, to embalm the dead and direct the living through the funerary maze. Before our father died, we bought the enterprise from him. His three daughters—ever his favorites— went to university and business schools and were installed in various key positions. Mary is the bookkeeper and pay mistress. Julie Ann is her factotum. Brigid handles trusts and insurance and preneed finance, and is the de facto comptroller at my brother Pat's funeral home. We call them the three furies and they travel between my establishment and Pat's bringing light and joy and accountability.

When I see them together—Mary, Julie, and Brigid—I often think of the headlands on the Dingle Peninsula called "The Three Sisters," which rise in a triad of sweeping, greeny peaks to protect the Irish countryside from the ravages of the North Atlantic. Like those features in the west Kerry topography, they are strikingly beautiful, immovable, and possessed of powers we know nothing of. They are, it is well known, Irish in origin—the powers, the sisters. The source of all that is holy and hazardous about them is a matrilineage that finds its way back to a kitchen and cauldron in a boggy parish in the old country where only marginally post-Celtic mystics bedded with poor farmers who never knew what they were getting into. It is a lineage of women who emigrated on their own, in numbers equal to or greater than men, enduring steerage and indignity, years of indenture, to better themselves and their American children.

The sisters come by their powers honestly. They are their late mother's daughters and have inherited that sainted woman's charms and spells, blue eyes and Parian complexion, intellect and idolatries. They are, as she was, devotees of the votive and vigil, rosary and novena, perpetual adorations, lives of the saints, imitations of Christ, statues of the BVM and Sacred Heart, stations of the cross, relics, waters, ribbons, and badges, prayer books and scapulars, all of which make them morally superior and spiritually dangerous. The arsenal of their godly wraths and blessed tempers would, in the best of circumstances be turned on their spouses, to their betterments. But as each has partnered and consorted with the most amiable soul mate, they've only to train their tantrums upon their older brothers whose puny potvaliances, collective and individual, are no match for the furies. It makes them, I suppose, easier women to come home to.

Wednesdays Mary and Julie come to my funeral home in Milford for payroll and accounts—receivable and payable. Brigid remains at my brother's office but calls to consult with her sisters three or four times on the day.

Last Wednesday, when Mary and Julie read my sympathy note they rolled their eyes and smote me with their disapproval. "How could you say such an awful thing about Baxter to your grieving sister?"

"What awful thing?" I asked. "*A beacon of faith and hope and love?*"

"This bit about the mum plant and stupor . . . couldn't you have just said something nice? Something about her loyalty?"

They did not see that stating the obvious about Baxter's life and times was central to the art of condolence and, a fortiori, the construction of the note's kindlier sentiment.

Truth told the dog was a disaster, which had worn out her welcome by eleven years with everyone except, of course, my sister, B. A female assigned a fashionably suburban, chicly Anglo-Irish, but still oddly mannish name, "Baxter Bailey" never seemed to know whether she was coming or going, whether to hump or be humped, whether she ought to lift a leg or squat. When she had just achieved adult size and indoor continence, she bit my sister—quite literally the hand that was feeding her—thereby missing the only requisite point of Dog 101, to wit: *don't bite the humans*. B. had her neutered. Later she growled and snapped at B's infant and toddling nieces and nephews as they approached to pet her. On the strength of these misdemeanors and distempers I once had B. talked into putting her down, citing the liability presented by a dog that might attack neighbors or their pets or children, houseguests, or passersby. I reminded her of the One Bite Rule, with roots in the Book of Exodus, near where the ordinances on the seduction of virgins are recorded, (alas, the emergent patriarchy!) which held that an owner would be called to account for the second infraction of a domestic animal. I'd gone so far as to set an appointment with the vet for the euthanasia and had Baxter leashed and loaded in the backseat and B. agreeably disposed to the good sense of it all. But when she got there she waffled in her resolve. She asked the vet, instead, for medication, something, she pleaded, "to calm her down"—Baxter, not Brigid. The cocktail of pharmaceuticals thus prescribed amounted to the non-surgical equivalent of lobotomy. She was given Phenobarbital to control her seizures, Lasix as a diuretic, something for her stomach disorders and insomnia, and a giant daily dose of canine Thorazine—enough I daresay to dull an orangutan—to quiet her demons, real and imagined. Baxter remained more or less on the edge of a coma for the rest of her life. Like some of those old lads you'd see in the pubs, the tooth gone out of them, supping up their daily sedation. She never snapped at anyone or anything again. She roamed about, bumping into the landscape and geography and furniture, like an outsized, spongy orb in a game of pinball or bumper-pool. At the lake, Mullett Lake—where we've recreated *en famile* for years and ruined the property values—she would sometimes walk into the water, as if some distant memory of her breed still flickered in her. Brigid would have to wade in and lead her ashore. People would toss Frisbees and tennis balls in her direction, hoping to engage her in the usual play. They would bounce off her snout and hindquarters causing not so much as a flicker in Baxter's glassy eyes. The customary commands—Sit, Fetch, Heel, Come—meant no more to Baxter than a recitation from the *Tain* or the *Annals of the Four Masters*. To the voice of her mistress or any human directive Baxter was uniformly non-responsive. The only trick she ever performed was "Breathe Baxter! Breathe."

"Where there's life there's hope," Brigid would say, ever the loyal human, as if the dog's damage were reversible. It was a sad thing to witness, this zombified miscreant working her way through a decade and then some of meaningless days. Her end was a mercy to all and sundry.

But what my sisters Mary and Julie seemed to be saying was that no empathy or fellow feeling could be tendered that did not include the ruse that Baxter was Rin Tin Tin done up in drag, or Lassie or Old Yeller—a great dog to be greatly grieved and greatly missed—a loyal, loving, exceptional specimen of Man's (read Woman's too) Best Friend. When I protested that Baxter would not want to be placed on a pedestal, or to be loved for other than the amalgam of distress and misfortune that she was, that authentic feeling could not be based upon a vast denial of reality, they both rolled their eyes in counter-clockwise turns and said, one to the other, "He just doesn't get it."

That I just don't "get it" is the conventional wisdom and the conversation's end with the several women in my life. Though I am the son of a good woman, now deceased and lamented, and sibling of three of them; though I am the father, friend, and spouse of females, like most of the men of my generation, and almost all of the men of my extraction, I just don't get it and maybe never will. A library of literature currently exists on the whys and whatnots about Irish men—with the notable exceptions of Bono and Liam Neeson—which render them denser than other specimens when it comes to getting it so far as women are concerned. The Irish American male is similarly disposed, unless there is a remedial dose of Italian, Mexican, or Russian in his genealogy, in which case not getting it gives way to not giving a wrap.

Five mornings out of every seven the woman across the street in the gingerbready Queen Anne manse with the Martha Stewart garden emerges with her two snow white toy poodles to attend to what Victorians called the duties of their toilet. Each is the size of a bowling ball and their tiny feces like wee, green, cat-eyed marbles, about which more, alas, anon. This daft and dainty pair of little sexless things is named for their mistress's favorite libations, "Chardonnay" and "Champagne," which are shortened in the diminutive to "Chardy" and "Champy," as she is heard to call out when they go bouncing about the neighborhood in search of somewhere to take their tiny designer shits. Most mornings the entourage looks a little dazed, as if they all might've gotten into the vodka and tonic late. But who am I to say?

She doesn't like me—the woman across the street. The list and variety of our quarrels and quibbles on civic, cultural, and neighborhood issues is a long and exhaustive one. I'm sure she thinks I just don't get it. Truth told, I'm not that gone on her. Except for the occasional wave or sidelong glance and nod, we make no effort at neighborliness. We knew from the get go we would not be friends. And though I admire her refusal to maintain any pretence or decorum, it is better to do so from afar. Maybe we remind each other of each other's former spouses.

Still, I uphold her right to her ways as she upholds my right to mine. This is America, after all. Though we hold forth from opposite sides of the street, the name of the street is Liberty. So the insipid little dogs, the fellow she's married to (who must on the weekends attend to Chardy and Champy's morning office), the overgrowth of garden—these are situations I accept like variations on the theme of weather. It could be worse is what I tell myself. In the same way she tolerates me and mine: the overflow parking from the funeral home, the mysterious vans arriving at all hours, the bright impatiens we plant every year among the uninspired juniper and yews and, the dear knows, my manifest personal foibles. Like me, she has much to tolerate.

It's only when she brings Chardy and Champy over to the funeral home to sniff about in search of a proper shitting ground that I take especial umbrage. To give her and her poodles their due, she always comes armed with a plastic bag and a rubber glove—the latter affecting the transfer of the turdlettes from my greensward into the former. She is, in keeping with local and regional custom, fastidious about the fecal matters. I think she uses them with her prized delphinium. But for some reason I cannot shake the sense that I and my real estate have been shat upon, and that there is a kind of message hidden in the act, that there is some intelligence she intends for me to "get" by the witness of it. Nor can I shake the temptation, so far resisted, to mosey on over and shit on hers. There's liberty in it and a kind of truth.

After my first wife and I divorced, I was the custodial parent of a daughter and three sons from the time they were ten, nine, six, and four, until I was married again, some seven years later, to the Woman of My Dreams. It's when I most wanted to be a feminist. The divisions of labor and money, power and parental duties—those good-for-the-goose-and-gander concerns of the third wave feminism of the day— were themes I found the most intriguing.   I read de Beauvoir and Friedan, Brownmiller and Millet, Germain Greer and Gloria Steinem. I read Robin Morgan's manhating rhetoricals on "cock privilege" and castration and Doris Lessing's *Golden Notebook* and Andrea Dworkin's sad and incomprehensible screed and wondered if there were miseries out of which such people could really never be put. I was a card carrying, contributing member of the N.O.W. I vetted my personal lexicon for sexist terms. Postman became mail carrier, chairman became chairperson, ladies became women. I never said "girl." I made my sons wash dishes and my daughter take out the trash and filed for child support from my former spouse, in keeping with the equal rights amends I was trying to make. I was encouraged by the caseworker from the Friend of the Court's office—a fetching woman with green eyes and a by-the-bookish style—who said the children should get 50 percent of their non-custodial parent's income. This, she assured, was a gender indifferent directive. The state prescribed formula called for 20 percent for the first child and 10 percent for every one after that. "It's what you'd be paying," she said matter-of-factly, "if the shoe were on the other foot." I figured I could save it for their higher educations.

The judge, however, overruled the caseworker's recommendation. Her honor conceded that while in theory our sons and daughter deserved the benefits of both of their parents' gainful labors, she could not bring herself to order a mother to pay child support, even one that saw her children but every other weekend. It was enough that the erstwhile missus was making her own way in a difficult world. Supplemental payments for the support of her children were more of an indenture than the judge was prepared to order. During the brief hearing I was advised by her pinstriped counsel to leave well enough alone. I just didn't get it after all.

In Ireland at the time they had no ex-wives and more than once I thought, "how very civilized." There was no shortage of domestic misery, of course, no shortage of abuse, just no divorce. It wasn't allowed. So people moved apart and lived their lives as, more or less, ex-spousal equivalents. There was a Divorce Referendum in 1986 but the priests all preached against it in the country places. It failed by a convincing margin. Still men and women wanted civil disunions and lobbied for them until the measure passed just as convincingly in '92. Now gay men and lesbians want to get married, and who could blame them, what with the bliss, for lobbying for the blessings and paperwork?

Back in those days I kept a lovely cur, free of any registered pedigree or jittery habits. She had a small head, a large body, and an agreeable temperament. We called her Heidi. When she was a puppy I walked her round our little city lot at the corner of Liberty and East Streets and the half block next door occupied by the funeral home and its parking lot and told her that she could come and go as she pleased but that if she showed up at home, more nights than not, she'd be fed and petted and sheltered well; she'd be loved and cuddled, bathed and brushed. In short, if she would do her part, we'd do ours. Such was the nature of our covenant.

And though Heidi traveled widely, she never strayed. She would follow the mail carriers on their rounds, forefending them from more vicious dogs. She'd find her way to the corner butcher shop and beg for bones and to the bakery on Main Street to beg for day-old donuts. She was particularly fond of custard-filleds. She would stare balefully into the doorway of the delicatessen for hours until someone proffered some Polish ham or Havarti cheese or some other succulent or delicacy. Later in the day she would make her way to the schoolyard to accompany my younger sons home from their day's studies. Evenings she'd position her repose in the driveway of the funeral home parking lot, acting the speed bump and sentinel whilst the children practiced their skateboarding or Frisbee or whiffle-ball. On weekends she'd be in Central Park, fishing with my oldest son or accompanying my daughter and her friends on their rounds through town, field-testing their ever changing figures and fashions. She died old and fat and happy and was buried under the mock-orange bush where she used to shade herself against the summer heat. Near two decades since she is still remembered with reverence; her exploits and loyalties are legendary.

Which is all I ever wanted out of love and husbanding, family and parenting—to be fondly regarded by the ones I loved; to be known for how I came home at night, minded the borders, kept an eye out for impending dangers, paid the piper, did my job, loved them all fiercely to the end. It was the dream I inherited from my mother and father for whom a division of labor did not mean a disproportion of power.

I was, in those times, a casualty of the gender wars that the men and women of my generation waged over duties and identities. It was, I suppose, a necessary battle, which we did not choose, and were powerless to avoid, damned if we did and if we didn't fight. We all took too seriously the carping and dyspepsia of a generation for whom sexism was a sin only men could commit, and only and always against women. Power and money were zero sum games. Sex and love were often trophies. Women of the day kept their litany of injustices—the glass ceilings, the hostile work environments, the sixty-three cents on the dollar deal, the who does the most work in the house debate. The little tally of inconsistencies I maintained kept driving me crazier and crazier. That the courts gave reproductive options to women but not to men was a bother. There was no clinic to which men could repair to terminate their impending paternity. If "choice" were such a fine thing, it occurred to me, oughtn't one and all, not one and half of the population have it? That my daughter might "choose" a career in the military but only my sons had to register for the draft struck me as odd. No less the victim-chic status of the feminist intelligentsia who were always ranting about "women and other minorities" whilst quietly ignoring the fact that women had been the majority for years. The planet was 52 percent female. That women not only outnumbered men, they outlived them—by years, not months, in every culture—seemed a thing that ought to be, at least, looked into. Never mind the incessant sloganeering, or the militia of women who blamed Ted Hughes for Sylvia Plath's suicide or who blamed their husbands for the history of the world or who turned men into the tackling dummies for their chronic discontents. Maybe it was all that "every intercourse is an act of rape" hysteria or "a woman needs a man like a fish needs a bicycle," or the way they joked about the man who had his penis cut off by his angry wife. I used to wonder what late night talk show host would survive any less than reverential comment about a woman's genitalia if the damage had been reversed. Violence against women was quite rightly abhorred whilst violence against men was generally ignored. Nothing in the literature rang more true to me than something I had overheard in a conversation between pathologists who were autopsying a fatal domestic case: "A man will kill his wife, then kill himself," one said grimly, "a woman kills her husband, then does her nails." Whatever else I did not get, I got that one loud and clear: the higher ground of entitlement that victims, self-proclaimed, could occupy. I'm certain there were additional grievances, like so much else, I've forgotten now.

In ways that were not so for my parents' generation and, please God, will not be so for my sons' and daughter's, the men and women of my generation suffered a kind of disconnect which left them each wary of the other's intentions, each ignorant of the other's changing, each speaking a dialect the other could not cipher, each wondering why the other just didn't get it. Such are the accidents of history and hers—that we make aliens of our intimates, enemies of friends, strange bedfellows entirely that crave the common ground but rarely really find it.

So it is with nations and neighbors, parents and children, brothers and sisters, family and friends—the list we keep of grievances keeps us perpetually at odds with one another, alone in a world that is growing smaller, more distant from each other, more estranged.

The sisters, Godhelpus, are praying for peace and reconciliation and forgiveness. They are praying to be vessels of God's love and mercy. They say it will take a miracle and that the world changes one heart at a time. They have unleashed the hounds of their Hibernian faith—the rubrics of which involve candles, moonlight, chrisms, icons, incense, and every manner of mystic unguents, passions, immersions, aromatics, and possibly herbs the recipes for which were no doubt published in the Gnostic Gospels, found in those jars.

I still don't get it. And I've quit trying to. Years of living with and among women have convinced me I'm as well off with no dog in that fight. My daughter, my sisters, my beloved wife (in the associative, not possessive sense), and no few women that I count as lifelong friends, the memory of my mother, aunts, and grandmothers—they've all been and remain powerful and courageous and selfless humans, gifted with a dignity and calm that has made me wish I knew them better and all the more wary of their mysterious medicines. Most days I recite a litany of gratitudes for the pleasures of their company, the beauty and beatitudes of their intellections. I'm resolved to say nice things about their dogs. It keeps me, so far, safe from the hounds.

Young neighbor couples and their designer dogs go walking with leashes now on weekend mornings. Their puppies and their babies are all pedigreed. Everyone is better trained and behaved. At every corner there are dangers and warnings, at every intersection, flashing lights and signs. The lesson, of course, is to mind the traffic. They learn to speak and heel and fetch and to return. The men, as is their custom, bark out wisdoms. They pose and sniff, they howl and growl and whine. Their wives and pets grow weary of listening. Some things only the dogs hear, some the women.

I ordered a mum plant for Baxter's obsequies scheduled for later this month at Mullett Lake. I asked the florist to write "Sorry" on the card.

I hope they get it.

Thomas Lynch is a poet and undertaker. He is the author of three collections of poetry: *Skating with Heather Grace, Grimalkin & Other Poems,* and *Still Life in Milford.* His collection of essays, *The Undertaking—Life Studies from the Dismal Trade,* won the Heartland Prize for non-fiction, the American Book Award, and was a finalist for the National Book Award. His work has appeared in *The New Yorker, Poetry, The Paris Review, Harper's, Esquire, Newsweek,* and *The Washington Post.*

KISS

LAURA HULTHÉN THOMAS

THE MORNING IRINA threw the dinner sausage into the River Moskva happened to be the same morning Victor was killed in the terrorist blast, the one that ripped apart his subway car just after the train left the Avtozavodskaya station. At the moment of Victor's incineration she was heaving the fat-flecked sausage over the railing of the Moscow River Bridge, the Kremlin at her back, the river below swollen but not completely constricted by ice. The city was still misty, a veil of frost that would soon burn off. Later Irina would think that she must have heard a sound, seen a plume of winding smoke rise from the death scene to the southeast, beyond the river's elbow as it wended south. But she hadn't. She couldn't have. Victor—the explosion—was miles away from where she stood in the center of the bridge in the center of Moscow. The wail of traffic, the suffusion of exhaust, blocked any revelation. She watched the sausage disappear under the bridge, a pound log of meat wrapped in oil paper, floating reluctantly out of sight like a flat-backed dachshund resigned to drowning, and felt no foreboding at all.

Earlier that morning they had fought, and in one of Irina's typically obscure gestures she decided to throw the sausage into the river. It would not, of course, have the same effect as in the Olesha novel, when Kavalerov contemplated throwing Babichev's newly-engineered, 70-percent-veal, 35-kopeck sausage into the Moskva. For one, the river was not trapped in the fist of winter; had Kavalerov actually tossed it over the railing, the meat would have splashed down with the torpedo effect he was hoping for, satisfying symbolism. But despite his disdain for the soulless new world he was facing, Kavalerov had not the will to free his fate from the sausage's, so fuck his symbolism. If her sausage's journey had the aspect of a sodden dog as it bobbed in what little current was free of the ice, at least Irina had the nerve to throw it away. Kavalerov may not have dared to deprive Babichev of his glorious accomplishment in industrial sausage design, but Victor could certainly do without his dinner if he was going to make so much out of one kiss. It was she, after all, who would have to struggle with what the kiss might mean.

She had not been unhappy with him, either. In the days just prior to the kiss and the carnage she had not been more restless than usual, although that morning, the last time she saw him, he had accused her of ennui, and falling out of love, and even revenge. It was not his last word to her, revenge; later, Irina was at least grateful for that. His last word to her before he had rushed out to make the train to work had, in fact, been sausage, a reference to their dinner that night, and the banality had enraged her, and she had thought how much she would like to fling his fucking sausage into the Moskva, and the impulse carried her straight to the center of the bridge, the same bridge and spot where Kavalerov had waffled and botched his only means of graceful protest. She had done it not only out of anger, not out of unhappiness, the restlessness he accused her of, nor capricious experimentation, another phrase he had used. He had judged her. It was his way to judge, and her way to jump to anger and want to do something ridiculous and wasteful and poorly timed. If he had ever known about the sausage, he would have laughed, forgotten the kiss, and for a moment his cumbersome depression that threatened to snare her, too, would have lifted for them both.

But after, in the shock of learning of his death and of his frantic trek through the tunnel with the other immediate survivors toward the Paveletskaya station, his emergence, after limping up the sweep of the escalator into that bitter frost of mist that should have soothed his smoked lungs and scorched skin but instead stoked unbearable pain, his begging for vodka from a shop owner before his death, a last request that made it into the foreign press accounts as being so fucking quintessentially Russian when it was merely quintessentially desperate; in the shock of it, the loss of him, the kiss was forgotten, subsumed, blasted apart in Moscow's deepest tunnel. Later, if she was ever to think of it at all, she would realize that it was the kiss—not the sausage, not Victor's death—that was the most ridiculous gesture, and she would put it out of her mind shamefully, as if it was the kiss after all that had murdered him.

He shouldn't have minded that kiss so much. Their own relationship began as an affair, the same night a year ago that he had first met her on the third floor landing after a fight with his lover. Irina had been on her way home from a job she would soon lose to the apartment she was afraid she would lose, now that the rent had tripled since privatization and her name wasn't even on the lease; and the neighbors were at it again. In the dim light of the landing—the bare fixture's bulb hadn't been replaced in months—she paused to listen to them, the diluted reverberations of anger drifting down to her like lazy petals on a mild breeze, and she wished she had reason to feel such passion. The voices had just moved in next door to her. There was reason to think they were connected in some way to the thugs who recently had seized possession of the building. The woman had the look of an unfettered government type, someone with connections and willingness to use them in the real estate grab that was still going on, ten years after Russia was supposed to be merrily market-driven. The man she had hardly ever seen. He was dark, reserved, thick around the waist, and he walked with a limp, all traits she associated with criminals. Irina had instinctively avoided them, but there was no avoiding them now as the door to their apartment at the top of the stairs burst open with a flurry of light and voice and chaos and he appeared, muttering a garbled reply to an accusation of some sort. He slammed the door after him, muffling any retort, and stood uncertainly in the hallway, clutching an oval vinyl suitcase, small and feminine, like a make-up case. He started down the stairs carefully, wobbling as if accustomed to using a cane.

Irina pulled her coat around her, preparing to walk past him, to pretend not to have heard. As she stepped from the shadows she averted her eyes, but the movement startled the man and he stumbled on his bad leg, dropping his case. The flimsy lock flew open. Papers, clothing, underwear, brushes and razors and soap scattered in all directions, more stuff than Irina would have thought could possibly fit into the small case.

And then, incredibly, strawberries.

She had to squint to recognize them and look again to believe it, but there they were, a quart at least, rolling down the steps languorously, like rubies, or royalty, the soft thud of the fruit as they fell from stair-step to stair-step echoing the pulse of anticipated embarrassment between them. She looked up at him, almost articulating—strawberries in winter? strawberries at all?—and saw him gasp, grip the railing to prevent his own fall as he watched his life and his berries tumble down to Irina's feet.

The man was mortified, and seemed to shrink into his frayed shirt collar. For a moment, Irina thought he might turn and flee back to his apartment and his altercation, leaving it all to her. It would have been better if he had run, easier for them both in the long run. Irina bent to collect papers, although of course it would have been more logical, more natural, to begin with the fruit. She wanted to pluck the strawberries from the uncompromising grime coating the old cement, gather the plump gems that still lay scattered on the steps like dropped beads, devour them before bruising marred their taste. It was even possible, she considered as she studied them, her paper gathering a ruse for her wonder, that they were not real. Plastic models of perfect fruit, perhaps. There was something false about them, their pristine shape, the rich color she could make out even in the dim light, and the aroma, ripe, sharp. They were domestic, not the wild ones she was accustomed to seeing in the summer markets, already rotted in transport from the Volga. She stacked the papers, but it was the fruit she wanted. She felt the usual wave of resentment at the connections he must have that made strawberries possible.

Her movements prompted him to move. With more speed than she would have expected, he joined her, kneeling awkwardly to snatch at the things that had come to rest on the bottom stair. Things other than the berries. Irina glanced at his lowered face. His expression was impossible to read. His hands shook as he grabbed the case that had landed upside down next to her, which she had not thought to right. The back of the hands bore scars; the tendons jutted out like steel rods. As he pulled the case toward him, she saw that his arms and shoulders under his shirt were as muscular as his hands. Silently, she handed him her neatened sheaf of papers and reached to gather his toiletries.

"You would help best by not helping," the man said suddenly. It was almost a threat. She glanced up at him, surprised, as he hastily twisted his underwear into a ball to stuff back in the case. He was older than she had judged by the sound of his vigorous voice through the wall. She now saw by the shavings of gray that dotted his beard's bristles that he was certainly past forty. Unlike a younger man, who might greet their reluctant rendezvous over his underthings with brash resignation, and even an opportunity for a flirtation, this man was bound to suffer over the sight of an unfamiliar younger woman assisting with his underwear and drawing conclusions about him from their condition, which, of course, she already had. Strawberries aside, he was certainly not mafia, judging by the worn look of all his clothes.

"If you have such little regard for help," Irina said shortly, "you should try to avoid having so much need of it." It irritated her that he could not see how his little drama ensnared them both. She could hardly walk up the stairs past him, any more than he could ask her outright to leave.

He would not look up. "You were listening in. Is your own life so uninteresting, then, that you must lurk about, waiting to be entertained?"

"Thank God you've tumbled so conveniently down the stairs to relieve my boredom."

She spoke without thinking. He sat back on his heels, swaying a bit as if in pain, meeting her eyes for the first time with a knotted stare, as if it was she who had hurt him and not his lover. "How rude," he said quietly. His voice was muted, cold and dense and slow, the velvet of fog.

"You've made your affairs mine," she replied steadily, wondering when the last time was that she had spoken to a man so closely, in failing light and rare isolation, stolen privacy that demanded gentleness, respect, even if they knew each other not at all, and it was not her way to speak so sharply to anyone. Yet he was so much like a sulky dog, crouched low, rocking on his hobbled heels, a dark, scrunched, wronged creature. To feel pity, to treat him with kindness, would be to take away his last hope of dignity. "There's nothing ruder."

It was the right thing to say. He almost smiled as he reached for the fruit, gathering with one unsteady hand, cradling with the other palm. His hand was broad enough to support a small pyramid until he deposited the berries back in the case, nestled them carefully in his clothing. It seemed, suddenly, a private matter. Irina could barely watch the careful way he handled them, dusting each with a quick flutter of thumb and forefinger before balancing it in his other hand. It felt more an intrusion than witnessing the little she had of the quarrel with his lover, or wife, whoever that woman was to him. He seemed very near; suddenly his presence was heat, his care of the berries deliberately sexual. She watched his fingers slide over the berries, and felt the scarcity of men more keenly than the scarcity of fruit.

But it was ridiculous to feel attraction simply because she had not had the opportunity to feel in some time. She broke her stare and resumed the cleanup. There wasn't much left to collect. "Where did you get them?" She had to say something, she thought, but to her dismay her voice echoed piercingly in the spare void of the stairwell walls. She had not meant to speak so loudly.

"Mila brought them." He glanced up briefly at his closed door, as if her name alone would bring her. "She knows the market."

Of course she does, Irina thought; she has the look of someone who does, steely and satiated. Irina loathed anyone connected to the market. She loathed the word itself, the clipped, elliptical sound of it. It was a Russian word, not a cognate; nevertheless, the pronunciation was unnatural, the look of it in print strained, incongruous. The market was debated, stroked, studied and manipulated, and still no one had got it right, right and stable and fair and functioning. Irina was poor with no hope of wealth. This man with his strawberries was as materially bereft as she, by appearances, and yet at least he had benefit of the sham free market, of knowing someone who knew someone who knew something of strawberries. For the

moment, he had thrown it away, but he had taken the berries with him. In time
he would have no choice but to return to his Mila, to markets, to corruption and
the spare hope of making it through these hungry days. It infuriated her suddenly,
that he had had something to sustain him and that she had been forced to hear it
through her wall, the arguments, the lovemaking, the passion and lack of peace they
had subjected her to, the passion and lack he could return to if he chose, and she
grabbed a berry that had settled at her knee and wiped it, and bit down, and the
burst of taste was tart and punishing. She coughed a bit, and a trail of juice tickled
her chin.

The man stared at her. Irina chewed, rubbed the juice from the corners of her
mouth, bit down again, nibbling around the nub of the green stem carefully. She
was angry but more aware of how good the fruit tasted, how startling and wonderful it felt to eat something fresh; she had been very much mistaken to think that
there was something fake about the berries. The man watched her eat, watched
her wipe her mouth and toss the stem aside, and said evenly, "They're flowers, you
know, not fruit."

"What do you mean?" Her voice was still too loud; she winced at the noise of
it, glanced up at the closed door.

"The seeds are on the outside. On the skin, not buried in the flesh. Flowers,
not fruit."

Was he flirting with her after all? She met his eyes. He was gazing at her with
a certain intensity, but a guarded one, and his voice was low and plodding. "What
kind of flower?" she replied quietly.

"Roses. Of the rose family." The landing was clean, his absurd little make-up
case closed and clasped. He leaned back to sit on the lowest stair. "You are our quiet
neighbor, then. A good girl, it would seem. I've rarely seen you. I've certainly never
seen you eat a strawberry. I think I would have remembered it."

"Since I rarely eat, it is a memorable experience," Irina said as she stood.

"You don't have the look of the hungry."

"The light is dim."

He paused, his face tilted up to her, and then replied steadily. "I can see well
enough to know you would fuck me for the rest of them."

He rose, blocking her way around him, and she was aware again of his broad
hands clutching the feminine handle of the little case. The vulgarity hung between
them, as out of place on that dirty, unheated landing as berries, or market connections, or love. She moved past him; she let him follow her. They entered her apartment, and, after a brief time of settling and silence and eating, made love. Mila had
the nerve to knock the next morning, too early. She wanted the strawberries, not
Victor. From bed, Irina listened to their argument, learned his name because Mila
used it, knew he would not leave her because Mila wouldn't yet have him back.

It suited him, she would think afterward, not to die young, but to die by the
violence of the times. The political murders, the apartment building blasts, the
horrible theater attack that had put an end to her desire to see any show, to be entertained at all; none of it fazed him. For Irina, Moscow was a deep tunnel, filling

with smoke and the shredded debris of safety and order, but Victor, for all his faults, would not put up with restricted, cautious movement any more than he had put up with the kiss. He had gone to see *Nord Ost* after the theater re-opened, even tried to persuade her to go. When she wouldn't, he took Mila.

After every attack he roamed the remains. The city opened wide to him. She didn't know why the bombs, the ruins, the hostage taking and predictably excessive government retaliation fascinated him so, seemed even to cheer him up. He would return home covered in the grime of tragedy with several rolls of film to process. He claimed the photos were for his Chechen course lectures, his apologia for those criminal separatists, but she knew his class had nothing to do with why he crawled over rubble and snapped pictures of bodies as if documenting newly excavated historical atrocities instead of fresh death. It occurred to her once, as he sat with Mila at the table examining photos of the shattered International Hotel lobby and the body parts of the suicide bombers littering the scene like erratic clumps of red dirt, to ask how he was able to slip past security to get such lurid shots, but seeing them huddled together, smoking, drinking Mila's coffee, talking languorously as if poring over family reunion photos, Irina did not question them. Mila probably arranged it for him somehow.

And Mila would watch her, sometimes, as Irina watched them, although their eyes never met directly. They never spoke to each other, not really. Whatever current of communication they ought to have had ran through Victor and came out wordless, helpless in the stasis of the unexpected circumstance that was working too well to question. Mila was arranging for her, too. Mila was looking at her. Her comments, when they were addressed to Irina too, were innocuous, lacking malice or envy. Mila was present and ubiquitous and Irina did not know her at all.

She knew Victor, however, knew he identified with the victims, although Irina never could understand why, untouched as he was by extraordinary suffering. His limp was due to muscle damage from a severe bout of reactive arthritis brought on by food poisoning. The scars on his hand she had noticed that night on the landing were remnants of a childhood burn. His parents were both living, had never been ill, had never been in the camps or prison. He was a beloved only child, encouraged in his pursuits, indulged in his failures. His circumstances, at least to all appearances, were steeped in the ordinary, the mundane rhythm of stability and luck. His violent, untimely death would be that family's first, a fact he would certainly find pleasing, even funny.

Irina's own past was checkered with the typical horrors of Soviet times, and she was deathly afraid of her own fate. Her mother's brother had been murdered by the State, her mother had committed suicide soon after his execution; her father had died of cancer. The family had fled Moscow years ago to avoid arrest; it was to Moscow Irina returned as a teenager, forging a city residency card, enduring a string of terrible jobs and crummy apartments as she worked her way through university. Then came the overthrow, the demonstrations at the White House, Yeltsin climbing the tank—his final honest moment, if, in fact, it was, and not the same old staged bullshit, a sanitized, televised velvet revolution.

Of course, nothing the collapse of the empire had promised to bring had ever materialized, not for the honest. For Irina, the jobs were worse, the apartments worse, food dwindled, hope evaporated, until one day she read an ad to apartment sit. The lease holder, a middle aged schoolteacher who was emigrating to America to get married, wanted to keep the lease on the apartment as a hedge against marital disaster. Despite the deterioration of the building, the apartment was in good repair, with a sunny kitchenette against the southern wall of the main room and a separate bedroom, freshly painted, roach-free. An automatic coffee grinder was built in to the stove. The rich, smoky aroma of ground beans overlay the odor of trash pitched heedlessly from tenants' windows to pile, untended, in the central courtyard. The schoolteacher wanted cash for her trip to America. Irina had the first month's rent with her. Her first decent apartment was also her first illegal market transaction.

The coffee grinder was the first thing Victor noticed. Sometimes she thought that the smell of the coffee was the only thing he loved about her. Mila, too, became an easy addict. When she began her visits that became so frequent it was as if they were all three living together, she would bring brown paper bundles of fresh beans, still warm from the roaster, for Irina to grind and brew. It got so that all they would drink was coffee, late into the evening. Eventually Victor gave up vodka entirely. Irina was not at all surprised he would ask for it, the vodka, as he lay dying on the cold pavement. He would have craved the crystal sting of it to purge his mouth of bombs and coffee. Mila's coffee.

Mila's coffee. Within a month of Victor's moving in with her, all they had came from Mila. After the first shock of insult—sleeping with a man who didn't love her, allowing his lover to bring them food, the unexpected cycle of odd circumstance that was fast transforming her into someone she didn't recognize, someone safe and full and calculating—Irina didn't care. She no longer worried about being found out as a sub-lessee, or about the illegal cash payments she made to the émigré lease holder's banker, because she knew that Mila knew the building owners. She ate well for the first time in her life, fresh vegetables from the south, berries of all types, even blueberries imported from America, steaks the shape of kidneys, pellets of fatty pork loin, real butter, pickles the size of bread loaves, eggs. Eggs were not scarce, as a general rule, but they were expensive, so much so they were sold singly to well-off consumers. Consumers. Another word to loathe; that is, until she be-came a consumer again, a consumer with connections. Before, she rarely thought of eggs. They were one more thing given up, and a minor thing at that. Now that she had them back, the sour aroma as they cooked sweetened by a film of butter over the yolks, she felt something in her years of deprivation that felt almost like grief, the sickly burn of regret, a hunger for the past, for her mother, perhaps; feelings she thought she had buried. Sometimes Victor would let her eat his egg, pushing his plate to her with the slight nod of sacrifice. She always took his food.

Victor was almost certainly sleeping with Mila during the day, while Irina kept books for the companies Mila lined up for her—one crooked company after an-other, concealing fraud with the same irritated efficiency as she would dispatch a blemish on her own face with a quick dab of cosmetic powder. She received bonuses; she became known as a good girl, a quiet girl, someone who knew some-thing about numbers. Her business grew. She brought in money, turned it over to

Mila after she paid her rent, and more clients called for her, and she worked long hours while Victor and Mila fucked in her sunny, coffee-filled apartment, and she didn't care that when she came home in the evenings—she, who was now someone who knew numbers and the market and how to grease the even flow of capitalism so she, too, could be comfortable—that when she came home to Victor, Mila was always there, steely, satiated, full from the sex she had taken from the man she was allowing Irina to borrow.

Irina was not unhappy. She didn't care that Victor's depression seemed to settle hardest after dinner, after they had eaten with Mila, drank the fine Arabica beans she had brought; after Mila left for the night. She didn't care that he shared his grisly photos and ridiculous rhetoric on the efficacy of terrorism to achieve rational political ends only with Mila. She didn't care that Mila seemed to understand his passion for violence and the crazy way it turned him happy for a time, as if she was privy to his private sense of injury, whatever it was in his charmed life that had caused his hurt.

"I don't want to know who she is," she told him suddenly one night. They never spoke of Mila, but Victor was not startled.

"You know who she is. You wouldn't tolerate her if you didn't," Victor answered.

And in fact she did know, or at least knew the rumors that came with accepting Mila's food and Mila's connections and Mila's man, and it came down to family, of course, as everything always did. She was somebody's daughter, or niece, perhaps, somebody who for years had been the head of Putin's personal security detail, so it all made sense, the connections and the exotic food that should not be exotic and the ability to fuck the market, fuck Victor, look calmly at his obscene photos of obscene tragedy, talk of bodies and bombs and terrorist efficacy, and smoke, and drink coffee, untouched by it all, secure. "I don't know who she is. Neither do you, it seems."

"What's to know?" he shrugged. "She's a fact; a thing that exists for us."

"A fact. A thing."

"Just that." He was tired. His old doglike ways were back. He slouched, pouted darkly at her.

They were sitting in on his university course, despite Mila and her connections. His lectures on the efficacy of terrorism—his sympathy with the Chechens, which she knew to be merely the attraction of fighting big power by small, grotesque means—had caught the attention of whomever's job it was to be attentive, and the monitor was depressing Victor, as if he had actually believed in the illusion of free speech; anyway, it should have excited him, this first whiff of pending persecution. And nothing had even happened yet. "Our 'Ophelia.'"

It pissed her off. He assumed that she, a bookkeeper, would think of Shakespeare, not Olesha, as if the slightest contour of obscurity was beyond her grasp. "And I'm the 'envier,' then?" She saw approval light him for a moment and felt her own enmity for him, and Mila, as a separate force, a fact, a thing. "And she the perfect woman of the future, the repository for our emotions, our sex?"

"Better than that, even. She's a boot maker now."

"Fuck off."

"No, I'm not kidding. She has ownership in a boot factory. Imagine our beloved plastic Soviet boots rolling off the assembly line once again."

"Retooling and thieving, then. A perfect woman for our times."

"It's honest," he laughed at her. She did brighten him sometimes, as if the addition of her to Mila, to himself, was the catalyst to it, them, working at all. "No refitting. I'm serious. She makes—remakes—crummy boots. Soviet chic. No one cares, now, that they are duds. The style's the thing. She's opened up a whole market for shoddy Soviet goods. Next it's perfume. Remember, how it used to stink like nests of dung under lilacs?"

It didn't matter. She did not love Victor, and she had become too practical during these market years to care how Mila's privileges came to her. If it took three to survive—Mila to feed her, Victor to sleep with her—she could accept it. Accept the triumvirate as a tool for survival. The morning of their quarrel, the morning of his death, the morning after the kiss, Irina had never felt more secure, less afraid, than she felt now that it was three of them. She had never felt such a complete lack of hunger. She would have lived this way for years, and she told Victor so during their quarrel. He had become angry then. He was more afraid of losing Mila, certainly, than her, had in fact told her as much when he suggested, no, commanded her, to prepare the sausage for dinner. It was fine sausage, not the cheap, fatty sausage with the first film of rot coating it that Irina was used to eating. Olesha again. As if she wouldn't understand the reference. Bookkeeping was never chic under any regime.

It was Mila's sausage, of course. She had procured it the previous evening, in fact was still holding it under her coat when she ran into Irina in the stairwell, on the landing where she and Victor had knelt over strawberries. The space was still unheated, but no longer dim. Mila had the bulb replaced weeks ago, and there was a proper fixture now, snug and unobtrusive amidst the cracks in the ceiling.

"You're not going out? . . . It's the dinner hour."

"Yes, only . . . I forgot an account detail report, and the office is still open, if I hurry." Irina paused before her, not from politeness, but from the fact that Mila was blocking the way down, her arm tucked unnaturally inside her coat. They never had been alone together; Irina would have preferred this coincidental passing to remain brief. But now that they had spoken, Mila wanted to chat, and Irina felt the pull of obligation. The report would have to wait. As Mila smiled at her, Irina was struck, as she often was, by how her mouth was too small to support a proper smile, and the bridge of her nose was broad, almost flat. Mila was not pretty, not that it mattered. Victor was clearly attracted to her for reasons other than looks. Why not go back to her, Irina had insisted a hundred times since Victor began sleeping with Mila again; you never fight, she listens to all your garbage about terrorists and our new world order and the shitty efficacy of it all, I can't imagine what you ever had to fight about at all, and Victor always laughed at this and replied, you'd have to live with her to know, and Irina would glare and say, I do; and he would kiss her, for once. Besides, it's you I love, he would say, your seeds are on your skin, not buried in your flesh, and it was this Irina was thinking of as Mila blocked her way down. It was only much later after Victor's death, after Mila moved out of the apartment next door and Irina had become used to not seeing them both, did it occur to her to question whether, with all Mila's connections and bounty and rumored ties to Putin, she could have warned them both to stay off the trains the next morning; whether she would have if it were not for the kiss.

"You're becoming successful," Mila told her, approvingly.

"Only thanks to you."

"Thanks to me; but never thanks to your own efforts. You're a good girl. Modest. And thanks to me, you're saddled with Victor, yes? We are a sad couple; you put up with us, I don't know why."

Mila was close, her odd, small smile slipping into a straight line of emotion Irina couldn't pinpoint—anger, or simply the dropping of pretense, the moment of surprise at being alone for the first time passing away into a comfortable acceptance that the trio was a success, even if Mila hadn't exactly engineered it. Irina didn't think she was looking for an answer, and with her own polite movement made to get around, but Mila took the sleeve of her coat.

"I don't know why you put up with us," she said again and leaned into Irina, parted her lips with her own, slid an arm around Irina's waist to pull her closer, the outline of the sausage pressing into her chest; Irina did not yet know what it was. She pulled back in surprise, because Mila had moved to kiss her so without breath, without thought, even without desire, and suddenly, with the imbalance of Irina's movement away from her, Mila dropped an egg. Irina hadn't noticed she was carrying it at all. It struck the cement between their feet and smashed dully, spattering the gelatin of the white like a dud firecracker, while the yolk nestled undisturbed in the middle of the mess, wiggling tidily. As choreographed as Irina suspected Mila's kiss to be, her answering kiss was impulse only; she saw the quiver of the egg, felt the hot, raised pressure of her lips, like a rash—Mila had pressed her hard—and stepped forward, slipping a bit on the slick film. They kissed again. Two kisses, although Victor witnessed just the second, the deliberate movement of Irina to Mila, not the careful ambush that preceded it. It felt experimental, a little cold, a little foreign. Mila's breath was sour, like cream just beginning to turn. The kiss was long; it took Irina's breath away, that a woman could press into her as insistently as a man, and needed no preamble. It just was. The sound of the kiss rustled in the stairwell, like leaves or petals about to detach in the breeze. Irina may have moaned.

Victor certainly did as he came upon them, shrinking into his coat, hands still cupped to his lips for warmth, and if only he had said something vulgar and rude, as he had that night over the strawberries, instead of turning and limping away, nearly tripping down the hard flight of crumbled concrete stairs, instead of causing Mila to follow him and quarrel with him and thrust the sausage at him as if it were a bomb and not precious food; if he had only said, with a grudging shadow of humor, I'd like to fuck you both, they might have ended up in bed together, all three. Perhaps even in their old apartment. But even had he said it, he would have boarded that train the next morning, that very train. He had an early class to teach. The class was being monitored. Perhaps he would be called in to the dean that very day, persecuted at last under the withering of free speech and order of any kind. Even with two women twining him, he would not have slept in.

She crossed to the other side of the bridge to watch the sausage winnow down the slow current. The cars were thick this morning; she could still remember a time when there had been so few cars that the whistle of one speeding by startled her. Yet then there had been so much more to life. More safety. More food, even if it hadn't been a bounty. There would be no end to the poverty of these days, not in her lifetime. At least she had a buffer now, in Mila, and the kiss that would bind them together for a little while longer, at least. As she walked along the railing toward the Kremlin and the Square and the Metro station at the mouth of Tverskaya, she felt her anger dissipate a bit, dissolve in the frosty mist that was evaporating under the thin winter sunlight, and it was not Victor she was thinking of then, but Mila, and how they would act when they saw each other again.

How the three of them would act together, after the kiss.

Laura Hulthén Thomas lived in Communist Moscow in the early nineties, when the staple diet was sausage, vodka, and revolution. Although she never got used to the highly questionable ingredients in the sausage, she fell in love with her Russian friends' tough but optimistic souls. Laura now teaches Creative Writing at the Residential College at the University of Michigan. She continues to write about Russia in her short stories and in a novel-in-progress, *Eve's Tears*.

X

NICHOLAS DELBANCO

WHEN HE TOOK the job in Ann Arbor he rented an apartment near the Farmer's Market. Lawrence liked the town, its coffee shops and jazz bars and, everywhere, its low-key Midwestern affability. As half-time adjunct assistant professor in the architecture program he made friends on the faculty and with those who worked downtown—designers and lawyers and real estate developers who asked him to join them at lunch. There were concerts and basketball games to attend; there were parties to go to and give. On his thirty-third birthday he joined a health club and started to work out four mornings a week; he enjoyed the anonymity, the nodding acquaintance with men on adjacent machines.

Again, he wrote steadily, liking his classes and liking the students, preparing his lectures with care. They would, he believed, make a book. His course on "Public and Private Space" was popular, and his editorial on "Urbanism and the Public Realm" was published in *Architectural Record*; this pleased him very much. Lawrence divided his time between the Art and Architecture Building and the local firm of Spence & Mills Design Group, spending Monday, Wednesday, and Friday afternoons on North Campus and the rest of the work-week downtown. At times—consulting on a shopping mall or the condominium complex adjacent to the golf course—he wondered what had happened to ambition. Early on he'd hoped to change the shape of things, to be a kind of Frank Lloyd Wright or Buckminster Fuller of his own generation; now here he was producing drawings for a downtown four-story parking garage . . .

Still, he felt at home in Ann Arbor; the city paid attention to its common space and parks. There were walkways by the river and playing fields and bridges where the students clustered, a pond out on North Campus where he sat and smoked. On fair days he would walk or jog through Gallup Park along the Huron River, and sometimes he drove out to Baseline Lake or Whitmore Lake and rented a canoe. He met his second wife in the Arboretum, drawing a willow tree with its roots exposed on the bank of the river. Janet was sitting on a blanket, and he stopped and praised the way she rendered sprigs of willow leaves.

Silent, she smiled and returned to her work. She was wearing a tie-dyed wrap-around skirt and a t-shirt with a Toxin sign.

"Do you do this for a living?" Lawrence asked. He introduced himself.

Squinting, she looked up at him; he was standing in the sun. She had a clip-board and a sketchpad and set of drawing pencils.

"I'm sorry, I don't want to interrupt . . . "

"But you're interrupting anyway," she said, and offered her hand. "Janet. Janet Atwan."

"I mean, you're very good at this."

"You're standing in my light."

"Oh, sorry. Is that a suggestion?"

"It is." Again, she bent back to her work.

In years to come he remembered the line, the way she instructed him to step aside. It was, Janet told him, a quote. Alexander the Great once made a pilgrimage to the beggar-cynic Diogenes, asking the seated man what he desired; you have only to ask for a favor, said the reverential Emperor, and it will be conferred. The philosopher had answered—or so the story went—with the phrase she repeated to Lawrence: Get out of my light, Lord, I'm cold.

All through their marriage it felt the same way: he standing, smiling, praising her, and she beneath him, elsewhere-focused, saying what bitter Diogenes said: You're casting a shadow. Move on.

Janet had her own career and proved successful at it, working as a bookkeeper for an insurance firm, and then as a certified public accountant, and then preparing taxes for well-heeled individuals and corporations in town. There were years she earned as much as him, and years when she earned more. But always she seemed to be nursing a grievance, always reminding him how much things cost—not in financial so much as emotional terms—and what she gave up to have sons.

They produced two of them—Andrew, then John—and in 1977 purchased a one-story home on a two-acre lot in Ann Arbor Hills. As the children grew, so did the house; Lawrence remodeled it, building a wing to the rear. He designed a series of glass-enclosed bedrooms facing the woodlot, gesturing at Philip Johnson's Glass House but from a respectful distance—as Johnson had gestured at Mies. There were skylights and free-standing chimneys and a wraparound Florida porch.

At Janet's urging, when Andrew turned three, they acquired a golden retriever the family named Daisy, and then a cat named Peek-a-Boo and hamsters and a parakeet and, until it grew too large to keep, an alligator called Rex. When the boys were old enough for school, and if the weather was pleasant, he and Daisy walked them there, through tree-shaded winding streets. The neighborhood children cried "Daisy" and ran to pet her fearlessly; she wagged her tail and rolled on the ground and let them scratch her belly and pull at her soft ears.

Lawrence liked being a "Dad." He had many happy memories—games of Frisbee on the lawn, the barbecue he built himself, springtime dinners at the picnic table where white azalea bushes and rhododendron bloomed. When he collected his children from school, they were always glad to see him and, hurtling out the door, would rush into his arms. He liked helping with their homework: the spelling and arithmetic and the building projects with cardboard and construction paper; he fashioned, in the basement, a platform for Lionel trains. It was bi-level, with tunnels and hills, and they spent hours together downstairs establishing freight yards and passenger stations and ramps. Fixing lunch for his sons was a pleasing routine: the peanut butter sandwiches and potato chips and chocolate chip cookies and boxes of fruit juice he packed into brown bags. They drove to the Toledo Zoo and Greenfield Village and the Henry Ford Museum when Catherine came to visit, on those rare occasions Annie sent her east. He tried very hard to be faithful, and to make his marriage a success.

But there were women everywhere: the lighting designer from Cleveland, the client from Grosse Pointe Shores in the throes of a divorce, the secretary in the office of the Dean of Engineering who wore tight skirts to work. Over time, it seemed to him, Janet grew more and more distant—preferring her Monday Quilting Club or Saturday morning live model class to staying home with him at night or staying, on weekends, in bed. He told himself he needed sex more often than she, more urgently, and if he lived in France or Argentina there would have been no stigma in acquiring a mistress; it would have been expected, and not an issue at home.

The woman from Grosse Pointe Shores owned a building site in Bay City and asked him to design a lake front house on the property. She had been referred to him because of his experience with solar panels and the Breuer house in Wellfleet, of which he'd made a model and on which he'd lectured in class. She came to his office in North Campus, saying, "Money's not an issue, not at issue anyhow, the main thing is getting it right. Don't you agree?"

He agreed. He asked her what she wanted, and she told him what she did and did not want—how she thought of the new structure as a getaway, a hideaway, a place to be alone. "I vont to be alone," she said, imitating Greta Garbo, and then she laughed and said, "Not really, that isn't at all vat I vont."

They made a site visit together, driving north, and that night she came to his hotel room with a bottle of white wine and said, "I'm lonely, aren't you lonely?" and undid her blouse. Her name was Marianne, and her husband turned out to prefer—to have a marked preference for—men. It undermined her self-esteem to be so obviously not the partner he wanted; did Lawrence find her attractive and would he object if she took off the rest of her clothes?

He did find her attractive and did not object. She was passionate beneath him, scratching at his neck and back, and he felt young again and somehow deserving, as though all of those days making breakfast for the children and all of those nights doing homework had earned him this session with reckless Marianne in bed. In the morning he visited her room instead, and they took a shower together, and she turned around and soaped herself and fitted him inside her, saying, "This is what Nathaniel likes."

"Nathaniel?"

"Nat. Mr-Soon-to-be-Ex."

When he returned to Ann Arbor Janet appeared not to notice the welts on his neck, and he settled back to his routine with a briefly slaked desire; he was solicitous with the boys and did the grocery shopping when tax time approached and his wife worked overtime. Lawrence remodeled the home of the man who owned the Porsche and Volkswagen dealership and then the loft of a couple who owned Main Street Music; he too spent long hours at work. But often he pictured Marianne beneath him, her brazen nakedness, and although she decided not to pursue the beach house project he did try to see her again.

She refused. When he called from the office, she said, "It's a bad idea, it would be too damn confusing, and anyhow we've gotten back together. Me and Nat, I mean, we're going to give it the old college try." To solace himself he slept with Dana the lighting designer, after her presentation on North Campus, in the motel she was staying in off Plymouth Road. She too was ardent, unrestrained, and when she left for Cleveland she said that she'd had a good time. "I'll see you next fall," Dana said. "Or you could visit me in Cleveland, if you want . . . "

Again for a month he felt happy at home, and that spring he planted a vegetable garden on the flat lawn up above the barbecue. He did not fence it, however, and rabbits and ground-hogs ravaged the lettuce and beans. Daisy ran after them fruitlessly, too fat and slow to catch her prey but enthusiastic nevertheless at the prospect of the chase. While John and Andrew watched TV he sat out at the picnic table, sketching a plan for a sauna; Janet joined him with a gin-and-tonic and a plate of cheese.

"This isn't working, is it?"

"What?"

"Marriage," she said. "Our marriage."

"Excuse me?"

"You know what I'm saying. You heard me."

"No."

"No you didn't hear me or no it isn't working?"

"No, I'm not certain I know what you mean."

"Come off it, Lawrence."

"No, really . . . "

She offered him cheese. There was stilton on crackers, a wedge of emmenthaler and sliced brie. "Dana called."

"Who?"

"Dana. She seemed surprised you had a wife. She tried to pretend the number was wrong, but I told her she was right. Correct, I mean, to think you won't be married soon."

"What are you talking about?" He looked at his sketch.

Janet took his pencil from the picnic table and reached across and X'd out the drawing thickly, twice.

"You don't want a sauna?"

"Denial. You've been into denial for years. Just because we don't discuss it doesn't mean I haven't noticed."

"What?"

"How unhappy you are, Lawrence. And how unhappy you make me."

"I do?"

"How we don't belong together, never did . . . "

Janet drained her glass, then emptied it out on the grass. She seemed matter-of-fact and bemused by his shock, explaining herself to him as to a child; she had known about his escapades, his little adventures, his—the word for it was—flings. Ann Arbor was too small a town for him to keep behavior hidden and she didn't love him, hadn't ever loved him maybe, didn't think she could forgive him and wanted a divorce. They had done what they could to pretend marriage worked and they belonged together, but in fact and all along they should have stayed apart. She should have known to start with they had made a mistake getting married, and for a while, for the sake of the children, she'd tried very hard to ignore her unhappiness and hope things would improve. But it wasn't working, wouldn't work, it was no favor to the children and they'd all get over it; she wanted him out of the house. This is, she said, the end of it; I need to get on with my life.

His own, he decided, had gone wrong. The schedules that his children kept no longer seemed to require him, the noise that once seemed a distraction now was a fuss he missed. Lawrence drank. He mourned the clattering ruckus of domesticity, the busy jumble of the house. In his furnished apartment on Ann Street, he tried to focus on his work, writing an essay on "Postmodernism" in which he praised Moore, Graves, and Tigerman, also acknowledging Venturi in "this rejection of the Modern Movement." Watching his sons play baseball or soccer, he kept his distance in the stands; he slept again with Dana, but the edge of desire had dulled. He was forty-eight years old, a bachelor, assailed by a sense of the passage of time and how it was passing him by; he consulted a therapist, twice.

The sessions were not a success. He positioned himself on a brown leather couch while the therapist—Alan McDiarmid, who had been recommended by a colleague—sat in a Barcalounger. McDiarmid had a close-shaved head but thick black eyebrows and a moustache and an attentive, purse-lipped expression; during the second visit he interrupted Lawrence, saying, "Let's get to the point."

"I'm not sure I know what you mean . . . "

"Meaning?"

"Point. Does there have to be something I'm after? Some problem I'm supposed to solve?'

"Well, why else are you here? Why did you make an appointment?"

"I thought maybe . . . "

The therapist seemed impatient. "Yes?"

"Maybe what I'm going through is, you know, representative? A predictable pattern in middle-aged men? A rite of passage, somehow . . . "

The wall clock audibly ticked. There were leather-bound books and a gas-lit fireplace and above it a framed painting of a stag bending down at the edge of a lake; outside there was traffic on Liberty Street. Lawrence coughed; he had been trying to decide, he said, if he wanted a permanent teaching position, if he should go up for tenure or be mainly a practitioner. He was at a turning point, he told McDiarmid, some sort of—what would you call it?—fork in the road, and could use help with directions.

"Oh?"

"What I'm trying to describe," he said, "is everything feels out of synch—like one of those movies with bad splicing. Bad editing maybe. I open my mouth and language comes out, except the audio is poorly dubbed, and there's a difference— a split-second difference—between what the character says and how his mouth moves, it just isn't right . . . "

"You called yourself a 'character.'" The man seemed unconvinced.

"Did I?"

"Why?" McDiarmid made a note. "Why would you do that, I wonder."

"Do what?"

"Why do you think you use the third person? Or talk about bad editing? You mean you're not able to say what you mean?"

He shook his head. "It's just I feel so far away from what I dreamed of early on, from who I thought I'd be, or be with."

"And this feels like a problem?"

"Almost everything feels like a problem, but none of it touches me really. I'm not really here, if you know what I mean."

"No . . . "

McDiarmid's therapeutic style, he recognized at last, was confrontational. "No what?" Lawrence asked.

"Who did you think you'd be with?"

"Does it matter?"

"If you think it does."

"This conversation makes no sense. All I do these days is work, and even the work isn't working . . . "

"Oh?"

Now he repeated what Janet had said: "We don't belong together, never did."

Still, his time with the therapist clarified things; he decided to stay in Ann Arbor. On the basis of two P/A Awards and *Ekistics and the Common Space*, the College of Architecture and Urban Planning proposed him for tenure; in 1991, he became a full professor. This promotion gratified him to a degree he found surprising, and he told the dean how thankful he was for the vote of confidence. "It's a slam dunk," said the dean. "We didn't break a sweat . . . "

While the boys remained in town he tried to be an active father, attending practice sessions and tournaments and concerts and car pooling with the other parents and paying the Greenhills tuition. With Janet's grudging permission he took them out on rafting trips and, for Tigers' games, to Detroit. They liked the Detroit Lions also, and he bought a set of tickets, but the games were long, and the Lions rarely won. Lawrence solaced himself with the notion that all children sooner or later leave home, but in the case of his children the process had been reversed.

While his daughter was in college they saw each other often; Catherine enrolled in Oberlin, a three hour drive away. She and her friends spent weekends in Ann Arbor, and if he himself went out of town he left her the key to the place. "Daddy-cool," her roommates called him, and this pleased him mightily, though he could not escape the suspicion that the nickname was intended as a joke. By junior year she began to display her mother's pampered recklessness; he worried for her safety and—when she argued with him—what he thought of as poor judgment. "Please be careful," he would say, watching irritation play across his daughter's face. Still, he urged Catherine not to drink and drive or trust in "the kindness of strangers"—Annie's phrase for casual sex—and, though he dared not be specific or too stern a moralist, could not keep from warning her about the risks she ran.

"Don't think I'm being . . . "

"Being what?"

"Oh, I don't know. Censorious?"

"A censor?"

"Someone you have to keep secrets from. Or someone you need to behave for."

"Why would I think that?" Catherine shook her golden mane at him and shrugged and turned away.

Then the boys too left for college and ceased being in regular contact. How did it happen, Lawrence asked himself, that the person in the mirror was sprouting liver spots and wrinkles and hair in his nostrils and ears? How did it happen that his wives and children found him an irrelevance, a stranger to be tolerated and, when possible, avoided? His waistline had thickened, his neck too, and he found himself comparing the price of real estate and cars and clothes with prices he remembered from a quarter of a century before. Increasingly he worried that the world of pleasure that once seemed so available was closed to him, foreclosed.

He went to his thirtieth Harvard reunion and reported to the tent where his classmates gathered, putting on badges and hats. They seemed old and fat or wizened and bald; at first he believed he had made a mistake and gone to the wrong tent. The class representatives had no difficulty recognizing him, however, and handed him his "Welcome" folder and slapped him on the back.

There were panels and speeches and parties; on Friday night there was a dance. Turn by turn he danced with classmates' wives and trophy wives and classmates, trying to enjoy himself, full of self-pity and scotch. Next morning, nursing a headache, he sat on a panel on "Urban Revitalization," comparing Newark and Birmingham and Atlanta and dealing with the three cities in terms of city-planning and the shift in profile of their population base. Lawrence took the position that the cutting edge of architecture was a serrated blade, or ought to be, and that what Dean Sert accomplished in the 1960s had been a conscious agenda: the Harvard Square they all dimly remembered was a kind of shadow footprint in the traffic pattern today. When it came his turn to talk he reached for the microphone and, remembering the couplet from Samuel Beckett, recited it: Spend the years of learning squandering courage for the years of wandering . . .

"That girl of yours," someone asked him at lunch. "Whatever happened to her?"

"Who?"

"What was she called, I can't remember. The one with all that hair, what, Harriet? Henrietta?"

"Hermia?"

"Hermia. Right."

"I don't know," Lawrence admitted. "We've dropped out of touch."

"Me, I've got grandchildren," said the man. "Five of them. Amazing, isn't it—remember that old Latin saying, Tempus, fugit." He laughed. "Bottoms up. It's what I tell my grandsons, bottoms up."

235

"Where are you living, Larry?" asked Tim Bell. Tim Bell wore a blazer and wide crimson tie.

"Ann Arbor."

"Oh. Retired yet?"

"Not yet."

"We've just done it," said Tim Bell. "The Missus and me and Betty makes three." He smiled. Then he explained that "Betty" was a forty-foot sloop, a rig he had brought up to Camden and was planning to sail back to Tortola before hurricane season, then winter over in the Virgins, and he told the others at the table there was nothing like it, nothing like a sailboat with a favoring breeze and the British Virgin Islands—Tortola, Virgin Gorda and the rest—for pleasure cruising, push come to shove; the Drake Channel made everything worth it, those years at the office spent sucking it up.

"I never would have figured you for the retiring type," said Sammy Lax, and everybody laughed.

"Did you say Virgin Gorda?" asked a man whose name he did not recognize. "Is that the one where the resort is Little Dix? No wonder it's still virgin—get it?—the Rock Resort is only Little Dix?"

Lawrence tried to join in the general merriment, but could not. The men were wearing crimson caps, the women crimson scarves. He looked around him at the dining tent—this herd of well-dressed well-fed citizens—and asked himself how he arrived at this place and how youth had drifted away . . .

Author and educator **Nicholas Delbanco** has taught at Columbia and Iowa Universities, as well as at Bennington, Skidmore, Trinity, and Williams Colleges. In 1977, he co-founded the Bennington Writing Workshops with the late John Gardner. In 1985 he went to the University of Michigan in order to direct the MFA in Writing Program at Ann Arbor, where he also administers the prestigious Hopwood Awards. The Robert Frost Collegiate Professor of English Language and Literature, Mr. Delbanco has published nineteen books.

DEAR MRS. BENDER-WONG
ELIZABETH KOSTOVA

To Mrs. Edith Bender-Wong
President, Guild of American Translators

DEAR MRS. BENDER-WONG:

I have a serious question for you. As a full-fledged dues paying member of the Guild of American Translators, I am writing to ask you for some advice. I joined the Guild of American Translators two months ago and I have to tell you it has done my career absolutely no good whatsoever. In the first place, I should explain that I am a long-term professional with serious goals. I have wanted to be a translator since I was in college. I started studying Burovian on a dare, because my roommate said it was the most obscure class she'd ever heard of. Also it was offered at 8:00AM, which was the most inconvenient time she'd ever heard of. She was shocked when I actually registered for it. She said even Russian or Swahili would have been a reasonable choice. I guess it wasn't the greatest reason to study a language, but I can tell you I got hooked right away. Our teacher was a native speaker married to an American and didn't mind that we had only three people in the class. She brought in some posters of the Burovian landscapes and also some crafts and traditional costumes. They were amazing. Also, we had lunch one Sunday all together at the home of a Burovian family she knew in Philadelphia. The other people in my class were too shy to say anything except "hello" in Burovian, but I tried out a few sentences. Wow! I could communicate. The mother of the household kept hugging me and giving me more lamb on skewers. She said in English, "This little one speaks Burovian." My teacher was beaming. I resolved then and there to devote myself to the language and try to work in the field someday. I guess you can understand from your own language experience what a thrill this revelation was to me. My teacher said she would help me go to Burovia for a summer seminar but unfortunately her husband got a job in Seattle and she became very busy moving out there, so we didn't organize it. When I was in my junior year I went abroad for one semester to London because I was also doing an English major while studying Burovian. I am very well read in Shakespeare, too, for example. You would think that would count on the market somehow. I decided I would go to Burovia from England during our vacation (in England they call it going on holiday) but that was when the hard-line coup took place there and they stopped letting foreign travelers in for over six months. Or maybe our State Department stopped it, I can't remember. Just my luck. I had to go home to Pennsylvania without even setting foot in Burovia, after all those hopes and dreams. When I got home I decided I would go to grad school in Burovian. That was a big decision because my dad's a doctor and my mom and dad wanted me to go to med school. Now I wonder if that wouldn't have been a good idea, seeing how little even joining a national organization has done for my career. But they were pretty supportive and so I started at Indiana University in their Burovian program, which I guess you know is world-famous. I was still having trouble with some verbs, especially the subjunctive and future present, but I eventually got that straightened out. I have to tell you it was an amazing program. I guess you know it has been discontinued which is pretty sad, especially since the Berlin Wall fell and there is a lot more contact now with people in Burovia. When I was at IU we even had a Burovian club. We had only eight people in the program and I guess we might have had an inferiority complex with all the Russian majors and Czech and Polish and everybody, but we really just had a good time. Our Burovian advisor wasn't a native speaker but his father was Burovian and you'd better believe he was pretty close. He said he thought I had a somewhat Burovian face and I felt very honored, because Burovian women are great beauties. I do have dark eyes and good eyebrows, which may be why he said that. I had a terrible crush on him after he secretly held my hand at one of our parties with the Ukrainian club. However, it didn't come to anything. The work was challenging and I was not exactly at the top of the class because there were several Burovian-American students and immigrants who obviously had an unfair advantage because they grew up speaking Burovian. They say you never can get the "l" or "x" sounds right unless you really do grow up with Burovian. We read some Burovian epic works, like Durshek's *Thirty Warriors Cavorting in the Mountains*, which has got to be one of the most heroic poems in the history of world literature. I can still say whole passages of it to myself, which I sometimes do when I have to unpack books at the back of the store and it gets boring. Some of the students in my program dropped out second year and went to law school or into business, but I was very determined. I applied for a grant to go to Burovia that year. However, the competition was intense—six people applied, including three from my program—and I made it only to the second cut, which wasn't too bad. Still, I was greatly disappointed because I'd been dreaming about Burovia for so long. I would fall asleep seeing these incredible mountains behind my eyelids, with goats climbing on them and villages full of people speaking Burovian in the streets. It was such a vivid picture I almost felt I'd been there already. One of the guys in our program sent me a postcard (I think he felt bad because we'd had a little fling and then he got to go to Burovia and he got involved with a Burovian student, whom he married eventually and moved to New York with). The postcard showed the National Mausoleum, where Burovia's dictators from the '60s and '70s are buried. It's built in the shape of an enormous village mountain hut to symbolize their origins among the people. But when I think of Burovia I think of those mountains in the tourist posters from my college class, where the thirty heroes fought and died. I could have picked that as a topic for my master's thesis, but I got excited about a different one, which my professor proposed after he took my hand and squeezed it at that party. I had been thinking about translating for a long time, so I wrote on contradictory translations of Middle-Period Burovian poetry. It was very intense; I just wrote and wrote and I did a major annotated appendix of my own translations. I really felt like I was onto something.

Plus, it seemed like it took me forever to finish! I was in grad school for a long, long time. In fact, I'm surprised this work has never gotten published. It is over four hundred pages long and was the longest thesis written in the IU Burovian program until someone else (a bilingual guy) came along and wrote one four hundred and fifty pages. But he did a lot more appendices than mine, so I don't know if that counts. You could say he had appendicitis. (I know—ha, ha.) I sent my thesis to three university presses. One never contacted me, one returned my manuscript with some coffee-rings on it, and one wrote to me that they were already doing a book on Uzbek astrology, and to try again next year. Well, that Uzbek astrology thing made me kind of mad, so I just didn't send it back. How can you compare a serious work of literature with something like that? It's not that I'm opposed to astrology. In fact, I'm a classic Gemini. But this was a very high-ranking university press. On top of that, the Berlin Wall had just fallen two years before, so Burovia was opened up to the world. My mom was so annoyed when I told her about it that she wrote the press a letter. However, she didn't hear anything back. I kept some copies of my thesis for my bookshelves but I started thinking about not teaching Burovian after all. It takes a lot of time to get a PhD, as you know, and on top of that there are only four positions to teach it in the U.S. and two of those are part-time. So if you're not a native speaker, it's pretty competitive. I decided to move to New York after graduation, where there's a Burovian community of immigrants, and do some translating while I applied for grants. I got a one-room apartment—actually, it was a closet—on the West Side but I definitely had trouble meeting Burovians there. Once when I was on my way to a job at a café that I thought I should take for a little while, I heard two people actually speaking Burovian on the subway. They were a tall, thin man in a suit with a long beard that curled up at the end, very traditional looking, and a tall graceful woman in a green dress. I tried to get close enough to really hear what they were talking about, but just when I finally heard him say something about "around the corner" and "potato" someone elbowed me back and then the two Burovians got off at that stop. I thought about calling some of my old friends from IU, but the only one I had heard about was working at the UN. So much for that job possibility! I didn't think he would do anything for me, anyway. So I kept writing proposals and eventually I got a grant to go to Burovia! You'll never believe this, but I got my acceptance letter on June 16, 1994! As you know, the day before the invasion of Burovia. It was so shocking. I heard about it on the morning radio news before I left for my new job at the health-food deli and started crying. Not just out of personal disappointment, either. I kept picturing the children and bearded old men of Burovia lying in the streets, like the ones they described. It was horrible. The presidents of several countries were interviewed condemning the invasion. Of course, the invaders lost their Most Favored Nation status and there was a blockade of oil, but still they never really got punished for what they did. My neighbor had a television and she let me sit there that night watching the smoke billowing out of Burovian villages and radio stations. I couldn't believe my eyes. I think that was the most publicity Burovia has ever received. I thought I should share some of my ideas and my experiences with Burovian culture, so I wrote a letter of protest to *The New York Times*, which unfortunately they

did not see fit to publish. I also thought it would be a good time to do some translating, since people might be more interested in Burovia with all the publicity. I
called a couple of translation agencies, but one of them had never needed any Burovian and the other already had a Burovian translator who specialized in mechanical engineering pamphlets, which was what they wanted. I kept thinking
about the war and waiting for something to happen. Finally, it came. By this time I
was working at the health-food deli full-time and had been promoted to bagels.
One morning a young man with a heavy accent walked in. He wanted a sesame-soy
bagel with lox. Something about the way he said "lox" gave me sort of a prickle of
extra-sensory awareness. He was wearing a blue-green suit made out of slightly
shiny fabric like raw silk, with the pants too long and pooling around his ankles. He
smelled like a fresh, strong, unusual cologne or soap. He had huge dark eyes and a
balding spot on his head. He definitely seemed foreign. I kept thinking I'd seen him
somewhere before. "Excuse me," I said on a hunch. "Where are you from?" He
smiled, but I noticed he looked kind of cautious. "Europe," he said. "Where in Europe?" I said. "I'm from Eastern Europe," he said, moving away from the counter. "I
mean, what country?" He smiled. "Oh, you have never heard of it," he said. He was
smiling from farther away. He had crooked teeth but a very sweet expression. I
asked, "Is it Burovia, by any chance?" He stopped smiling and stared at me. I said, in
Burovian, "Are you from Burovia?" "Yes," he said, very surprised. Then he switched
back to English. "But you're American? How do you know Burovian?" I felt very
proud. "I went to graduate school in Burovian," I told him. "I'm actually a translator." He started smiling again, but not showing his teeth. "You are from a Burovian
family?" he said. "No," I said proudly. "My parents are German Lutherans! I learned
Burovian in college," I said. I said this in Burovian but he kept speaking English. "It
is surprising," he said. "You work as a translator?" "Oh, yes," I said. I gave him his
bagel with lox, which I'd been holding onto. I kept wondering if I could get his
phone number, or at least get him to speak to me again in Burovian. We were just
standing there looking at each other and I suddenly realized he might be a refugee
from the war; maybe his town had been burned or bombed and he had come here
to keep from being killed. I started making another bagel with lox for him. (My
boss is out of the store in the morning.) I made two or three and I said anything
that came into my head in Burovian. He was almost smiling again and he leaned on
the counter. Then the store door opened and a young woman walked in and
grabbed his arm. "Boriz!" she said. She had a loud voice. My first thought was, she
was trashy. She had streaked hair and long maroon fingernails and a very short red
skirt. Boriz said, "Oh, this is my wife." "I'm glad to meet you," I said politely in
Burovian. "Oh, no," Boriz said. "She doesn't understand you. She's American." Boriz's wife frowned at me and combed her hair with one hand. "Well," she said. "I
understand that we're going to be late soon if we don't get going." Boriz smiled at
me with his teeth this time. "Sorry," he said. He said it just like that: "Sorry." His
wife took his arm and started pulling. I almost let them get away. Then I remembered and held out the bags of bagels with lox. That's when I should have stuck to
Burovian, but I forgot all about it. I called out, "Wait! I made you some extras.
They're for free." But Boriz's wife yanked him out the door and they disappeared.

When I turned around, my boss was standing right there, behind me. He never comes in before noon. So my question for you is, how can I get some translating through the Guild? Since I lost my job three weeks ago I've been trying to find some translating work. Joining the Guild, which I did promptly the day after my boss told me not to come back, has had no results for my career. I didn't ask for a recommendation from him for the bookstore, you can be sure. As a dues paying full member of the Guild, I would certainly like to see some results. Could you please send detailed suggestions and a list of contacts as soon as possible?

Thank you for your assistance.

Elizabeth Kostova was born in Connecticut in 1964. She writes fiction, poetry, and essays. Her first book, *1927: The Good-Natured Chronicle of a Journey,* appeared in 1964. Her first novel, *The Historian,* was published by Little, Brown in 2005. She loves 826.

ANN ARBOR ART FAIR 2005

RICHARD SOLOMON

> I sit in one of the dives
> On fifty-second street . . .
> —W.H. Auden
> September 1, 1939

Surrounded by hundreds of combat boots
Lined up like gravestones, I'm sitting in the Diag
Where thirty years ago I drove my MGB onto the 'M'
And had to be chased off by security police. Back then
I listened to "Machine Gun" stoned in black light.
My draft number was forty-nine. I got out with a bad back 1-Y.

Now I'm listening to names: soldiers and families
Who've died in Iraq, his disembodied voice
Flat somber monotonous calling each one out.
A mournful flute. The carillon of Burton Tower
Playing now for thirteen minutes. High noon.
The shadows of oak leaves on this page.

There were no weapons of mass destruction!
We invaded a country without provocation!
I've written my senator but haven't
Burned myself in the square

In July a hundred thousand invade the town
Ravage the beauty and leave.
I'm eating sour blueberries from the farmer's market.
My pocket full of business cards from the artists I loved.
Like the Rothko-esque landscapes in thick gold frames.
The artist and I could have been lovers.
On Liberty packed like Bourbon Street during Mardi Gras
I bought *Seize the Day* and *Dangling Man*
At Dawn Treader's sidewalk book sale
Where the old crone told me about the boots.

'Chief warrant officer William I. Brenner 36'

Burton Tower has been playing for thirteen minutes now

The sun shining on this page. Rising too fast
The moral limits beyond which the mind snaps.

'Ranwaal Mohammed, age unknown.'

A beautiful woman in a wheelchair, lips pierced,
Wearing beads, in black; black hair pulled back
Pensive among the boots listens to the names.

The dead accumulate. If you'd have been there
You might have been affected forever or
Dropped a bomb on a whole city and been glad.
You should have seen the giant Bear Made of Nails
Tom Monahan, the Dominoes Pizza tycoon, bought it.
The farther I got away the less it bothered me

Richard Solomon is a developmental pediatrician in private practice in Ann Arbor. Recently he has published his poetry in the *Michigan Quarterly Review*, *5am*, *freefall*, and *Krax*. A chapbook of poems, tentatively titled *The River Through Your Eyes*, is due out eventually. He and his wife of thirty-two years live in Ann Arbor. He has two adult children—and a grandchild.

EPISTOMOLOGY OF LOVE

ONNA SOLOMON

Dad would get fed up
with the mess in the fridge,
pull a chair up to it, sit down,
and frowning at the wasted food,
he'd begin chucking things into the bin,
molded jars and soggy lettuce,
all the neglected goods.
One time when I was eight or nine,
he picked up an over-ripe plum
from the drawer and tossed it
to me. I caught it. The skin was loose
and thin. If I had dropped it,
it would have ruptured, that perfect
darkness ruined. When he
finished cleaning out the junk,
he cut the plum in half and we ate
and laughed as juice ran down our chins.
Now this is love, he said. I wasn't sure
what he meant and now
I'm still not. Was it the salvaged
plum's perfection or the sharing of it?
Or that he tossed this
faultless thing to me, trusting
I would catch it?

Onna Solomon recently moved back to Ann Arbor after finishing her MA in poetry at Boston University. Her writing has appeared in *32 Poems, Diner, Van Gogh's Ear,* and *Punk Planet.* The only critical acclaim of her life's work had nothing to do with writing and was part of a restaurant review in the *Toledo City Paper.* Tom Szor wrote, "special mention must be made to our server, Onna, who with style and a smile, not only waited on us exceptionally well but also engaged my party and me with her trenchant insights into the existential condition of life, love, and dining at Seva, enhancing our already well-presented table."

TELEGRAM SAM

PAUL A. TOTH

"**HAVE YOU NOTICED** the clover this summer, Writer John?" Farmer Pete said, boots crossed on John's desk.

"Of course I notice. It's coming down like a blizzard."

"But Weatherman Mary, she don't know. She keeps saying, Farmer Pete, you don't need a—well, you know. Sometimes I think we should call her Tangled Up in Bob. She's a weather woman, after all, but don't try telling her that."

Their children had left this junked commune at first opportunity. It seemed as oppressive to them as any refugee camp. Their elders called the place Picturesque, a spot on the map nestled by intersecting mountains, invisible from any highway. John pulled his own beard, which he had been considering shaving for some time, all the men chin-burdened yet feeling no wiser despite their wizardly facial hair. They lived on beans and sprouts, their children semi-nourished until that day when they had made their trek to the highway, found a bus and went somewhere, anywhere, that sold a better variety of food. Then they found the rest of the world, returning one day to announce a marriage or some fatal disease—if they returned at all.

"I sweep it up," Farmer Pete was saying, "but it blows right back. Then it flows through the trailer like feathers."

"Like bone dust. I think it's beautiful."

"Summer snow, I prefer to call it, but it's ruining the crops."

"Maybe it's time—"

"What?"

"Time we leave."

"And do what, go to a senior citizens home with our Social Security checks? Let 'em know we've got enough socked away for a two-week stay? I don't plan to be around that long, anyway."

"There's two sticks marking the fields back there, and what's underneath fertilizes the gardens. Six of us live on: you; me; Weatherman Mary; Seamstress Sally; Builder Bob; Fix-It Fred. We plant, we document, we predict, we sew, we build, we fix, but we've long ago fixed everything that can be fixed, used all the wood we could find, run out of thread, learned to smell the rain coming, have nothing much of a history to record and—no offense—could all go for a cheeseburger. Maybe we should track down our kids in the world."

John blew clover from his desk. Farmer Pete sneezed and shook his head. In the shower of white fluff, he was hazed, blurred, one moment looking older still, the next reminding John of the college boy he had recruited so many years before.

"We need a Scientist Sue," Pete said. "The summer snow's always gone by now." He dusted himself almost free of white. "Goddamn it."

"Why don't you make some dandelion wine, Farmer Pete? We could use some."

"Oh, right. The orgy days are over. They ended when the kids came along."

"I'm talking about having some wine and thinking things over."

Farmer Pete uncrossed his legs. When he stood, a gust came through the door. "What's with this goddamn wind? We do need a weatherman. Weatherperson. A real one. Somebody. Somebody who knows why."

"How long for the wine, Pete?"

"I've got twenty bottles under my bed. That's how I sleep alone at night."

Later, they would gather in what had become a shed of the broken, shredded and frayed and where they once had voted on everything. Democracy became unnecessary. They each had their own campers shared with lovers, except for John and Pete whose women lay underneath the beanstalks. Weatherman Mary lived with Builder Bob, Seamstress Sally with Fix-It Fred. They all did their chores without need for communication. They said "good morning" and "goodnight" and sometimes commented on the weather but otherwise waited, John believed, for their own place under the underground. John's archives—meant for historians who would trace the history of this, one of the sole surviving sixties' communes—had become diaries of nonsense and gibberish, pleasing rhymes that came to mind or useless proverbs like, "If the hungry bird won't touch the worm, don't blame the worm," and so forth. He hoped one day the book would be unearthed along with his bones, that future theologians would unleash his Dr. Seuss prophesies. Perhaps a new church would evolve from his whimsy, one that would only confuse people and thereby serve as an improvement over their other spiritual choices.

Dusk settled on Picturesque in blue neon rays. As John knocked on the doors, the summer snow still fell. John interrupted Weatherman Mary and Builder Bob playing blackjack, Seamstress Sally and Fix-It Fred trying to force their bent screen door into place, and Farmer Pete finishing a bottle of wine. He told everyone to meet in the shed and then helped Pete carry the wine there.

Enough light remained that they could see one another, but they avoided looking and grabbed the bottles. John planned to let them drink a while, get drunk enough to listen and possibly even talk. The couples whispered and laughed together, while John and Pete tapped their feet. Finally, John rose, holding his volume of wisdom in hand for authority.

"Hello?" came a yell from the field.

"Sam?" John said. "Is that my son?"

They walked out of the shed into the still blue fields. Somehow, Sam had managed to drive his SUV from the nearest road, between the mountains down to the hiding place. He walked toward them. John opened his arms. Sam walked into them and waited until he was let go.

"It's been years," Pete said.

"Five, to be exact," Sam said.

Mary started to say, "We were—"

"Getting drunk," Sam said, his tone suggesting he thought that's what they did now—all they did. "I'm afraid I haven't come with good news."

"What happened?" John said. "Are you all right?"

"Not me; Milo."

"Milo?" Sally said.

"Your son was—he was—it happened in Afghanistan."

Fred said, "What happened?"

"The explosion."

"Explosion?" Fred said. "What was Milo doing in Afghanistan?"

"Relief work, UN, something like that. It was terrorism. And I—well, it was fatal terrorism."

"Milo's dead?" Sally said.

Sam nodded. The rest huddled around Sally. She knelt, pulling clover from the ground. Standing back, Sam sneezed. Fred helped Sally to her feet and led her away to their trailer.

"What's going on out there?" Pete said.

"Jesus," Sam said, "no news at all gets here, does it? September 11: That date mean anything to you?"

"Somebody's birthday?"

"Not exactly."

Sam explained everything, the tumult that had eluded his elders. "All this clover," he said, kicking a cloud of it. "That's what the paper looked like spinning down from the towers."

"I never even heard of those towers before," Pete said.

John, still holding the master volume, said, "Where's the funeral?"

"That's just it: New York City. It's in two days. Which means if anybody wants to go, we'd have to drive to the airport tomorrow. But I don't know how you'll get back. I used all my vacation getting here in time to make it to New York. Then it's back to work in Chicago. I've got money. You can use it. But like I said, I don't know how you'll get back from the airport."

"You're not coming back," Pete said.

Weatherman Mary and Builder Bob held each other's hands as though they would lift into orbit should they let go.

Bob said, "Maybe if we had a Doctor Dave. We're getting older."

"You mean," Pete said, "if we had a doctor, some of us wouldn't be dead, is what you mean."

"It's true," Weatherman Mary said. "They might both be alive."

"People get sick out there, too," Pete said, pointing. "Medicine ain't magic. It can't fix everything"

Sam looked at his watch as if he had somewhere to go.

"Come on, Sam," John said.

The group collapsed into couples but for Pete, who staggered, then fell to the ground. As the rest walked away, he reached for the moon, tried to snatch it and missed, then slipped into a reclining position he would maintain the rest of the night.

"Where's Mom?" Sam said to John.

"Why don't we go to your car and talk? I'm sick of that trailer. I'd rather roll down the windows and keep an eye on Pete. Did you notice him holding his stomach?"

They climbed inside the SUV. Sam put his keys in the ignition as if he wanted to drive away from the impending conversation, but he left the ignition off.

"Your mother's gone, Sam."

"I was figuring that."

"Pneumonia, we think. We tried to find a way to a hospital, but she wouldn't have gone if we had. I won't say she didn't suffer, but she didn't suffer long."

Sam held the steering wheel, then let go.

"Are you okay?"

"I knew before I got here. No, I didn't have a dream. I just stopped feeling her breath on my back. And so I started getting scared more often, anxiety attacks. I tried to forget you both, and then I couldn't stop thinking about you after everything that happened, especially Milo dying. I'd been in touch with Milo over the years. He inherited what I didn't. He made you guys relevant again, or what you thought was relevant, anyway."

"It was all a dream, like that clover back there. But after the funeral, I'm going with you—if you don't mind."

"With me? I got a couch, I guess. But Chicago? Sure you can handle the change?"

"You just get me through New York. I'll take care of Chicago. I'm sick of this Monet valley. I need some clarity."

At sunrise, they met outside the trailer of mourning. Sally and Fred opened the still-bent screen door looking as though they had taken hallucinogens the night before, backed-up dreams orbiting their eyes in rings of black. They squinted in the sun, Bob's hand on Sally's back like a ventriloquist with no words to offer himself or his mate. Pete appeared no better and kept looking behind at the place where the women had been buried. Mary and Bob had their hands in their pockets, digging for comfort or rabbits' feet. Sam checked his watch. John turned Sam's wrist so that time faced elsewhere.

"Well?" John said. "Who's coming? I am. Sally, Fred, I know you're coming. Mary and Bob, now's your chance. Pete?"

"Staying."

"You can't stay here alone," Sam said.

"Yeah? Feel this." Pete took Sam's hand and placed it on his stomach.

"Christ, you've got to see a doctor."

"For what? I already know what it is: same thing that killed my dad. This is where I want to die. I don't want no radiation."

"But you'll need help."

"It won't take long. I've got company here."

"Right," Bob said, "because we're staying. We've got no business out there."

"None," Mary said. "We're history."

"Pete," John said, "you know I've got to go."

"I know. You're a writer. You should be writing about whatever's happening now, not all this nostalgia."

John held out his palms and caught the drifting clover.

"Consider that," Pete said, pointing at the particles in John's hand, "your kisses, your hugs, your toasts goodbye."

"Right," Bob said.

Sally, Fred, John and Sam walked to the SUV. They drove away. As the vehicle rose with the incline, the air clearing with the climb, John finally realized the valley had been sucking the clover down from its surroundings. He opened a newspaper and read aloud various items, until the wind snapped the paper from his hands, shredding it to ribbons behind the car.

Paul A. Toth has published two novels, *Fizz*, and its successor, *Fishnet*, both available from select retail stores and all major online outlets. *Fishnet* and a third novel will be published in Russia. His short fiction has been nominated for the Pushcart Prize and *Best American Mystery Stories*. For more information, please see www.netpt.tv.

CONCEIVED
DAVID LAWRENCE MORSE

OUR VILLAGE IS built on a great fish—Ceta—so sizeable we have room for nineteen huts, built with the bones we find floating on the sea. Osa always thought it more precarious than it is—we have the huts lashed down with great belts of kelp, for those rare moments when the seas get aggressive. Our huts are grouped in two rows, facing each other across the bony length of Ceta's spine, extending from her dorsal fin to her blowhole. My hut is closest to the blowhole, so I can monitor it, keep it free of debris—fish lice like to force their way into those warm, wet recesses. And even a small child, crawling loose and free, is liable to fall in, become wedged in the delicate tracheal membranes, suffocating our gentle Ceta. Who knows what she would do in such a situation? Thrash and flail the sea, flinging our meager posts and provisions miles across the deep? Perhaps, but Ceta is the gentlest of beasts, and also the wisest—she would see the futility in such aggression, knowing with a beast's instinctual wisdom that there's no cure for calamity once it has lodged itself inside. No, I imagine her simply sinking calmly into the sea, giving her flukes one last flip as if in apology, or farewell. Either way that would be the end of us.

It is my duty to see that Ceta has everything she needs. I swim into her mouth daily, clutching the great bony beak of a swordfish, with which to pick her baleen clean—the bigger fish sometimes get stuck between those hard, horny plates, causing her some discomfort. Of course it's not easy work, finding my way in that great black chasm, swimming through the whirling swirl of krill, but Ceta is patient and tries to keep her gullet shut so I won't get swallowed up inside. Sometimes these days I think of giving in to the temptation, of releasing my grip on the baleen, letting my body be taken up in that violent stream, swallowed along with millions of krill for the sake of a larger life. But that would mean abandoning my duty, and I assume Ceta's stomach would have no room for the likes of me—I'm a stubborn man and probably not easily digested.

Other villagers take care of the remaining matters—harvesting the fish lice, our primary source of food, also a danger to Ceta if too many accumulate too quickly. Lice attach themselves to her skin, trying to suck the very life out of her. But if you know how to grip them—just above the gut—they pluck right off, and make for easy eating—succulent, nothing but muscle, tasty raw or pickled in vats of brine. And our drinking water must be collected—every few minutes Ceta spouts forth a mighty mist, the water always remarkably warm no matter the temperature of the sea, and free of any trace of salt.

Osa loved Ceta almost as much as I did, but was afraid she might suddenly make a dive for the deep, giving up her commitment to a surface existence. But Osa had many such fears. I never knew anyone who regarded the simple things of life with such simultaneous passion and suspicion. She was afraid of drowning, though she loved to swim. Afraid of swallowing her own teeth (they might make a meal of her from the inside out), though she loved to eat. Her greatest fear was of being misunderstood, though the life she lived was a mystery. But not a mystery to me, or at least I thought as much at the time. Understood? What is there to understand? We live on a fish on the sea. We eat fish lice and occasionally a lung fish, a tench, or a snook. We play with our children and make love with our wives. Life is good, life is not so good. We are glad, we are not so glad. What is there, I would ask my Osa, to understand?

I call her my Osa, though she was never properly mine—not my wife, anyway—only my companion. Companions are not allowed to marry unless and until they have produced a child—human life is too precarious to allow a couple to pass through life without propagation. If after a few seasons the companions have not succeeded, then they are separated and a new pair is arranged. I was Osa's second companion. Her first was set adrift on a raft of bones after he was discovered to be impotent, which is not punishable in and of itself (we are not, after all, pitiless) except combined with his deceit—the couple, it was judged, had flaunted our customs regarding fertility in order to attend to their own notions of togetherness. Osa herself never confessed—it was her younger sister Tama who overheard them discussing it and told the elders. Osa was only spared the same sentence because as a childbearer she was entitled to another chance.

As for me, I was surprised to find Osa was interested at all. Her first companion, Conger, was one of the men who rode bareback on the dolphins, hunting with spears the larger game—swordfish, mako sharks—as much to protect our Ceta from attack as for fresh meat and hides. Osa would often ride the dolphins with them—not on the hunts but at other times, just for fun—and I would sit in envy, not of their prowess but of the wonderfully free way in which they rode. But some months after Conger had been exiled, Osa began to join me in the sea when I would inspect Ceta's sides for signs of illness or evidence of attacks. We would swim underneath her, admiring her massive dimensions, her jaws yawning open and her throat swelling to twice its size, swallowing the sea. Once we found a fresh wound on her belly—a gash of jagged flesh as long as my arm, the tooth of a mako shark lodged in the fat—which fascinated Osa so much I couldn't bring her to leave, even with another shark attack surely imminent. Wounds, scars, scabs, blisters, sores—the evidence of injuries and how they healed—these captivated her. The body and its processes was her passion, and the reason she became obsessed with me, too—caretaker of the largest body in the sea.

Though ours was not her first companionship, I was surprised to find she approached it with the passion and even ingenuousness as if it were. In our first weeks together, we were en route on our fish from the seas of summer to those of fall, the cool darkness of the deep, by degrees, seeping closer to the sea's surface. We moved together into one of the huts set aside for companions, and she brought with her many additions—variously colored sea stars to surround our pallet and a briny ball of orange, with brilliant, serpentine tendrils, to hang like the sun from our ceiling. The waters were still moderately warm at that time and we spent our days splashing and laughing and swimming with the others, the quicker swimmers among us catching tench for all to eat, the smaller children taking turns on the blowhole to be shot wriggling into the air, a few of us lying flat on Ceta's flukes to be flipped high into the sky, and my own Osa climbing onto the backs of the dolphins and holding on for the ride. At her goading the two of us dove down into the cold sea-deep, and there, unseen, lost in darkness, suspended together in the giant writhing silence, I first knew the reach and rush of lust.

And yet she didn't conceive, and soon our fish had brought us to winter seas, stretching before us calm and cold, Osa said, as a corpse. The sun far-flung, for months unmoving above, and I found my Osa gradually given to fits of ill-humor. She hated the cold and monotony of those winter seas, where nothing much exists but ourselves and the occasional shadow of something silent in the deep, and her body began to show it. Her brown hair, a surge of curls and tresses, began to wilt, become long and sodden as seaweed. Her eyelids thickened; the soft corners of her mouth hardened with suspicion. In winter we rely almost entirely on the fish louse for food, but Osa lost her taste for these, needing variety. And while others enjoyed the weather of these winters—the crisp, brisk touch of the sun—Osa was always chilled.

Her younger sister Tama—who had told the elders of Conger's impotency— didn't help matters—there were no boys her age to flirt with, and she was having to wait for male attention until she grew a few years older. Tama frequently frustrated my efforts to care for Ceta, hiding the swordfish beak I used to clean the baleen, or worse, using the beak to dig holes into Ceta's skin, which I would then rub down for hours with vats of shark fat. But when I mentioned this to Osa she refused to scold her sister and insisted that I leave her alone as well. "She's harmless," Osa said, "just a girl really. And can you blame her if she's bored?"

"Bored?" I asked. "How could one be bored? We're surrounded by the sea, the sky, the stars. Every day Ceta swims us somewhere different—the colors of the waters—see how they're changing!" But Osa's sympathies seemed to be more with her sister than with me, and the two of us grew increasingly hostile. She was suspicious in her misery, sure that I disapproved, which was true, except I would not admit it, instead offering limp, bitter sympathies. I could be caretaker, but only of something I thought deserved being taken care of—what reason did Osa have for her petty ways? "What reason?" she asked. "What reason does Ceta have for bringing us here?" I told her Ceta didn't need a reason—any more than did the sun for sinking into the sea. "Then I don't need a reason, either," she said. "Maybe one day I'll be riding a dolphin and decide to keep holding on, and never let go. Dolphins know where the warm waters are, and never leave them." In such moments Osa would become perfectly still, riveted by her own resentments, her cheeks reddening—in her anger she would forget to breathe. I was infatuated with her passions but angered when the passions ran her the other way—from love of our life to hatred of it. She began to grant me little intimacy, though even at our most estranged I was fervent for it, from sheer lust, but also from the growing realization that our time together would soon be ended by the elders unless our love proved fruitful.

The days were long in those winter waters and the nights nonexistent. Osa spent much of the time on our pallet, preoccupied with picking the calluses from her feet, or from mine, when I would let her. Or she would lie on the pallet resting on her elbows, studying the gray patterns of Ceta's skin. When she did leave the hut, she would wander about looking for the sunburned boys—bribing them until they agreed to sit still while she peeled off their skin.

Our village spent much of these white nights in revelry, amid music of the drum and fife, spinning and slipping and dancing across Ceta's mottled skin, free from the haunts and sluggishness of sleep. I often observed these revelries—finding it enjoyable to watch others enjoying themselves—but Osa remained much in our hut, determined to sleep—even with no night to necessitate it—so she would not miss her dreams.

Sometimes she would describe these dreams to me, full of things none of us had ever seen: beings like fish that swam through the air rather than the sea; an expanse of surface, like our Ceta's back except more vast, more firm, and fixed; and from that surface, things growing upward, like seaweed but without need of water for support, fixed instead of floating, whispering in the breeze. She told me these were things she had dreamed into existence. She said that life inflicted wounds and that dreams were the mind's means of healing. She asked me if I ever dreamed and I—taken aback and even offended by her visions—lied for the first time in my life and told her I didn't. I told her dreams were the things of fools and prophets. She assumed I meant her to be a fool and left me alone on the pallet; I might have stopped her but found I couldn't. In truth I didn't know which she was—fool or prophet—and didn't know if she knew, either.

Yet we maintained a fascination with each other—there were still flashes of passion. As once when we crawled onto our hut's roof, a shelf of kelp, to watch the winter lights—great green glowing bands dancing in the sky. Swoot swoot BOOM went the blowhole, and the spout shot high into those green sky lights, and we were awash in the heated mist, the seaweed soft and supple under our backs, and Osa asked me what did it all mean. I didn't know any more than she did, but I did know that wasn't what she wanted to hear, and for once I obliged her, and gave her meanings—fool that I was—as I understood them right then: that there was no such thing as time, only the glow of the moment; that there was no such thing as truth, only the blur of feeling and belief. She gasped and her eyes regained their wide, wild delight. "We shouldn't be up here," she said. "We could fall through." And then we fell to each other with such force that that is exactly what we did—fell through—the kelp suddenly letting us go so quickly and completely that it seemed impossible it had ever held us, and as we fell we remained embraced, suspended for a moment, blind in the green misty light, before we landed on the pallet, on Ceta's forgiving back, with an unforgiving thud.

"Where have you been?" she asked afterwards. She was resting on my chest, her head rising and falling with my breaths.

"Where else? I've been right here."

"You mean with me?"

"Well, yes."

"You only love the idea of me. And I love the idea of you. But that's not enough. Our love needs a body."

"That's what a child is," I said, "or could be."

She was quiet for awhile. Every few minutes the blowhole boomed. "No," she said. "No it's not. A child would just be floating right along with us. We wouldn't love our child, just the idea of our child."

"What's wrong with floating?" I asked. "That's the way the world works."

"But what if we weren't living on Ceta anymore? What if Ceta were free to swim and dive and leap out of the water like other fish, and we were free, too, without clinging to her back like lice. What if we found a place where what was under us wasn't always moving? Then I could settle down with you."

"What do you mean 'then?'" I said. "There's no such thing as 'then.' There's only now. Now is the same as it's always been. And always will be."

Again she was silent, and said bitterly, "I see." And I could feel the bones in her back stiffening, feel them constricting, until she rolled off my chest and away from me, and we lay there silently, separately, rising and falling with Ceta's tremendous breaths.

I can't remember which arrived first that spring—the rumors or the bird. The rumors said that the elders were already thinking of separating Osa and me; it was no secret, though I'd tried to keep it so, that we were having difficulties. She now refused intimacy except on rare occasions, though at the same time, she refused to be finished with me. She thought she could somehow win me over to her dreams of things, and didn't believe me when I said I never dreamed. "You talk in your sleep," she said. "Sometimes you cry out—that's how I know you're lying." And it was true I was having dreams, but not like Osa's—her views had gotten under my skin, and I had secretly begun to fear what would happen to us if Ceta ever died. We had lived on her back for generations, so that we could no more imagine her dying than the sun itself, but then again, wasn't she a fish, just like the other fish of the sea? I began having nightmares, dreaming of an ocean of bones and foam and blood. I dreamed of Ceta sinking, and of the villagers lashed to her back, sinking through an abyss of krill. And yet my role as Ceta's caretaker was a sacred responsibility I could not easily disavow—as long as I continued to administer to her needs, then surely she would continue serving us dutifully as she had always done. And besides, I asked Osa, where were we to go? She was determined that I admit the possibility of her nightly visions, and I was determined that she admit the actuality of our situation.

I tried to seduce her while she slept, but she would wake, angry, and leave. She would go back to her father's hut. Sometimes when this happened Tama would make her way down Ceta's long bony spine, balancing, her arms outstretched like fins. She would sing to herself, "Osa's home, Osa's home," loud enough that the villagers in their huts on either side might hear. When she arrived at my hut she would stop in the doorway, a hand on the frame, looking at me, and announce, "Osa's home."

"Yes, I know."

"Do you know why?"

"Because she loves her little sister."

"Don't be a fool," she would say—reproving me, but reproving Osa, too, whose love could not be had or held so simply. And then she would make up a preposterous list of reasons why her sister had gone home: Osa lost her eyes again—Papa is gluing on new ones. Osa forgot to kiss the great fish in the sky goodbye before she was born—she has to go back and be born again. Osa likes to sleep with Papa. Osa peeled off all her skin.

One day she didn't stop at the doorway but slipped inside, keeping her hands behind her. She started again on her list: Osa swallowed a fish louse whole. Osa exploded. Osa came home to find her sister but her sister turned into a bird.

"What's a bird?" I asked.

"Here," she said, and held out her cupped hands. Inside them was the strangest thing I'd ever seen, like something out of Osa's dreams. A snout like that of a swordfish, long and beaked, which opened and shut and emitted strange squeaks. A plump body, shaped more like a large fish egg than a fish itself, with a thin, wrinkled membrane of skin, and strange, soft fins that alternately extended and were tucked away.

"What is it?" I asked.

"A bird, silly," Tama said. "Osa created it in one of her dreams. But she's never seen a real one. I'm the only one who has. Me, and now you, too."

"Where did you get it?"

"It got me. It landed on my head. Here, you can hold it," she said, and reached toward me, but the bird sprang out of her hand and began swimming through the air, beating what I only knew then to call its fins. "That's okay," she said. "In Osa's dreams that's called flying." The bird flew out my cabin door but Tama remained unconcerned. "It'll come back," she said. "I'm its new home."

Only the bird didn't come back, but was seen by various villagers swimming—flying—in and out of huts, over heads and under arms, until it landed in the hands of Tope, one of the elders, a timid man with enormous eyes, who clutched at it and almost broke its neck before his wife got it into a makeshift cage. There was a commotion in the village such as had not been seen since years before, when an old woman named Daee declared our great fish pregnant, and it was only after many speeches from me that I convinced the village Ceta wasn't pregnant but was only suffering from indigestion. "How could she possibly conceive?" I told them at the time. "She's twice as big as any fish out there."

Everyone took the bird's arrival as a sign—the question was, of what? Some thought it meant the end of times, which brought leaping and laughter from some, crying from others. Some quarreled, hitting each other in the knees with bones. Others played the fife and drum, marching up and down Ceta's spine. Others feasted, opening up the reserves of pickled plaice, or plucking off fresh fish lice and biting them in half. Games of gobo, shinny, and battledore, wrestling and fencing, spouting contests among the boys. Only in the uproar, the villagers lost track of the bird itself, and when a line formed around Tope's hut, waiting to give him his ceremonial, congratulatory whacks on the back for a notable deed done, it was discovered that Tope himself no longer had the bird—he said it was at Turbot's. Turbot said it was at Tautog's. Tautog said it was at Sprat's. Sprat didn't know where it was, or even that it existed, Sprat having died the previous week. His widow beat the villagers out of her hut with a dead lungfish.

Late that night, Osa returned to the hut, as I knew she would. There was no moon and the night was black and the sea winds unusually strong for the season, and I felt as if I were lost and swirling inside the sea-filled jaws of a beast even greater than Ceta, without even her bony baleen to hold onto, to keep me from giving myself to the rush of darkness swallowing us all. Osa paused in the doorway; I couldn't see her but could feel her presence, her eyes wide and fixed on where she knew my body would be lying. She feared doorways—that feeling of being caught in between—but she lingered there, as her sister had done so many times before.

"Would you believe me if I told you I conceived the bird in a dream?" she asked, her voice trembling, her words tumbling down onto me as if from a great height. I was staring into the night through the tattered hole in the roof, which she'd insisted I never repair, so that the mist from Ceta's breaths was continually drizzling down upon us.

"No," I said.

"Would you believe me if I said the bird flew to us from a great expanse of something called land, and that we could live there, you and I?"

"No," I said.

"Would you believe me if I said I have conceived a child? Our child?"

My heart kicked at my breast, but though I wanted to believe her, again I said no. To believe one of her conceits was to believe them all, and to believe them all was to risk the ruination of the precarious life it was my responsibility to preserve.

"I see," she said and was silent. Ceta's spouts boomed and the warm mist fell upon us, and I could feel Osa sinking away from me, sinking back into the night.

By noon the next day the entire village had been given to understand that Osa was with child—it was Tama who triumphantly spread the word. The village decided the mysterious bird must have been a messenger bringing the news, and there were whispers that Osa was to bear a child of great strength and courage. Most were pleased that the end of times was to be put off after all, though a few dissenters said the child might be the one who would one day wreak the ruin. All of the men—including Osa's father—lined up to whack me on the back (some of the shark hunters hit harder than they should), and in the afternoon three elder women arrived with pillows and fragrances and a tiara of pike teeth for the blessed mother-to-be. Only Osa had not yet returned to our hut from the night before, and I had not gone to find her—from preoccupation and obstinacy. The women stumbled about in the hut, embarrassed and concerned and titillated, adjusting and readjusting the pillows on the pallet and chattering.

"It's a hardness on a woman, who's with child."

"A man's no help anyways."

"Could be a demon-child."

"No telling what a woman might do."

"Come to her good sense eventually."

The villagers were befuddled. Marriage festivities were in order and yet couldn't proceed if the couple didn't seem inclined to be together. As for me, in the following days I busied myself in the sea with Ceta. Now that she'd returned us to warmer waters I had many duties: cleaning the yellow algae from beneath her flippers, rubbing down her flippers and dorsal fin with vats of shark fat, filing the barnacles off her flukes. Routine duties, but pleasurable all the same, keeping me busy in the sea and out of my vacant, newly fragranced hut. As for Osa, I missed her terribly, and strove to know if what she said was true—that she had conceived a child. And yet I remained tormented by my own suspicions. What of what she'd said did she herself believe? We were suffering, as we had all along, from two different kinds of obstinacy—Osa's driven by the fervency of dream and belief; mine more like a disease, trapped within the accumulated fat of habit, insulation against a fear of the mysterious, that would not let me yield, and would not let me go.

A week passed. One of the elders—Tope himself, who had found and lost the messenger bird—came to me, his enormous eyes drifting in his cavernous sockets, and questioned me tepidly about the nature of our disagreements, suggesting I do what I could to solve them. Tama could be heard about the village, singing out "Osa's home" to whomever looked as if they might want to hear. But she did not come again to my doorway, instead solving everyone's problems by coming to the elder women late one afternoon, crying and saying with a mixture of shame, anger, and dismay that Osa was not pregnant after all. Osa had neglected to throw away the strips of kelp she'd used to clean herself, and Tama had found these and was here bringing them to the elders. The elders made their decision swiftly, this being Osa's second offense against fertility, that she was to be put on a raft of bones and set adrift at sea.

The entire village seemed in agreement, except her father, who tarried in the doorway when the shark hunters arrived to carry her away. But even he put up little fight—just a gatherer of fish lice his entire life. It was said Osa seemed willing to go, that she seemed to have salvaged from her suffering if not dignity then at least a degree of defiance. It was said she forgot to kiss our Ceta, the great fish, goodbye. It was said she took nothing with her. It was said that her raft didn't drift at all, but seemed moved by unseen currents, and that a bird flew overhead, leading, circling, following.

It was Tama who said these things, lingering, swinging in my doorway. It was Tama who told me proudly that it was her own blood that had bloodied the kelp, her first time, and just in time, for Osa really had conceived a child, but had placed her sister under oath not to tell.

"Why?" I asked, cringing, my airways constricting. "Because she wanted to die?"

"Oh, don't be such a fool," she said.

Only now I have little choice but to be the fool, love-lost, fearful of what may become of us, lying on my back by night, showered by Ceta's mists, admiring and scrutinizing the nature of her spouts. Are they coming less frequently? Are they blowing at not quite their former height? Is our Ceta slowing down? I do not know, and cannot, nor can I know what became of my Osa alone out there on a raft of bones, but every day I keep watch on the horizon for that mysterious expanse of something called land, and imagine my Osa running and spinning and dancing across it, our child clinging to her back, laughing, holding on for the ride.

David Lawrence Morse grew up in south Georgia and attended the University of North Carolina at Chapel Hill. Since then he has lived and worked in Washington, D.C., Iwakuni, Japan, and Ann Arbor, Michigan, where he completed an MFA in fiction and now teaches writing and literature. He is currently working on a novel about a rice farmer in coastal Georgia, as well as a collection of stories. "Conceived" was included in *The O.Henry Prize Stories 2006*.

FOUR HOLLOWS

DEANNE LUNDIN

vibrate

The size of our lives terrifies
I mean the way

Some days I can't find it

Just now   we're between
The traffic & the bruise

All the way down we're ecstatic
A sweetness survives

A survivor is how many times

May Day from Magdelen Tower
The town swings its bells out over the river

But what does it do in July

They say
The view is striking

Can the body be tuned like a fork

Jesus if I had a hammer
I'd ring like that

abandon

Wild as a hot scrap torn
From the back of a scarlet chevy

Ripe with boys

On a mission

To slit some asphalt

Whose doesn't matter

Night is a road
We believe in it

Feral to the primer
We know

There will be towns without names

We can name them
And get some disease for ourselves

Call them Fever & Hole & Disaster &
Somebody's Little Sister

She lets us just hanging on to the fender

We shine like that
It's an echo we like

Hey America hey u r us

We're your long overdue
Colonic irrigation

The roughage you can't get enough of

The key
In your back door turning

Snatch of neon curling down

Each bare throat
Wind rip the scream from

Heaven

Who wants you

sear

Soul itch a
Bruise so deep it feels good when you find it

This isn't about the body

But only its alias

Shine
Ghosting up from the surf

How it claws at the sand & pretending to faint keeps on coming

You are the man with a packet
Of ruptured sky

Your fingers are stained with it

Slice up this night for confetti
I want to scatter you

All down the Avenue of Stars

While the city unwinds
Its sirens like watches from Mexico

O love undo me

You can
Leave off the skin

open

She used to say it's never too late
For a hippy childhood

Wearing her beads fandango
And doing

The cockroach stomp on a table

I don't believe our
Lives ever slammed like that

You hear her whisper like dust on your screen

Open yourself &
Let the noise out

Or take some more in &
hey I'm bad but I'm good at it

We laugh
& the light howls in through the hole

What pierces the heart is darkness

A few rusted notes
Nailing the sky

Keeping it open

Deanne Lundin's work has appeared in journals such as *The Kenyon Review*, *The Georgia Review*, *Tarpaulin Sky*, and others. She is the author of *The Ginseng Hunter's Notebook* (poetry, New Issues Press) and one of her stories was a winner in *Glimmertrain*'s 2005 Open Fiction. She directs the Work-in-Progress Reading Series at the Crazy Wisdom Bookstore.

KODAI CON

HEATHER NEFF

I RECOGNIZED KISHO by the sprouts of celery-colored hair spiking out of his battle helmet, which had been sprayed to an air-brushed tint of Corinthian Silver and Pagan Bronze. His tunic, made from a fawn-toned fabric covered with nubs of tiny knotted threads, billowed out when he mounted the stage, offering us a quick glimpse of corded athletic thighs in spandex shorts. His feet were encased in leather boots that buckled at the calf. Bridget prodded my ribs with her elbow and whispered "*utsukushi!*" in a not-so-low voice.

Utsukushi, indeed. The guy really was gorgeous—so gorgeous, in fact, that I nearly forgot that I was about to make a complete fool of myself by following him up on that stage. Though I tried to see more, my Curtain of Fire hair completely covered my left eye, and even worse, I'd left my glasses on the table next to my bed. As I got dressed that morning I tried to convince myself that the important thing about the Con was to be seen rather than to see—meaning that much of what was going on around me was reduced to a soft kaleidoscope of texture and color. Even the Neo-Seraphim insignias of our magenta battle suits looked like fuzzy, shifting hieroglyphs as we moved through the crowd.

Still, I wished I could see this Kisho better as he flicked his electron lasso to the cheers of his admiring spectators. By tilting my head I managed to free up my line of vision enough to make out the twinkling emerald tip of his left ear, which was peeking out from beneath his visor. The arms he raised to welcome the swelling applause were gently muscled beneath his silver undershirt, and he was wearing a thick onyx ring—the source of Kisho's immortality—on his right middle finger. He'd put some serious effort into that costume.

"Well, what do you think of Number Sixteen, folks? Pretty excellent Kisho, isn't he?"

The MC, wearing a floor-length black cloak with a lavender *obi* in the tradition of a *Kodai* Warrior Priestess, was grinning so hard that I thought her lips were going to jump off and start doing cartwheels. He was an eyeful, all right. But that wasn't really the point.

Now his turn was over and he leapt lightly to the floor and was instantly swallowed up by his personal fan club of *Nami*-clones, all of them adorned in shimmering golden tutus with thigh-high button-up plastic boots.

"Stupid cows," Bridget snapped as she followed them with her eyes. "They should at least get matching wigs if they're going to be his groupies."

I thought of our wigs—stiffly gelled orange plastic humps that rose up off of our heads like traffic cones, with a thick swath of hair fixed like a shower curtain over one half of our faces. Our battle suits, made from a stretchy polyester that shone in the spotlights like translucent wine-colored snakeskin, were so tight that neither one of us could completely exhale. We'd even managed to find spike-heeled black ankle boots in both our sizes.

Bridget worked equally hard to get our faces just right. Our heavily painted Cleopatra eyes were offset by a mask of thick white Geisha makeup. Better yet, our mouths looked like wads of chewed bubble gum, thanks to a lipstick called Raucous Pink.

We were matching, all right. It didn't matter that we looked like fugitives from a Dr. Seuss nightmare. We were the most perfect imitations of *Mine* Maidens at the entire Con.

Coming to the Con had been Bridget's idea. Everybody she admired at school was into cosplaying, and she figured that just showing up would score us some points on a certain social register. Let's face it—neither one of us was ever going to get asked out by a jock and we didn't have the rags to roll with the preps. So, as she suggested, maybe hanging out with the *Manga*-fanatics would help us fit in somewhere.

Now the MC pointed at Bridget and me. "And here we have Numbers Twenty-Two and Twenty-Three! Looks like two more *Mine* Maidens," she announced cheerfully, mispronouncing "*Meen-eh*" as "mine." She gestured that we should take our place beneath the spotlights on the stage. I reluctantly followed Bridget, who had already strolled out and struck a combat-ready pose, her *kendo* stick poised in front of her like she was preparing to pole-vault.

There was a polite round of applause that seemed to diminish slightly when I arrived by her side. I knew that my battle suit was particularly snug and that the circular *kodai* insignias looked a little bit like binocular lenses placed on my boobs and butt. I tried to edge my way into Bridget's shadow, but the MC waved her arms, encouraging me to move up alongside her.

"These maidens are sworn to protect the secret location of the Seraphim-Sanctuary," she read from an index card, "and are trained as samurai. Ladies, perhaps you'd like to show us how you defend the *kodai* priests!"

That got another weak round of applause and a few encouraging hoots from the back of the ballroom. I tried to smile, but I had a feeling that the hot pink lipstick had smeared on my teeth, and my makeup was already flaking off. Bridget raised her brows, signaling me to assume a battle pose. I drew my brows together in refusal. She responded by pivoting around and lifting her stick very slowly.

Feeling like a marionette strung on razor wire, I too hoisted my arms. Bridget psyched a pass at me, slamming her stick noisily against mine. I knew that twisting my body would offer the crowd an unobstructed view of my magenta rear, so I scuttled across the stage like a lobster in a tank avoiding the hands of the cook. Bridget didn't seem to take the hint. She waved her stick fiercely back and forth, moving toward me with great loping strides as if she was suffering from gravity-deprivation.

"What the hell are you doing?" I whispered after she cracked her stick hard against mine for the fourth time. By then I was backed up against the wall and one step away from plunging into another pair of *Mine* Maidens who were waiting for their turn on the stage.

"Come on, *act*," she muttered between clenched teeth, a strand of her blond hair sneaking out from under her wig.

"Chill out, you tae kwon *doofus*!" I answered coldly. Hearing the no-joke in my voice, she froze, then reluctantly turned to face the crowd. I turned, too, and we bowed half-heartedly.

"There you have them, *Kodai Warrior* lovers!" the MC announced enthusiastically. The fact that we looked like idiots was emphasized when only two or three people clapped. I followed my friend down from the stage, so glad it was over that I forget how pissed I was at her.

Once freed from the spotlights I realized that sweat rings were blossoming out from my underarms and a rip had opened up at my left shoulder. I didn't need a mirror to know that my Curtain of Fire was drooping and I sensed that in our little combat demonstration one or two of my insignias had come undone.

"Look, Bridge—I'm changing clothes!" I shouted above the crowd's appreciative roar at the sight of the *joshikousei* who followed us—fake schoolgirls clad in pink *fukus* with pleated skirts so short that everyone could see their color-coordinated panties.

"But you look great, Kenya."

"My face itches, my feet hurt and I'd enjoy being able to breathe!"

"You've got to be here for the judging!"

"Like we're going to win something."

"We might. You know as well as I do that we're the best *Mine* Maidens in the place!"

"Then you can accept the prize for the both of us," I said, stomping away.

The Con was being held in the ballroom of the downtown Holiday Inn, the closest thing to a luxury hotel in our town. At least fifty vendors had set up booths offering everything from bootleg DVDs to the armbands worn by the mercenaries in *Tokyo Dragons*. There were stands selling Japanese juice-drinks, rahmen, and sushi, too. One guy had a table loaded with toy kittens, the mascots of the *Neko Knights*.

A group of *Botan* girls—servants to the *Kodai Hime*, or ancient princess, were guarding the door to the women's john. They were done up in cheerful orange shifts with periwinkle knee socks and baby-jane shoes, like the girls on the television animé. I knew that the real *Botan* girls—I mean the ones in the original *manga*, or graphic novel—wore ballet slippers that laced up to the knee. I pushed through them, ignoring the barbed laughter that followed me.

The restroom was done up like a mini-Versailles, with red velvet walls and dripping chandeliers poised between the gilded mirrors. Aside from the occasional roar of the crowd as yet another priest or warrior mounted the stage, the place was mercifully quiet.

I'd just dropped my backpack on a plush chaise lounge when the door opened and Bridget hustled in behind me.

"Kenya, what are you doing?"

"I already told you I'm getting out of this thing," I said, twisting around to reach the zipper.

"But why?"

"Reality check, Bridget: I don't belong here."

"What are you talking about?"

"I'm talking about those people who came here to strut around on the stage to win a prize. Those girls with color-coordinated panties who only showed up to get a guy. The people who don't even know that these characters come from books with detailed plots and storylines!"

"But you got up on the stage—"

"Only because you wanted to, Bridget!"

"Aren't you having fun?"

"Can't you tell I'm having a great time?"

Bridget opened her mouth to answer, then closed it. I could see the hurt in her eyes.

"Listen," I said more softly, "you're my best friend. We've been friends since graham crackers and naptime. But sometimes we've got to be ourselves, right? Now you should go on out there and enjoy yourself. I'll change clothes and catch up with you in a few minutes."

Be myself? I thought as the door exhaled to a close behind her. *What's the point in that?*

I learned long ago that being myself wasn't real easy. Nobody wanted to know who I really was. It made things simpler to see me as the girl with hair like a reggae singer, who dressed like a rugby player and talked like a guy. It's true that I had a dangerous tendency to say what was on my mind. It decreased to zero the number of guys who were willing to ask me out, but on the other hand I didn't have to waste a lot of time on knuckleheads. Well, except maybe knuckleheads like Bridget.

Of course, Bridge really was my friend, though she'd nearly tipped the boat with those magenta *Mine* Maiden costumes. Though they were perfect to the detail, neither one of us was really built for polyester. But who cared? I didn't know anybody at the Con, anyway.

I pulled a pair of nylon warm-ups and a t-shirt from my backpack, then peeled myself out of my battle suit. I had a hard time removing the Curtain of Fire, because Bridget had used at least a dozen hairpins to clamp it to my hair. I'd also forgotten to bring a change of shoes, so I was trapped in my dog-hating spike-heeled boots.

Fortunately I'd remembered to pack a couple of baby-wipes in a plastic bag. Unpeeling them carefully, I began the Herculian task of excavating my face. It wasn't easy, but once the glitter make-up and ridiculous lipstick were cleared away, I finally dared to look at myself.

The dreads I'd started growing the year before stood up like the spikes of a black dandelion around my face. My eyes were still ringed with eyeshadow, a new look for me. I was still kind of sweaty from the costume, but I sort of liked the sheen it gave my coppery face. All in all, I figured I could emerge from the bathroom and nobody, not even the stupid *gakis* by the door, would recognize me.

Outside the place was all noise and movement. More people had arrived and the soundtrack from *Kodai Warriors II: Gallidora's Gateway* was blaring from the speakers. The lights had been dimmed so the cosplayers could see the newest episode of the animé, which was being projected onto a giant screen behind the stage. I hadn't walked two paces before I noticed that the *Nami* groupies were now standing near the door to the men's john, checking out the *Botan* girls and chomping down on Pocky.

The door swung open and a guy in dark clothes came out. He was moving fast—so fast that when he brushed by me I nearly lost my balance on those stupid boots.

Man, I'd had enough of the Con for that day. I was all about finding Bridget and seeing how fast she could drive us home. Shouldering my backpack, I inserted myself into the crowd and started making my way back toward the stage.

"Oh—dang!" Without meaning to I banged right into the guy, who'd stopped at a booth selling *Kodai Warrior* figurines. He turned around. He was tall and broad-shouldered, but in the darkness there wasn't much face to be seen between his knitted cap and dark hoodie. I apologized and waited for him to say something crappy—after all, I'd hit him pretty hard—but instead he just stared down at me.

"You look familiar."

"I do?"

"Yeah. Where do you go to school?" He speaking in a low voice, but somehow I could hear him beneath the roar of the crowd.

"Western."

"What year?"

"Junior."

"Me, too."

"Really?" I tried to get a closer look, but he was wrapped up like somebody in the Witness Protection Program. "I don't think I've ever seen you before."

"I transferred in this semester. My family moved here from Maryland." He flicked his head toward the table. "That's why I'm at this Con. Some of my friends back home are really into animé and I thought I'd grab a few things for them."

"You don't want that stuff," I replied bluntly.

"Why not?"

"It's junk. Anybody who's really into the series can see that."

There was a moment of silence as he glanced over at the rows of plastic Kishos, Namis and *Mine* Maidens. Then he looked back at me.

"So what's wrong with them?"

"They've been prettied-up for kids who don't know anything about the original *manga*," I explained. "The *Kodai* Warriors are reincarnations of people who felt like outsiders in their earlier lives. They don't fit in anywhere, so they just sort of hide out until it's time for them to fight. Even when they're scared they put up a front so that nothing can get to them."

"Then you know the series pretty well?"

"It's the best *manga* out there."

"That's why you like it?"

"I like it because—because I know how they feel."

He paused. "Do you cosplay?"

"Well, sort of," I replied, hoping he wouldn't recognize me as one of those goofy girls in the magenta body suits. "And you?"

Now it was his turn to hesitate. "I did today, but I got out of my costume."

"Why?"

"I wasn't feeling it. Too many of these folks think this is a game."

"It's not?"

"Not for me. I come to Cons to leave that stupid stuff behind. I can't stand people who're obsessed with store logos and expensive kicks and being popular. And I really can't take it when those people show up at places like this."

"Right," I answered, surprised.

"What about you?" he asked.

"What about me?"

"I don't see many Black girls here."

"So?"

He laughed. "I didn't think it was *allowed*."

I was all set to remind him that slavery ended one hundred and fifty years ago when he did something unexpected: he reached up, pushed back his knitted cap and scratched his ear.

That's when I saw the twinkling emerald stud.

"*Utsukushi*," I whispered.

"What?" he leaned closer to me and I gasped as I made his face out for the first time.

"You—you're Black, too," I stammered.

"Correction: I'm Blasian. My mother's Korean and my Dad's African American. I was raised as a Black person, but people remind me all the time that I don't really fit into either category."

"Well, I don't see any other Blasians here."

"Of course not," he said, laughing again. "Everybody knows that the only thing Blacks can do is play basketball, and Asians are too busy trying to score a 1600 on the SAT."

"What about you?"

"I'm just me."

We stood there for a few seconds, looking at the carpet. I was suddenly shyer than I'd ever been in my life.

"So—who's your character?" he asked.

"I'm a *Mine* Maiden."

"Really? I didn't see you in your costume."

"Yeah, well, it was kind of itchy."

"I'll bet. Did you get the hair?"

"Sure. It's right here." I indicated my backpack.

"Would you show me?"

I swung the backpack down from my shoulder and began to open it.

"No," he said, reaching out to touch my hand. "I mean, would you put it on again?"

"You've got to be kidding."

"No. I mean it."

"But—"

"Come on. You don't really expect me to get idea about how good it looks when it's balled up in your backpack."

"But what's the point?"

"The point is that you're supposed to be downtown buying clothes so you can look like the girls in the gangsta videos, just like I'm supposed to be somewhere doing Calculus or shooting hoops. That's the real thing I like about these Cons. When I come to a Con I can be whoever I want. For a couple of hours my race really doesn't matter."

I glanced around us. The hotel ballroom was packed with people pretending to be everything from fantasy demons—*oni*—to *manga* gods. Officers of the elite Pilot Corps were chatting with *hime* princesses who battled like ancient samurai. I even saw a few *Inochi* priests, dedicated to teaching our ragtag humankind how to protect and preserve the natural world. I turned back to the guy.

"Alright," I said. "I'll put my costume back on. But only if I get to see yours, too."

"*Yoshi,*" he replied.

It's bizarre how fast I got back into my battle suit. Even the Curtain of Fire slipped easily onto my head. I let go of the makeup. I didn't need it.

There was something different about Kisho, too, when I found him waiting just outside of the restrooms. He'd let go of his helmet, revealing his toffee-colored skin and beautiful, almond-shaped eyes. His curly-nappy hair formed a rough halo around his face.

"Very *kawaii,*" he remarked, his eyes flickering appreciatively over my costume.

"You're pretty *subarashii,* yourself," I concurred.

He grinned. "Hey—you didn't tell me your na—"

At that moment the voice of the MC burst through the noise of the crowd. "*Kodai* Warriors, the judges have come to their decision and we are ready to announce the winners of the Best Cosplay Contest."

A sudden hush fell over the entire ballroom as everyone turned in the direction of the stage.

"The prize for the best *Kodai Hime* goes to contestant thirty-five. Thirty-Five, are you still in the house?"

A woman in a rippling aqua robe with deep purple lining jogged up on the stage to enthusiastic applause. The MC handed her a framed poster of the *Kodai Warrior* animé characters, signed by the artists. The crowd roared as she began acting like a possessed Miss America, grinning wildly and blowing kisses through her tears.

"Congratulations, congratulations," the MC continued as she shooed the Princess to the rear. "Alright, folks—the prize for the best *Mine* Maiden goes to let me see—Number Twenty-Two. Are you still here, Twenty-Two?"

A shrill scream went up and I saw Bridget clamber up the steps. More blond hair had escaped from her Curtain of Fire, but it was hard to tell because she was acting like the stage was a trampoline. The MC grabbed her shoulders to steady her and everyone laughed.

"On behalf of the judges, I'd like to present you with a complete sixteen-disc set of the *Kodai Warrior Animé* on DVD."

Bridget screamed again and her knees buckled as if she'd bought the winning Magic-Millions Lottery ticket. The MC guided her gently to the back, where she fell into number thirty-two's arms.

"And now," the MC continued, "it's time to present the prize for Best Cosplay at *Kodai* Con. This year, the First Prize is a pair of tickets to Chicago to the *Kodai Warriors* Regional Con, one of the largest Cons in the entire country. So—by unanimous decision, the First Prize goes to Number Sixteen—Kisho!"

When no one reacted the MC shielded her eyes against the spotlights and peered into the audience. "Come on, Sixteen—I know you're out there somewhere."

A restless murmur swept over the crowd as everyone began to look for the renegade Kisho. I glanced over at my companion and saw him reach up and pull something off his tunic and ball it up in his fist.

"Hey," I said lightly. "Wasn't that your number?"

"Number?" He turned to me with a shrug. "What number?"

"*Kodai* Warriors," the MC said, "since we seem to have lost Number Sixteen, the prize will pass on to the judges' second choice. Contestant Forty-Seven, are you here?"

We watched as another guy in a Kisho costume climbed onto the stage to a roar of applause.

When the noise subsided my companion smiled. "You know, I never got your name."

"It's Kenya."

"*Aisatsu*, Kenya. I'm Daniel. So tell me—what other *mangas* do you enjoy?"

After graduating from the University of Michigan, **Heather Neff** studied at the Sorbonne in Paris and earned her PhD at the University of Zurich in Switzerland. A professor of African American Literature at Eastern Michigan University, Neff is also a poet and the author of four novels: *Blackgammon*, *Wisdom*, *Accident of Birth*, and *Haarlem*. Her writing reflects her interests in travel, world politics, and issues of race and economic class in the United States and abroad. Neff lives with her husband, daughter, and calico cat in Ypsilanti, Michigan. You can visit her website at: www.heatherneffbooks.net

SOLSTICE IN A NATURAL,

OR HOW COME YOU DON'T GOT NO "WHERE I'M FROM" POEM?

ADAM FALKNER

I'm a bluesbaby
cradled by my father
on Sunday mornings
born into the arms of a new hip
      hop scotch picassos
on danda-lined sidewalks
talking shit early,
was *that* kid on the playground.

first freeze to last bloom.
I ride the swell of a season in its cycle:
rinse, repeat . . .

lingo twisted thick
in a tongue I'd later learn
      to love by
      to live by
      to believe the bond of beat
      tie stronger than single motherhood . . .

my coming of age
through time is music
its melody pulls
like red wagon to peer pressure
progressions of its chords play
gepetto puppet strings stuck to the sun
sucking daylight
and returning it
to begin again
when the encore fades like watercolor.

I am June:
the sound of leather pounding
in summer comes sacred
till sunlight swallowed in
the mouths of cicadas
      hums a hymnal

for the afternoon to erode like hairlines
splashing in drain pipes
and muddy fights in waist high,
bedtime yarn of class cut
and bad-ass
belly born Detroit boy mischief
spinning from grandfather's lips.
life lessons like
       "sing before you speak"
       "dance before you walk"
       "and cry prior to falling
            so you know what it feels like when you do, son
because you will, son."

October:
the walnut crumble of
autumn under timbs
wind whips lung puncturing;
bleeding heat of breath;
arthritic,
tickling trees into blushing
bus stop jive shit
colorful then,
funky then,
like chilly morning
woodchip-cigarette passing laughter
at steam from chapped lips...
I'm a group caboose
squeezing from skin tone like sweat
and aching to fit hand-me-down hoodies.
two sizes
too big
       too early to
know the smell of good weed
like home cookin.
one less way to see the world naked
before it gets bitter like baby-mamas
still that kid on the playground
but starting to improvise
covered slide into tunnels from teacher vision
this is the pull of my seasons
from red wagon to peer pressure

I am January:
firewood crackle in flame snap

like fumbling rookie unfastening strap, stuck
as fifteen going on virginity.
winter feels
thick like air in waiting rooms
suffocating
a shepherd of sheep
whose ship
he's told could sink whiskey water
I am learning
to double knot laces
when shoes are too big to fill
and how to laugh at somber jokes
a cracking tenor tone held
accidental after cut-off silence
so still that breaking ash becomes gunshot.

I am April
when lemonade and lilacs gots
attitude once again
till riverbed humidity licks
sticky salt from skin.
mosquito alley am-track
tin can
rattles back:
through double-dutch
slaps on concrete
as palms in congregation
race back:
through crawl space closet forts
and furniture tent kisses
first little league hit
      first beer, first Mrs.
first real scar with ya
first set of stitches
and ya first real job
from jiminy-cricket wishes,
waiting
for that long front rim rebound
back:
to the first high
that worst high
      to be young, in summer,
untouchable high . . .
when lip corners salivate,
to bake on blacktop

drop with the radio loud
when being tardy is on time
the days are molasses
and the sound of leather pounding comes sacred

but until then
I ride the swell of season in its cycle:
Rinse, repeat
step on toes when we waltz,
      drift,
capsize,
let it beach me
lungs heaving
and begin again
when the encore fades like watercolor.

Born and raised in Ann Arbor, **Adam Falkner** is a student in the Residential College at the University of Michigan. With declared majors in Creative Writing and Race Relations, he produced his first solo hip-hop album last spring, entitled *Control the Circle*. Having competed at national slams for the last several years in Chicago, San Francisco, and Philadelphia, he just recently returned from a short tour out east to a number of small colleges in New York state. He is a regular at Burns Park Elementary where he works as a noonhour supervisor and spent last semester teaching weekly creative writing workshops at Cooley High School in Detroit. He continues to believe strongly in the power of word as the foremost tool for educating young people everywhere. He is a founding member of Ann Arbor Wordworks, the 2005 Ann Arbor Book Festival Poetry Slam Champion, and a two-time member of the UM Poetry Slam Team. "RIP Richard Pryor."

2006 ANN ARBOR YOUTH POETRY SLAM TEAM

The 2006 Ann Arbor Youth Poetry Slam Team was formed through three brutal evenings of poetry competion with over forty poets competing for the cherished six slots on the squad. One of the finest group of young poets ever to represent Ann Arbor, the team participated in the Brave New Voices National Youth Poetry Slam Festival in New York City. Out of forty-plus teams from around the country, Ann Arbor finished in a tie for seventh in the nation and was invited to perform as a special feature during the finals in front of fifteen hundred people at the historic Apollo Theater in Harlem. It was the eighth consecutive year Ann Arbor either qualified for, or was invited to feature on the finals stage.

THE WOMAN

COURTNEY WHITTLER

I murdered a woman
Bruised her when she needed something to be fresh inside of her

I've woken too many afternoons and
Had to clean the blood off my bathroom floor
I don't like brown anymore
It used to be my favorite

I buzz on a loss for words every time
And I'm starting to get numb to
Knocking my knuckles together—grind gritty bone
Of blaze and siren
It's just a mess, It's hectic
And brown
I still like red

Mix red . . . orange, blue—
Flow through night, wake mornings . . .
Windex evenings of sleepless sirens
Mix love and lust and you get brown
I don't like brown anymore
I love blue

And I tear like love that builds bridges
And grows rust: moldy and ill
Until I infect the mouths of others.

Rape and self destruction
Are woman and ally
She was bruised on a Friday night
After a taxi cab ride with her assailant
I cut myself
I am the murderer of myself and woman
I watch her fall limp as
My liver crumples out of function
I pull women from my veins
Mocking their sorrows
Watching red seep to the surface
And stain my floor brown

Cleaning it up in the morning is ignoring the struggle.
So, I'll taste the iron while I still can
Before it's just stain clinging
To pink down comforter spreads
And hospital bed sheets
Surgeon and ER understand why
Brown is death and
Blue is blood
Why red is the transition
They understand why cuts scab

It's not sex anymore

Siren, scream of a victim trying to find the end
Mold reality, bend
If I could choose where I was going
I'd go backward
A long way before I figured out what it looks like on the inside
Of an ambulance

Don't rape me of my blue
Don't clean out my arteries
Like they were my womanhood

I used to wonder how a woman could have a baby
Dilate 10cm
Push out a life
And then shrink back into mortality
As if she hadn't just witnessed her body's miracle
As if she was bungee cord
I was told it was because the walls of a woman's vagina are very forgiving
And so I ask,
Well what about the woman?

She calls me when she gets home
To tell me she got there safe
Even when I don't ask her to
Because she knows that I love her
Too much to wonder
If the screams I hear are hers
I don't want to
Cover my ears
and
Close my eyes
If it's her tinting those sheets,
And it is
Every time

Drawing lines between
Suicide and overdose
Ambulance and hospital
Doctor and nurse
Mother and sister
Rapist and murderer
But, what if it's your own blood you're looking for
She forgave me with her eyes wide open

If only she could forgive with her womanhood
If only she didn't have to
If only she knew how I bled for her
Blue, red, brown
Life, rape, murder
Cut like a siren through the thick of her screams,
The sound is perfect torture
And there is no answer

But, what about the woman?

Does she have to forgive with her organs
Before she can wake up in the morning
And press her feet to clean tile?
What about the woman?
Her sirens
Her being
The sheets
The force, agony
The rush, the rape
The afterward, scars
Bathroom floors, sisters, and depression
The mother
   . . . it just keeps wailing . . .
The ambulance
The brown sheets
The murder
and
The woman

Courtney Whittler was born and raised in Ann Arbor. She loves playing soccer, laughing, scrapbooking, and spending time with her sisters. Courtney has been writing poetry since middle school but only started getting involved in slam poetry her sophomore year at Pioneer High School. She will be attending Washtenaw Community College in the fall of 2006.

MAGIC MARKERED CUNTS

MAGGIE AMBROSINO

We are not humans who walk here yet
And I can't classify you
Not a sister and not exactly a best friend
You have made your home somewhere between companion and ally
This summer you were my chrysalis
They must see us as pair a duo
A bff clique who trade lockets and hair tips
When really

Here we are

Two manged spitting hyenas
Hidden over the forest and beneath
Grinning and cackled
with tartared bones for teeth
We cling to backs and tear flesh for nutrients
I will wear antelope hide like a bathrobe
You will sip marrow like a strawberry shake
our hair nests ear wigs and gnats

We are liars
I stutter
You walk with a limp
Venus horizons
We trap you fly

I whisper
You hum
I rock my head
To your backbeat
And disregard what is said to me

We are two written letters
dusty and tampered with
We worry about salutations
And never mention how we feel

We are shit-faced Barbie dolls
Skirts too short collars too high
We slur and stumble and get dunked in the Huron River

We wear too much mascara and not enough cover up
We write Genesis quotes on douches
And pick the fleas from each other's hair

You teethe me when you're nervous
And I kick when I am restless
We are raw bleeding bitches
Cut with the same knife
Blood like smoke into Al Gon Quian
Stuffed full of cinder
Washed clean of ash
Rotting from our throats
We decay of the same sickness

We are magic markered cunts
Blue dilated pores
We are spayed and flowering
Menstrual mud veins down our thighs
I am six velvet weighted drapes like eyelids
You are a lavender lampshade too taut too thin
We are bitches
We are fuck ups
We are fucked up
We are summer sucked photo albums
And rusty tactless rings
We are two celibate water beetles
iridescently tenting our wings
I peel under your toenails
And take a nail file to your scabs
you slice my spine seam
strip my rib meat like jerky
to gnaw on during math lectures

We shut our mouths chew our gums
Our pheromone stench clouds us
We trail after each other
Each leading
Both behind
Epileptic and shuddering
Like moths

Maggie Ambrosino is a senior at Pioneer High School in Ann Arbor. She is the 2004 Ann Arbor Youth Poetry Slam Chapmion and a three-time member of the Ann Arbor Youth Poetry Slam Team. She has appeared on the finals stage at the Brave New Voices National Youth Poetry Slam and is a cast member of the poetic drama *Lay Your Comfort Down*.

TO BE YOUNG GIFTED AND FAT

BEN ALFARO

I am a titan of all things digestible
A colossus
Well beyond mere behemoth
I am a truffle-shuffling monstrosity
The deity of every burned Richard Simmons cassette
As if Fat Albert and the Michelin Tire Man
Procreated
I am fat
Not just "are these jeans too tight" fat
Or "maybe I should go see a doctor" fat
I'm so big
My mom's C-section scars stretch from her chin to her ankles
I get winded taking escalators
And sweaty watching toddlers play Putt-Putt golf
I've been habitually criticized for my size and stature
To the point where
Calling me overweight is no longer an insult
I'm bigger than that
I'm the one who's pointed at
When political agendas need a booster seat
Failing to put pressure on the school system
Or to pave libraries through project yards
Politicians preach the reason our nation is crumbling
Is due to the pudgy love-handles
of kids too scared to take their shirts off in a pool
Kids mocked by a greasy burger shop every other block
And told to spend premature incomes
On SlimFast and Food for Dummies
They tell me that for fifteen dollars
Off working minimum wage hours
I can read my way to skinniness
They can brand name build me
Into an immaculate toned-torso body
In the same manner they brand name buried me
Into the shape I've carried my whole life
But a page past the introduction

Of every Atkins weight loss grapefruit handbook
My mouth waters like a hammer-cracked hydrant
My sweet teeth yearn for every last calorie
That can corrode their enamel physique
I drool so much that I have to spread mayonnaise across the cover
Place a slice of provolone between the glossary and index
Embed the book between four slices of Texas Toast
And devour it faster that you can say "Willy Wonka"
If a healthy lifestyle
Is made of sucking the chlorophyll from celery stalks
And chomping down shit-brick energy bars
Then let my waistline grow so monumental
They make a statue out of it
Let my chubby cheeks drown every school picture
Let my bust rival my mother's
Before I was known as the fat kid in class
Before I was more worried about my gym final than my history exam
I was that small developing bud growing in the darkness
Taught to stand straight and be polite
To not listen when the other kids laughed when I walked by
To let pride take back seat to ridicule
To let the voices accumulating under my bedroom door
Crawl into my full axis abdomen
I've learned to be hungry
For every time I got picked last for anything
For every crumb quickly consumed
To spare the agony of being watched in public
For every morsel shamelessly swallowed
To outweigh the criticism
And for every fat kid told he was nothing more than that
Never the smart kid or the prom king

I am young gifted and fat
The pimpled plump pumpkin
Rotting on your doorstep
The product of feeding the fire that burns you
Of eating until the anguish and aggression
Don't have enough fiber
To push themselves out of my plump fists or wet lips
I want to double dip my chance to be someone
I want to come back for second helpings
And scrape the past sixteen years from my plate
Down to the last intestine-splitting
Pant button-bursting Skittle
I have always been told

Being overweight is being worthless
But I have always been fat

I have always been hungering
For something
To tip the scales

Ben Alfaro is a junior at Pioneer High School in Ann Arbor. He is a member of the Board of Directors of the Neutral Zone.

LETTER TO A WOMAN WHO SAW GOD IN COLOR, BECAUSE JANIE, YOU ARE SO MUCH MORE THAN JUST A CHARACTER

CARONAE HOWELL

(This is dedicated to Zora Neale Hurston, because she was watching God.)

Dear Janie,

You must have been born below a pear tree because nobody glistens quite like
you.
Nobody's got that soft, green earthy flesh like yours,
nobody. But I'm afraid
maybe I underestimated you.
I guess I thought you were only a memory knotted up in ink.
But I forgot about those generations of slave women that came before you,
pounding their hands into the dust and their feet into the cotton fields, Janie
after reading you I feel like I must be missing something.
I feel like I am a shade of turquoise yet to be splashed onto orange canvas,
I feel like I am a bruised purple woman,
lying on the ground with my hips pushing against the dirt.

Will you remind me what it tastes like to be bursting, Janie?
I want my mouth to swell scarlet.
Will you press your heels into the road so God knows how it feels
to be a woman of so many colors?
Sometimes, I wish I understood your story more
and sometimes I am very, very frightened.
I think you are the ripest pear on the branch.

I've never known someone who loves the way you do, Janie,
like celadon butterfly wings or
muddy brown bean fields.
I've never known so many colors knotted up in plain, black ink.
So many horizons penciled down on paper.

Janie, your words are a midnight shadow cast by a tangerine sun.
You are a black woman's reason
why white men should be ashamed because
Janie
you are no Goddamn mule.
Mostly

I think you are an adventure where
the dragons are men who love your body too much
and the princesses are bright colors,
and you,
a gleaming, chestnut unicorn.
Let us fold our thighs together and lay them neatly beneath
the front porch,
where no one will watch us make love.

This must be a growing up poem
or a growing out poem
or I'm growing gray just thinking about you, Janie, and
(I hope it's not too late
because I know you are more than a memory,
more than the horizon in June).

I wonder if you meant for God to be something spiritual,
some yellow-tinted force,
some golden woman with arms like pyramids.
Or maybe God wasn't really a God at all,
but a river or a reason
I don't know, but Janie, I'm ready and now
I can see clearly why you wondered in color,
and I wonder how you felt when men
shoved their penises inside of you.
Your silence was a tattered sheet
and I wonder what burrowed beneath it.

I've got a million questions queuing up for you, Janie,
waiting patient, but
there is one more urgent than the rest,
itching against the sides of my skull:
I want to know where your pear tree is
so I can sit under it
and start my own journey.
I want to know where your pear tree is
so I can sit under it
and worship that green, fleshy fruit.

Caronae Howell is a senior at Pioneer High School in Ann Arbor. She is the 2006 Ann Arbor Youth Poetry Slam Champion and has appeared on the finals stage at the Brave New Voices National Youth Poetry Slam. She is also a member of Pioneer's National Champion Girls Swim Team.

DAUGHTER OF
TONIESHA JONES

If I had a knife, I would stab you
carve my name into your carcass
just like your bullets did my mother's

I want your cold blood
to exit your flesh in gallons
leave your skin dry and empty . . .
just like my heart

The thought of you
tricking me into believing
you were this ideal man
curdles and crumbles my stomach

Looking at you now
I can't believe I spent so many nights
crying myself to nightmares
I was afraid your next bullet
was gonna be aimed at me

Because of you
I'll never be able
to put my trust
in the hands of a man

You proved palms can be deadly

You made me hate Father's Day
I can't celebrate Mother's Day
and all you got was twenty-five years in prison
chance of parole in fifteen
if you maintain good behavior?

You executed my mother
and all you got was free
phone calls, bedroom, bathroom, basketball courts?

You couldn't even wait a day
after my little brother blew out those eleven candles
to take away the one who conceived him

You shot her four times in her heart
with me, my sister, and my brother watching

Did you not see us?
Did you not care?

First bullet—I'm in the store buying candy
I hear my brother scream, "He shot Mama!"

Second bullet—it's a little blurry, my eyes are straining
to see who's controlling my mother's life
inside that car

Third bullet—I recognize you—Stepdad
I can't believe it. Just five days earlier
you were giving me allowance
telling me you loved me

Fourth bullet—the passenger door opens
my heart pauses, I was hoping my mom
was going to breathe life
instead she swallowed her final gasp

I covered myself in her blood
soaked her life through my pores

I called 9-1-1
and her spirit answered

I am the daughter of

> A car radio singer
> who didn't care if she was in tune
> as long as her voice was heard

> An old school supersonic
> living room dancer

> A woman who strapped
> three kids to her side

and put the world
in her backpocket

For she, my mother, was more than just a statistic in the *Ann Arbor News*

You tried to control my mother's life
but you couldn't
you never can

Although her body may be lifeless
she is not dead
her blood is flowing in me
and it's your spirit that died
three years ago
the day you pulled that trigger

Toniesha Jones is a senior Pioneer High School in Ann Arbor. She has appeared on the finals stage at the Brave New Voices National Youth Poetry Slam.

HOW I FOUND THE GARDENIA IN HER HAIR AND THE "I" IN NIGGER

ANGEL NAFIS

Leo Africanus
Nat Turner
Scottsboro
Sink into
Rwanda
Richard Wright
Ruby Brown
Dipping back, breathing, and feeding.

Billie chants the tales of slaves
Before and after the emancipation
Which by the way
freed no one

Legends sewn in and sucked between her teeth
Indigo, Sapphire, Lavender swaying
It's like watching the living slip
From ankles that graze the mouths of eager tree trunks
It's like leather whips lusting after brown flesh on broad backs
Like niggers
Hanging from trees
Choking
Hyperventilating
Leaving legs limp
History impotent

I attempt to keep this ankh tamed on my thumb
Binding me to branches
Perpetually linking me
Mapping me to ancestors in charred soil
So when two things rub together
There's bound to be sparks
And that night
Conversation was ignited

Friend Dan breaks a link

Turns to me and says
I didn't know that you took that stuff so seriously

Brotha . . . that stuff?
You mean
This tree on my back?
You mean dozens of copper carcasses smacking waves
Belly first
Like round coins in a well
Sinking

You mean you can't hear Billie?

Lady Holiday was rising, black skin blazed metallic
Hovering, whistling hollow
From her unyielding brass throat
That's right now
singing only to you
Lighting dead voice underneath
Brotha
Can't you hear her?

This is street poetry
The kind of stanzas that knock down your door
After asking politely for four hundred years
The kind of strange fruit from a vine that winds
The loop of a tightly woven rope around southern accents
That slur adjectives
Because if lives on the tongue then we're nurturing it.

It's about awareness
Sambo
Uncle Tom
Aunt Jemima
Don't get solicited, subjugated, broken, demoralized, exploited
I'm keeping conscious of these names reciting them
Mohammad, Martin Luther, Marcus Garvey
Because they're somebody, and I want to be somebody

I am trapped in epidermis cocooned in brown
But I want to be
Burning plus signs in my backyard, tessellating crosses
Draining me off brick walls and border lines
Then bloating me with
The queen of swing

Swinging loose black calves
small combo lady whose subtle art scared the blues away
From night clubs and evening cabarets
Pinning it down, improvising on a fella

Her pupils welled with foot fights
On ballroom floors and alley way asphalt
Pinning her name on your hips
She spins a story like painted throat
Blows on metal
Revolves mic into porcelain
Turns cigarette scratched vocals into gold
Can't you hear her?

There's a whole life in her voice
Like we were all stranded in the same big star
Stranded on uprooted avenue
And brow beaten boulevard
Where opportunities have been snatched like fruit from vine
I wish I could understand why the letter "I"
In nigger is the boldest of the six
And I wish I could show you why,
n-i-g-g-e-r or n-i-g-g-a
It doesn't matter cause' either way it's a racial slur
Because if it lives on the tongue than we're nurturing it

This is for every black man who's ever been great
Dred Scott, Mandela, Dubois
This is for every time I've fried my hair straight
This is for the busy bustle of Billie's blues
How she bends notes, bends brown bodies that float
Can't you hear her?

I can
I can feel her

So excuse me, brotha
If I take this stuff
So
Seriously

Angel Nafis is a graduate of Huron High School in Ann Arbor. She is a two-time member of the Ann Arbor Youth Poetry Slam Team and has appeared on the finals stage at the Brave New Voices National Youth Poetry Slam. She is a cast member of the poetic drama *Lay Your Comfort Down*.

aBOUT 826michigan

826michigan is a nonprofit, totally free center for kids dedicated to supporting students ages six to eighteen with their creative and expository writing skills, and to helping teachers inspire their students to write. 826's services are structured around the belief that great leaps in learning can happen with one-on-one attention and that strong writing skills are fundamental to future success.

Through after-school drop-in tutoring, field trips, workshops, writing rooms, in-school projects and various other means, 826's main goal is to inspire young people and foster their creativity. 826michigan takes kids very seriously in an often not-so-serious way. All programs are free of charge.

DROP-IN

During the school year, 826 offers drop-in tutoring Monday through Thursday from 3-5:30PM, allowing students an opportunity to work on schoolwork with adult mentors.

All summer long, in place of tutoring, 826 offers drop-in writing time from 3:30-5PM on Tuesdays, where students and volunteers of all ages work together on different writing exercises.

WRITING WORKSHOPS

Year round, 826 offers evening and weekend creative writing workshops centering around a variety of topics, from College Entrance Essay Writing to Poems of Audacity and Weirdness. 826 also brings their programs into the community, hosting numerous workshops at local schools, libraries, and bookstores.

PUBLISHING OPPORTUNITIES

826michigan feels that it is important to give students a serious platform on which to make their voices heard. It is with this in mind that they offer a number of publishing opportunities for students. *Vacansopapurosophobia: Fear of a Blank Page*, the literary journal they put together in conjunction with a high school editorial board from the Neutral Zone, is just one example.

826 Valencia was started in San Francisco by famed writer (*A Heartbreaking Work of Staggering Genius*) and editor (*McSweeney's*) Dave Eggers. In 2002, he decided to start a nonprofit organization that focused on mentoring kids in creative writing. Founded by local writer Steven Gillis (*The Weight of Nothing*), 826michigan opened its doors in the fall of 2005, joining 826NYC, 826LA, 826 Seattle, and 826 Chicago.

If you are interested in more information about 826michigan, please visit www.826michigan.org, or call (734) 761-3463.

THE NEUTRAL ZONE

aBOUT THE NEUTRAL ZONE

Neutral Zone was founded by teens to provide Ann Arbor area high school youth with a venue for needed social, cultural, educational, recreational, and creative opportunities. The mission statement, written by youth, continues to be the voice and heart which drives the center's creative programs and opportunities:

> *The Neutral Zone is a diverse, youth-driven teen center dedicated to promoting personal growth through artistic expression, community leadership and the exchange of ideas.*

Neutral Zone offers unique literary arts and performance opportunities:

SHORT STORY WORKSHOP

Teens gain experience and skills writing short fiction and short short fiction. They read favorite published works, workshop one another's stories, and write, write, write.

VOLUME YOUTH POETRY PROJECT

In addition to writing and performing nationally recognized, award-winning poetry, VOLUME publishes a bi-annual magazine, between six and twelve individual artists' poetry chapbooks per year, and record and release poetry CDs on the YOR label. VOLUME also hosts the annual capacity-crowd Poetry Night in Ann Arbor, and the Ann Arbor Youth Poetry Slam Competition, whose winners go on to represent Ann Arbor at the national level.

2ND TUESDAY MONTHLY VISITING AUTHOR SERIES

In partnership with the Ann Arbor Public Library and 826michigan, Neutral Zone runs this popular evening of literature, readings, poetry, music, live interview, and Q&A with the author. CR Credit is now available for participation in the monthly book club held at the Ann Arbor District Library (whose participants receive a copy of the book for free).

In addition, Neutral Zone offers an after school drop-in program, engaging programs in education, community leadership, music and technology, and digital and media arts, and special events and concerts.

Please check out their web page for a detailed program description and the latest special events: www.neutral-zone.org, or call (734) 214-9995.